Engineering Electronic Negotiations

A Guide to Electronic Negotiation Technologies for the Design and Implementation of Next-Generation Electronic Markets—
Future Silkroads of eCommerce

SERIES IN COMPUTER SCIENCE

Series Editor: Rami G. Melhem
> University of Pittsburgh
> Pittsburgh, Pennsylvania

ENGINEERING ELECTRONIC NEGOTIATIONS
A Guide to Electronic Negotiation Technologies for the Design and Implementation of Next-Generation Electronic Markets—Future Silkroads of eCommerce
Michael Ströbel

FUNDAMENTALS OF X PROGRAMMING
Graphical User Interfaces and Beyond
Theo Pavlidis

INTRODUCTION TO PARALLEL PROCESSING
Algorithms and Architectures
Behrooz Parhami

OBJECT-ORIENTED DISCRETE-EVENT SIMULATION WITH JAVA
A Practical Introduction
José M. Garrido

PERFORMANCE MODELING OF OPERATING SYSTEMS USING OBJECT-ORIENTED SIMULATION
A Practical Introduction
José M. Garrido

POWER AWARE COMPUTING
Edited by Robert Graybill and Rami Melhem

Engineering Electronic Negotiations

A Guide to Electronic Negotiation Technologies for the Design and Implementation of Next-Generation Electronic Markets—
Future Silkroads of eCommerce

Michael Ströbel
BMW Group
Munich, Germany

Kluwer Academic / Plenum Publishers
New York • Boston • Dordrecht • London • Moscow

ISBN 0-306-47413-1

©2003 Kluwer Academic / Plenum Publishers, New York
233 Spring Street, New York, N.Y. 10013

http://www.wkap.com

10 9 8 7 6 5 4 3 2 1

A C.I.P. record for this book is available from the Library of Congress

All rights reserved

No part of this book may be reproduced, stored in a retrieval system, or transmitted in any form or by any means, electronic, mechanical, photocopying, microfilming, recording, or otherwise, without written permission from the Publisher, with the exception of any material supplied specifically for the purpose of being entered and executed on a computer system, for exclusive use by the purchaser of the work.

Printed in the United States of America

Preface

When I left my job as a consultant with the goal to earn a PhD, eCommerce was still in its infancy. I was excited to do research in this new and thrilling field, which pushed the fusion of economics and information technology to the extreme crossroads I had already been approaching during my graduate studies. In particular, the matter of negotiations in eCommerce presented uncountable challenges for a scientist, since social, emotional, and cultural factors interplay with the rational, computational analysis one would initially like to pursue.

Later, while I was buried deep in my thesis work, all around me the eCommerce hype was raging and one after another of my former or current colleagues left to join start-ups – leaving me wondering what I was doing in blue-sky scientific research surrounded by a booming new economy with pockets full of venture capital. But as I was just completing the last pages of my dissertation, the bubble burst, and soon prudent rationality started gradually to replace boundless enthusiasm. Restricted to the role of an observer I could draw my own conclusions from this phenomenon: to me, electronic markets are not dead. But they are not as simple to create and operate as many people might have thought. In addition to a solid business model (no surprise) they require careful analysis and skilful development as well as ongoing care. I hope the methodologies and technologies proposed in this book support an approach to eCommerce that fulfils these properties.

"In general it will be better to pursue not substitution but complementarity. We want ATMs that will supply us with money, not ones that will spend it for us " (John Brown, Paul Duguid: The Social Life of Information).

Acknowledgements

This book would not exist without the contributions of many people: first of all my colleagues from IBM's Zurich Research Laboratory (ZRL) where I found all the time I needed to roam: Markus, my PhD advisor, not only for constantly reminding me of the 'offer configuration' problem, but also for always asking the right questions; Simon, not only for insisting on price dependency but also for all the freedom he gave me; Heiko, not only for refreshing runs, but also for the always-available sanity check. And of course the rest of the eBusiness group for not letting me rot away in my office – especially Jörg, who contributed elements of the SILKROAD code (and the Space Night CDs), and Keith, who pushed me to find a hot name for my project. Thanks as well to Lauren and Christian, who sifted voluntarily through the drafts for semantic and syntactic bugs.

Additional credits need to be given to my PreDoc comrades at ZRL, who distracted me from the dark side of thesis writing with lake trips, boarder breaks, or blue lagoon tournaments – most of all Joy; To my fellow PhD students at the mcm Institute, for the 'real' student feeling and lots of fun (Vienna!) and to Ulrike, for steering me through the PhD seminars.

I have also drawn liberally on many ideas circulating in the eNegotiations community – thanks to Dirk, Gregory, Martin, Morad, and Stefan. This book is based on my dissertation, which I submitted in 2001 to the University of St.Gallen, Switzerland. My thesis project was only possible with the support of my advisors – Prof. Beat Schmid and Prof. Christof Weinhardt – and the support I received from the IBM Research Zurich Research Laboratory.

One very special person needs no explicit acknowledgement, she knows. To all those whom I failed to mention, apologies and thank you.

Overview

1. INTRODUCTION 1
2. ASSESSMENT..11
3. FOUNDATIONS 39
4. ELECTRONIC NEGOTIATION SUPPORT.................................73
5. ELECTRONIC NEGOTIATION DESIGN..................................111
6. ELECTRONIC NEGOTIATION ARCHITECTURE..................153
7. APPLICATION 185
8. EVALUATION, EXPLORATION, AND CONCLUSION..........219
APPENDIX 255
BIBLIOGRAPHY 279
INDEX 297

Contents

CHAPTER 1 ....INTRODUCTION

1. Remarks..2
2. Motivation and relevance..4
   2.1 Why negotiate?..4
   2.2 Why negotiate in electronic markets?..5
   2.3 Why negotiate with electronic media?...7
3. Outline 8

CHAPTER 2 .... ASSESSMENT

1. Research contributions..11
   1.1 Classic negotiation research...12
   1.2 Electronic negotiation research..14
      1.2.1 Decision support systems 14
      1.2.2 Group support systems 15
      1.2.3 Autonomous agent systems 17
      1.2.4 Combined approaches...18
2. An evaluation of the state of the art..20
   2.1 Classic negotiation research revisited..20
   2.2 Electronic negotiation research revisited 22
   2.3 Beyond research..23

2.4 Lessons learned 27
    2.4.1 Challenges for electronic negotiation technologies 27
    2.4.2 First conclusions and directions 30
    2.4.3 Core problems in multi-attribute negotiation support 33

3. Summary **36**

CHAPTER 3 .... FOUNDATIONS

1. Negotiations **39**

2. Electronic negotiations **40**

3. Formal model **45**
    3.1 Negotiation situation 46
    3.2 Negotiation interaction 50

4. Reference model **55**
    4.1 Development and deployment 56
    4.2 Roles 57
    4.3 Execution 58

5. Taxonomy **59**
    5.1 Taxonomy structure 60
    5.2 Endogenous classification criteria 60
    5.3 Exogenous classification criteria 67
    5.4 Taxonomy application 69

6. Summary **70**

CHAPTER 4 .... ELECTRONIC NEGOTIATION SUPPORT

1. Definition **73**

2. Requirements **77**

3. NSC external view - behaviour **79**

4. NSC internal views **81**
    4.1 MatchNSC 81
    4.2 ScoreNSC 87
    4.3 MediateNSC 92

5. NSC candidates 97

- 5.1 BundleNSC 97
- 5.2 BidNSC 100
- 5.3 ContractNSC 102

6. Combining NSC operations 104

- 6.1 Example MatchNSC/MediateNSC 105
- 6.2 General interdependencies 107

7. Summary 108

CHAPTER 5 .... ELECTRONIC NEGOTIATION DESIGN

1. Approach 111

2. Analysis 114

3. Design 116

- 3.1 Communication design 117
  - 3.1.1 Offer context ontology design 118
  - 3.1.2 Offer state structure design 121
- 3.2 Organisation design 124
  - 3.2.1 Entity types and instances 125
  - 3.2.2 Design language 128
  - 3.2.3 Design rationale 131
- 3.3 Integration design 134
  - 3.3.1 Offer context assignment 134
  - 3.3.2 Model validation 137

4. Implementation 139

- 4.1 Communication design representation 139
  - 4.1.1 Offer base schema 140
  - 4.1.2 State-dependent customisation 142
  - 4.1.3 Ontology-dependent customisation 144
  - 4.1.4 XML instance document examples 147
- 4.2 Organisation design representation 148

5. Summary 149

CHAPTER 6 ... ELECTRONIC NEGOTIATION ARCHITECTURE

1. Architecture model **154**
    1.1   Requirements 154
    1.2   Rationale 155
    1.3   Model structure 157
    1.4   Model behaviour 160

2. SILKROAD **164**
    2.1   Technical architecture 165
    2.2   Application architecture 168
    2.3   Tool support 170
        2.3.1 Development 171
        2.3.2 Deployment 175
    2.4   Run-time processing 177

3. Summary **183**

CHAPTER 7 .... APPLICATION

1. Potential usage **185**
    1.1   Online buying/selling 186
    1.2   Electronic market intermediation 186
    1.3   Dynamic outsourcing 187
    1.4   Negotiation service provisioning 188

2. Scenario cases **188**
    2.1   Bilateral offer exchange: DSP-V1 case 190
    2.2   Supported offer exchange: DSP-V2 case 196
    2.3   Multi-attribute auction: DSP-V3 case 203
    2.4   Service bundling: DSP-V4 case 211

3. Summary **217**

CHAPTER 8 .... EVALUATION, EXPLORATION, CONCLUSION

1. Intended scope and assumptions **220**

2. Solution approaches revisited **222**
    2.1   Electronic negotiation support 222
    2.2   Electronic negotiation design 228
    2.3   Electronic negotiation architecture 233

3. Future work 236
3.1 Support extensions 236
3.1.1 MatchNSC 236
3.1.2 ScoreNSC 238
3.1.3 MediateNSC 239
3.1.4 Negotiation support meta-components 240
3.2 Design extensions 242
3.2.1 Model simulations 242
3.2.2 Reference models 243
3.2.3 Dynamic models 244
3.3 SILKROAD extensions 247
3.4 Further exploration of the enMedia framework 248

4. Summary 251

APPENDIX 255

1. NSC Interface Definitions 255

2. SILKROAD data model 259

3. Sample scenario case specification 264

4. JSP agent adapter class diagram 268

5. XML schemata examples 269

6. Acronyms 278

BIBLIOGRAPHY 279

INDEX 297

Figures

Figure 1. Book outline 9
Figure 2. Negotiation research streams and communities 11
Figure 3. INSPIRE negotiation example [Inte02] 15
Figure 4. Offer editing in the SeCo system 16
Figure 5. Negotiation strategy definition in Kasbah [Kasb02]. ... 17
Figure 6. Multi-attribute auction interface (from [Bich99b]). 19
Figure 7. BargainAndHaggle negotiation example 24
Figure 8. Haggleware negotiation example 25
Figure 9. RFQ system example from [Perf01] 26
Figure 10. Single-/multi-attribute negotiation problems 28
Figure 11. Negotiation intermediation versus direct offer exchange ... 32
Figure 12. Interaction phases of an electronic transaction 41
Figure 13. Configuration of electronic negotiations 44
Figure 14. enMedia in the MRM 45
Figure 15. Negotiation situation model 51
Figure 16. Spaces in the negotiation process 52
Figure 17. enScenario development and deployment tasks 56
Figure 18. enProcess execution tasks 59
Figure 19. Taxonomy criteria categorisation 60
Figure 20. Sequential decision-making model 74
Figure 21. Conceptual NSC model 76
Figure 22. NSC behaviour – external view 80
Figure 23. MatchNSC operation 84
Figure 24. Scoring result example 88
Figure 25. Utility function examples 89
Figure 26. MatchNSC output example 105

Figure 27. Negotiation intermediation with NSCs 108
Figure 28. enMedia development action-model 112
Figure 29. Business analysis approach 114
Figure 30. Design meta-model 116
Figure 31. Communication design approach 118
Figure 32. Offer context ontology example 120
Figure 33. Extended organisation design meta-model 125
Figure 34. Types of offer states 127
Figure 35. Organisation design state-chart semantics 131
Figure 36. State-chart example 132
Figure 37. Offer context assignment example 135
Figure 38. Event and view authorisation example 136
Figure 39. XML schema generation and customisation process 140
Figure 40. Negotiation intermediation with run-time specifications 150
Figure 41. Architecture and system layers 156
Figure 42. enMedia architecture model components 158
Figure 43. Functional architecture component distribution 159
Figure 44. Offer submission run-time use case 162
Figure 45. NSC invocation run-time use case 163
Figure 46. Three-tier technical architecture 165
Figure 47. Support package UML class diagram 169
Figure 48. SILKROAD client application user interface 171
Figure 49. enScenario designer window in the SILKROAD client 172
Figure 50. Communication design with SILKROAD 173
Figure 51. Organisation design with SILKROAD 173
Figure 52. Integration design with SILKROAD 174
Figure 53. Ontology design with SILKROAD 175
Figure 54. Generation and deployment of run-time specifications 176
Figure 55. Retrieval of generated XML schemata 177
Figure 56. SilkRoadLogin.jsp run-time example 179
Figure 57. SilkGetTemplate.jsp run-time example 180
Figure 58. Run-time processing UML sequence diagram 182
Figure 59. Complete enMedia framework negotiation intermediation 183
Figure 60. DSP offer context ontology 190
Figure 61. O2S states in DSP-V1 191
Figure 62. O2S transitions in DSP-V1 192
Figure 63. Event authorisation in DSP-V1 194
Figure 64. Prototype interface for buyer agents in DSP-V1 ... 195
Figure 65. O2B states in DSP-V2 197
Figure 66. O2B state chart for DSP-V2 198
Figure 67. O2B transitions in DSP-V2 199
Figure 68. O2S transitions in DSP-V2 200

Figures xix

Figure 69. Corrected O2S transitions in DSP-V2 201
Figure 70. Prototype interface in-tray example for DSP-V2 203
Figure 71. O2B states in DSP-V3 204
Figure 72. O2B transitions in DSP-V3 205
Figure 73. O2S transitions in DSP-V3 207
Figure 74. O2S event authorisation for sample states in DSP-V3 208
Figure 75. Corrected O2S state chart for DSP-V3 209
Figure 76. Prototype interface for raising AGENT.BID in DSP-V3 210
Figure 77. Offer context ontology for DSP-V4 211
Figure 78. O2B transitions in DSP-V4 212
Figure 79. O2S transitions in DSP-V4 213
Figure 80. O2S event authorisation in DSP-V4 214
Figure 81. O2B view authorisation in DSP-V4 214
Figure 82. O2S view authorisation in DSP-V4 215
Figure 83. Prototype interface for reading result-sets 216
Figure 84. Intended scope of the enMedia framework 221
Figure 85. Three-way-NSC-operation architecture model extension 237
Figure 86. Decision support component architecture model extension 239
Figure 87. Negotiation support meta-component extension 241
Figure 88. Round-trip engineering of enScenario models 243
Figure 89. Run-time processing for dynamic enScenario models 246
Figure 90. UDDI and Web services prototype extension 248
Figure 91. Electronic negotiation engineering language stack 249
Figure 92. SILKROAD data model 259
Figure 93. JSP agent adapter class diagram 268

Tables

Table 1.	Roles criteria	61
Table 2.	Process criteria	61
Table 3.	Information revelation and strategy criteria	65
Table 4.	Generic NSC interface	79
Table 5.	Flight reservation example	96
Table 6.	MediateNSC input example	106
Table 7.	Offer state structure elements and notation options	121
Table 8.	O2X.ADVERTISED state template	123
Table 9.	enMedium manager operations	126
Table 10.	Event and view authorisation example	137
Table 11.	enScenario model test conditions	138
Table 12.	State-machine table representation	149
Table 13.	Attributes in the DSP offer context ontology	191
Table 14.	Offer session example	195
Table 15.	SUPPORT.BID action property definition in DSP-V3	206
Table 16.	MediateNSC compensation example	239
Table 17.	MatchNSC interface	256
Table 18.	ScoreNSC interface	257
Table 19.	MediateNSC interface	258
Table 20.	Relations in the enMedium repository	260
Table 21.	Relations in the offer repository	261
Table 22.	Relations in the in the run-time specification repository	262
Table 23.	Relations in the in the design-time model repository.	262
Table 24.	Acronyms	278

Chapter 1

Introduction

Why electronic negotiations?

Research in the domain of electronic negotiations is a rather new and very interdisciplinary field that is gaining more and more attention due to the industry hype and momentum regarding electronic commerce (eCommerce) and electronic markets. Until recently, electronic markets have been dominated by fixed pricing. Offers or classified ads (such as in an online catalogue) are posted electronically, for example by sellers, and buyers can either take these offers at the advertised price or 'leave'.

Such posted offers obviously bear the risk of not matching the requirements of all potential buyers. But fixing a price also imposes another risk on the seller – the price might not always reflect the current market balance of supply and demand and the specific valuation of a single buyer. Whereas static offer schemes are still prevalent today, price-focused negotiation systems such as electronic auctions address the risk related to fixed pricing with an easy way of price discovery by soliciting a wide range of bids from multiple parties. Most eCommerce systems today support dynamic pricing, but only few allow buyers and sellers to exploit differences in their valuations beyond price in order to achieve win-win solutions with joint gains. This may be one of the reasons why current electronic markets struggle for acceptance, liquidity, and prosperity – traditional negotiations often comprise the discussion of additional attributes of a deal, e.g. delivery terms or payment conditions. Hence, support for complex multi-attribute negotiations may become a critical success factor for the next generation of electronic markets. In response to this development, this book investigates multi-attribute negotiations from many different perspectives and introduces novel technologies for the development of multi-attribute negotiation systems.

Regarding its theoretical relevance, this book is situated at the intersection of the information systems, game theory, economics, and computer science disciplines:
- From an information systems perspective, this book demonstrates an approach for the structured development of electronic negotiation systems, which is based on artefacts and sound engineering principles.
- From a game theory perspective, this book illustrates how formal solution procedures for tasks in negotiations can be applied and adapted to practical negotiation problems in an eCommerce setting.
- From an economics perspective, this book investigates the role of negotiations in electronic markets and provides a foundation for the design of, and experimentation with, new market mechanisms.
- From a computer science perspective, this book contributes to the emerging shift from interactive computing to proactive collaborative computing, from human-centred to human-supervised computing.

Because of this interdisciplinary context and its practical relevance for eCommerce, this book addresses the scientific as well as the industrial community. Its findings should be valuable for researchers and practitioners who are interested in the state of the art of electronic negotiations, or who are themselves facing the challenge of designing and implementing electronic negotiation systems. In addition, this book has something to offer for readers interested in new IT developments, since the featured implementation examples illustrate how software building blocks such as Enterprise JavaBeans, Java Server Pages, or XML Schema can be combined to create state-of-the-art eCommerce systems.

This introductory chapter continues with remarks regarding the relationship of this book to key topics in negotiation research, such as auctions and security. These remarks are followed by a discussion of the context and relevance of this book, which is formulated as answers to the questions 'why negotiate?', 'why in electronic markets?', and 'why with electronic media?' Finally, an outline of the book's structure is presented.

1. REMARKS

In a first definition, a "negotiation is a form of decision-making with two or more actively involved parties who cannot make decisions independently, and therefore must make concessions to a achieve a compromise" [Kers+91]. The focus of this book is on a special type of negotiations, namely commercial negotiations, which deal with decisions regarding transactions of objects such as money, products, or services between buyers and sellers (the parties) in markets. The realm of eCommerce provides a rather structured environment for negotiations compared to, for instance, political or social disputes, where negotiations also play a vital role.

For the further characterisation of the context, motivation, and approach of this book a number of basic terms have to be briefly introduced – more formal definitions for these terms are provided in Chapter 3. An electronic market is a market where the exchange of economic products is coordinated through the electronic exchange of data, eventually resulting in deals among the market participants. Subject to a commercial negotiation in an electronic market are typically attributes associated with a deal such as delivery or payment conditions. A deal can comprise one or more transactions, which transfer the ownership of goods or rights to services from one market participant to another. A negotiation scenario describes the rules defined for a negotiation process. If the negotiation is conducted through electronic media, for example an electronic market, an electronic negotiation takes place.

Negotiations in electronic markets, and especially those types of electronic negotiations that allow discussions between buyers and sellers beyond the price of a transaction, constitute the context of this book. The notion of electronic markets, as understood in this book, extends to electronic exchanges in a wider sense, and includes general means beyond specific support for buyer/seller relationships, such as systems for the coordination of complex electronic interactions among organisations (e.g. virtual organisations).

In respect to the current practical and theoretical importance devoted in today's electronic markets to auctions, the relation of this book to the domain of auctions requires an introductory remark. Not all negotiations in electronic markets are, or have to be, electronic auctions. But the converse is true in the understanding of this book: all electronic auctions are electronic negotiations. Since negotiations in electronic markets are the focus of this book, auctions will be covered as specific types of negotiations with certain characteristics, e.g. the necessity for a priori fixed rules and competition among the participants. In addition, the success of auction protocols as coordination mechanisms in electronic markets requires special consideration, because this observation allows understanding the implications of specific electronic market characteristics for the effectiveness of other types of negotiation protocols. A negotiation can be regarded as playing a game with certain rules. If the rules change, the game has to be played differently.

Especially for the domain of electronic auctions, but also for other types of electronic negotiation protocols, security is an important issue, which has traditionally gained a lot of attention in research and practice. The reason for this awareness is that negotiations require an exchange of confidential information, e.g. preference structures, which could be exploited to the disadvantage of the discloser if intercepted by a malicious party. In addition, negotiations typically require the rigorous surveillance of rules to guarantee properties such as fairness. Through the introduction of electronic negotiation media, new security issues have to be considered (e.g. computational exploitation). On the other hand, it is generally easier to ensure compliance with pre-defined rules in a programmed environment.

The matter of security in electronic negotiations opens up a whole new field of research and discussion, which is outside the scope of this book. Security issues are addressed only if there are strong implications on the concepts presented in this book – an example are the different modes of electronic contracting.

The following conventions are used throughout this book. **Boldface** indicates the introduction of new terms where they are defined. *Italic* is used for examples. `Courier` is used for formal definitions and code samples.

2. MOTIVATION AND RELEVANCE

Three questions are discussed in this introductory section in order to outline the motivation for this book and its relevance. First, why do sellers and buyers engage in the complex and potentially cumbersome process of negotiating instead of simply advertising fixed offers or accepting the best offers? Second, given the characteristics of electronic markets can we expect to see more or fewer agreements based on negotiations in eCommerce than in traditional markets? Lastly, what are typical incentives to negotiate electronically?

2.1 Why negotiate?

In general, there are many reasons already prevalent in traditional markets to negotiate the attributes of a deal as opposed to relying on the advertisement or selection of the 'best' fixed offer (classified ad). It is, for instance, difficult to fix a price for transactions of objects that are unique and non-repetitive (e.g. excess inventory), that are subject to diverse buyer valuations (e.g. fashion goods, art), that are perishable (e.g. food, newspaper advertisements), or that face very dynamic demand (e.g. network bandwidth, electrical power).

Furthermore, a fixed offer, from the perspective of a seller, always imposes the risk of failing to satisfy the requirements of potential buyers or of misinterpreting the current balance of supply and demand. Negotiations allow sellers to tailor their offers of goods and services to individual buyer needs and to leave the determination of the value to the marketplace where resources are allocated in a fair manner to those buyers who value them most

Motivation and relevance

[GuMa98a]. Buyers on the other hand, may, for instance, use negotiations to imply competitive pressure on sellers in order to achieve better prices.

Overall, the motivation to execute a negotiation process is always either that without a negotiation no agreement can be found, or that buyers or sellers expect to achieve a 'better' agreement than by merely accepting fixed offers. Nevertheless, the decision whether one should enter into negotiations or not, and especially the estimation of a potential negotiation benefit, is very complex and subject to many uncertainties. At any point in a negotiation process a buyer or seller has the following choices:
- to have no agreement and to abandon further negotiation,
- to accept the current offer,
- to create a counteroffer,
- to convince the other party to change its offer,
- to choose the best alternative to a negotiated agreement.

The choice, which has to be made, can, in general, be influenced by the following considerations:
- All variables to be reflected in this decision are subject to uncertainty: the reservation value of the other party (e.g. the minimum amount a seller is willing to accept), the expected profits and the total negotiation costs, the proximity or probability of a future agreement, or the understanding of the current economic situation (e.g. the potential demand or competition).
- The decision usually cannot be isolated from other factors such as the general relationship to the other party (e.g. long term trade partner, most wanted customer, new market entrant, etc.), the current business situation (overstocked, declining sales…), and decisions in related negotiations. In real estate scenarios, for instance, there might be concurrent negotiations between buyer/seller and buyer/bank.
- Negotiations can be very expensive and if not successful, all the negotiation costs are sunk. Costs are mainly caused by the necessity for human intervention (e.g. to create a counteroffer with new options) and the time required for the negotiation process.

Nevertheless, negotiations are the dominating coordination mechanism in traditional markets (see for example [Andr01]). Historically, the usage of fixed offer schemes with uniform prices only found widespread acceptance when industrial processes allowed the production of standardised, uniform goods and advances in transportation (e.g. the railroad system) enabled an efficient distribution of these goods [CoSt98].

2.2 Why negotiate in electronic markets?

The answer to this second question abstracts from the actual means of negotiation support. One could imagine a scenario where a company uses an electronic market to advertise its products, but still negotiates in a traditional non-electronic way, e.g. by exchanging written offer documents.

Key to a specific view on the need for negotiations in electronic markets are low transaction costs and especially low search costs, which are typically prevalent in electronic markets [WiBe95]. If search costs for price information are zero, buyers will enjoy perfect price information. This typically leads to price wars. When so-called 'involuntary electronic winner-take-all markets' are created by software agents [CrMa01], sellers either block the automated agents gathering the price information, or face the following alternatives: make price comparisons more difficult, differentiate their products, create markets that emphasise product information over price information [Bako91]. None of these strategies is compatible with fixed advertised offers but rather they require some form of negotiations as shown in [Ströb00b].

A different argument for more negotiated agreements in electronic markets relates to the concept of negotiation power. Low transaction costs also enable the constitution of buyer consortia such as the ones organised by LetsBuyIt [Lets01], which perform an accumulation and coordination of demand, leading to an increase of the resource controlled (in this case buyer money) in a negotiation. Resource control is one of the sources of power that might be used to influence an opposing party in a negotiation (see Section 4.5.1.2). With aggregated negotiation power, the likelihood of negotiations taking place is increased, as equal powers of buyers and sellers lead to mutual dependency, which is a necessary prerequisite for negotiations (c.f. the definition of a negotiation in Section 3.1).

The conclusion is that one can expect more negotiations to take place in electronic than in traditional markets. Support for negotiations in electronic markets is therefore not only a necessity but also a critical success factor for many eCommerce market ventures.

The market for air travel is the most popular and most intensively studied example of an electronic market that demonstrates a pattern of virtualisation, price wars and differentiation/discrimination strategies. Currently it is easy to search for convenient flights but finding the best rate is cumbersome, because the number of different rates is enormous. Airlines deliberately introduced this discriminated price structure (for example with early reservation discounts, frequent flyer bonuses, or weekend tariffs) to reduce market transparency after a phase of open price competition [Pico+97]. The next move away from fixed offers came when airlines started to run auctions for unsold seats. Nowadays, services such as Priceline [Pric01] allow buyers to specify the amount they are willing to pay for a ticket. Upon a request, Priceline queries the market to see if an airline is willing to accept this price. Differentiation strategies are also manifested in new bundled offers that, for instance, combine business class tickets with free rental cars. This shows that the air travel market, as an example for a complex service market, is constantly moving towards more variable prices and more differentiated offers, resulting in more negotiated agreements.

2.3 Why negotiate with electronic media?

Buyers and sellers might participate in an electronic market to exchange their goods, but negotiations could still be conducted outside the electronic market, using other types of media such as letters or the telephone. In this case, tasks such as searching potential partners, advertising offers, or executing a payment might be supported by the electronic market medium whereas negotiation processes are not, which is often the case in practice [Rung98]. Sustained benefits can be achieved for the market participants if the support of electronic markets is consistently provided for negotiator interactions across all phases of an electronic transaction, overcoming the need to complement the electronic transaction paradigm with traditional interaction outside the electronic medium.

The preceding two sections developed arguments favouring the usage of negotiation processes to reach an agreement. In many cases, though, negotiation mechanisms, as means of market coordination, will not be applied because of potentially high costs and uncertain benefits. Electronic negotiation media propose to increase the efficiency of negotiations through the assistance and automation of decision tasks (see Section 3.2) This increase in efficiency and the associated reduction of negotiation costs can lead to the following potential benefits:

- The electronic negotiation medium can take over structured negotiation tasks whereas human negotiators can focus on complex decisions, which have to be made under uncertainty and lack formal representations or well-defined solution approaches.
- The complexity and uncertainty of the remaining non-automated decisions in electronic negotiations can be reduced – e.g. due to higher information availability.
- It is also possible to apply complex electronic negotiation scenarios for the transaction of goods or services with low revenue margins.
- The number of potential transaction partners can be increased, thus leading to more options, more competitive pressure, and possibly more efficient agreements.
- With multi-attribute negotiations, which allow sellers to emphasise product over price information, automated price comparison efforts and related price wars, enabled through the high transparency of electronic markets, can be avoided.

- Through the removal of visual and verbal factors, electronic negotiations might become less emotional and more objective or rational. Long haggling processes with psychological tricks or intimidation tactics can be avoided. It has been shown, for instance, that focussing on facts, leads to more efficient negotiation results [PrLe75].

Not in all cases will these benefits be realisable. There undoubtedly exist many cases where the transfer of a traditional negotiation process to an electronic negotiation medium does not provide any advantages, does not produce sufficient returns to justify the investment, or even results in less efficient negotiation processes and outcomes. Common examples are negotiations in a business context with long-lasting and personal relationships among the negotiating parties or with complex and a priori unknown dimensions or rules. Furthermore, users of current electronic negotiation systems are often confronted with various open issues such as the strategy paradox or the ontology problem (see the critical discussion of the state of the art in Section 2.2). Hence, the restrictions of an electronic negotiation medium as well as the requirements of a specific business context have to be explicit in order to assist stakeholders in the decision to introduce an electronic negotiation.

Abstracting from individual cases, this section argues that the advent of electronic markets motivates a general need for electronic negotiations. As an answer to this need, this book proposes new ways of developing electronic negotiation systems and enables new types of negotiation scenarios for electronic markets. The following outline of this book illustrates the distinct elements of its overall contribution.

3. OUTLINE

This book is based on findings from several years of applied electronic negotiation research, which was undertaken by the author at IBM's Zurich Research Laboratory. Having its roots in applied industrial research, the goal of this book is not merely to achieve an understanding or explanation of the needs and problems identified in the domain of electronic negotiations, but to contribute to their solution in a practical way. This foundation is also manifested in the book's structure as illustrated in Figure 1 (next page).

Outline 9

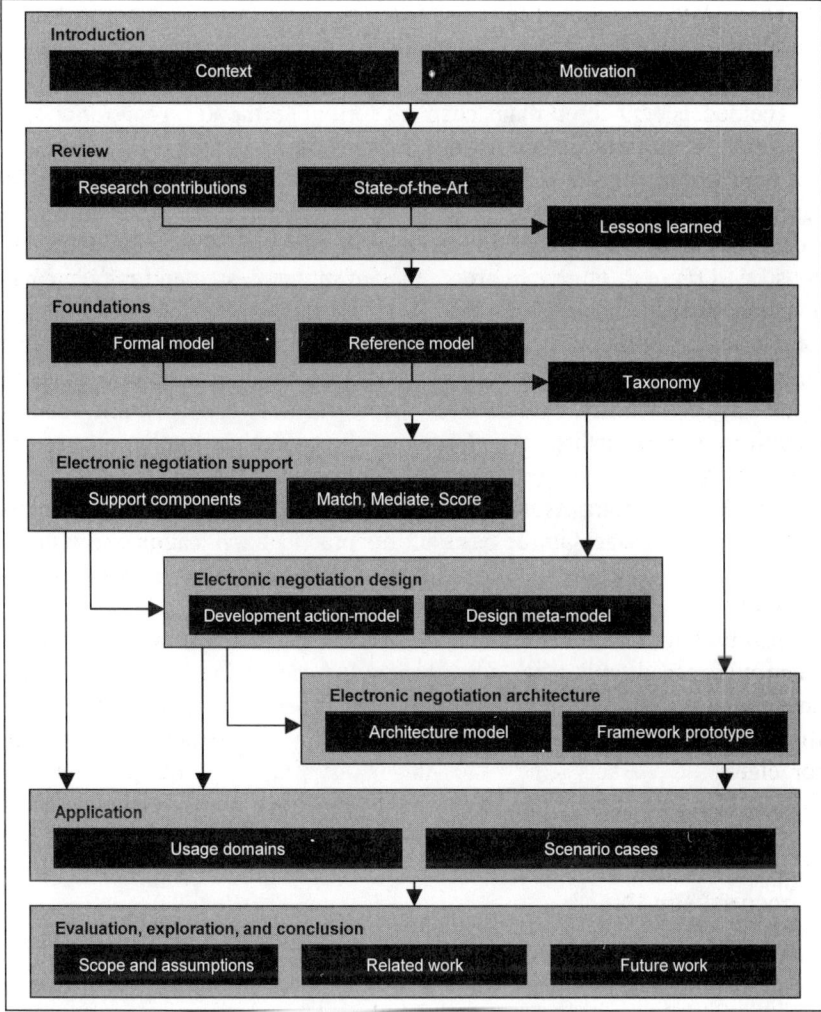

Figure 1. Book outline

After the present introduction to the context and motivation of this book, existing scientific and practical approaches to electronic negotiations are discussed in Chapter 2. This includes pointers to break-through electronic negotiation systems from research and currently available of-the-shelf products. On the basis of a review of the state of the art, core problems that need to be solved for the future are derived. The foundation for the presentation of the key propositions of this book is provided through the definition system in Chapter 3, which introduces a formal model for elements of electronic negotiations, a reference model for electronic negotiation development and execution processes, as well as a taxonomy for the classification of electronic negotiations.

The subsequent three main chapters formulate the key propositions of this book: the notion of negotiation support components for the modularisation of solution procedures for tasks in electronic negotiations in Chapter 4, a design approach for electronic negotiations in Chapter 5, and an architecture model for electronic negotiation systems in Chapter 6. These core contributions build on each other and are integrated in one design and implementation framework for symmetric multi-attribute negotiation intermediation in electronic markets, the enMedia framework. An implementation of this framework, the SILKROAD prototype, is also presented in Chapter 6, in order to provide preliminary evidence for the correctness and feasibility of the claims postulated in this book. Chapter 7 illustrates the application of the book's propositions, namely the enMedia framework, through the discussion of generic usage domains and the detailed presentation of electronic negotiation scenario cases. On the basis of this practical application and a theoretical argument regarding the properties of the solution approaches, the propositions of this book are evaluated and compared to related work in Chapter 8. This final section concludes with an elaboration on future work that can be based on the enMedia framework, addressing its current limitations but also foreseeing potential extensions. These extensions may eventually realise the vision of this book – an electronic negotiation engineering paradigm.

This structure is complemented with an appendix, which features technical details (such as a data model for the prototype implementation), the list of references, and an index with pointers to the definition and further usage of frequent terms.

Chapter 2

Assessment
On the state of the art

A negotiation is a complex, ill-structured, and uncertainty-prone process, which might be subject to half-truths, tricks, and other means of psychological warfare [Syca90]. Accordingly, its multitude of aspects and dimensions is reflected in the diversity of related research [Hols+95]. This chapter aims to capture the primary contributions of research in the domain of negotiations in order to critically review the current state of the art.

1. RESEARCH CONTRIBUTIONS

This first section examines the contributions of two research streams, classic negotiation research and electronic negotiation research (see *Figure 2*).

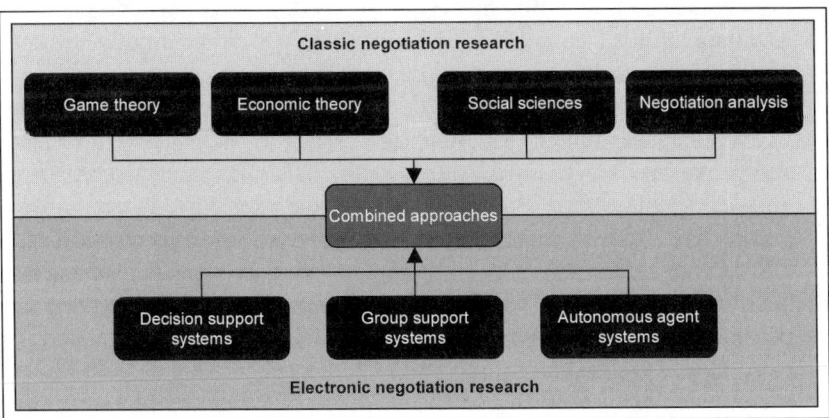

Figure 2. Negotiation research streams and communities

The discussion in this section covers also scientific communities associated with classic and electronic negotiation research as well as the combination of these two research streams.

1.1 Classic negotiation research

Research on negotiations without regard to electronic negotiation media is conducted within a number of scientific disciplines and referred to as 'classic' negotiation research in this book. In general, negotiations have been explored from the more constricted abstractions of game theory to the broad practical perspective of social sciences [Hols+91]. The following overview summarises the primary disciplines dealing with classic negotiations, as well as their respective research questions. Not considered are scientific disciplines such as decision science, which is often used for the discussion of negotiation phenomena, but does not explicitly address specific aspects of negotiation situations or problems.

- **Game theory**
  For game theorists, bargaining is a synonym for negotiation [HaSe87] and bargaining situations are investigated as 'non-cooperative zero or non-zero sum games'. For the field of descriptive game theory, the focus is on the potential outcomes of these games (e.g. the Nash equilibrium [Nash51]), whereas prescriptive game theory suggests normative strategies the players (agents) should use [Raif82], or mechanisms with specific outcomes and specific actor behaviour [McMc96]. Mechanism design is a dedicated branch of game theory that does not take the rules of a game as given but asks about the consequences of different types and combinations of rules [Bich01, p.70]. A primary contribution originating from game theory is utility theory [NeMo44] and its extension to Multi-Attribute Utility Theory (MAUT, [KeRa76]), which is currently still one of the primary instruments used in the analysis of negotiations.

- **Economic theory**
  Economic research on negotiations emphasises investigations of the price and market mechanism, mechanism design, and experimental analysis. Research in the design of mechanisms is undertaken from an economic perspective and has resulted in proposals for auction protocols such as the Vickrey auction [Vick61]. Experiments with existing mechanisms have uncovered relations such as the implication of the bidder's arrival process on the negotiation outcome [VaSe00]. As negotiations are a price-discovery mechanism for markets, research in microeconomics has investigated many properties of negotiations (e.g. indifference and contract curves [Fran96, 557ff.]) and defined optimisation measures, e.g. the overall market welfare or the aggregate surplus [TeMa00]. Finally, eco-

nomic pricing strategies [Phli83] can be used to support the bargaining tactics of agents.
- **Social sciences**
  The interest of this discipline is the behaviour of humans in negotiations. Negotiation skills are seen as critical for management activities [LaSe86] and social science tries to give advice on how humans can negotiate in the most effective way. Empirical research with experiments is often used to interpret common phenomena in negotiations. Questions of interest are, for example, whether the willingness to concede is influenced by the existence or absence of visual contact between the opponents [Shef92], or what the effect of the information available to the agents is on the efficiency of the final outcome [Thom89]. From an analytical perspective, sources of negotiation power such as resource control, information, or location are investigated [Lewi97, 182ff.].
- **Negotiation analysis**
  The negotiation analysis discipline integrates decision science and game theory with the goal of bridging the gap between descriptive qualitative models and normative formal models of bargaining. Whereas the focus of game theory is mostly on outcomes, negotiation analysis focuses on the negotiation process. It seeks to develop useful advice for negotiators and third parties and aims at situations that are not fully specified in advance [Sebe92]. From a conceptual level, the contributions of negotiation analysis are the concentration on possible agreements and value 'left on the table' rather than searching for equilibria, or the acceptance of pragmatic goal seeking rather than the assumption of rational behaviour [Kers00]. Negotiation analysis investigates questions such as the negotiators' dilemma, which postulates that competitively claiming value in a negotiation drives out the possibility of cooperatively creating value [LaSe86]. Contributions of negotiation analysis comprise, for instance, methodologies to assess tradeoffs in negotiation situations [BaPe76], or value tree analysis [Keen+83], whereby preferences of large groups can be assessed for decision-making purposes.

This overview does not aim for completeness. The motivation is to demonstrate the multitude of contributions that have been made to analyse negotiation situations or processes and to provide support for negotiators. Outside the scope defined for this book, additional research on negotiations is conducted within the disciplines of politics (e.g. for the design of voting schemes), industrial relations, and organisational management. It is also very difficult to separate distinct research communities, as it is not unusual that, for example, game theorists join economists to design mechanisms or to analyse certain strategies, which are then evaluated on the basis of social experiments (see for example [PrLe75]).

1.2 Electronic negotiation research

Negotiations executed through electronic media and the exchange of electronic data constitute a major application area for generic solution approaches or methodologies developed within the computer science and information systems discipline. Due to the complexity of negotiations, a number of specific aspects, such as the generation and choice of strategies, or the coordination of distributed negotiators, provide isolated problems for the application of algorithms or protocols and the combined representation thereof in a system. The results of this synthesis are various forms of electronic negotiation systems. However, to date, no dedicated electronic negotiation discipline within computer science or information systems has emerged. The various approaches to electronic negotiations can be illustrated based on their scientific community roots.

1.2.1 Decision support systems

Within a negotiation process, negotiators have to make a number of decisions. Decision support systems (DSS, [DeGa87]) can be used to support negotiators in making these decisions. Through DSS, decision science has an implicit impact on negotiation research. In DSS negotiations are defined, for example, as a set of issues, options, offers, objectives, preferences, tradeoffs, utility functions and opposition levels [KeNo99]. Decision problems (how to evaluate an offer, the choice and the level of compromise) are modelled, and systems such as INSPIRE [KeNo97] or NEGOTIATOR [BuSh96] are designed to support, based on these models, negotiators in finding pareto-optimal or integrative agreements in an efficient way. *Figure 3* shows a collection of screenshots from the INSPIRE system. The graph is a post-negotiation analysis of the interaction history, which illustrates the differences from one party's (*Misty*) own valuation of an offer to the other party's (*Smiley*) valuation of this offer. Two attributes constitute the negotiation object, *price* and *warranty*. In this case, offer [4] was acceptable for both parties, but a more efficient package could be found by the system on the basis of the preference information available (in *Misty's* case the table in the bottom-left corner of *Figure 3*). This package was suggested by INSPIRE in the post-settlement state to *Misty* and *Smiley* and accepted in this example as final agreement [5].

Research contributions

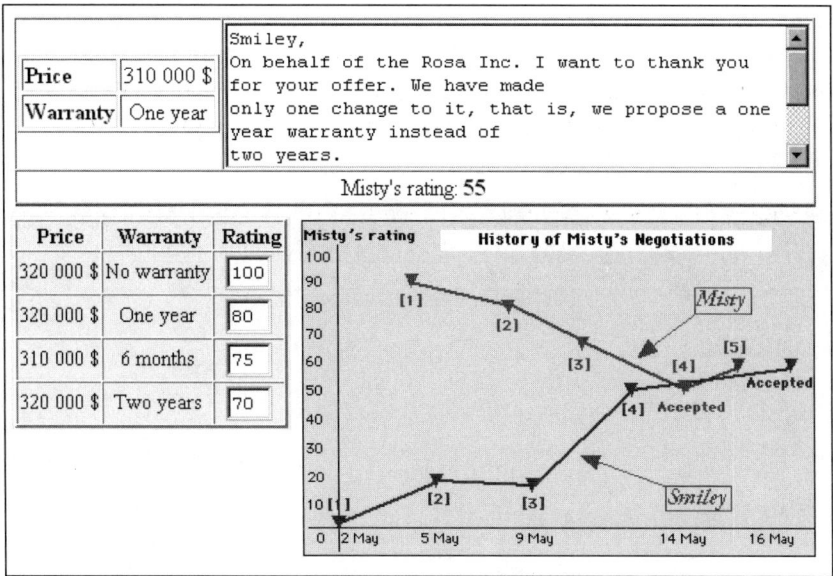

Figure 3. INSPIRE negotiation example [Inte02]

Different representations in DSS are, for instance, influence diagrams, which can illustrate decision situations in bilateral negotiations where 'accept', 'reject' or 'counteroffer' are the possible choices for the decision nodes [MuVa00]. In summary, the core research problems for decision support are the analysis of human decision-making under risk or under uncertainty and the representation of decision-making in models such as the analytic hierarchy process or conjoint analysis (for an overview see [Bich99a]).

1.2.2 Group support systems

Due to their inherent joint problem-solving nature, negotiation processes have become a major application area for work in the field of computer-supported cooperative work or group support systems (GSS, e.g. [Nuna+87]). For the application of GSS the agreement in a negotiation is considered to be a decision that has to be made within a (potentially distributed) group of decision-makers. GSS assist negotiators with facilities for sharing information or mediating agreements. For instance, some systems model the interaction in negotiations as a process of cooperatively editing rich documents (see for example [HaHo99]). *Figure 4* shows an example for such a GSS in the domain of negotiations – the SecureContracts (SeCo) system [Greu+00]. SeCo allows users to exchange and edit offers as XML documents, which contain next to the offer details also information about the contracting process (e.g. the status and a trace) and the negotiation protocol. Through digital signatures, these offers are rendered into electronic contracts.

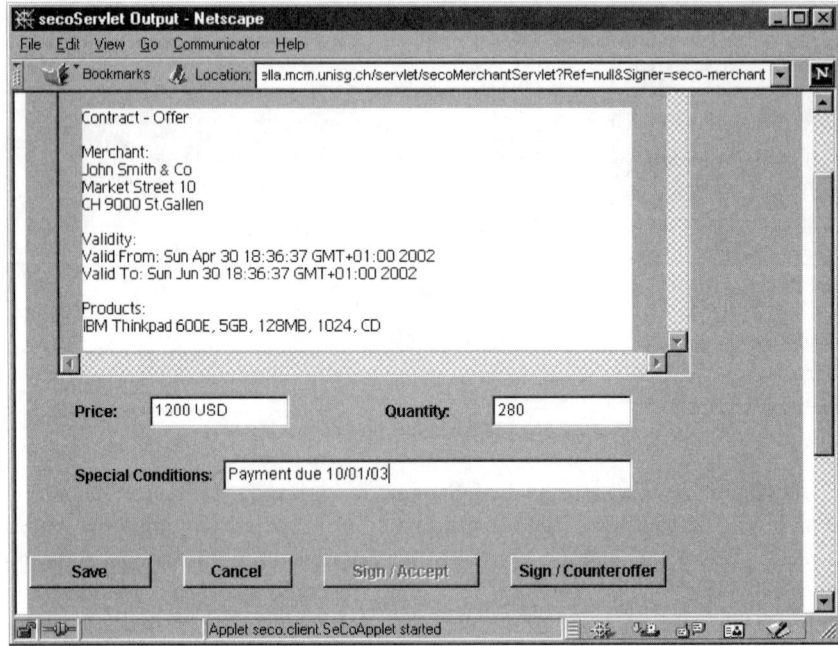

Figure 4. Offer editing in the SeCo system

Another research direction in this discipline is communication management, which introduces a language-action perspective to negotiation support. In this approach the basic units of communication are speech acts (e.g. directives or assertives), which are mapped to actions and document exchanges in negotiation processes [ScQu01]. [Yuan+98] presents a GSS for negotiations that focuses on community aspects by supporting real-time online collaboration with message channels, discussion support, or common windows. Finally, if negotiations are analysed and modelled from a process perspective, another type of GSS, namely workflow systems, can also provide a foundation for negotiation support systems ([Rebs99] or [BeKe00]).

Research contributions 17

1.2.3 Autonomous agent systems

An autonomous software agent can be defined as persistent software, which is typically personalised, that is able to carry out certain tasks autonomously for its user, represents its user towards third parties, and proactively interacts with its environment in a meaningful way [Mouk+00]. Negotiation research in this discipline mainly focuses on formalisations of negotiation strategies, which enable agents to negotiate automatically on behalf of their user. This also includes the development of appropriate protocols (rules of encounter). The term 'automated negotiations' usually represents the efforts related to electronic negotiations in this discipline (see for example [Sand00b]). Definitions of the negotiation problem from an agent's perspective include the rules restricting the agent interaction, aspects of tactics (e.g. the generation of proposals on the basis of certain criteria), and the usage of different tactics over time [Card+99].

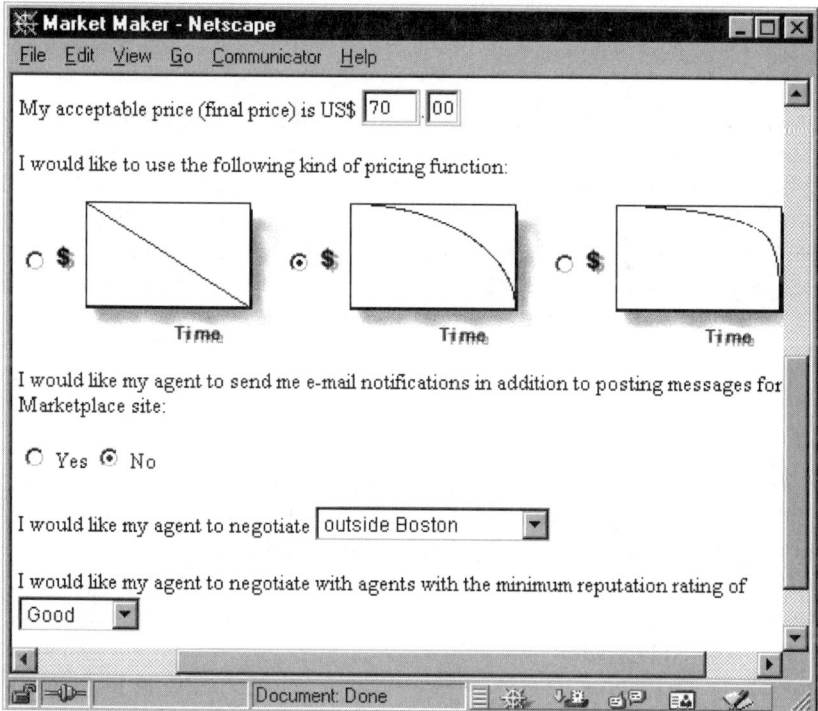

Figure 5. Negotiation strategy definition in Kasbah [Kasb02]

In the simplest case, the user has to manually define or choose the strategy for the agent. In the early Kasbah system [CaMa96] this was done through pricing functions. The user can express risk attitude by choosing different price curves, which determine the degree of concession over time, as illustrated in *Figure 5*.

In more advanced systems, these negotiation strategies and tactics are, for example, derived in a formal way [RoZl96] or generated on the basis of genetic algorithms [Tu+00]. Another area of research within the autonomous agent discipline addresses formal aspects of argumentation and conversation, leading to, for instance, systems with agents that reason and negotiate by arguing on the basis of linguistic exchanges [Pars+98]. Finally, in order to reach high degrees of autonomy, many agent negotiation systems rely on learning or adaptation technologies from artificial intelligence (AI) such as case-based reasoning [Wong+00], planning [Syca90] or fuzzy logic [KoBu00]. Within the AI community, a negotiation is often regarded as a search problem [Oliv97].

1.2.4 Combined approaches

In most cases, laboratory electronic negotiation media combine a number of findings from both classic and electronic negotiation research. The degree of application of classic negotiation research depends on the inherent level of formalism and the associated assumptions. Whereas social science is often based on practical settings, many of its findings are informally expressed maxims and therefore not suited for automation efforts. Game theory, on the other hand, tends to produce very formal outputs. The validity of the results, however, is restricted by numerous constraints (see Section 2.2.1).

To give examples for combined approaches, the integration of auctions with multi-agent systems and pricing mechanisms is often used to provide efficient, distributed, and autonomy-preserving methods for solving task- and resource allocation problems ([Gomb+00] or [Sand00a]). Furthermore, agent systems often use decision support methodologies in order to elicit and represent the preferences of the user [BeSe97]. In another example, the strategies applied by the agent within the negotiation process, can be determined with game-theoretic considerations [Benn+99]. In the opposite direction, solution approaches from computer science, such as heuristic search or learning techniques in the AI field, can help game players with bounded rationality to locate an approximate solution strategy [ZeSy98].

Another aspect of combination is that theories, e.g. from economics, on the behaviour of negotiators or the outcome of negotiations can be evaluated through experiments with electronic negotiation media. The efficiency of multi-attribute auctions, for instance, was analysed with the experimental prototype system in the domain of financial derivatives pictured in *Figure 6* [Bich99b]. In this example two negotiable attributes were subject to the negotiation between buyers and sellers of derivatives: *strike price*, and *volatility* (*duration* and *style* were fixed in advance). The buyers needed to specify a scoring function for incoming bids (shown in *Figure 6* for the *strike price*).

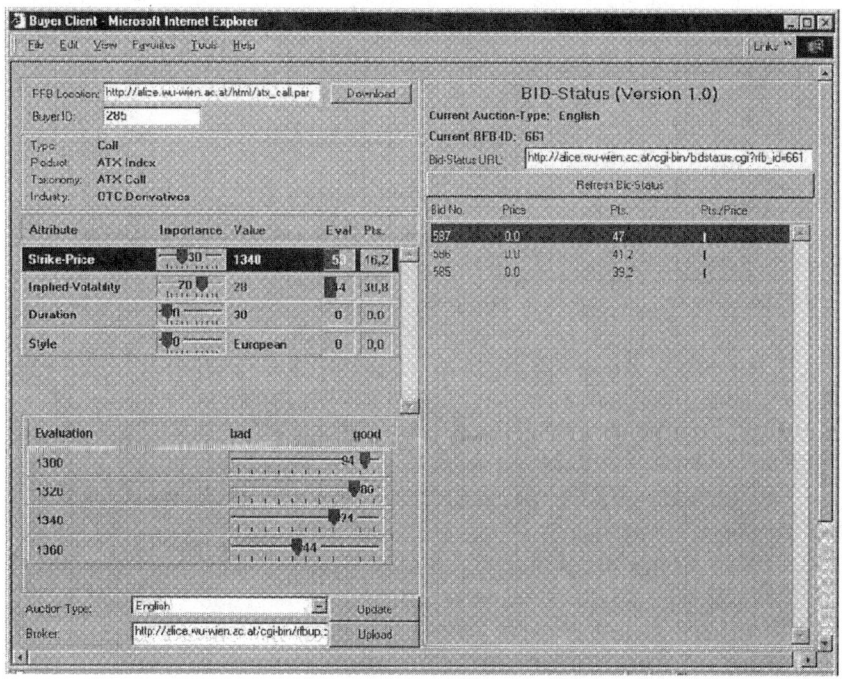

Figure 6. Multi-attribute auction interface (from [Bich99b]).

The experiment revealed, for instance, that the utility for a buyer in a multi-attribute auction is overall higher than in a single-attribute auction. But the setting also demonstrated that the complexity of the decision-making is dramatically increasing with the number of negotiable attributes. In the case of bidders this means, for example, increasing difficulty to determine the combination of attribute values providing the highest utility for the buyer. In another example, Kephart et al. use simulations to study the collective behaviour of large populations of software agents employing a variety of economic protocols, in order to find out whether an information economy of software agents behaves in a different way than today's economy of human negotiators [Keph+98].

2. AN EVALUATION OF THE STATE OF THE ART

If there is a growing need for negotiations in electronic markets, and if electronic negotiations propose many benefits – which is the conclusion of Section 1.1.3 – what assets can be used, as of today, for the implementation of electronic negotiation media?

In this section, the results available from classic and electronic negotiation research are discussed, with respect to their relevance for practical implementations as well as with regard to their unresolved issues.

2.1 Classic negotiation research revisited

Game theory certainly contributes a large part of the theory concerning negotiations. However, many criticisms of the results of game theory have been suggested. As early as 1967, Bishop discussed five game-theoretic approaches to bargaining situations and concluded that even under favourable circumstances (rational bargainers with complete domain knowledge) no results can realistically be applied or tested because no theory can explain how ordinary fallible mortals will play these games [Bish67]. Game theory may be useful in understanding repeated negotiations in well-structured situations, but also suffers from a lack of prescriptive usefulness [Sebe92, p.19]. Holsapple et al. add that game theory tends to emphasise conflict and to neglect important factors that are difficult to quantify such as organisational norms or negotiation power [Hols+91]. This criticism is summarised by Loui and Moore [LoMo97] who state that a "negotiation is usually not considered enough constrained by rules to be called a game."

The impact of economics on electronic negotiation practice is focused on pricing mechanisms and results from auction theory. Real world auctions such as the U.S. frequency auctions were reviewed and designed according to recommendations from economists [CrSc00]. The difficulty for this application domain was to design an auction, that on one hand allows bidders to change bids on frequency bundles in response to price changes, but on the other hand prevents them from concealing their interest and postponing bidding to the last minute [BiSe01]. In this example, a thorough economical and game-theoretic analysis suggested the usage of a multi-round auction.

Auctions, as special types of negotiations, are very efficient coordination protocols (see Section 2.2.3) in electronic markets, but a number of problems have to be considered ([GuMa98b] and [Strö00a]):
- **Rings and shills** – bidders can form rings to acquire the objects at relatively low costs and then distribute the gain among them. Sellers themselves can bid to push the price higher (with after-sales evaluations and rating schemes this risk can be reduced).

An evaluation of the state of the art 21

- **Winner's curse** - the winning bid is usually higher than the common market valuation (a problem addressed by the Vickrey auction).
- **Lot size and frequency** – although sellers leave the determination of the price to the market, the right choice of the frequency and size of auction lots for production goods that are, in principle, unlimited resources (e.g. digital music) is not trivial.

Depending on the design of the negotiation scenario, these problems usually can be addressed. But there are also fundamental limitations, which imply that one should not focus all efforts on the investigation of auction protocols. Auctions typically have a fixed timeframe (the exceptions are continuous protocols such as a double auction), which tends to be long in order to capture a critical mass of bidders, thus resulting in slow market coordination. Moreover, auctions are by nature distributive as the issue is typically one attribute, namely the price. Distributive negotiations are of a win-lose nature and consequently the agreements are not as economically efficient and desirable as agreements based on integrative negotiations (see [Raif82, 33ff.] and Section 3.3.2).

Regarding the usage of findings from social sciences, one major question arises: can outcomes from experiments be transferred to practical negotiation scenarios? The performance of dyads is usually reflected in some monetary reward or comparable incentive (e.g. credits for university classes). However, especially in real world negotiation scenarios, decision-makers are typically economically involved themselves, which is difficult to model in experimental settings. If, for instance, the behaviour of dyads negotiating a manufacturing contract is subject to an investigation, the consequences of a bad performance cannot realistically be reflected in the loss of a $50 reward in the experiment. The risk attitude, reservation levels etc. might be different.

Another problem related to the contribution of social sciences to the domain of negotiations is that when the designers of negotiation systems were looking for clear terminology and well-defined mechanisms or processes, they were often confounded by the conflicting studies and prescriptions. Gulliver noted early in his seminal work on negotiations, that "the social science literature is somewhat confused and contradictory about the definition and application of some basic concepts that are used in the study of negotiations" [Gull79, p.69].

Finally the contributions of negotiation analysis need to be discussed. The focus of negotiation analysis is more on unstructured, dynamic or non-repetitive negotiation situations with incomplete information. In the domain of electronic markets though, many negotiation situations are simple, reoccurring, and well defined. For the support of these scenarios, negotiation analysis does not provide many formalised mechanistic solution approaches, which could be used, for instance, to automate tasks. Nevertheless, negotiation analysis is very useful to examine a negotiation situation in order to assess its complexity (e.g. the interests of the stakeholders, the space of alternatives, or value creation processes), and to decide which solution approaches available from other research disciplines can be applied.

2.2 Electronic negotiation research revisited

Applying classic negotiation research to the development of electronic negotiation media requires a preceding discussion on how research findings can be transferred to and represented in actual negotiation systems. In contrast, the results of electronic negotiation research are in most cases already packaged as systems. However, the major problem related especially to the results available from the decision support and autonomous agent community is that MAUT, which underlies most approaches, often fails to reflect the true preferences of negotiators owing to the following shortcomings (c.f. Section 8.2.1.2):
– The conditions for the application of MAUT, such as independence of issues or complete knowledge of all issues, are often not met in real world negotiation scenarios [RaSh97].
– If these conditions hold, utility functions are still subject to severe assessment errors and inconsistencies – this is especially the case if there is a wide range of options [KrDu80].
– It cannot be assumed that preferences are constant in a negotiation because pressures or new knowledge can alter these preferences at any time [KeSz86].

Although this is actually a criticism of classic negotiation research, the impact of these shortcomings for electronic negotiations is a loss in trust of the user towards the representation of preferences and accordingly towards potential automation efforts.

Beyond user preferences, agent systems also require a formalisation of the user's negotiation strategy. Regarding the prospects of strategy formalisations, Beam et al. expressed their criticism in a **strategy paradox** [Beam+99]: if a strategy is simple enough to be formalised, then it probably can be deciphered by the opposing agent – if it is too complex, it cannot be formalised.

Brown and Duguid present in [BrDu00] additional arguments against fully automated negotiations among autonomous software agents:
– Agents might happily destroy an electronic market as long as they can maximise their goal (i.e. their profit).

An evaluation of the state of the art   23

- If the owner of an agent has to take responsibility, then the owner requires control over and insight into the agent. But to a non-expert, agent interaction is mostly intransparent and unexplainable.
- Agents end up with autonomy without accountability. The owners of the agents might have the accountability but lack means of control.
- Considering the open issues identified, the question arises as to what extent electronic negotiation media have been used in real world electronic markets. This question will be discussed in the next section.

2.3 Beyond research

In today's electronic markets, single-attribute (namely price) negotiation scenarios dominate [Kers+00]. Single-attribute negotiation scenarios are usually referred to as **dynamic pricing** solutions [CoSt98] as opposed to 'true negotiations', which go beyond the discussion of price. Dynamic pricing is defined as a pricing strategy in which prices change either over time, across buyers/sellers, or across product/service bundles [KaKo01]. Forrester Research projects that dynamically priced transactions will grow twenty-five-fold over the next years – reaching $746 billion in 2004 [Kafk+00]. Andren summarises in [Andr01] the evolution of electronic markets by stating that "negotiation is the most commonly used form of dynamic pricing offline, but it was the last to emerge in e-business, lagging behind auctions and bid/ask exchanges."

Single-attribute negotiations with multiple buyers and/or multiple sellers are well established in eCommerce practice. Numerous examples can be found of single-sided (only buyers or sellers can bid) scenarios such as consumer-to-consumer (e.g. eBay [eBay01]), business-to-consumer (e.g. Lufthansa Infoflyway ticket auctions [Info01]), and business-to-business auctions (e.g. DoveBid capital asset auctions [Dove01]), which is also the case for double-sided exchanges (e.g. Band-X physical network capacity or minutes traffic trading [Band01]). On the other hand, support for structured bilateral (one-to-one) single-attribute negotiations is scarce in electronic markets. One example is the BargainAndHaggle market [Barg01], which supports customers who do not want to participate in auctions with a bilateral negotiation scenario. Once the seller posts an object with an asking price, buyers can make binding offers and enter a negotiation, during which either side can ask questions, accept the sale terms, make a counteroffer, or 'walk away' (see *Figure 7*, next page).

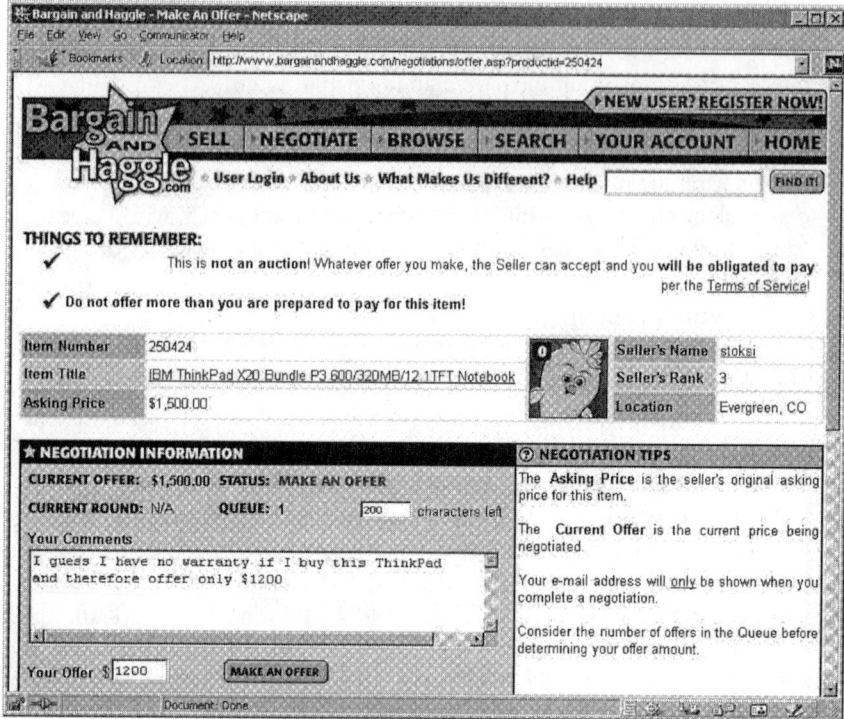

Figure 7. BargainAndHaggle negotiation example

An earlier example was the Haggleware[1] site where buyers could bargain with life-like characters representing the shop owner, as illustrated in *Figure 8* (next page). The course of the negotiation and the strategy of the virtual seller were influenced by a number of parameters such as the degree of concession demonstrated by the buyer or the buyer's transaction history.

---

[1] At the time of this writing the Haggleware site is not operative anymore and therefore cannot be referenced with a URL. The screenshot in *Figure 8* was taken by the author in early 2001 from www.haggleware.com.

An evaluation of the state of the art 25

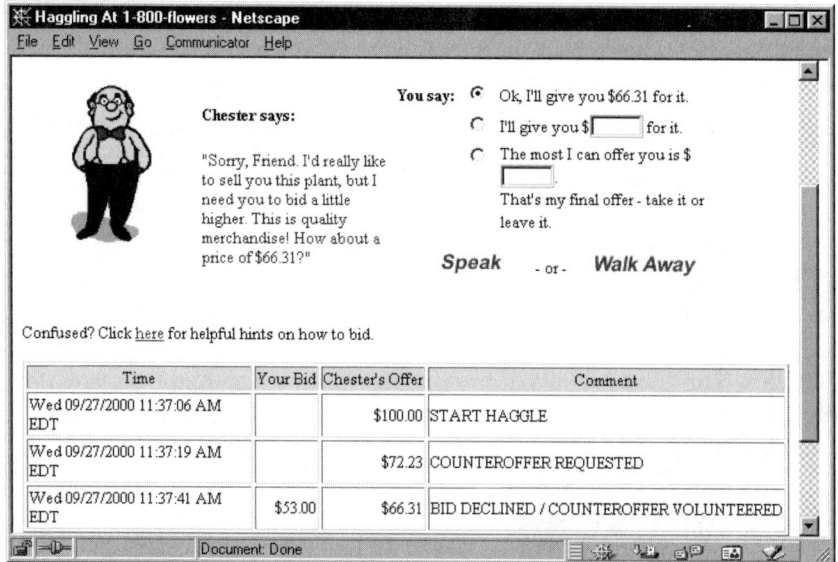

Figure 8. Haggleware negotiation example

A number of reasons can be found why single attribute, and especially multilateral negotiation scenarios, such as auctions, are very successful in electronic markets today, and probably, according to the forecast for dynamic pricing mentioned, will continue to be in the future (c.f. [Ströö00a]):

- Interactions in these scenarios are limited to the communication of offers (asks and bids) with one attribute, the price. Coordination is therefore easy and inexpensive to automate compared to the more complex exchange and analysis of information that would be required for multi-attribute negotiations.
- The competition inherent in multilateral mechanisms forces bidders to unveil their true valuation. Overall this leads to more efficient prices than in bilateral negotiations, where a negotiator can always try to demand a bigger share in the hope the counterpart will back down because she or he is not aware of alternative agreements.
- Open cry negotiations, which constitute most multilateral mechanisms, are public and can be delegated to independent third parties [Milg89], which reduces the opportunity for 'behind the scenes agreements' and creates an image of fairness.
- Network externalities are exploited: an increased benefit for sellers with increased number of buyers and vice versa [Whin+97, 516ff.]. This effect is based on the ubiquitous and cheap connectivity of the Internet, which helps achieve a critical mass of bidders.

The main limitation of dynamic pricing solutions is that by nature the agreements are restricted to be distributive, i.e. of win-lose nature. Especially for differentiated markets with complex products and services, where neither should buyers compare nor do sellers want to be compared based on just one attribute, multi-attribute negotiation scenarios with the potential for win-win agreements are advantageous.

In today's eCommerce many complex multi-attribute negotiations are conducted via electronic channels such as e-mail or video-conferencing, but in a free-form manner without explicit rules [Andr01]. Structured negotiation media with support for multi-attribute negotiations and enforced rules are just on the verge of finding widespread support in electronic markets [Butt+00]. This is especially the case for systems supporting request-for-quote (RFQ) processes such as Moai LiveExchange [Moai01], Perfect Sourcing [Perf01], or the Ariba Platform [Arib01].

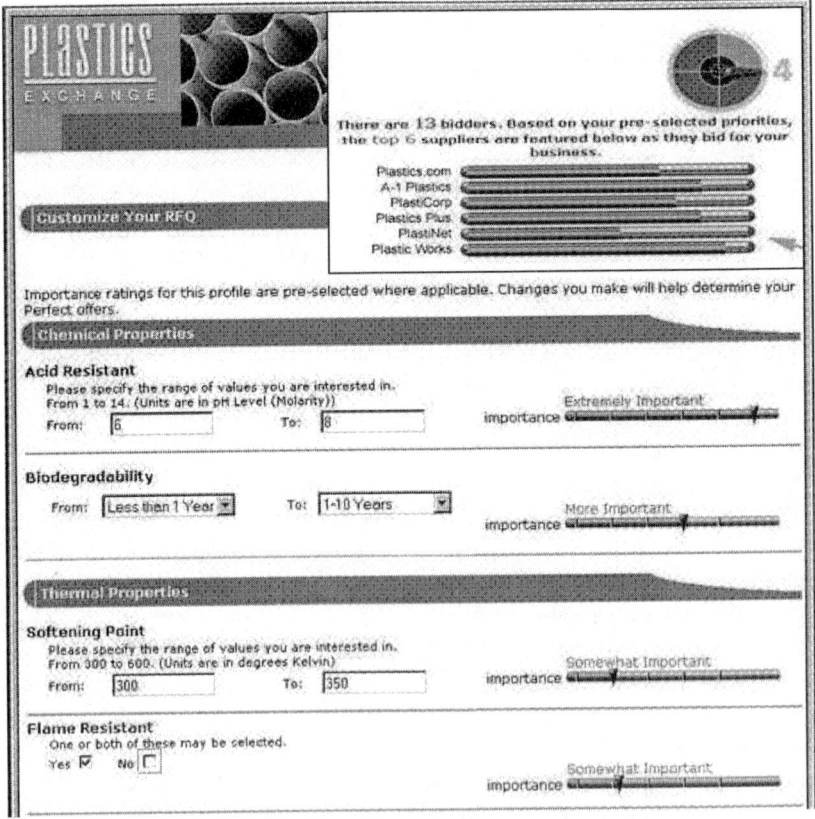

Figure 9. RFQ system example from [Perf01]

An evaluation of the state of the art 27

Figure 9 shows elements of a sample RFQ system from Perfect, which allows users to define multiple criteria for the evaluation of incoming quotes.

However, the automation provided by these systems is very limited (e.g. to filter and notification rules) and focused more on the support of the negotiation process and communication (with workflow or document management technologies) than on specific negotiation tasks.

Another shortcoming of these negotiation systems is the asymmetry of the buyer and seller roles. The mechanisms available to a buyer often differ from those available to a seller. Whereas a buyer in a RFQ platform usually is provided with some functionality to rank incoming bids, the seller has in general no means to compare and score multiple requests from different buyers. The same is true for constraints a buyer can define to filter bids – sellers in most cases do not have possibilities to define constraints towards the buyer requests they are interested in receiving.

2.4 Lessons learned

After the extensive collection of pitfalls and perils in the previous section, the reader may start to wonder about the maturity of electronic negotiation technologies in general. Some practitioners might also have a map of necessary building blocks in mind that now shows far too many white spaces. But these apparent shortcomings a) have to a large extent their roots in several specifically tough challenges in the domain of electronic negotiations, b) clearly define the future direction of research (what needs to be done), and c) can be broken down into smaller problems, which are feasible to address one after another. In the corresponding next three sections, these lessons learned from the analysis of the state of the art are presented.

2.4.1 Challenges for electronic negotiation technologies

The preceding review of electronic negotiation research and the brief analysis of electronic negotiation technology usage in today's eCommerce world unveils a large discrepancy between theory and practice. Whereas in research, experiments with, for example, fully automated negotiations among communities of autonomous agents with learning capability are undertaken (see for example [Keph+00]), simple price auctions with minimal automation (e.g. through bidding agents) are leading-edge applications in operative electronic markets.

This discrepancy cannot be attributed only to a typical technology adoption cycle and the common human resistance to the simplifications of automation – factors which inhibited other information systems / computer science innovations attempting to replace human communication and decision-

making (e.g. methodologies from operations research). In the case of negotiations, the reason lies also in the fact that electronic negotiation technologies face
- already discussed shortcomings in theory (see above)
- many uncertainties in negotiation situations (see Section 1.1.1)
- one really 'hard' problem (see below), and
- resistance motivated by social and cultural issues.

The hard problem is the need for creativity. In the negotiation literature a common saying is that a pie needs not only to be divided but also to be enlarged before it can be cut to everybody's satisfaction (c.f. [Lewi+97, 74ff.]). If a negotiation gets stuck because the parties cannot achieve an agreement on the current set of issues, often the best solution is to redefine the negotiation problem – e.g. by adding or removing dimensions of the negotiation object.

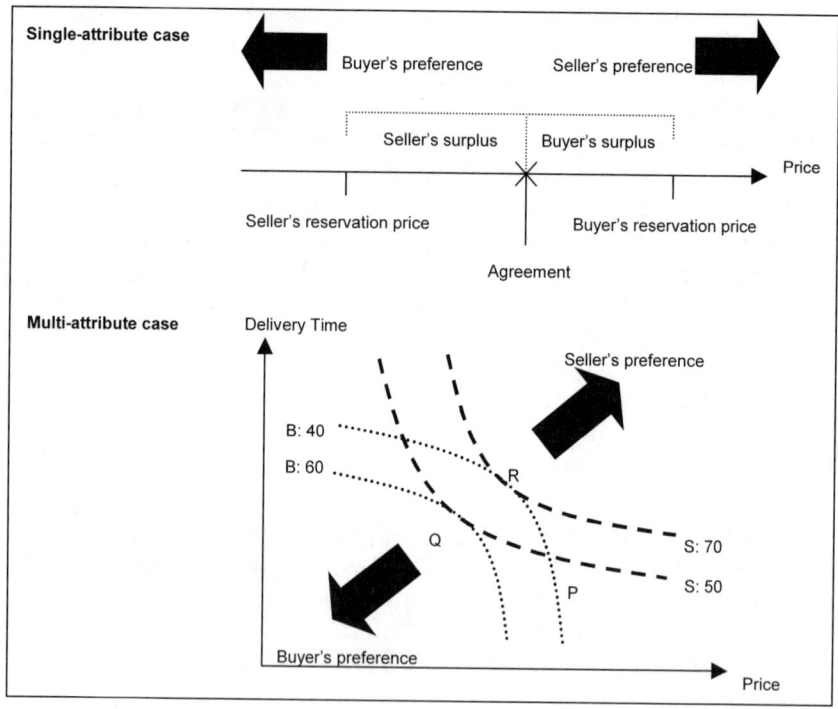

Figure 10. Single-/multi-attribute negotiation problems

In a simple example, two parties might debate only one attribute, the *price* for a certain transaction. Obviously one party wants to pay less, the other receive more. If no agreement is in reach, one approach is to add another attribute, e.g. the *delivery time*. Maybe now, through mutual compromises in a two-dimensional space, an agreement is possible that can be accepted by both parties. This change to the nature of the negotiation problem is illustrated in *Figure 10* (previous page).

In the multi-attribute case in *Figure 10*, the preferences of the seller and buyer towards the negotiation outcome are indicated through iso-value curves (see [Raif82, 156ff.]). All combinations of *price* and *delivery time* on an iso-value curve return the same utility (are indifferent, see Section 3.3.1), e.g. a value of 60 for the buyer. Initially the negotiation process might be stuck at point 'P' where the seller expects a utility of 50 and the buyer a utility of 40. If the seller now agrees to reduce the price but in turn has more time to deliver, this trade-off for him to the new point 'Q' still returns a utility of 50, but due to a different valuation of this trade-off, the buyer expects now the utility of the transaction to be 60. If both parties manage to discover another similar trade-off with favourable outcome for the seller, the prospects for an agreement are certainly better than in the initial situation. The points on a line between 'Q' and 'R' represent improvements for both parties, and the line is called a contract-curve. This search process may result then in a typical example for a win-win solution, which could also be pareto-efficient – no other solution can be found which is better for one party without being worse for the other (see [Fran96, 558ff.] and Section 3.5.2.2). However, multiple attributes are not a necessary condition for win-win solutions. If the parties have opposing interests and corresponding valuations across all attributes, no win-win solutions can be found (see the debate on the measure of opposition in Section 3.3.2).

If all attributes are known, this 'log-rolling' game can be solved computationally. The true hard problem, though is to 'bring new attributes on the table' – to find new attributes so that the preference structure of the parties allows for mutual improvements. This includes defining exactly the meaning of this new attribute so that all involved parties share the same understanding towards the outcomes regarding this attribute. Up to now, in none of the mentioned research disciplines has a solution for this problem been suggested and as a consequence, real world negotiators have a tough argument against their electronic counterparts.

This argument is often complemented with a variety of social and cultural issues. In traditional commerce, long established relationships among trade partners play a big part in negotiations. Negotiators tend not to restrict their view to the current negotiation situation but rather often have a larger picture of the relation to the other party in their minds. In fact, negotiations are often the means to get to know the other party and to build a relationship with a certain degree of trust.

As a result of this, for example in Latin or Asian countries, the negotiation process itself may sometimes be more important than the result [Ulji+01]. Therefore, reducing a negotiation situation to an exchange of numbers with a computational optimisation strategy is in many real world cases clearly not a substitute for the multi-faced aspects of the traditional way of business interaction.

In addition, the math behind the suggested negotiation algorithms is a mystery to most real world negotiators, and since the required capture and formalisation of the negotiator's preference structure remains obscure, trust regarding the loss of control and transfer of responsibility to, for instance, a software agent, remains the primary obstacle for widespread acceptance.

2.4.2 First conclusions and directions

Not only regarding the mentioned challenges, but more generally one can say, "standard auction formats are the low hanging fruits" [Kers00]. As a consequence, electronic negotiation media for price-based auction scenarios are proliferating in eCommerce. However, the preceding assessment of the state of the art unveils a lack of electronic negotiation media that considers both, the need for multi-attribute negotiations and the value of the intended transaction. The goal of electronic markets is to increase the efficiency of the market process by achieving low transaction costs comprising fast market coordination. Without this benefit there would be no incentive for business organisations to coordinate their transactions through an electronic market. One major means of achieving this efficiency is to provide a high level of automation and integration for all phases of market interaction. However, as has been shown, in practice support for negotiation processes is insufficient if an agreement on multiple attributes of a deal is required.

If there is a need for multi-attribute negotiation because a negotiation scenario cannot be reduced to a matter of price, but the value of the transaction is low, major electronic market benefits cannot yet be achieved because automation support is missing and intensive human involvement is needed. This human involvement increases the transaction costs and slows down the coordination process. If the transaction value is high, the necessary agreement on the various attributes can be achieved through intensive human interaction, which is expensive and requires time. But the benefit of reaching an efficient agreement will in most cases exceed the costs involved, and low transaction costs in other phases are still prevalent. Hence, traditional offline negotiation is currently used for large, complex deals, whereas electronic negotiation is used to work out smaller, price-based, and more routine transactions [Andr01].

An evaluation of the state of the art

From this discussion a need for multi-attribute negotiation support providing low transaction costs and fast coordination can be derived. One way to achieve this efficiency is automation. But, regarding the shortcomings of current research approaches (see above), it is still an open question whether complete automation in the multi-attribute negotiation space will ever succeed.

Kersten and Noronha express a need for hybrid (partly automated) negotiation media, owing to the fact that despite all advances in automation, humans still need to be involved in negotiations [KeNo99]. Schoop and Quix also argue that "human negotiators cannot and indeed should not be replaced by software agents and the aim should be to provide support for electronic negotiations rather than to automate them completely" [ScQu01, p.154]. In **hybrid** electronic negotiation media, structured or formalised tasks are automated, and decision support mechanisms are used to assess unstructured tasks, whereas humans interactively control the execution of the electronic negotiation and perform exception handling.

The intermediary paradigm is well suited for the implementation of hybrid negotiation media, because an **intermediary** expects input from the negotiator for the task execution, returns results, and waits for subsequent actions. Intermediaries interpose themselves naturally between buyers and sellers and replace direct communication in order to support the coordination in the market ([ClLe99] or [ZaBr99]). Most formal negotiation media approaches focus on supporting the communication of decision-makers and/or automating the decision-making of a single negotiator, whereas a model where the medium suggests decisions to, or processes decision tasks for, multiple negotiators seems not to be explored extensively in electronic markets. This is especially remarkable since intermediaries or brokers generally play a vital role in electronic markets owing to their efficient hub position, which offers the capability to create trust and to provide value-added services (c.f. [Sark+96]). Negotiation intermediation offers many opportunities such as economies of scale through standardisation or the derivation of reusable negotiation patterns (see Section 8.3.2.2). Furthermore, though negotiators typically refrain from revealing confidential information such as their preferences to the counterpart in a negotiation, they might be less hesitant if this information only has to be disclosed to a trusted third party, i.e. the intermediary.

Figure 11 below illustrates the focal point of negotiation intermediation, which is the central enforcement of rules and support for communication and decision-making processes abstracted from the internal view of negotiators, whether they are human or software agents. In contrast, negotiation offer exchange focuses on support and rule mechanisms, which are private to a negotiator. An online auction system, for example, acts as a simple negotiation intermediary, since it enforces communication rules (e.g. 'who can bid when') and executes one central decision (e.g. 'who is/are the winning bidder/s').

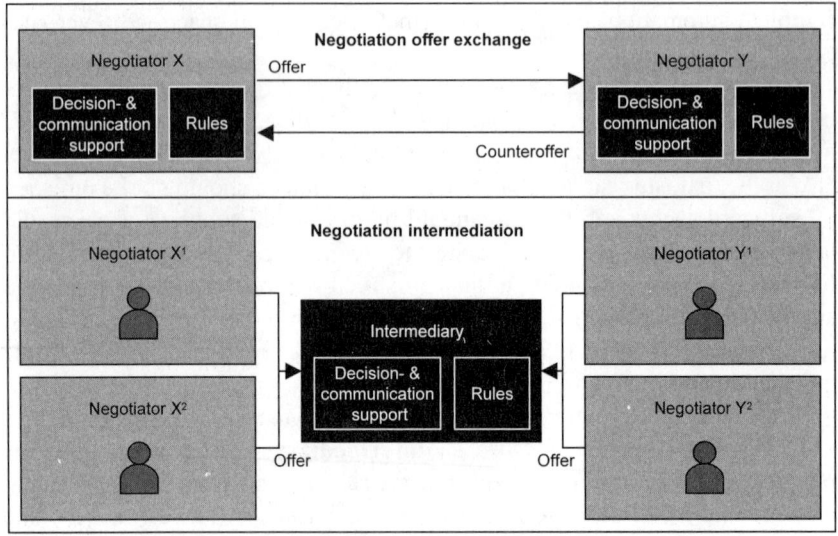

Figure 11. Negotiation intermediation versus direct offer exchange

In addition to insufficient support for multi-attribute negotiations, the analysis in this section also identified a lack of symmetry in existing commercial negotiation media. Although a mutual dependency is a necessary condition for negotiations to take place, in practice electronic negotiation media tend to provide richer functionalities and representations for either buyers or sellers, thus jeopardising fairness and consequently the incentives for participation. **Symmetry** in negotiation refers to a unified view towards the roles of buyers, sellers and third parties (e.g. market makers) participating in an electronic negotiation. All parties have, in principle, the same options to act and react. The intermediary approach also provides a natural foundation for a symmetric media conception.

On the basis of this review of the state of the art in classic negotiation research and electronic negotiations, the focus of this book is narrowed to the domain of electronic negotiations where critical open issues are currently not addressed, but which also offers significant practical relevance: **symmetric multi-attribute negotiation intermediation in electronic markets**.

An evaluation of the state of the art 33

2.4.3 Core problems in multi-attribute negotiation support

This book does not suggest a solution for the creativity problem discussed in Section 2.2.4.1, nor does it specifically address the social and cultural challenges that electronic negotiation technology is facing. The stage for this book is multi-attribute negotiation intermediation in electronic markets (for the reasons outlined in the previous section), and its part is to solve a number of problems in this domain, which currently inhibit for solely technical reasons a practical application of this approach. Hence, if the proposed solutions are successful, the challenges discussed in Section 2.2.4.1 still remain – but we are certainly one step further.

So what are the core problems related to multi-attribute negotiation? As outlined, electronic negotiation media are, as of today, available for single-attribute negotiations in a very efficient way, but negotiation support still faces open issues for multi-attribute negotiations. Communication processes in multi-attribute negotiations such as sending an offer to counterpart, or posting a multi-attribute RFQ on a public bulletin board and receiving notifications for every incoming bid, are well supported with means that do not necessarily originate from electronic negotiation research (e.g. e-mail and document management technology). However, automation and assistance is insufficient for decision tasks in multi-attribute negotiations, such as for decisions on the following issues:

- Which party is the best to negotiate with?
- What issues are subject to the negotiation?
- How can one get closer to an agreement?
- How does this offer compare to another one?
- Should one accept this offer or counteroffer?
- What kind of trade-off can be proposed?
- Should this negotiation process be continued?

As stated above, the goal of electronic markets is to increase the efficiency of the market coordination through low transaction costs on the basis of a high level of automation and integration for all phases of market interaction. In practice though, automation support for negotiation processes is insufficient if multiple attributes of a deal have to be considered. Thus, the following first problem in the domain of electronic negotiations can be formulated:

Problem I: Automation or assistance for multi-attribute negotiation decision tasks in electronic markets is not sufficient to attain low transaction costs.

The undesirable consequence of this problem is that in many cases, creators of electronic markets might try to reduce negotiation scenarios to simple price mechanisms and the application of multi-attribute negotiations remains limited to transactions of high value, which justify extensive human interaction and high coordination costs. Hence, those electronic markets that were constrained to price conflicts, but in reality would require more complex negotiations will fail, for instance by the means of price wars and seller exits. Another consequence could be that economic transactions, whose coordination does not comply with the assumptions of currently available negotiation media, will not be executed through electronic markets but remain subject to traditional offline trading.

In addition to these dangers of market failure, agreements achieved through multi-attribute negotiations are potentially more desirable than outcomes of single-attribute negotiations because of the possibility to achieve win-win solutions. Therefore, availability of multi-attribute negotiation support in electronic markets would provide an additional incentive for market participation, which may result in increased market volumes.

But it has also been shown that it is not a realistic goal to demand the complete automation of multi-attribute negotiations in electronic markets. In most cases this will be impractical owing to decision complexities and uncertainties (c.f. Section 1.1.1). By and large, human interaction will remain necessary in real world negotiation scenarios. Thus, following the notion of hybrid negotiation support, electronic negotiation media have to offer means to automate and assist those communication and decision-making processes in electronic negotiations that are structured enough to be formalised, as well as interfaces for human decision makers to evaluate the results of support operations in order to decide on the next process steps (c.f. [Kers98]).

A second problem related to the design of electronic negotiations can be identified in the domain of this book. For the acceptance of an electronic negotiation it is necessary to achieve some commitment from the potential users of the electronic negotiation medium on the rules restricting actual negotiation processes, including the distinct roles of the involved negotiators. This a priori agreement has to address a number of questions such as: should all attributes be negotiated at the same time, or one after another, and in which sequence? Can one negotiator counter an offer by including or requesting additional offer attributes (e.g. a currently not included product warranty)? What happens if an offer is not signed within a certain timeframe?

Like any other information system, the creation of an electronic market can be structured along the system development phases of analysis, design, and implementation. For a market intended to support electronic negotiations, the design activity has to comprise the negotiation scenario, which defines how potential transaction partners reach an agreement on the attribute values of the deal. Choice and further specification of this scenario will vary depending on the business context requirements identified in the analysis phase. In the implementation phase, the design including the rules defined for the negotiation, i.e. the negotiation scenario has to be mapped to the system architecture.

However, there are no common means by which the creator of the electronic market and the stakeholders can reason about the potential rules for the negotiation. Holsapple et al. [Hols+91] identified this need for general models of negotiations, which could be used to characterise formally the nature and process of the negotiation and still have the flexibility to describe a wide range of possible structures and interactions. But the construction of comprehensive modelling paradigms has been largely neglected in negotiation research, rendering it difficult to discuss and communicate negotiation scenarios on a conceptual level. Furthermore, design efforts cannot be reused and refined in a formal way in the implementation phase. In principle, general modelling approaches from game theory or computer science can be applied to represent negotiation scenarios, but these approaches still have to be examined and potentially tailored regarding the specific requirements of the electronic negotiation domain. "What is so special about the design of electronic market mechanisms is the fact that a designer has many more possibilities to design a mechanism than in physical markets. Computer networks make it easy to communicate large amounts of information relevant to a market transaction, not just price quotes" [BiSe01, p.138]. The second problem is therefore postulated as follows:

Problem II: Comprehensive and well-suited model representations for the design or discussion of negotiation scenarios in electronic markets are not available.

Given that comprehensive models for negotiation scenarios, which capture all possible dimensions of rules, are missing, it is also more difficult to come up with new negotiation scenarios that exploit the potentials of the combination of electronic markets with enhanced negotiation support technologies. Hence, in many cases, existing negotiation scenarios from traditional markets will only be copied to an electronic market setting, without specific consideration to a potentially changing environment and new possibilities.

Finally, a problem related to the current status of electronic negotiation media is that a large variety of media for different negotiation scenarios exists, but there is no system or architecture available that can support a broad range of negotiation scenarios. For certain negotiation scenario types, flexible media architectures have been developed, e.g. the Michigan Auction Bot [Wurm+98] for multilateral single-attribute negotiations (i.e. auctions). But to support a negotiation scenario with a round of bidding that leads to a synchronous bilateral negotiation between the highest bidder and the auctioneer, requires, for instance, the integration of auction technology with one-to-one cooperation tools. This lack of generalisation creates the undesirable consequence that unique and proprietary electronic negotiation media are created again and again, and huge efforts are spent on integrating isolated building blocks. Thus, a third problem can be identified:

Problem III: There exists no flexible media architecture model for electronic negotiations that can support a broad range of negotiation scenarios.

As long as this is the case, the implementation and setup costs for electronic negotiation media remain high and outsourcing opportunities, which require some level of standardisation, are limited. Hence, technology will drive, or rather constrain, the strategy of electronic market providers, forcing them to focus on those types of transactions that are assisted by negotiation support systems already available for the chosen medium architecture, or affordable to add and integrate as an extension.

This research intended to conclude in solutions for these problems followed an applied research and design science approach. Applied research means that the relevant problems are discovered in practice (as demonstrated above) and the research undertaken aims to provide the solution to the problems in a normative model, which again has to be useful in practice. This normative model is the enMedia framework and accordingly the research results presented are prescriptive. Design science (c.f. [MaSm95]) generally attempts to construct artefacts, such as the enMedia framework, and to assess their utility on the basis of criteria (e.g. the artefact's completeness, consistency, simplicity, elegance, understandability, and ease of use). This necessary assessment is also presented in this book (see Chapter 8).

3. SUMMARY

This chapter reviewed the theoretical and practical contributions in the domain of this book. The assessment comprises a summary of existing scientific approaches to electronic negotiations and a critical evaluation of the state of the art in electronic negotiation research and practice. On the basis of this review, a first conclusion is drawn. The primary focus of this book is narrowed to symmetric multi-attribute negotiation intermediation in electronic markets, as this domain offers real world relevance and many practical prospects, but currently faces a multitude of open issues such as the inability to achieve low transaction costs. These issues defined the core problems to be addressed in this book. The consecutive exploration in the upcoming chapters provides claims about and evidence for how these problems can be solved.

Summary

A first contribution of this book is manifested in the next chapter, which introduces a stringent and comprehensive definition system for electronic negotiations as a foundation for the following presentation of the suggested concepts and solutions.

Chapter 3

Foundations
Terms, formalisms, and a taxonomy

In this chapter a specific foundation for the presentation and discussion of the research results is developed for this book. This foundation complements the theoretical and practical assets for electronic negotiations reviewed in the previous section. The definition system in this chapter comprises:
- the introduction of a set of basic concepts and especially the notion of electronic negotiations and negotiation support,
- the development of a formal specification for describing a multi-attribute electronic negotiation situation and process,
- the characterisation of elements of a reference model for electronic negotiation development and execution processes, and
- the profile of a taxonomy that can be used to classify distinctively different types of electronic negotiations.

These four building blocks are a necessary basis for the precise formulation and understanding of the findings presented in this book, and therefore will be used extensively in its remainder. The formal specification, for instance, provides the foundation for the specification of negotiation support solution procedures in Chapter 4 and for the offer language syntax in Chapter 5, whereas the reference development process is reflected in the deployment tool functionality of the prototype presented in Chapter 6.

1. NEGOTIATIONS

Humans negotiate all the time, though rarely over commercial issues such as price or delivery dates. Most often humans negotiate behaviour, barely conscious about it, in order to get along with each other: "...when negotiations surface and people do become aware of them, it is usually a sign that implicit negotiation has broken down..." [BrDu00, p.49]. Next to the most apparent explicit domain, commerce or trade, negotiations also take place in, for instance, political (e.g. Camp David) or legal conflicts (e.g. divorces). However, for the purpose of this book, the domain is restricted to commercial negotiations.

The outcome of a successful negotiation is usually some sort of contract. This contract may in a simple case just state one or more facts that all involved parties agree to (e.g., 'the name for the new joint venture is ...'). More complex contracts on the other hand, usually constitute a plan for future actions that is described through rights and obligations (e.g. 'X delivers goods and Y pays for the goods').

According to Lewicki et al [Lewi+97, p.5] "negotiations occur for one of two reasons: (1) to create something new that neither party could do on its own, or (2) to resolve a problem or dispute between the parties." Accordingly the activity of negotiating can be characterised by a set of common properties:
- There are two or more sides, represented by two or more parties.
- The parties are searching for a solution to a problem, which may be a conflict of interest.
- Through decision-making this solution (agreement) has to be accepted by all parties.
- There is a mutual dependency between the parties. The solution cannot be reached through unilateral action.
- The parties communicate because they want a better solution instead of simply accepting what the other side will voluntarily give them.

This definition clarifies that a negotiation is a **communication and decision-making process** and that this process can be distinguished from a pure decision-making process, in which no communication might occur. Depending on the area of research, more formal definitions of negotiations have been suggested (see Section 2.1).

2. ELECTRONIC NEGOTIATIONS

A **transaction** transfers the ownership of tangible or intangible **objects** (e.g. *goods*, *money*) or rights to services (e.g. *insurance*) from one **agent** to another and vice versa. The specification for one or more transactions, for the objects of the exchange, and for the agents involved, constitutes a **deal**. A number of deals similar in kind can be classified with a **deal type**.

The basis for introducing the notion of **electronic negotiations** is the concept of media and the media reference model (MRM, [Schm98]). **Media**

Electronic negotiations

are platforms where transactions are coordinated through agent interaction. Media can be described in terms of three main components:

- **Channels**
  Agents access a medium via channels that can transport the data to be exchanged.
- **Logical space**
  The syntax and semantics defined for the data that the agents exchange.
- **Organisation**
  Roles describing the types of agents and protocols specifying their interactions.

An **electronic medium** in particular is a medium with electronic (digital) channels that transport electronic data. The agents, however, might still be humans or organisational units and do not necessarily have to be software agents. If economic goods are exchanged through agent interaction, the medium constitutes an **electronic market** (EM).

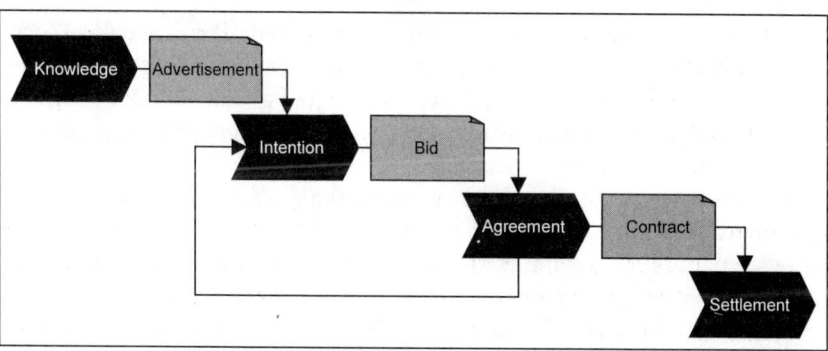

Figure 12. Interaction phases of an electronic transaction

In *Figure 12* the phases of interaction in the MRM are outlined. Offers issued by agents are possible, and in practice the dominating means of representing this interaction in electronic markets (see for example [KeNo99]). Depending on the actual phase transition, offers may assume different states of formality and structure [Strö01b]:

- **Advertisement**
  In the knowledge phase agents gather information concerning the objects offered or the profiles of other agents. An offer in the form of an advertisement can be issued in the knowledge phase. This advertisement might relate to a general class of objects (e.g. the types of products or services offered by this agent) and is typically not related to another offer from a counterpart, but targeted at a group of potential transaction partners. An

advertised offer is also persistent in the sense that it is valid for a certain period of time.
- **Bid**
In the intention phase, demand and supply are specified. An offer in the form of a bid can be a response to an advertisement, and is therefore specific to the transaction, object, and agent specification proposed in the advertisement. Bids might also result from an advertisement that 'spawns' bids specific to received requests. This is, for instance, often the case if the object is customisable or has certain options. In such an example, an interested agent might bid to buy an advertised object with certain options and the advertisement 'generates' a complementary bid with a total price for this choice of object options. The validity of a bid is limited by the validity of the associated advertisement or complementary bid, but is usually constrained even further (e.g. 'please respond to this bid by…'). The agreement phase is initiated on the basis of one or more bids.
- **Contract**
As a result of a successful agreement phase, a final offer in the form of a contract can seal mutually accepted bids with legally binding signatures of the agents. A contract, which is persistent beyond the duration of the agreement phase, marks the transition to the settlement phase where the agreed-upon transaction is executed.

For the purpose of this book the following distinction is made: an **agreement process** represents the complete agent interaction in the intention and agreement phase for the coordination of one or more transactions. The goal of an agreement process is to come to a mutual agreement between agents regarding the specification of one or more future deals. The agreement process might comprise a negotiation process, but an agreement can also be reached without any negotiation. This will be the case if one or both agents merely accept the offer of the counterpart.

A **negotiation process** takes place when the first agreement phase fails – i.e. when based on the offers made in the intention phase, either an agreement cannot be reached or the agreement has the potential for optimisation and the agents intending to carry out the transaction want to discuss their offers. From the perspective of one agent, negotiating is characterised by the modification of one's own offer or the efforts to change another agent's offer [Strö00b]. This relation of the agreement and the negotiation process can be compared to the definition of negotiations in the wider and the narrow sense in [Rung00, 77ff.].

Referring to the negotiation processes, the notion of offer modification can be narrowed to modifications in reaction to the behaviour (offers made) of the other agent(s) or to parameters related to the negotiation situation (e.g. the remaining time). Predefined dimensions of offer specification (e.g. with associated price functions), which allow the counterpart to select the preferred deal configuration (typically with electronic product catalogues) do not constitute offer modifications in this narrow sense but represent a fixed offer with predefined choices.

If a negotiation process is executed, the core activity of revising offers requires agents to alternate between the intention and the agreement phase, for instance to generate a counteroffer. Within the agreement phase the agents will evaluate the offers of potential transaction counterparts and decide, based on their negotiation strategy, on the subsequent action. In summary, a negotiation process is always part of an agreement process, but an agreement process might not necessarily include a negotiation process.

An **agreement scenario** defines the environment for the execution of an agreement process. The description of an agreement scenario consists of a set of rules (or policies) restricting agent actions and agent interaction. An electronic medium supporting negotiation processes in the intention and agreement phase is denoted an **electronic negotiation medium** (enMedium). An enMedium provides **electronic negotiation support**, meaning the assistance or automation of decision-making or communication tasks within negotiation processes.

A negotiation classifies as an **electronic negotiation** in the context of this book if it is restricted by at least one rule that affects the decision-making or communication process, if this rule is enforced by the electronic medium supporting the negotiation, and if this support covers the execution of at least one decision-making or communication task (c.f. [RaSh97]).

If a negotiation process is conducted using an enMedium, an **electronic negotiation process** (enProcess) is executed. In the case that an agreement scenario leads to a negotiation process and is supported by an enMedium, it is referred to as an **electronic negotiation scenario**, or enScenario for short. An actual enScenario executed within an enMedium in a specific business context is denoted an **electronic negotiation instance** (enInstance).

Figure 13 (next page) illustrates the relation among the introduced electronic negotiation elements. An enScenario might be deployed to several enMedia (see Section 3.4.1). An enMedium resides within a specific business context and may support several enScenarios, the combination thereof constituting an enInstance. One or more enProcesses can be executed in one enInstance.

Depending on the level of support provided by the enMedium, electronic negotiations can be: **automated** or **hybrid** (partly automated), **communication-supporting** and/or **decision-supporting** (c.f. Section 4.1). Assistance for an enProcess can already be realised with electronic means for exchanging or discussing offers such as e-mail or video-conferencing. An enMedium does not necessarily assist all communication and decisions in the intention and agreement phase. Tasks outside the core negotiation process such as *pricing* in the intention phase, or *contract validation* in the agreement phase, may not be supported by the enMedium.

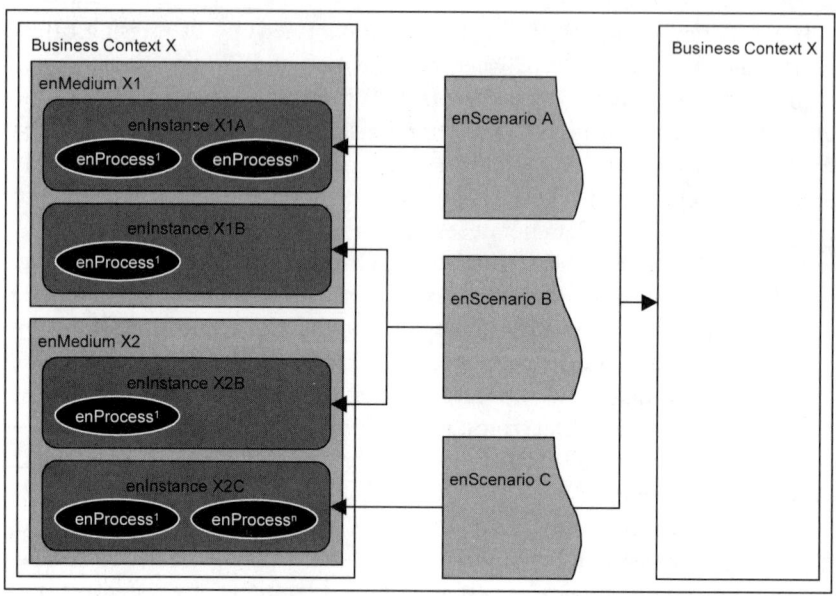

Figure 13. Configuration of electronic negotiations

A multitude of technologies can be used to build enMedia. These technologies are the results of development efforts that have historically come to be known as negotiation support systems (NSS, [JeFo89]). The notion of enMedia comprises NSS as services on the transaction layer of the MRM. *Figure 14* (next page) summarises the most important definitions developed in this section on the basis of the holistic media reference model perspective. An agreement process on the implementation layer can, but does not necessarily have to, include a negotiation process. Accordingly, an electronic market medium must support agreement processes with services in the transaction layer, but does not necessarily include an electronic negotiation medium with support for electronic negotiation processes.

Formal model

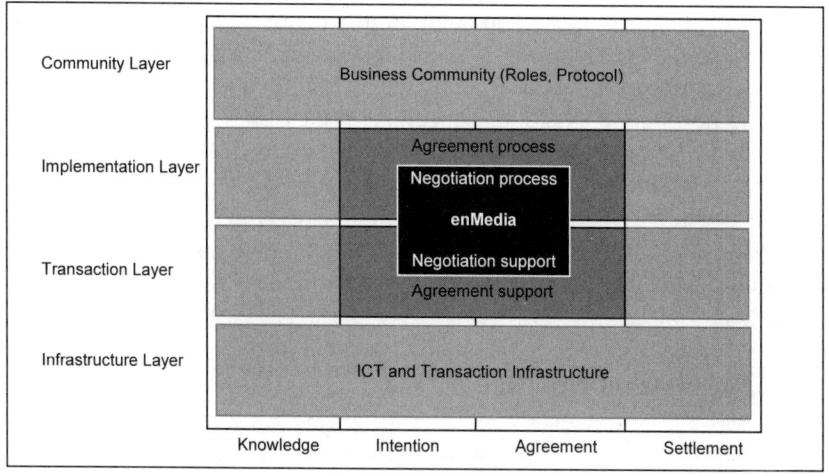

Figure 14. enMedia in the MRM

Finally, negotiation support is not restricted to electronic media. For instance, if a human mediator joins the negotiation process to suggest a compromise to settle a dispute, this also constitutes a negotiation support activity, but not a form of electronic negotiation support.

3. FORMAL MODEL

In this section, a formal specification for common negotiation situation and interaction elements is introduced on the basis of relational algebra. The goal for this formalism is to be rich enough to express a variety of potential negotiation scenarios, but also formal enough to allow for the definition and characterisation of structured, machine-readable negotiation scenario representations.

In principle, this specification should apply to both traditional and electronic negotiation situations. However, its main purpose is to provide a foundation for electronic negotiation support[2]. The formal model was used to

---

[2] The usability of a formal definition approach for the support of electronic negotiations is also demonstrated in [BaLo00], which suggests a comparable formalisation for a generic architecture to support local reasoning of negotiating agents in the form of propositional constraint optimisation.

formalise the negotiation support solution procedures in Chapter 4[3], such as a matchmaking operation, and it also provided the basis for an offer language, as manifested in the offer XML syntax specified in Section 5.4.1.

First, a negotiation situation is specified in general. Then the definitions are extended to views of two or more agents on a negotiation situation, including a characterisation of the negotiation process.

Readers who are less interested in formal aspects may skip this section and advance to the process model in Section 3.4, since the definitions provided in the preceding section are already sufficient for the further elaboration in this book.

3.1 Negotiation situation

The following specification elements are used to represent a negotiation situation. An **agent** in a negotiation has an associated role, which may be of the type buyer, seller, or intermediary. In electronic negotiations, autonomous proxy agents can represent all of these types and automate certain aspects of the agent behaviour.

Definition 1. Agent (synonym: participant, party, negotiator)

$ag \in AG = \{ag_1, ag_2, ..., ag_n\}$

Definition 2. Agent type

$ay \in AY = \{buyer, seller\}$

Definition 3. Agent role

$ARO \subset AG \times AY$

The goal of commercial negotiations is to conduct one or more transactions between some of the agents involved in the negotiation process. A transaction, the associated object(s), and the agents involved constitute a deal, which can be described with a set of **attributes** such as the *delivery time* of the transaction, the *colour* of the object, or the *location* of the agent.

Definition 4. Attribute (synonym: property, terms & conditions)

$at \in AT = \{at_1, at_2, ..., at_n\}$

Definition 5. Attribute operator

$ao \in AO = \{<, \leq, =, \neq, \geq, >\}$

Definition 6. Attribute value

$av \in AV = \{av_1, av_2, ..., av_n\}$

The set of possible attribute values for one attribute specifies the **domain** of an attribute, which can include a **unit** measure (e.g. *USD* or *MHZ*) and may be specified to be **dynamic**. Dynamism is used to express that concrete values cannot or are not intended to be defined for this attribute in this nego-

---

[3] The complete formal specification of the NSC solution procedures is available in the original dissertation underlying this book.

Formal model

tiation situation until some knowledge about the offer of the counterpart or some external data (e.g. the current oil price) is known. A typical example is found in the insurance industry, where quotes are usually dependent on the *age*, *medical record*, or *driving experience* of the customer. An example of a dynamic domain is: *(price,=,*,USD)*.

Definition 7. Unit

```
un ∈ UN = {_,un₁, un₂,…,unₙ}  (the symbol '_' stands for 'no unit')
```

Definition 8. Domain

```
DOM ⊂ AT x AO x AV x UN | AT ≠ {}
DOMₐₜ = at x AO x AV x UN
```

Definition 9. Dynamic symbol

```
dy = *
```

Definition 10. Dynamic domain

```
DOMₐₜ,* = at x AO x dy x UN
```

Instantiations of domains can assume different characters:

– Point domain
 Only one tuple with one attribute value and the '=' operator is specified.
 Example: *(colour,=,blue,_)*
– Discrete domain
 Several tuples with a '=' operator are defined for one attribute.
 Example: *(colour,=,blue,_) (colour,=,green,_)*
– Steady domain
 One or several tuples with other operators than '=' are assigned to one attribute.
 Example: *(disk,≥,6,GB) (disk,≤,9,GB)*
– Exclusion domain
 Point and discrete domains become exclusion domains if the '≠' operator is used instead of the '=' operator.
 Example: *(colour,≠,blue,_) (colour,≠,green,_)*

Tuples of agent, transaction, or object attributes with corresponding attribute values and operators specified by an agent define the elements of a **deal space**. The deal space represents the possible configurations of a deal.

Definition 11. Deal space

```
DSP ⊂ AG x DOM
DSPₐg ⊂ ag x DOM
DSPₐg,ₐₜ ⊂ ag x DOMₐₜ
```

The **intention space** represents not only possible, but also acceptable, deal configurations from the perspective of one agent. This space is usually private to the agent and not communicated to counterparts in a negotiation. Domains restrict the set of potential values for one attribute and therefore can be denoted unary **constraints**. Binary constraints express relations between two attributes on the basis of a constraint operator. Accordingly, the intention space is defined as the joint finite set of unary and binary **constraints**. An agent may have multiple internal intention space representations (e.g. for different types of transactions or objects).

Definition 12. Constraint Operator

$co \in CO = \{<, \leq, =, \neq, \geq, >\}$

Definition 13. Unary Constraint

$ucs_{at} = DOM_{at}$

Definition 14. Binary Constraint

$bcs_{at^*,at^\wedge} \in BCS_{at^*,at^\wedge} \subset (at^*,AO,AV,UN) \times (at^\wedge,AO,AV,UN)$

$bcs_{at^*,at^\wedge} \in BCS_{at^*,at^\wedge} = (at^*,co,at^\wedge)$

Definition 15. Intention space

$ISP_{ag} = (ag \times UCS) \cup (ag \times BCS)$

Definition 16. Intention space attributes

$ISA_{ag} = \{at \mid \exists ucs_{at} \in ISP_{ag} \vee \exists bcs_{at,at^*} \in ISP_{ag} \vee \exists bcs_{at^*,at} \in ISP_{ag}\}$

Definition 17. Constraints for one attribute (domain constraint)

$ATC_{at,ag} = UCS_{at} \cup BCS_{at,at^*} \cup BCS_{at^*,at}$

In the following intention space example, the first tuple illustrates acceptable attribute value combinations for two attributes, the second specifies that the payment should take place after the delivery of the computer:

((X,(disk,<,6,GB)),(Y,(RAM,>,64,MB)),(X,(payment_t>delivery_t))).

Constraints restrict the set of all possible combinations of attributes to a smaller set of desirable combinations. Given the constraint-based intention space definition, a standard constraint satisfaction problem (CSP, see [Will+00]) can be defined. The solution to a CSP is an assignment of attribute values to attributes such that none of the constraints is violated[4]. The solution may not contradict any of the unary or binary constraints. One CSP can have several solutions. **Deal configurations** represent solutions to the intention space constraint satisfaction problem of one agent. In a deal configuration exactly one attribute value has to be defined for each attribute in the intention space – the cardinality of the set of attribute values in all domains is thus '1'.

Definition 18. Deal configuration

$DCF_{ag} = \{(at,ao,av,un) \mid \forall at \in ISA_{ag}: \exists (ag,at,=,AV,un) \in ISP_{ag} \wedge |AV|=1\}$

One could argue that alternative attributes in the intention space specification (e.g. *graphics accelerator* or *DVD drive*) do not require an attribute value for each attribute. For constraint satisfaction purposes, however, such alternatives can be reformulated as alternative combinations of value tuples

---

[4] Solving CSPs for non-discrete (steady) attribute domains is still very inefficient. Therefore it is often assumed that only discrete domains are used in order to guarantee efficient solutions.

(see the definition of 'options' below). In some cases it might also make sense to relax the restriction of single attribute values, because agents often finalise a deal including well-defined value ranges for certain attributes (e.g. acceptable size tolerances in manufacturing).

An agent can express a willingness to modify the intention space, if, for instance, an agreement does not seem to be possible on the basis of the initial intention space definition. Technically, all constraints that define the intention space can be **negotiable**. Of course, this does not make sense for all attributes assessed by constraints – a constraint for the agent *location* attribute, for instance, will usually not be negotiable. Constraints that are tagged 'negotiable' are denoted 'soft' constraints, as opposed to the non-negotiable 'hard' constraints in the intention space definition.

Definition 19. Negotiability assignment

```
NEG = ISP → {true,false}
```

Definition 20. Soft constraints

```
SCS_ag = {isp | isp ∈ ISP_ag ∧ NEG(isp) = true}
```

Definition 21. Attributes with soft constraints

```
ASC_ag = {at | at ∈ ISA_ag ∧ ∃at c_at ∈ SCS_ag}
```

In an example case, the constraint *(X,(disk,<,6,GB))* could be negotiable but also a complete binary constraint such as *(X,(payment_t,>,delivery_t))*, indicating that the agent might also agree to a settlement where the payment takes place before the delivery. An agent could as well decide to make elements of the intention space dynamically negotiable, during the course of the negotiation process, e.g. due to competitive pressures.

What is the difference of negotiable constraints to discrete or steady domains? The answer is that in the case of negotiable constraints, the agent is willing to make a concession – to agree to a deal configuration outside the initial intention space specification, maybe in return for another agent's concession (see the definition of negotiations in a narrow sense in Section 3.2).

In summary, the specification of an intention space as introduced so far, may comprise the following elements: unary constraints, binary constraints, and the negotiability assignment. In other words, the intention space can be defined by the joint set of unary and binary complemented by the labelling function indicating which of these constraints are soft constraints. The minimal definition of an intention space is a non-empty set of attributes. All other elements introduced in this section (attribute values, operators, units, negotiability, etc.) are optional. This reflects the fact that in practice the scope of negotiations might not be clear at the beginning of the intention phase.

In addition to these fundamental definitions, a number of terms commonly used to characterise negotiation situations can be defined on the basis of the specification introduced. The number of attributes in the intention space defines its **dimension**. If there are only two attributes, for instance *price* and *quantity*, the intention space is two-dimensional. A typical example for a one-dimensional intention space is an English auction, where the agents want to agree on one single attribute – the price.

Options in the intention space can be defined on the basis of binary constraints if the value for one attribute is paired with a set of two or more alternative values for the other attribute.

Example: $bcs^1_{RAM,mouse} = (X,(RAM,=,64,MB)),(X,(mouse,=,track,\_))$
$bcs^2_{RAM,mouse} = (X,(RAM,=,64,MB)),(X,(mouse,=,stick,\_))$

Constraints also enable the specification of **dependencies**. In the case of dependencies the selection of one attribute value for a particular attribute determines the attribute value of another attribute. If, for example, an agent chooses to increase the size of the hard disk for a computer this will certainly have an impact on the price from the seller's perspective.

Example: $bcs^1_{disk,price} = (X,(disk,=,8,GB)),(X,(price,=,900,USD))$
$bcs^2_{disk,price} = (X,(disk,=,12,GB)),(X,(price,=,950,USD))$

If *price* is the only attribute defined in the intention space (that is, the intention space is one-dimensional) and the agent defines a steady constraint, the boundary is often referred to as the **reservation price** [KeSz98].

Aspiration levels (desired deal configuration elements, see [KeSz86]) can be represented as attribute values of negotiable domains. A steady domain might, for example, be defined as follows: *(CPU,>,600,MHZ)*. If this domain were tagged 'negotiable', the agent would aspire to get a computer with a processor speed greater than *600 MHZ*, but would also settle for less, if compensated appropriately.

3.2 Negotiation interaction

In the previous section, the discussion of negotiation concepts and terms was focused on a rather static view of the negotiation situation. This restriction is now omitted in order to investigate how two (or more) agents may come to an agreement.

An **offer space** is an expression of will concerning the attribute values associated with a deal. Offer spaces are subsets of an agent's intention space that the agent intends to communicate to another agent as proposed dimensions of a deal configuration. The structure of the intention space limits the structure of the offer space. If the intention space, for instance, is just minimally specified with a set of attributes, an offer space can only be a subset of these attributes and cannot contain additional attribute values/operators. In another scenario, the intention space definition might comprise soft constraints, though the initial offer space contains only a set of attributes without constraints.

Formal model

Definition 22. Offer space

$OSP_{ag} \subset ISP_{ag} \cup NEG_{ag}$

The information that an agent might have represented internally at the beginning of the agreement phase, before the actual negotiation process takes place, can be summarised as depicted in *Figure 15*.

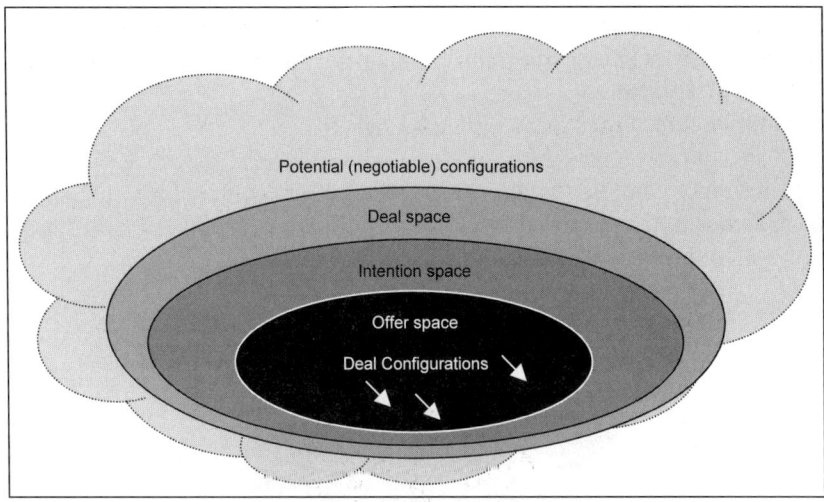

Figure 15. Negotiation situation model

From the perspective of one agent, an offer space is usually a subset of the intention space (because agents tend not to advertise the complete intention space), which in turn is a subset of the deal space. A deal configuration represents one point within the offer space. A fuzzier notion of negotiable deal configurations surrounds the more explicit representations introduced in the preceding section. Offer spaces as well as intention spaces may change during the course of a negotiation, and the deal configuration might not be part of the initial offer space. These dynamic aspects of negotiations are discussed in this section.

Let us assume that two agents have an internal representation for their intention spaces and offer spaces, and that they initiate the negotiation process by exchanging initial offer space instances. The originator of an offer assumes one of the agent roles buyer or seller, and thereby defines the offer as either an **offer-to-buy** (O2B) or **offer-to-sell** (O2S).

Definition 23. Offer space instance (Synonym: offer, bid, ask)

$osp_{ag} \subset OSP_{ag}$

Definition 24. Offer category

$ct \in CT = \{O2B, O2S\}$

Definition 25. Offer assignment

    OFA = osp → CT

Definition 26. Offer-to-buy

    o2b_ag = osp_ag : OFA(osp_ag) = O2B

Definition 27. Offer-to-sell

    o2s_ag = osp_ag : OFA(osp_ag) = O2S

Those attributes of the intention space whose value domains are specified through unary or binary constraints in the offer space are called **offer space instance attributes**.

Definition 28. Offer space instance attributes

    OSA_osp = {at | ∃ucs_at ∈ osp ∨ ∃bcs_{at,at*} ∈ osp ∨ ∃bcs_{at*,at} ∈ osp}

For further analysis of the dynamic view on a negotiation interaction, the agent association is removed, which allows for the derivation of joint spaces with well-defined semantics.

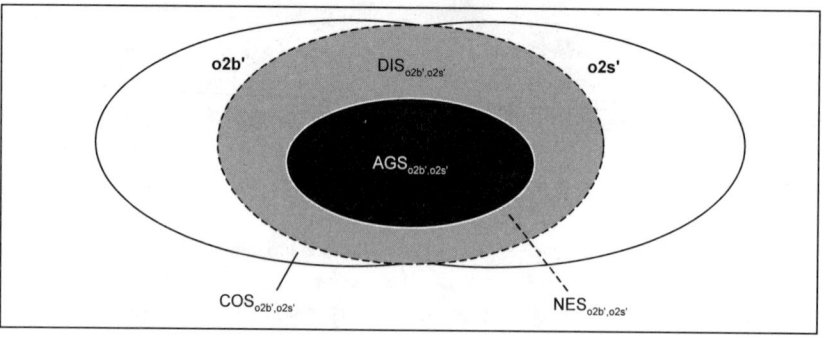

Figure 16. Spaces in the negotiation process

Definition 29. Anonymous offer space instance

    off' = {(at,ao,av,un) | (ag,(at,ao,av,un)) ∈ osp_ag}

Definition 30. Agreement space

    AGS_{o2b',o2s'} = o2b' ∩ o2s'

Definition 31. Negotiation space

    NES_{o2b',o2s'} = o2b' ∪ o2s' : OSA_{o2b'} = OSA_{o2s'}

Definition 32. Disagreement space

    DIS = NES \ AGS

Definition 33. Conflict space

    COS_{o2b',o2s'} = (o2b' ∪ o2s') \ AGS_{o2b',o2s'}

For all constraints in the **conflict space** COS (see *Figure 16*), the interacting agents do not even agree on the attributes that are supposed to be part of the deal and subject to the agreement. The agents do agree on the attributes of the constraints in the **negotiation space** NES. However, in the

Formal model 53

disagreement space DAS, which is part of NES but excludes AGS, the agents still disagree on the attribute values. Finally, the **agreement space** AGS represents elements of deal configurations that are compliant with the constraints defined in the offer spaces of the agents at the current state of the negotiation.

In practice, it will in most cases be impossible to determine the agreement space in this formal way because the intention space specifications of the agents will either not be complete, or will not be revealed completely through offer space instances. A trusted and objective third party, though, could assess the agreement space for particular negotiation situations and thereby evaluate the feasibility of a solution. The issues of a negotiation are defined as those offer elements (constraints), which are not part of the agreement space.

Definition 34. Issues

$$ISS_{o2b',o2s'} = \{isp \mid (isp \in o2b' \lor isp \in o2s') \land isp \notin AGS_{o2b',o2s'}\}$$

The agreement space can be empty, thus indicating that based on the current definition of the offer spaces no agreement is possible. On the other hand, the agreement space could as well contain all dimensions defined in the respective agents' intention spaces, thus indicating that an agreement has already been reached and only a detailed specification, meaning a selection of one deal configuration among the set of possible configurations, remains to be undertaken.

Once the agreement space is determined, an agent will try to evaluate the potential deal configurations in order to reason about the feasibility of an agreement, its potential value, and the future negotiation strategy. For this purpose let us assume that the agent associates a certain value with a deal configuration[5]. Different deal configurations might return the same or different values. Agents typically have a preference towards deal configurations, which can be formalised as a transitive order relation.

Definition 35. Deal value

$$va \in VA = [0...1]$$

Definition 36. Deal configuration value assignment

$$DCV_{ag} = ag \times DCF \rightarrow VA$$

Definition 37. Preference

$$PRF_{ag} \subset DCF \times DCF$$
$$PRF_{ag} = \{(dcf^*, dcf^\wedge) \mid dcv_{ag,dcf^*} > dcv_{ag,dcf^\wedge} \land$$
$$(dcf^*, dcf^\wedge), (dcf^\wedge, dcf') \in PRF_{ag} : dcv_{ag,dcf^*} > dcv_{ag,dcf'}\}$$

In many cases the deal configuration value is fixed. The buyer, for instance, might have configuration choices, but the deal configuration value expected from the execution of the transaction is fixed by the seller (for

---

[5] Means to determine this value are discussed in Section 4.4.2.

instance to a certain profit margin). Other sellers might accept an agreement within a certain deal configuration value range, though preferably with a high value for them. If a high value is not possible (because no buyer is willing to accept any deal configuration with high value for the seller) the seller may concede.

Definition 38. Offer spaces with fixed deal value (buyer side)

$$OSX_{buyer} = \{osp \mid \forall dcf \in AGS_{o2b',o2s'} : dcv_{buyer,dcf} = dcv_{fix}\}$$

Definition 39. Offer spaces with flexible deal value (seller side)

$$OSL_{buyer} = \{osp \mid \forall dcf \in AGS_{o2b',o2s'} : dcv_{buyer,o2s'} \in [dcv_{min}..dcv_{max}]\}$$

The level of disagreement between the agents can be estimated using a measure of **opposition** that was suggested by Kersten and Noronha in [KeNo99].

Definition 40. Opposition

$$OPS_{buyer,seller,dcf} = dcv_{buyer,dcf} \times dcv_{seller,dcf}$$

Opposition is a concept that represents the differences in values that agents may assign to various deal configurations in the agreement space. As an example, the buyer might consider the deal configuration suggested in the joint agreement space to return a value of *0.8* whereas the seller might assess a deal value of *0.5*. The $OPS_{buyer,seller,dcf}$ in this example would be *0.4*, the low value indicating strong opposition.

The process of negotiation takes place, if, for instance, the initial agreement space is empty, or if it does not contain a sufficient number of attributes to specify a deal configuration that both agents agree to (sufficient condition). During the process, agents may modify their intention space specifications (aspiration levels, dimensions, dependencies etc.) in order to reach an agreement. Hence, intention spaces may assume different states (with different dimensions and structure) over the time of the negotiation process[6]. Accordingly a **negotiation** can be defined as a process of changes to the definition of intention spaces (c.f. [KeSz86]). The goal of the negotiation process is to find an agreement space definition that contains at least one complete deal configuration.

When is a deal configuration complete? A formal and objective measure of completeness cannot be defined, as it is the very nature of the negotiation process that agents not only have to agree on the attribute values, but also on the set of attributes which are part of the agreement. This is reflected in the concept of the negotiation space. Informally, a deal configuration is complete if both agents are willing to accept this configuration and to execute the associated transaction according to the specification in the deal configuration.

---

[6] This relation of spaces, such as the offer space, to states is the basis for modelling the dynamic aspects of negotiation processes in Section 5.3.2.

To further characterise the negotiation process, the distinction between distributive and integrative negotiations is often used. This classification is primarily based on the number of issues that are subject to negotiation. Kersten et al. demonstrated in [Kers+00] though that single-issue negotiations can be integrative while multi-issue negotiations can be distributive. In the original sense, distributive negotiations are characterised by their win-lose nature – the fact that a gain (increase in deal value) achieved in the negotiation process for one agent is necessarily a loss for the other agent. Integrative negotiations, on the other hand, allow the agents to achieve win-win solutions.

A stricter characterisation of negotiations according to the suggestion in [KeNo99] can be achieved on the basis of the formal model introduced in this chapter. **Distributive** negotiations take place if the agents, on the basis of their initial intention spaces, cannot find any deal configuration that returns both agents a higher deal value. Likewise, a negotiation process is **integrative** if the agents achieve a mutual higher deal configuration value.

Definition 41 Distributive negotiations

$\forall$ dcf*, dcf^ $\in$ AGS$_{X,Y}$: dcv$_{X,\text{dcf}*}$ > dcv$_{X,\text{dcf}^\wedge}$ $\rightarrow$ dcv$_{Y,\text{dcf}*}$ < dcv$_{Y,\text{dcf}^\wedge}$

Definition 42 Integrative negotiations

$\exists$ dcf* $\in$ AGS$_{X,Y}$ $\leq$dcf~ $\in$ AGS$_{X,Y}$: dcv$_{X,\text{dcf}*}$ > dcv$_{X,\text{dcf}^\wedge}$ $\wedge$ dcv$_{Y,\text{dcf}*}$ > dcv$_{Y,\text{dcf}^\wedge}$

Achieving win-win solutions might require changes to the intention space such as adding new dimensions or changing attribute domains or constraints. The negotiation situation may also allow for tradeoffs (log-rolling) that can lead to a higher mutual deal value.

This final characterisation of the negotiation interaction concludes the specification of the formal model from a descriptive perspective. In the next section, a prescriptive model for common electronic negotiation task elements is introduced.

4. REFERENCE MODEL

In keeping with the goal to define electronic negotiations from multiple perspectives, this section specifies two referential processes with associated tasks and roles: the meta-level electronic negotiation development and deployment process, and the actual electronic negotiation execution process. The latter provides the framework for the introduction of a taxonomy for electronic negotiations in Section 3.5.

4.1 Development and deployment

The creation of an enInstance, comprising an enScenario and an enMedium as negotiation support system, can be structured along the system development phases of analysis, design, and implementation.

On the basis of the assumption that an enMedium able to support multiple enScenarios exists, the main task in the process of creating an enInstance is reduced to developing enScenario models and deploying them in an executable representation to an enMedium. Accordingly, two main phases with related tasks can be distinguished in the lifecycle of an enScenario: the **design-time** phase and the **run-time** phase (see *Figure 17*).

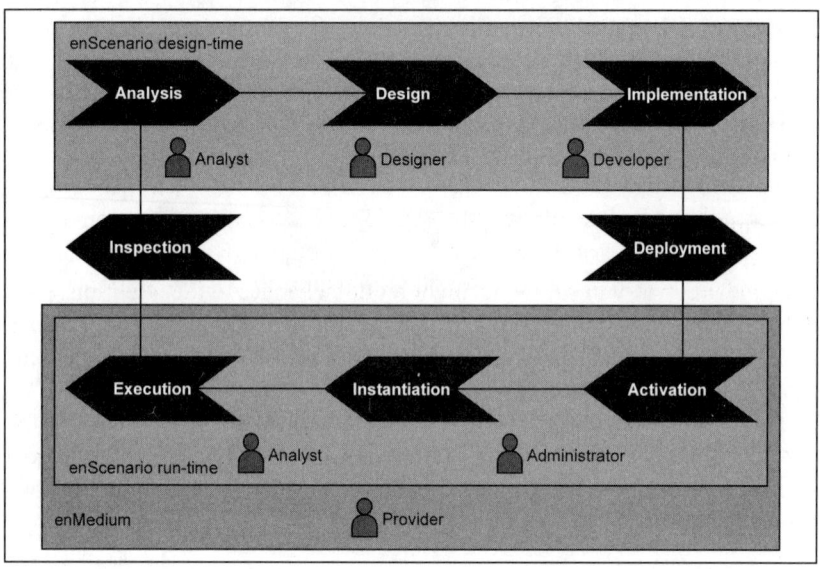

Figure 17. enScenario development and deployment tasks

During the design-time phase, a model for the enScenario has to be designed on the basis of a business context analysis, and implemented in such a way that an enMedium can 'understand' the enScenario rules. Through a deployment step, the executable enScenario representation is transferred to an enMedium. In the run-time phase, the enScenario needs to be activated, so that real agents may engage in electronic negotiations according to the scenario rules. If an agent chooses, for instance, to submit an initial offer for a new enScenario type, an instance of this enScenario will be created by the enMedium and the subsequent enProcess will be executed (see Section 3.4.3). During or after the execution, the enScenario (its enProcesses) might

Reference model 57

be monitored (e.g. to validate agent behaviour) or its results might be inspected (e.g. for data-mining purposes).

Eventually an iterative cycle of enScenario development and deployment is supported, where necessary changes or refinements may be discovered at run-time and lead to a modification of the enScenario at design-time.

4.2 Roles

On the basis of the enScenario life cycle a number of roles for the defined process can be identified (see *Figure 17*):

- **enScenario analyst**
  The task of this role is to analyse a business context in order to derive guidelines and requirements for the design of the enScenario.
- **enScenario designer**
  The designer will use the recommendations of the analyst in order to come up with a detailed design of the enScenario on the basis of the underlying enMedium capabilities.
- **enScenario developer**
  Using the completed design, the developer has to perform the conversion from the enScenario design-time specification to a run-time specification, which is supported by the enMedium. This run-time specification can then be deployed to one or more enMedia.
- **enMedium provider**
  The organisation or individual assuming this role provides an enMedium, which may host multiple enScenarios, for a purpose such as supporting an electronic market. The provider typically charges for the use of this enMedium.
- **enMedium administrator**
  The administrator has the task of managing enScenarios that are deployed to an enMedium. This may comprise activating or deactivating a specific enScenario, authorising agents to use this enScenario, or monitoring the actual enProcesses taking place in an enInstance.
- **enMedium analyst**
  On the basis of the data gathered during the execution of one or multiple enProcesses, the analyst can evaluate enScenarios for the fulfilment of quality goals such as efficiency or fairness (see Section 3.5.2.2). Conclusions can be compiled into suggestions for changes to a specific enScenario design, or more general recommendations towards the design of enScenarios in a particular domain.

4.3 Execution

The MRM was used in Section 3.2 as a general foundation for the distinction of electronic transaction phases. The resulting definition claims that a negotiation process usually includes interactions in the intention and agreement phase of electronic transactions. In this section, typical tasks within these two phases are identified from a high-level perspective (c.f. [Strö00b]). Each of these tasks may be split into several sub-tasks. The assumption for this task classification is that all interaction between negotiating agents is based on the exchange of offers. For the intention phase the following tasks related to the offer exchange in electronic negotiations can be identified:

- **Offer specification**
  The agents have to specify offers indicating their constraints and preferences towards the deal. This specification may also include the provision of signatures or the definition of timestamps (to express offer validity).
- **Offer submission**
  Submitting an offer can range from the active task of sending an offer to a specific agent or group of agents to a notification of completion of the offer specification task and the provision of the offer in an accessible manner (e.g. through a public advertisement).
- **Offer analysis**
  Upon reception, offers are usually not only stored and processed but also checked for compliance with certain conditions or rules.

For the agreement phase additional tasks may be necessary:

- **Offer matching**
  The goal for this task is to find pairs of offers that firstly classify as potential candidates for a transaction execution (e.g. by fulfilling mutual constraints defined in the offers, see Section 4.4.1). The scoring of candidates may also be part of the offer matching task. The extended goal for scoring is to find the 'best' pair of offers among the set of candidates, taking into account criteria such as agent preferences for the comparison of a candidate pair towards competing pairs (see Section 4.4.2). Finally, a selection among the candidates might be necessary.
- **Offer allocation**
  Using the results of the offer matching and scoring, this task has to determine the result of the enProcess execution ('who gets what') and thereby defines the duties of the agents involved in the manifested deal. If the selected offer still features value ranges or options, a configuration resolution may also be part of the offer allocation task.

Taxonomy

– **Offer acceptance**
In this final task, buyers or sellers have to accept or sign one or more offers in order to execute the transaction associated with the agreed-upon deal.

On the basis of the resulting process schema in *Figure 18*, electronic negotiations can be characterised and classified, as will be demonstrated in the next section.

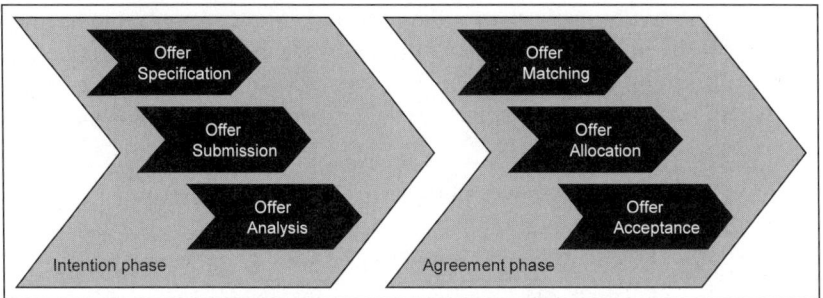

Figure 18. enProcess execution tasks

The reference model does not specify an absolute sequence of task executions. Depending on the enScenario rules, some of these tasks can be passed over. Offer allocation, for instance, may not make sense in a negotiation between two agents where only the price is discussed, but is necessary in an enProcess where the configuration of an offer is possible. Other enScenarios, however, could explicitly allow iterative cycles of task executions so that, for example, the sequence of offer matching and offer allocation is executed multiple times until one agent accepts an offer.

5. TAXONOMY

The main goal for the taxonomy introduced in this section is to provide a common language for the descriptive characterisation and classification of enScenarios, enMedia, and enInstances. Furthermore, this taxonomy supports the conceptualisation of new enScenarios as it prescriptively outlines potential design dimensions and corresponding enMedia configurations. It combines a number of common criteria for negotiations, and for electronic negotiations in particular that have also been suggested in other classification schemes (e.g. [Wurm+01] or [Lomu+01]), but aims to be more generic and is not targeted towards a specific group of enScenarios (e.g. auctions or automated negotiations).

5.1 Taxonomy structure

The taxonomy (c.f. [StWe02] for the following[7]) distinguishes between exogenous and endogenous, as well as explicit and implicit, classification criteria. The combination of both categorisation approaches results in four criteria categories (see *Figure 19* and the subsequent sections).

A **criterion** represents a distinctive electronic negotiation property, which is typically represented as a **rule** and is associated with a number of potential criterion values (or rule expressions). These values embody the variation of the semantics that can be defined for an electronic negotiation regarding a certain property or rule. The sum of all criteria values assigned to a specific enScenario, enMedium, or enInstance constitutes its **type**.

	Exogenous criteria	Endogenous criteria
Explicit criteria	Rules or quantifiable knowledge about the business context, e.g. laws or statistical data for agent behaviour or object transactions.	Choices made by the enScenario designer, e.g. the termination of the negotiation process or a certain matchmaking algorithm.
Implicit criteria	Domain knowledge which cannot be directly determined or represented in a formal way, e.g. ethical standards.	Facts determined through assessing the negotiation process execution, e.g. the fairness or efficiency achieved.

Figure 19. Taxonomy criteria categorisation

From a design-time perspective, exogenous criteria have to be analysed and rendered directly into endogenous explicit criteria, i.e. into a configuration for a specific enInstance. The operation and results of this enInstance can then be evaluated with endogenous implicit criteria at run-time (or on the basis of a theoretical run-time approximation such as a simulation or experiment), whereas exogenous or endogenous explicit criteria are known or determined already at design-time.

5.2 Endogenous classification criteria

Endogenous criteria represent the choices made, the parameters determined within the design of an enInstance. The main focus of the taxonomy is set on

---

[7] A first version of the following taxonomy was initially developed as joint work of the participants at the London DEXA 2000 eNegotiations workshop [DEXA01], and was revised at the Montreal 2001 eNegotiations seminar [Mont01].

Taxonomy

endogenous and explicit criteria, which are presented in the next section. A high-level characterisation of potential implicit criteria and complementary endogenous criteria is provided consecutively.

5.2.1 Explicit criteria

All criteria expressions in this category can be combined arbitrarily in one type classification – that is the criteria are orthogonal. For non-dual criterion expressions only the extreme expressions are listed (e.g. 'two' or 'many' but not 'n'). The first set of explicit classification criteria examines the roles defined for an electronic negotiation.

Table 1. Roles criteria

Participation	Two (**bilateral**) sides, e.g. a buyer and a seller, enter the enProcess.
	More than two sides (**multilateral**) engage in the enProcess.
	In the **intermediated** case, one trusted impartial party joins the negotiation process, for instance to suggest a fair agreement.
Agents	**One** agent per side is negotiating
	Multiple agents on each side are negotiating.
Admission	There is no restriction on the admission of agents (e.g. buyers and/or sellers) into the electronic negotiation (**open**).
	There are restrictions on the admission for agents (**closed**).
Collusion	If collusion is **approved**, agents and/or sides can collaborate in order to achieve mutual benefits.
	Collaboration or coalition formation among agents is **prohibited**.

The categorisation for the second set of classification criteria refers to the enProcess reference model execution tasks identified in Section 3.4.3.

Table 2. Process criteria

Overall rules	
Variation	The rules for the enProcess are **fixed**.
	The rules are **flexible** within the enProcess, but the range of possible rules is defined a priori. Active rules are selected from the predefined rule set.
	During the enProcess execution the process rules themselves can be modified (**dynamic**) by agents (e.g. through a preference specification), by exogenous parameters (e.g. timeouts), or by endogenous parameters (e.g. the liquidity of the market).
Rounds	In a **single**-round negotiation the enProcess is passed through only once.
	If an enProcess to reach one single agreement is repeated (e.g. by re-starting the process with different information available to the agents), the electronic negotiation is of a **multi**-round type.
Stages	In a **single**-staged electronic negotiation the rules are the same from the beginning to the end of the enProcess (i.e. from the offer specification to the acceptance). This is also the case if the process is of a multi-round nature (see above).

Overall rules	
Stages	If rules are allowed to change, then each time they do, a new phase in the enProcess is initiated and the electronic negotiation is **multi**-staged.
Concurrency	If one negotiator can only engage in one negotiation session with one other agent at a time, concurrency is explicitly **prohibited**.
	In an enScenario with **possible** concurrency, one agent could also run multiple-bilateral or -multilateral negotiation sessions at the same time.
Offer specification	
Attributes	Only a **single** attribute (or dimension) describing the transaction, object, or agent (see Section 3.2) in the offer can become an issue of the negotiation.
	The **multiple** attributes case is met if more than one attribute of the transaction, object, or agent context might be negotiated and used in the offer specification.
	The number and kind of attributes might also be **undetermined**, i.e. not constrained by any rule, and thus might vary within the enProcess.
Values	Attributes in an offer specification may have associated values. For some enScenarios only a **single** value can be defined, e.g. *(price,=,100,CHF)*.
	Ranges or choices for attribute values can be subject to the negotiation in the **multiple** values case, *e.g. (price,>,100,CHF)*
Relaxation	An agent might be allowed to specify values as **negotiable**, in order to indicate potential concessions in the enProcess.
	All attribute value domains are **fixed** in an enProcess where agents cannot a priori indicate flexibility in their offer specification.
Structure	The number and kind of attributes for the offer specification is **fixed**.
	During the enProcess execution, the number and kind of attributes is **flexible** according to predefined rules.
	The number and kind of attributes can be changed in a **dynamic**, a priori unknown way, during the enProcess.
Relation	An **independent** electronic negotiation does not allow for any dependencies between offers.
	In a **synchronised** (also: simultaneous, parallel) electronic negotiation there are n deals. An agent can make a smaller number of m distinct offers on m distinct deals. The offers are made simultaneously.
	If the n deals are negotiated individually one after another then the electronic negotiation is **sequential**.
Object	An offer might be specified for only a **single** object, or only a single, fixed, and indivisible bundle.
	One offer can specify **multiple** homogeneous or heterogeneous objects.
	In the multiple objects case, the offer is **bundled**, if it allows an agent to specify different valuations for different quantities.
Offer submission	
Sides	Only a **single** side (e.g. sellers or buyers) is allowed to submit offers within the enProcess, i.e. buyers or sellers are offer-takers only.
	All (**multiple**) sides are allowed to submit and receive offers.
Position	In a **single** position negotiation, agents can assume only one position (or role), such as buyer or seller.
	If the negotiation is of a **multi** position type, one agent can, for instance, create offers-to-sell and offers-to-buy (potentially for the same object) in one negotiation process. A typical example is a double-auction.

Taxonomy

Offer submission	
Activity	In an enProcess with **unrestricted** activity the agents might submit as many offers as desired – all offers are received and processed.
	For enProcesses with restricted activity, the receipt of offers from one agent may be limited through a **time-based** termination, i.e. the enProcess closes at a specified point in time and no offers are received or processed after this deadline.
	An enProcess with a restricted **event-based** activity rule will end if a certain event occurs, such as a period of inactivity.
Direction	A **reverse** electronic negotiation takes place when there are two sides, buyers and sellers, and a buyer posts an offer (request) for a deal while sellers compete with offers for the best conditions which the buyer will accept.
	An electronic negotiation is said to be **forward** if sellers advertise a deal and buyers submit offers.
	In a **haphazard** negotiation process the direction of offer submission might change within one phase.
Overall analysis	
Value	An enProcess is said to be **ascending** if a new valid offer has to provide a higher value (price) than the current best offer.
	The enProcess is **descending** when new offers have to be lower than the current best offer.
	In an undefined case, there is no rule regarding the value relation of a new offer to other current offers.
Threshold	If the offer has to provide a higher value than a certain threshold (e.g. the reservation price) then the enProcess is **low-cut**.
	The enProcess is **high-cut** if the offer has to be lower than a defined threshold.
	An enProcess with **undefined** threshold does not perform this kind of validation.
Offer matching	
Sorting	For a **satisfying** sorting, agents can define in their offers constraints towards the potential transaction partners, which have to be satisfied for the offers to match. Depending on the type of match (full compliance, negotiable violations, etc.) matching pairs of offers are assigned to classes.
	The enProcess sorting is **broadcast** if no difference is made among the potential transaction partners – all are qualified in the same way for the consecutive enProcess.
	In the case where potential transaction partners are a priori chosen, for instance by one agent, the classification is **exclusive**.
Offer matching	
Evaluation	In a **ranking** enScenario, offers are ordered according to the preferences of an agent in order to find out the 'best' offer among the set of matching offers. Ranking can be applied to the results of a preceding classification.
	If no offer scoring is executed, the enMedium is just **listing** the matching offers (which still might be classified).

Offer matching	
Resolution	The enProcess has a **defined** resolution if a rule-driven selection (e.g. 'one offer from each seller or class' or 'only three offers') is executed for the set of classified or scored offers and only suitable offers are considered for the consecutive enProcess.
A defined resolution may be complemented with a **tie-breaking** rule, which defines how selection conflicts are resolved. Conflicts arise if, for instance, there are multiple candidates for the execution of the transaction found through sorting and/or scoring, but only one can be chosen.
If no resolution or tie-breaking rules are defined, conflicts are **forwarded** and have to be resolved by the agents.
Schedule	Offer matching takes place in defined time intervals (**clocked**).
Offer matching is **triggered** by events (e.g. the submission of an offer).
Permanent execution of offer matching (**continuous**).
Offer allocation	
Distribution	In a negotiation with **discriminatory** value distribution a distinct unique price (value) may be determined for each winning offer.
On the basis of a **non-discriminatory** value distribution one uniform price (value) is set, and every originator of a winning offer has to pay the same price.
Provision	Through **offer-dependent** value provision a winning bidder has to pay the price (provide the value) specified in the winning offer.
In a negotiation with **offer-independent** value provision, the price (value) specified in the winning offer is not necessarily the price the originator of the offer has to pay (provide). An example is a 'second-price' auction.
Configuration	In an electronic negotiation with **mediated** configuration, candidate offers with defined value ranges *(delivery_date,<,10,day)* or options are resolved to offers with single values *(delivery_date,=,3,day)*, for instance through third party mediation.
If the configuration is **open**, agents can decide which final offer configuration to choose among the possible choices defined in the offer space.
Overall acceptance	
Commitment	The offers in an enProcess might be **binding**, meaning that they cannot be retracted, and the agents are forced to execute the transaction according to the agreement.
With an **indicative** offer the agent is not forced to execute a transaction as specified in the agreement but rather has the option to retract the offer.

Finally, explicit classification criteria for the information revelation and the strategy defined in an enScenario are provided in *Table 3*. The strategy represents the implementation of the exogenous business model[8].

---

[8] This notion of strategy from a negotiation designer's perspective should not be confused with a negotiating agent's strategy and tactics.

Taxonomy

Table 3. Information revelation and strategy criteria

Information		
Communication		The communication in the negotiation maybe **offer-restricted**, which means that the agents can only exchange offers.
		In an **offer-extended** case an offer might be complemented with additional remarks (e.g. comments, inquiries).
		A **free-form** communication allows agents to exchange all sorts of messages, e.g. offers or comments.
Transaction		The history of past deals resulting from previous enProcesses is available to the agents (**logged**).
		No deal history information is available (**unlogged**).
Negotiation		The interaction history of the current enProcess execution is available to the agents (**logged**).
		No interaction history can be accessed (**unlogged**).
Transparency		The current status of the enProcess (e.g. the best offer) is available to all agents (**public**). A common term for public transparency is 'open-cry'.
		Only the agents involved in the actual enProcess can access the status information (**protected**).
		The status information is restricted (**private**) to the agent to the moment of offer submission, i.e. in the form of submission feedback, and to the third party evaluating the (sealed) offers.
Identity		An electronic negotiation is said to be **anonymous** if any assignment of agents to their offers and identification of agents is impossible based on the information exchange provided within the enProcess.
		Identification of agents and the tracing of enProcess information to agents is possible in an **exposed** case.
Content		The level of information is **unrestricted**, i.e. all elements of the winning offer, such as price quotes or constraints, are revealed.
		Only **selected** offer or status information (e.g. not the reservation price) is provided by the enMedium.
Timing		If the information is revealed in defined time intervals, the timing is **clocked**.
		An enScenario could also specify that the information is refreshed if a certain event occurs (**triggered**), e.g. a new 'best' offer was received.
		If the information is always updated and can be accessed any time, a **continuous** timing is defined.
Strategy		
Fees		The enScenario defines fees for agent actions (e.g. offer submission) or enMedium actions (e.g. the invocation of an offer matching service) within the enProcess (**transaction-based**).
		Fees may only be defined for successful enProcess completions (**success-based**).
		Through **access-based** rules, fees might vary depending on the views (available information) or functionalities provided to the agents.
		No fees related to the actual enProcesses are charged to the agents (**free**).
Arbitration		Violations of enScenario rules result in penalties (e.g. exclusion, behaviour restrictions, or payments) for the agents (**punishing**).
		In case of a violation no related penalties are exerted – the action causing the violation might nevertheless be denied or rolled back (**tolerating**).

Strategy	
Arbitration	Compliance to the rules is gratified with benefits such as additional rights (e.g. to take actions, to view specific information) or payments (**rewarding**).
Ratings	Past behaviour of the agents results in the assignment of certain properties (e.g. recommendation levels or punishments) through the enMedium provider or other agents (**appraisal-based**).
	No ratings are assigned to the agents during or after the enProcess (**neutral**).

5.2.2 Implicit criteria

Implicit classification criteria allow an enMedium analyst to evaluate an enInstance or a number of enInstances (e.g. for classification purposes) and the agreements achieved by the agents using this enInstance. This evaluation might be useful to compare the enInstance to other activated enScenarios or to assess the fulfilment of predefined goals or requirements. In general, an enInstance (i.e. an enScenario and the associated enMedium within the business context) supports agents in finding a solution to a resource allocation problem and therefore can be compared to the notion of a mechanism in economics or game theory. Hence, implicit criteria for the classification could be derived from the set of criteria used in economics to evaluate mechanisms (see [Hurw73]). Other criteria such as fairness may be found in the field of negotiation analysis (see Section 2.1.1). The following list suggests potential criteria:

– **Pareto-Efficiency**
   A solution to a negotiation problem is economically pareto-efficient if, depending on the preferences of the agents, there is no other agreement that is better for one agent without being worse for another agent.
– **Social welfare maximisation**
   If the negotiation process ensures that any agreement maximises the sum of the utilities of all negotiation participants, the solution is maximising the social welfare.
– **Fairness**
   A solution is fair if it is not more beneficial (advantageous) to one side of agents (e.g. buyers or sellers) than to the other. Hence no agent envies the counterpart – all sides have the same opportunities, rights, and obligations. Accepting the rules defined for the enScenario is in the best interests of all negotiation participants.
– **Convergence**
   It is important to know whether an electronic negotiation process converges towards a solution/ compromise and if it produces a determined allocation. This solution or allocation might be unique. The speed of

Taxonomy

convergence - the time or number of steps needed until the electronic negotiation process converges towards solutions – or the uniqueness of the solution can also constitute an implicit endogenous criterion.

- **Stability**
  A solution is stable if there is no subset of agents who could have done better by coming to an agreement outside the enInstance. If a solution is stable, then it is efficient, although the converse is not true [Varian92, p.388].
- **Truth revelation**
  Each negotiating agent is motivated (that is, it is a dominating strategy for the agent) to reveal true preferences and to offer truthfully irrespective of the behaviour of other agents (incentive compatibility). No advantages can be gained by modelling other agents or having additional information (strategic behaviour).
- **Nature of gains**
  An enProcess is distributive (of win-lose nature) if a gain for one agent is necessarily a loss for the other agent (see Section 3.3.2). In integrative (win-win) negotiations, joint gains are possible either through simultaneous improvements (trade-offs) based on opposing preferences or through the extending the possible alternatives (e.g. addition/invention of new attributes/options) during the enProcess.

As stated before, the focus for the taxonomy presented in this book is on endogenous and explicit classification criteria. The given list of implicit criteria is just a suggestion, which requires further theoretical foundation and practical evaluation. The same is true for the following discussion of exogenous criteria.

5.3 Exogenous classification criteria

Exogenous criteria are mostly determined by the business context in which the enInstance is supposed to be situated and cannot be influenced by an enScenario designer. These criteria should typically be identified on the basis of the chosen business domain and business model before the design activity is initiated.

5.3.1 Explicit criteria

Explicit criteria are parameters with formal representations (e.g. quantifications, or the possible rule expressions, or the dimensions of support, which an enMedium could in principle provide).

Research towards explicit classification criteria for the business context from an electronic negotiation perspective is still immature. Once a set of well-defined criteria becomes available, an analyst would be empowered to distinctively classify a target business domain and business model, and to suggest the corresponding most appropriate enScenario design (c.f. Section 3.3.4).

The current state of the taxonomy defines a high-level categorisation with some examples for potential low-level criteria. Two criteria categories are suggested:

– **Business domain**
  Criteria for the business domain should cover the relation of the agents operating in the business domain (e.g. buyers and sellers). A set of explicit criteria could be based, for instance, on microeconomic market structures (e.g. monopoly, oligopsony, polypoly, see [Bich00]) and the nature of the negotiation object (homogenous versus heterogeneous, private value versus public value, see [Lomu+01]). Other explicit criteria could assess the stability of the buyer/seller relation or the transaction volumes and frequency in the business domain.

– **Business model**
  The business model defines the role of a business (e.g. the enMedia provider) within the described business domain. More detailed explicit criteria may address the value creation or revenue generation process, or the effects of technology as an enabler or a constraint for the business model.

5.3.2 Implicit criteria

Implicit criteria assess the consequences of explicit criteria, e.g. the characteristics of the enProcess execution and the resulting agreements for a particular enInstance. These criteria are not 'written down' or implemented but might be determined, for instance, through observation of the market customs. The high-level categorisation suggested in the previous section can also be used to structure the implicit criteria.

– **Business domain**
  Exogenous implicit criteria might describe the culture of the market community (e.g. from a trust perspective) or the prevalent implicit ethical standards (for example, regarding the disclosure of confidential competitor information).

– **Business model**
  The definition of the business model usually comprises implicit criteria on a high level such as the organisation's mission with a value proposition (potential benefits) and strategic goals, or the sources of revenue [AlZi01].

5.4 Taxonomy application

The taxonomy can be used to determine, for instance, the type of one enScenario that is commonly used by online auction sites such as eBay – the English auction (see for example [KuFe98]).

Regarding roles, the English auction is classified to be of the type *bilateral-participation* with *multiple-agents* on the buyers side and *one-agent* on the seller side. Typically an *open-admission* is used in combination with *prohibited-collusion* (in order to avoid rings or shills, see Section 2.2.1).

The English auction process is *single-phased* and *single-staged* with *fixed-variation* (i.e. the rules of the auction cannot change). Concurrency is usually *possible*, which means that one can participate in multiple parallel auction sessions. It allows only for *single-attribute, single-value, fixed-relaxation*, and *fixed-structure* offers. One attribute with one value can be specified in the offers (bids), namely the *price*. In addition, offers are usually specified for *single- or multiple-objects*. As only the buyers are allowed to submit offers, the scenario is *single-sided* and *single-positioned*. Offers have to be submitted with *forward-direction*. In addition, the offer submission is typically subject to an *event-based-activity* rule (e.g. a timeout is defined dependent on a period of inactivity) and *ascending-value* restrictions (new offers need to have a higher price than the current best offer). If a reservation price is defined, the process is due to its forward-direction with a *low-cut-threshold*. Offer matching occurs with *continuous-schedule* and *exclusive-sorting* – buyers submit their offers directly towards a specific offer-taker. A *ranked-scoring* is used in the sense that the buyers' offers are ordered according to the offered price. Offers with the same price can still be selected based on a simple *tie-breaking-resolution*, which establishes precedence through the submission timestamps. For the allocation, *discriminative-distribution* is used, i.e. the winner has to pay the price specified in the winning offer, the price to pay is *offer-dependent*, and *mediated-configuration* results from the fact that only single-values are allowed for attributes. Through *binding-commitment*, the auctioneer ensures that the winning bidder is forced to execute the agreed-upon transaction.

Concerning the information available within the enProcess, an English auction is always with *offer-restricted communication*. In most cases the auction is *transaction-logged* and *negotiation-logged*, which means that the agents can lookup the past transactions as well as the bid history. Through *public-transparency*, an *exposed-identity*, and *unrestricted-content*, competing bidders know who submitted the currently winning offer and which price is specified in that offer. This information is updated each time a new bid arrives and therefore with *continuous-timing*. With regard to the business model implementation, English auction providers tend to impose *success-*

based-fees, for instance by charging some percentage of the overall deal value to the seller. Another common example is *punishing-arbitration* where providers try to prevent sellers from bidding in their own auctions. In many cases *appraisal-based-ratings* are used to create a level of trust between buyers and sellers.

The explicit classification criteria can also be used to evaluate and compare enMedia or negotiation support systems. First of all, the dimensions of negotiation support (i.e. the flexibility of the enMedium) can be assessed by checking whether a specific enMedium supports certain criterion values, i.e. rule expressions. Second, the level of automation or decision support can be evaluated based on the enProcess execution reference model. Some enMedium systems might, for example, support offer matching with filtering and selection rules, whereas other types of systems (or platforms) leave the task of matching offers to the offer-taking agent.

In general, one enMedium may host several enScenarios and corresponding enInstances with varying rules and, accordingly, different classification types. Depending on their requirements or intentions, agents choose the most suitable enInstance. Often the enInstances available to an agent are defined by the enMedium provider. A typical example is an electronic market for financial derivatives, where, depending on the level of experience, agents may participate in enProcesses for different objects (e.g. *options* or *futures*).

6. SUMMARY

This fundamental chapter introduces key definitions and models for the domain of electronic negotiations. The presented holistic conception of an electronic negotiation and its elements constitutes the first core element of this book, which will be used for the subsequent presentation of the research findings.

Core to the understanding are the notions of the enMedium as a means to support electronic negotiations, the enScenario as a container for all the rules constraining electronic negotiations, the enInstance as the fusion of an enMedium and an enScenario within a specific business context (e.g. the *electricity market*), and the enProcess as a representation of the actual electronic negotiation interaction within the enInstance. Based on this general understanding, a formal model for electronic negotiations was presented, which can be used to specify an electronic negotiation in a machine-readable way, and which provides the foundation for a further analysis of electronic negotiation situations and interactions.

Summary

These two descriptive deliverables, the definitions and the formal model, are complemented with a prescriptive electronic negotiation reference model, which covers the development and deployment process of an enScenario as well as the execution of an enProcess. Finally, a taxonomy for electronic negotiations was introduced, which can be used for descriptive as well as prescriptive purposes and covers aspects such as the roles, process, information revelation, and business model implementation of an electronic negotiation.

In summary, this chapter defines the universe of discourse for this book, focused on its underlying research goals and defined context. Although striving for broad application purposes, the definitions and models introduced might not be suitable for other contexts or research directions in the domain of electronic negotiations, whereas the taxonomy presented does claim to be suitable for a broad spectrum of electronic negotiations.

In the following chapter, the foundation provided by the definitions and models of this chapter will be used to investigate automated solution procedures that can be applied on the basis of a formal electronic negotiation representation. These solution procedures provide different means of negotiation support, which are conceptualised on the basis of a common novel paradigm – the notion of negotiation support components.

Chapter 4

Electronic negotiation support
From matchmaking to contracting

In this chapter, the concept of support for symmetric multi-attribute negotiation intermediation in electronic markets is conceptualised through the paradigm of negotiation support components (NSC). On the basis of a conceptual definition, requirements are derived that can be used to identify NSC candidates. Additional criteria for the final selection and construction of NSCs from a set of candidates are suggested. This addresses the first problem identified in Section 2.3, which declared that automation or assistance for multi-attribute negotiation decision tasks in electronic markets is insufficient to attain low transaction costs. The specification of NSCs in the design of electronic negotiations and the integration of NSCs in a generic electronic negotiation architecture model will be discussed in Chapter 4 and Chapter 5.

1. DEFINITION

Negotiation support components (NSCs) automate communication and decision-making in electronic negotiations. An NSC constitutes a component of an information system, namely, a reusable unit of code for an enMedium. Referring back to the media reference model introduced in Section 3.2, NSCs are situated in the media transaction layer for the intention and agreement phase and thereby provide generic services for the transaction processing. In general, **components** have two characteristics: they can easily be connected to make a new system, and the user of the component does not know how the components are implemented [Faya+99, p.13]. To conceptualise the NSC paradigm in greater detail, a number of theoretical foundations are required.

In general, tasks in information systems are either transformation tasks or decision tasks [FeSi93, 31ff.]. A **transformation task** corresponds to a generic input-output system, thus receiving information (input) and creating information (output) depending on the input. The object of the task is the input received. The intended state and structure of the output is defined in the goals of the task ('what has to be done'). An additional source of input, objectives, are necessary for **decision tasks**. Objectives refer to the quality aspects pursued by the execution of the task ('how it has to be done') and determine the behaviour of the task. Accordingly, the output information of a decision task is optimised regarding the underlying objectives. From a formal perspective, a task is based on a solution procedure [FeSi93, 166ff.]. The solution procedure may consist of several actions, which are controlled by an action controller. This controller invokes the actions upon receiving a trigger. The actions, the controller, or the trigger might be executed in an automated way. A task is fully **automated** if all three of these elements are performed by a system and not by a human agent.

A second foundation for the NSC paradigm is that the context of one agent in a negotiation process can be represented with the general notion of a **sequential decision-making model** [ZeSy98]. Basic characteristics of a sequential decision-making model are (1) a sequence of decision-making points; and (2) a decision-maker who updates her/his knowledge based on feedback received within the process.

Combining the sequential decision-making model and the introduced definition of tasks in information systems, an electronic negotiation from the perspective of one agent conforms to a sequence of decision-making points at which decision tasks have to be performed (see *Figure 20*).

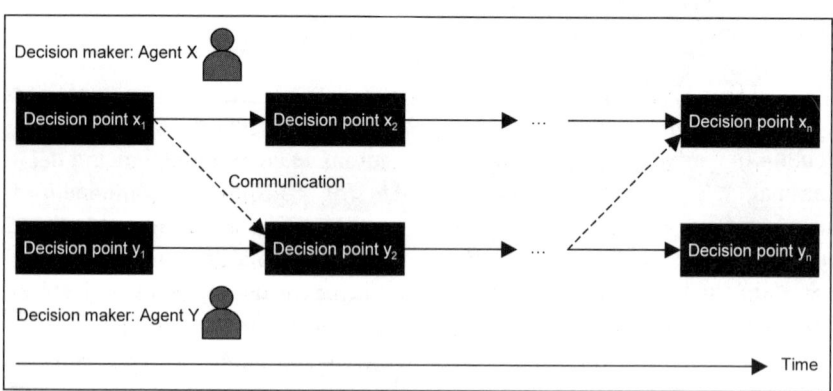

Figure 20. Sequential decision-making model

Definition 75

Through transformation tasks the inputs for the decision tasks might be processed or generated and the outputs may be communicated to other agents in the negotiation process.

NSCs represent automated decision tasks in electronic negotiations with static goals. If a transformation task is associated with the input or output of the decision task, the NSC may also automate this transformation task. The objectives for the decision task are either set by the human agent triggering the execution or by the action controller. This is an important criterion to distinguish objectives from the other inputs, namely, offers. Offers are usually private to the agent issuing the offer, but a third party might want to control the execution of an NSC by settings its objectives with a certain policy.

The actions of an NSC are automated, which is also the case for the action controller. However, NSCs are always triggered by a human agent or another element of the information system, and therefore do not operate in a fully automated fashion. This distinguishes NSCs from the concept of software agents, which demonstrate autonomous behaviour [ZaBr99]. In addition, NSCs are also not location-autonomous (which is a feature attributed to mobile software agents, see for example [Tu+98]), but must be permanently located in one enMedium.

The decisions in a sequential decision-making model can be transformed into offers [Kers+91]. Hence, the input and output information of NSCs in an electronic negotiation are sets of offers. The offers are differentiated into one **initiating offer** and one or more **target offers**. The output of an NSC provides the inputs for subsequent transformation and decision tasks. Decision-making points might require human intervention either to perform a decision task that cannot be automated, or to provide objectives. However, human intervention is not required for all decision points in an electronic negotiation. This is the case, for example, if a sequence of automated decision tasks is executed in the negotiation process.

NSCs may either automate the decision task of one agent, or a decision problem shared by multiple agents. Objectives are usually set by one agent, who might be a buyer, seller, or third party (see *Figure 21*, next page). Therefore it is possible that a third party sets the objectives, while inputs are received from buyers and sellers. In some enScenarios it might make sense for multiple agents to set objectives. This can be realised in either a disjunctive way or with priority rules (e.g. 'if the third party did not specify this objective, the buyer can set the value').

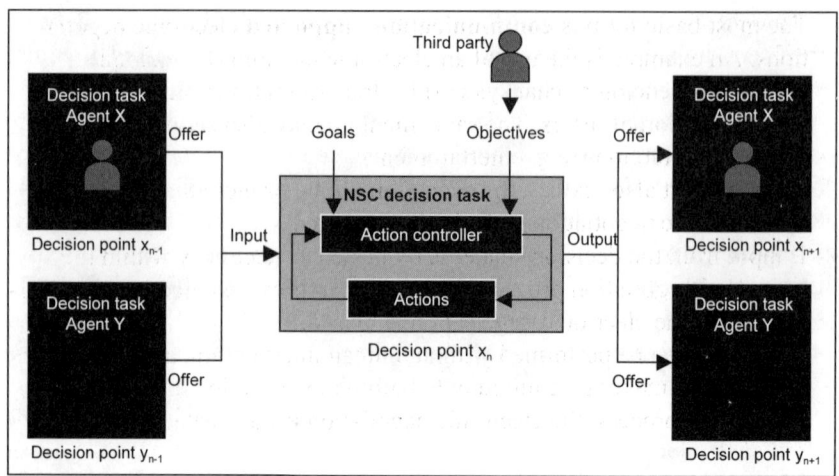

Figure 21. Conceptual NSC model

Two or more decision-makers have to be considered in an electronic negotiation. Some of the decision tasks to be performed by one decision-maker (agent) will typically require a preceding decision from the counterpart (e.g. the definition of a counteroffer). The operation of NSCs will naturally synchronise decisions for which inputs and/or objectives are required from more than one agent (which is usually the case). Hence, the complete notion of a negotiation can be represented with a set of sequential decision-making models, interconnected through additional communication.

By automating some decision tasks within an enProcess, NSCs assist the execution of the remaining decision tasks through human agents, e.g. by providing additional input information. This definition of NSCs and the underlying sequential decision-making model reflects the hybrid nature of intermediated negotiations (c.f. Section 2.2.4).

In summary, NSCs automate or assist decision tasks and associated transformation tasks in order to support decision-making and communication in an electronic negotiation. In an enScenario, an arbitrary number of NSCs of different types can be used. It is also possible that one NSC is executed multiple times – in a repeated fashion, triggered by different agents or potentially also at different stages of the enProcess.

Finally, beyond the level of single NSCs, the sequential decision-making model and the concept of information system tasks allows the definition of the following types of electronic negotiations, which differ with regard to the level of support and automation provided by the enMedium:

- The most basic form is **communication-supported** electronic negotiations. An example is the use of an electronic medium (for example a video-conferencing or chat system) for transformation tasks such as the communication of offers. The same medium may also serve other purposes of interactions (e.g. entertainment).
- If the support also realises the execution of one or more decision tasks, the electronic negotiation is decision-supported.
- If input from the decision-maker is requested or necessary within the supported negotiation process, for instance to provide objectives for decision tasks, the electronic negotiation is hybrid.
- If all tasks can be performed without human intervention, and input from the decision-maker is required only before the execution of the negotiation process, the electronic negotiation is automated.

2. REQUIREMENTS

In this section, the defined conceptual model of an NSC is used to derive requirements for the design of NSCs. These requirements are useful to (1) find candidate NSCs; and (2) construct new NSCs. The following set of requirements can be identified:
- NSCs perform a decision task and may perform associated transformation tasks in electronic negotiations – the task execution is optimised towards objectives.
- The represented decision task is always an intermediating task requiring inputs from more than one agent.
- An NSC operation is never modelled to represent only the decision task of one specific agent role (e.g. buyer) or to receive different inputs from different roles. The interaction with an NSC is always symmetric and it operates in the same way for objectives of buyers, sellers, or third parties.
- The goal of an NSC is static. Its objectives might be variable and set dynamically by multiple agents before the NSC operation.
- NSCs receive one or more offers as inputs and produce one or more offers as outputs in a result-set. Offers received as inputs might be modified during the NSC operation.
- The operation of NSCs can be preceded or succeeded by the operation of any other NSC, but it is never interrupted by an associated NSC operation. It is possible to define necessary preconditions for the operation.
- The last requirement in this list is important, because in most cases more than one NSC will be used in an enScenario. Some NSCs might only be practical and valuable if they are applied in combination with other NSCs.

The agent triggering an NSC operation is denoted the **initiator**. The determination of objectives and inputs for NSCs from the perspective of one agent relates to the notion of tactics and strategy in autonomous agent systems (see for example [Card+99]). Tactics are generally used to generate a proposal such as an offer. Strategies define either how tactics change over time (e.g. based on feedback and learning), or a certain sequence of actions [Lomu+01]. However, to provide maximum flexibility, the NSC model abstracts from the variety of potential agent tactics and strategies. Through objectives and inputs, an NSC simply provides means to represent a predefined strategy. On the other hand, NSCs can be related to the concept of mechanisms in economics and game theory. A mechanism supports agents in finding a solution to a resource allocation problem based on the information that is known by the agents [Bich01, 70ff.]. Hence NSCs can be regarded as mechanisms that assist agents in finding solutions for the resource allocation problem in electronic markets. From mechanism design theory the following additional requirements can be derived:

Generally, "mechanisms have to be designed so that each agent is motivated to follow the strategies that the designer wants it to follow" [Sand00b]. A mechanism design should give agents an incentive to share their private information in order to reach an efficient allocation. In other words, NSCs have to be incentive compatible, meaning that the triggering agents have an incentive to provide truthful input offers and objectives and are not enticed to demonstrate strategic behaviour. If multiple agents provide inputs for an NSC operation, the decision should be fair and efficient from the perspective of all agents, in order to achieve common acceptance of the decision.

The outcome of a mechanism should be feasible, non-wasteful, possess some equilibrium, and represent a uniquely determined allocation (c.f. [Hurw73] and Section 3.5.2.2).

Are all decision tasks in negotiations that fulfil these requirements NSC candidates? Potential decision tasks comprise the questions specified in the problem definition in Section 2.3, such as the selection of the most promising agreement candidates or the definition of the set of negotiation issues. Fulfilling the requirements is a necessary condition for automating the decision task and the corresponding construction of an NSC. An additional sufficient condition for an NSC construction is the **efficiency** of the task automation (c.f. [FeSi93, 183ff.]). To check this condition an analysis is necessary which compares human execution of the decision task with the proposed automated execution – considering factors such as execution costs (including human/computer interactions), necessary control, associated risk, execution time (computational and communication efficiency), availability, or transparency. If there are potential benefits of an automated task execution, these benefits have to be set in relation to the costs of the NSC construction (e.g. the formalisation and implementation of the solution procedure). A positive overall result of the costs/value analysis is the final sufficient condition for the NSC construction.

3. NSC EXTERNAL VIEW - BEHAVIOUR

This section outlines the general behaviour of NSCs, thus abstracting from their internal view (the formalisation of the solution procedure and the input/output information). To comply with the paradigm of a component in an information system, all NSCs have to demonstrate identical behaviour. The methods in the generic interface of an NSC, including their potential parameters and return values, are defined as follows:

Table 4. Generic NSC interface

createNSC	
Explanation	This method creates an instance of the NSC type and registers this instance with the enMedium. The unique ID can be used later to retrieve the NSC and its results in an enProcess.
Parameters	None
Returns	Unique ID
setInitiatingOffer	
Explanation	With this method the initiating offer is passed to the component and represented in its internal state. In the lifecycle of an NSC instance, this method can be called only once and by one agent.
Parameters	The initiating offer ID
Returns	Success (upon validation of the initiating offer)
setObjectives	
Explanation	This method might be called multiple times by different agents before the NSC operation. If specific objectives are already defined by one agent, but passed a second time through another agent, a conflict occurs.
Parameters	The objectives for the NSC operation
Returns	Success (failure if a violation or a conflict occurs)
addTargetOffers	
Explanation	Using this method, agents can specify which offers are supposed to be the targets of the operation. The NSC will try to retrieve these offers and check them for compliance with the preconditions. If target offers cannot be found, the NSC will retry after a certain time interval. If offers are invalid, the NSC will persist the associated error message in the result-set.
Parameters	References to offers or wildcards (e.g. all offers with a certain state)
Returns	Success (upon acceptance of the target offers)

removeTargetOffers	
Explanation	This method removes target offers before or during the NSC operation
Parameters	References to offers or wildcards
Returns	Success (acceptance of the removal)
getErrors	
Explanation	Errors of the NSC operation can be retrieved with this method.
Parameters	None
Returns	ErrorMessage
executeComponent	
Explanation	Invocation of the NSC operation. The execution might consume an arbitrary amount of time. Hence no immediate result is passed back to the caller. The execution ends when either all input offers are processed, an error occurs, or the operation times out (depending on an objective).
Parameters	None
Returns	Nothing
getResults	
Explanation	This method might be called anytime within and after the NSC operation to retrieve the current or finalised definition of the result-set.
Parameters	None
Returns	A result-set with references to processed target offers and additional meta-information. The meta-information might comprise result-codes for each offer and associated offer element (e.g. constraint) codes. The meta-information can be evaluated by the caller to reason about the overall result-set structure (e.g. the number of failed operations).

The complete behaviour of an NSC from an external view can be represented with the state diagram in *Figure 22*.

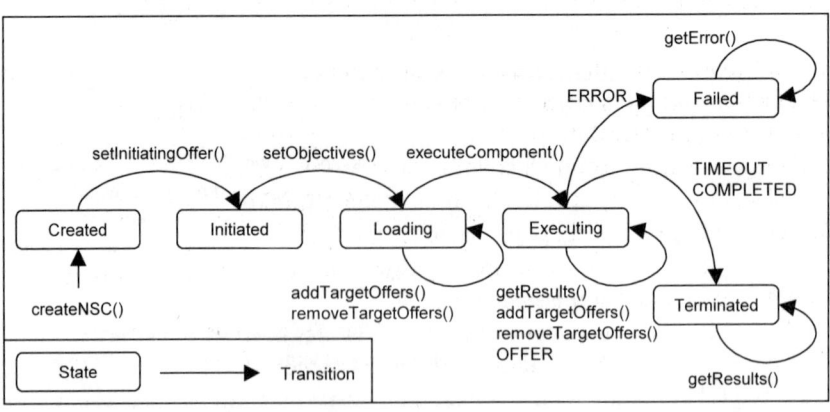

Figure 22. NSC behaviour – external view

This state diagram shows that it is valid, for instance, to execute an NSC without passing any references to target offers (through calling *addTarget-Offers*), which is still possible later in the 'Executing' state. In addition to the interface defined in *Table 4*, an NSC can raise four events: *TIMEOUT, COMPLETED, ERROR*, and *OFFER*. The *OFFER* event is used to signal the generation of new offer instances or the modification of target offers through the NSC operation.

4. NSC INTERNAL VIEWS

Whereas the previous section described common elements of all NSCs, this section proposes specific NSC examples, thus focussing on the internal view of NSCs. For each NSC presented, the solution procedure, the internal information structure for the inputs and objectives, and the structure for the outputs will be defined. A detailed discussion of the characteristics of the proposed NSCs, as well as an assessment of potential extensions, is provided in Chapter 8.

4.1 MatchNSC

The goal of a MatchNSC is to find agreement candidates on the basis of a set of advertised offers-to-buy and offers-to-sell (see [StSt01b] for the following).

4.1.1 Incentive

According to the formal model introduced in Section 3.3, both the seller and the buyer can specify offers with a set of constraints on the value domains of the attributes for the intended deal. Hence, a symmetric constraint satisfaction problem (CSP) with buyer and seller constraints can be formulated (c.f. [KoBu01]). It is possible to solve this CSP automatically, and the mechanism to find a solution (a set of compatible attribute values in a deal configuration) is referred to as a **matchmaker**. Typically, a matchmaker will return a successful match if, for each attribute specified in both offers, an instantiation of attribute values can be found such that all constraints are satisfied at the same time.

The seller advertises, for instance, to sell an object of the type *notebook computer* with the constraints *(CPU,=,600,MHZ)*, *(RAM,=,128,MB)*, and *(disk,=,6,GB)*. Additional constraints for the transaction may be *(price,=,2000,USD)* and *(delivery_time,>,10,day)*. A buyer, on the other hand, might offer to buy a notebook with the attribute value domains *(RAM,>,64,MB)*, *(disk,≤9,GB)*, and *(price,≤2000,USD)*.

In general, the matchmaking operation is performed for a set of offers with the goal of determining the set of successful matches. The outcome of 'no successful match' is particularly unsatisfactory in cases, in which values for perhaps only one attribute were incompatible, and that, by only a marginal attribute value difference. In the previous example, one additional constraint of the buyer that specified a minimum speed of *666 MHZ* for the *CPU* of the notebook would have resulted in incompatible values for the *CPU* attribute and accordingly, in 'no successful match' with the offer-to-sell. But maybe speed is not that important to the buyer, or it is not critical that the speed is at minimum *666 MHZ*, or maybe the buyer would agree to a lower speed if the price were lower as well.

To address this issue, a first NSC, the MatchNSC, is proposed, which is able to identify negotiable agreements in the case where genuine constraint matching does not provide (enough) successful matches and where buyers and/or sellers are willing to relax some of their constraints.

4.1.2 Solution procedure

The proposed MatchNSC first tries to find a solution to the constraint satisfaction problem defined by the constraints of the initiating offer and the complementary offer. The **basic matchmaking operation** proceeds for a pair of one O2B and one O2S instance in the following way:
– For each attribute defined in the O2B and the O2S instances for the transaction, object, and agent context, the attribute value domains defined by the domain constraints are determined.
– Those attribute values that are part of both attribute value domains constitute the compatible attribute value domain (CVD).
– If the CVD is empty, the domain constraints in both offers are violated and the attribute represents a match conflict. A violation is always mutual.
– If the CVD contains at least one value, this attribute has been matched successfully.
– If all attributes can be matched successfully, the original pair of O2B and O2S constitutes a successful **match**.

To give an example for the violation of constraints, let us assume that in the previous example the buyer specifies a constraint *(price,<,1900,USD)*. In this case the constraints in the O2B and O2S are violated because the seller's price, *2000 USD*, does not intersect with the value domain *< 1900 USD*. If the seller defined *(price,>,1800,USD)*, the attribute would match successfully, but result in an **agreement value range** of *1800 USD < price < 1900*

NSC internal views 83

USD. This means that for this pair of offers, the buyer and the seller still have to agree on a specific value within the agreement value range. An agreement value range does not have to be steady but can also feature a discrete set of values (e.g. {*black, white*}).

Binary constraints are violated if the defined domain operation (e.g. 'smaller than') fails for all combinations of values belonging to the respective attribute value domains of the complementary offer. This can also be illustrated in the sample constraint *payment_time* < *delivery_time* in an O2B. If the O2S specifies attribute value domains of $t + 2 <$ *payment_time* $< t + 5$ and *delivery_time* $= t + 3$, both attributes would match successfully.

What happens if no constraints, or constraints from only one agent, are defined for an attribute? To resolve such **null-attributes** the following approaches can be suggested:

- This situation is generally avoided. The matchmaking operation requires the agents to specify constraints for all attributes defined in the deal type associated with the offer.
- The matchmaking operation requires at least one domain constraint from either agent for all deal type attributes. If only one agent expresses a domain constraint, two options exist: the attribute is matched successfully and the CVD is defined by this domain constraint, or the attribute creates a match conflict.
- The matchmaking operation is restricted to the attributes with domain constraints and the null-attributes are marked as open issues.
- The deal type definition may include default attribute values, which represent best practices or common trade standards. These default values are initially suggested for the null-attributes.

4.1.3 Adaptation

Using the foundation of the basic matchmaking operation with genuine constraint satisfaction, the MatchNSC can perform an **extended matchmaking operation**, which takes the notion of soft constraints (or 'negotiable' constraints, see Definition 20 in Chapter 3) into account. Negotiability does not specify to what extent a constraint might be relaxed in case of a conflict, if at all. It does not require the agent to actually change the negotiable constraint; it only indicates an agent's willingness to do so. The actual decision to compromise might be subject to various considerations, such as the potential compensation regarding other attribute values. The extended matchmaking operation is specified as follows:

- If the O2B and O2S instances constitute a successful match, the Match-NSC determines whether one or more successful attribute matches result in agreement value ranges. If not, the O2S instance is added to the matching agreements set (MAS). If yes, the O2S instance is moved into the distribution agreements set (DAS).
- If one or more attributes created matchmaking conflicts, the MatchNSC checks for each attribute whether the violated domain constraints are negotiable.
- If both the seller's and buyer's constraints are negotiable, the constraints are marked as **double-sided negotiable constraints** (DNC) and the O2S instance is moved to the negotiation agreements set (NAS).
- If this is true for only one agent, the negotiable domain constraints of this agent are marked as **single-sided negotiable constraints** (SNC) and the O2S instance is also moved to the NAS.
- In the case where neither the buyer nor the seller issued negotiable constraints for the attribute creating a match conflict, the extended matchmaking operation fails for this pair of O2B and O2S instances.

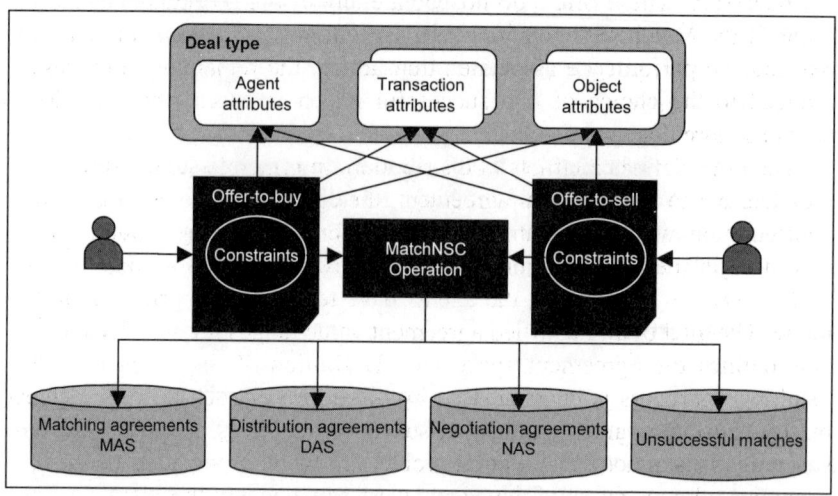

Figure 23. MatchNSC operation

In principle, the basic and extended matchmaking operations can be executed on a set of n initiating offers and m complementary offers, thus forming $n \times m$ **match candidates**. The result of the MatchNSC operation is then a classification of the match candidates into four sets (see *Figure 23*):

NSC internal views

- A set of match candidates where no constraint violations occurred and the CSP solution contains only compatible attribute value domains with single values (MAS).
- Match candidates where no constraint violations occurred but the solution contains agreement value ranges (DAS).
- Match candidates where negotiable constraints from the buyer and/or the seller were violated (NAS).
- A set with unsuccessful matches.

4.1.4 Results analysis

All match candidates in the MAS, DAS, and NAS are referred to as **agreement candidates**. Depending on the configuration of the MatchNSC operation, agreement candidates with open issues (see the discussion on null constraints above) might be identified and classified as well. The discovery of open issues is also a valuable input for subsequent decision tasks.

For agreement candidates in the MAS a negotiation process is typically not necessary. These offers do not violate any of the constraints of the initiator of the MatchNSC operation and accordingly, an agreement is already reached. To perform the associated transaction, the remaining enProcess is reduced to the choice of one successful match in cases where the MAS contains more than one candidate.

The DAS defines conflicts of distribution. In principle, no constraints are violated, but to reach a final agreement, the agents have to agree on a deal configuration with single attribute values for all agreement value ranges identified in the CSP solution. If the MatchNSC returned a range of *1800 USD < price < 1900 USD*, the agents have to agree on a price within that range. The total of all identified agreement value ranges for an O2B and O2S pair defines the agreement space (see Definition 30 in Chapter 3). The resulting enProcess is characterised by the desire of each agent to achieve optimal attribute values within that space, on the basis of their preference structure. This is not a negotiation problem in the narrow sense, because, in principle, all constraints of the agents were satisfied and therefore any solution should be acceptable. However, the agents still face a conflict of surplus distribution, comparable to a situation of overlapping reservation prices. In practice, agents might even risk missing a viable agreement in order to maximise their returns. One approach to this configuration problem is to use joint maximum utility gain as the optimisation criterion (see for example [Teic+98]).

True negotiation processes, which require compromises from at least one agent in order to reach an agreement, are necessary for the offer pairs in the NAS. The required negotiation process can be further analysed on the basis

of the marking performed during the extended matchmaking operation. Those attributes that created a match conflict for a pair of offers in the NAS are referred to as **negotiation issues**. The semantics of the associated domain constraint markings are as follows:
- Single-sided negotiable constraint (SNC)
  Only the originator of this constraint is flexible towards this issue. The corresponding domain constraint(s) in the complementary offer is (are) not negotiable.
- Double-sided negotiable constraint (DNC)
  Both agents declare flexibility towards this issue.

Constraints originally tagged as negotiable, but not marked within the MatchNSC operation, are not relevant in the agreement candidate analysis. The flexibility indicated by the agents was not operative (i.e. used) in the operation, since no actual violation occurred for these constraints.

Each offer in an agreement candidate pair in the NAS may comprise single-sided as well as double-sided negotiable constraints. This result is denoted a **negotiation signature**. The combination of the two negotiation signatures of the two offers within an agreement candidate defines the disagreement space (c.f. Definition 32 in Chapter 3). A disagreement space comprises the negotiation issues, the value boundaries for these issues, and the constraint markings. The complexity of the enProcess for a disagreement space can also be assessed on the basis of the following primary constellations:
- Single-sided disagreement space
  Only one offer features (in this case, single-sided) negotiable constraints.
- Double-sided disagreement space
  Both offers contain negotiable constraints.

For single-sided disagreement spaces an agreement depends on the flexibility of one agent. The constraints that caused a violation are tagged as negotiable and are marked to be operative. Thus an agreement can be reached if the agent relaxes these constraints accordingly. For instance, if the seller offered *(guarantee,=,6,month)*, an agreement is possible with the buyer if the resulting attribute value domain is changed to *(guarantee,=,12,months)*. Double-sided disagreement spaces, on the other hand, require mutual concessions in order to reach an agreement.

One possibility to further extend the analysis of the disagreement space is to assess the number of negotiable issues for each agreement candidate. One can distinguish **single-issue** and **multi-issue disagreement spaces**. A double-sided disagreement space can still be of single-issue nature, if both offers contain only one double-sided negotiable constraint.

Another possibility is to determine the range of disagreement for an issue by evaluating the difference between the boundaries of the attribute value domains for the negotiation issues. If the O2S specifies *(price,=,2000,USD)* and the O2B's constraint is *(price,<,1900,USD)*, then the range of disagreement is $100. This is obviously less meaningful for non-metric issues such as *colour*. The extent to which agents are willing to negotiate certainly depends on this attribute value boundary difference. But further analysis of the disagreement space on a general level is not possible because the importance of the issues to the buyer/seller and the range of intended or acceptable flexibility will vary from case to case. If the seller needs to relax only one constraint, but this issue is crucial to the seller and small concessions may already result in a big revenue loss, then the probability of an agreement might be lower than in a case with multiple issues of minor importance and greater boundary differences.

Finally, the subsequent enProcess can also be characterised on the basis of a result-set analysis. Let us assume the NAS comprises multiple agreement candidates with single-sided disagreement spaces in which only the buyers need to be flexible. This NAS structure suits well the requirements of an auction-type enScenario. Depending on the number and homogeneity of the issues, a single- or multi-attribute auction component [Bich99a] can support the subsequent enProcess. In a mirrored single-sided NAS structure, a set of sellers may have offers with only the *price* attribute operative negotiable, and thus a reverse single-attribute auction can be initiated.

Comparing the different result-sets might also provide additional feedback. There could be, for instance, only one agreement candidate in the MAS, but several candidates in the NAS. Whereas an agreement for the candidate in the MAS is straightforward, the effort invested in negotiating additional agreements with the candidates in the NAS might pay off, particularly if these agreements exploit win-win tradeoffs and thereby achieve overall higher benefits for the initiator than the agreement in the MAS.

4.2 ScoreNSC

The ScoreNSC models the decision task 'what is/are the best offer/s' from the perspective of one agent (buyer or seller). To execute this decision task the ScoreNSC requires a set of evaluation criteria from the agent. On the basis of these criteria the ScoreNSC then calculates an aggregated multi-attribute utility value for each offer in the set of target offers. The offers with the highest utilities are the 'best' offers according to the preferences of the agent.

4.2.1 Incentive

Multi-attribute decision analysis, which prescribes theories for quantitatively analysing decisions involving multiple, interdependent criteria, is a critical enabler for multi-attribute negotiation support [Bich99a].

The task of comparing a set of competing offers is a complicated decision, which typically requires assessing multiple interdependent criteria. A buyer might, for instance, use three criteria to analyse a set of competing offers: *quality*, *performance*, and *service*. For each of these criteria several choices (alternatives), which can be quantified, exist across the set of offers. Criteria typically represent objectives that the agent wants to achieve by executing the transaction. In one example, the buyer might want to purchase a number of notebook computers, thereby receiving *high quality* notebooks with *high performance*, and *good service* from the seller. Accordingly a criterion is supplemented with an indication of **preference** or an aspiration level (c.f. Section 3.3), which defines, for instance, whether the agent strives for *high quality* or *low quality*.

Digital Cameras	PointSum	LendsMaxZoom
Canon PowerShot A5	282.2	35.0
Olympus C1400L	269.0	110.0
Kodak DC 260.0	268.2	115.0
Nikon Coolpix 900.0	267.0	115.0
Fujifilm MX-700	250.7	35.0
Olympus C840L	240.7	36.0
Agfa ePhoto 1280.0	237.6	114.0
Olympus C1000L	232.6	150.0
Konica Q-M 100.0	212.7	39.0
Kodak DC 210.0	210.9	58.0
Olympus C820L	205.9	36.0
Kodak DC 200.0	198.1	39.0
Casio QV-5000SX	172.4	unknown
Ricoh RDC-4300	168.3	105.0
Agfa ePhoto 780.0	148.8	50.0
Umax MDX-8000	132.3	50.0

Figure 24. Scoring result example[9]

The task of comparing a set of offers can be identified as a core process in the agreement phase of electronic transactions and is referred to as **scoring** ([Stol00] or [Strö00a]). In *Figure 24* an example for the result of a scoring operation in the domain of digital cameras is illustrated. For each

---

[9] Screenshot from the ScoreCat application developed at IBM's Zurich Research Lab [Stol99], [Scor01].

NSC internal views

criterion, a score can be calculated. And an aggregated and weighted score can be calculated, which takes into account the scores of all criteria for a specific offer. The final decision can then be based on a comparison of the aggregated scores for all competing offers.

Decision analysis provides techniques for both eliciting evaluation criteria and scoring. For the elicitation, procedures such as the Analytic Hierarchy Process (AHP, based on hierarchical decomposition of criteria, pair-wise comparison, and re-composition, [Saat96]) or Conjoint Analysis (focusing on relative importance of criteria, [GrWi73]) have been proposed. The assumption for the proposed ScoreNSC is that a definition of evaluation criteria is already available and provided as input to the ScoreNSC operation. The task of criteria elicitation does not require intermediation among several agents and therefore does not comply with the NSC paradigm.

4.2.2 Solution procedure

If only one attribute of an offer is evaluated, the scoring procedure is trivial: the offer with the agreement value domain containing the most preferred attribute value is the best offer.

If more than one attribute needs to be taken into account, Multi-Attribute Utility Theory (see Section 2.1.1) provides a solution procedure for the ScoreNSC operation. MAUT allows defining the relationships (e.g. trade-offs) between preferred values for multiple attributes. For every decision, a distinction has to be made between the choices (the alternatives manifested in the offers), the characteristics of the alternatives (quantified by measures) and the relative desirability of different sets of characteristics (c.f. [Bich99a]).

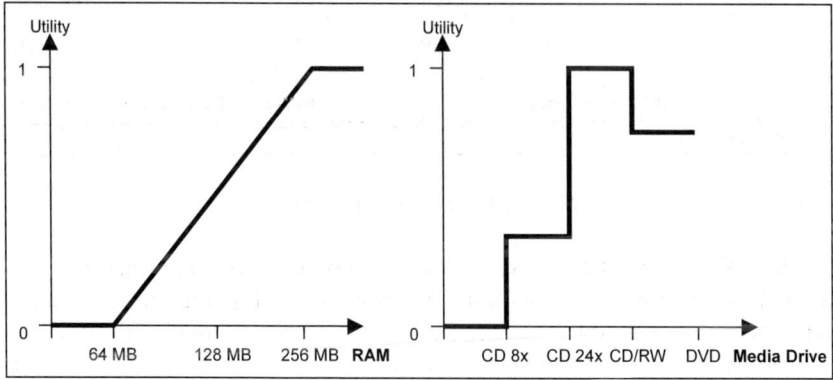

Figure 25. Utility function examples

Each utility function $U(x_i)$ assigns values of *0* and *1* to the worst and best outcomes for that particular objective. Utility function examples for two attributes, the *RAM* size of a notebook and the type of its *media drive*, are illustrated in *Figure 25*. Using the additive utility function[10] for any alternative (offer) *i* that has values $x_1 \ldots x_n$ for the *n* attributes and associated weights $w_1 \ldots w_n$, the highest overall utility is given by $U(x_1 \ldots x_n) = \Sigma\, w_i U(x_i)$ and $1 < i < n$. The alternative with the largest additive utility is the most desirable one.

4.2.3 Adaptation

For use in the ScoreNSC, the foundations of MAUT are complemented with the concept of evaluation criteria. The following hierarchical definition of the criteria evaluation procedure is introduced for the ScoreNSC (c.f. [Stol00]):

An evaluation criterion can be defined as an objective (e.g. *high performance* or *good quality*) for the execution of the transaction. One **criterion** can assess one or more attributes (its associated attributes) of an offer and can be defined itself on the basis of several other criteria (its sub-criteria). If an offer specifies evaluation criteria it has to feature one **root criterion**. A utility function assigns utility units to attribute values. If one criterion assesses several attributes the overall **score** (utility) for a criterion is defined through the criterion utility function, i.e. the relation of value tuples to utility values. The relative importance of criteria can be specified through weights, so that the final score of an offer is defined as the utility of the root criterion, which is the weighted sum of the score for its sub-criteria. The best offer is the one with the highest root criterion score.

On the basis of the formal model introduced in Section 3.3 the solution procedure of the ScoreNSC could be represented as follows. A utility function can be specified as a set of attribute values with associated utilities and a functional expression for the intervals between these points (e.g. linear ascending). The notion of preference was already introduced in Definition 37 in Chapter 3 on the level of deal values. A preference of the agent towards the attribute values can be defined as the direction of ascending utility.

Criteria are associated with attributes defined in an offer and, accordingly, the value of a criterion is derived from a tuple of associated sub-attribute values. The performance criterion for a notebook computer, for example, could depend on the tuple of attribute values for its *on-board cache memory, processor speed* and *bus system*.

---

[10] Multiplicative utility functions, as an alternative to the presented additive function, are discussed in Section 8.2.1.2.

These basic definitions allow the specification of a hierarchical **scoring tree**, which has the root criterion at the top and attributes or criteria as leaves. The weight of each leaf is the product of all weight arcs leading to the leaf. The specification of criteria can be illustrated with an example:

$CRD_{quality}=\{(quality,guarantee), (quality,service)\}$

To assess the quality of a notebook, this agent refers to the *guarantee* and the *service* attribute specified in the offer of the manufacturer. The value tuples are defined as follows:

$CRV_{quality}=\{(3years,2yearsOnSite),(2years,1yearOnSite)\}$

To complete the definition of the criterion, weights and utility values have to be assigned. In the following example, the weight is *0.25* and the utility value is *1.0*:

$CRS_{quality}=\{((3years,2yearsOnSite),0.25,1.0),...\}$

Using the definition of a set of criteria, the overall deal value can alternatively be calculated as the weighted sum of the second-highest-level evaluation criteria utilities, or the utility of the root criterion.

Special consideration is necessary for the ScoreNSC operation if target offers include attribute value domains or agreement value ranges. In this case the ScoreNSC has to search the set (e.g. a combinatorial tree) of all possible offer instantiations and to return the maximum utility achievable within this set as the score for this offer.

4.2.4 Results analysis

In general, the ScoreNSC will return an ordered set of offers with associated scores. Let us assume the following sample result-set: $RS = \{(OF\_003, 0.92), (OF\_001,0.88), (OF\_008,0.88), (OF\_005,0.87), (OF\_007,0.81)\}$

Obviously *OF_003* is the best offer since it has the maximum score according to the evaluation criteria specified. This is a subjective order of the agent submitting the evaluation criteria. If the criteria change, or are specified differently by another agent, the order might change completely. The offers *OF_001* and *OF_008* have the same root criterion score, which means that the agent specifying the evaluation criteria is indifferent towards these offers and they might be substituted for one another.

It is difficult to generalise the interpretation of the scoring deltas. The utility distance from the offer with the maximum score to its first successors in the example result-set is $score(OF\_003) - score(OF\_001) = 0.04$, to the third successor $score(OF\_003) - score(OF-005) = 0.05$. On a very abstract level, these deltas could be interpreted to mean that *OF_001* is only 'a little bit' better than *OF_005*, but *OF_003* is 'much better' than all the others. In more detail, the utility increase from *OF_005* to *OF_001* is *1.1%*, whereas the utility increase from *OF_001* to *OF_003* is *4.5%*.

4.3 MediateNSC

The goal of a MediateNSC is to suggest a settlement for two agreement candidate offers (see [Strö00c] for the following). The task it represents is an interdependent decision of two agents: 'how can we find an agreement for a set of negotiation issues?' Through its operation, mutually beneficial agreements can be reached with minimal effort by the agents.

4.3.1 Incentive

In 1996, the game theorists Brams and Taylor suggested adjusted-winner (AW, c.f. [BrTa96] and [BrTa99]) as the only efficient, envy-free, and equitable procedure for fair division. AW is also non-manipulable unless one agent has advance information about the exact preferences of the other agent.

The application scenarios presented by Brams and Taylor fall into the category of dividing an existing set of items such as the possessions in a divorce or land rights in a political dispute. Yet, the issues to be 'divided' in an electronic market setting are incompatible attribute value domains in an offer-to-buy and an offer-to-sell. Therefore, for application in an electronic market, AW has to be used to resolve who wins the right to determine the value domain for which attribute in the final deal configuration.

If the initial offers of buyers and sellers do not match, three approaches are possible to reach an agreement: the buyer, the seller, or both agents make a concession and adjust their offer. By using AW, both the buyer and the seller have to make concessions in order to reach an equitable agreement. But there could also be cases where unequal entitlements are performed, for example because the seller is only willing to agree to a ratio of *60/40*, which is also supported by the AW procedure [BrTa99, p.67].

The criteria of satisfaction used by Brams and Taylor to evaluate the AW procedure are transferable to the EM context. Envy-freeness, for instance, is the characteristic of an agreement such that no agent envies the other for the set of attribute value domains it determined in the final deal configuration.

In addition to the conditions necessary for the application of the AW procedure (mainly the independence of the negotiation issues, see below), supplementary conditions for the usage of AW as a negotiation support component can be defined.

The first condition is that the offers have to be binding in the sense that an agent cannot 'walk away', that is, retract its offer. The issues that are subject to the agreement are not fixed like real estate objects – they are expressions of will or promises. If the option to retract exists, a malicious agent could heuristically identify with conjured offers the reservation values of

NSC internal views

another agent and then modify its true offer accordingly (e.g. by specifying a price offer just above the reservation value of the seller) in order to achieve mediation results in its favour.

The second condition is that the division is only fair if the marginal utilities of the agents are constant and the boundaries of the utility functions for an issue, which have a utility of 0 and 1, correspond to the negotiable attribute value domains and are vertically mirrored. To give an example, let us assume the following scenario: agent X specifies the utility of the payment mode to be 0 if it has to pay *on receipt*, and to be 1 if it has to pay within *four weeks of receipt or later*. For agent Y on the other hand, the utility is 0 for a payment within *four weeks of receipt*, but 1 if it succeeds in getting agent X to pay within *five days of receipt* or earlier. In this case, depending on the outcome of the AW procedure, the agreement is no longer equitable because one agent might achieve a higher utility than the other. Non-linear utility functions leading to unfair division in this scenario may exist if for agent X the utility gain of moving from a *two-week* to a *four-week* payment period is not the same (but rather, for example, maybe twice as high) as that of moving from payment *on receipt* to a *two-week* payment period.

The assumption for the solution procedure of the MediateNSC is that these conditions hold. In the evaluation in Section 8.3.1.3, countermeasures are discussed for situations where this is not the case.

4.3.2 Solution procedure

The procedure presented by Brams and Taylor uses the following approach to reach an agreement:
- Agents X and Y have to define the set of issues that are subject to the agreement and what winning and losing means for each of these issues.
- Each agent has 100 points to assign to the identified issues – the more points assigned, the more important it is to win this issue. At least one point has to be assigned to each issue by each agent.
- Issues have to be independent, meaning that if agent X wins two issues, the value earned for this particular combination is not greater than the sum of the points assigned.
- Agent X wins the issues on which it puts more points than agent Y and vice versa.
- Tied issues are awarded one-by-one to the agent with the lower number of total points at the current state of the division.
- If the total number of points that each agent wins is the same, the procedure is completed.

- Assuming that agent X won more points than Y, then X has to give back items (or fractions of items) to Y until both agents have won the same number of points (equitability adjustment).
- The giveback starts with the item with the smallest preference ratio (SPR).

There is no other assignment that can give both agents more points at the same time, and therefore the procedure is efficient. As both agents achieve at least 50 points, they will not desire to have what the other agent achieved, which guarantees envy-freeness. Lastly, the adjustment ensures equitability because both agents win exactly the same number of points.

4.3.3 Adaptation

For the MediateNSC, a procedure for fair division has to be applied to a deal configuration problem in which there are not always issues to divide. If a buyer wants to purchase a specific notebook with *256 MB RAM*, but the manufacturer is not able to ship it with this configuration, there is no way the buyer can 'win' this issue. Therefore it is critical to determine those issues where both sides can accept that the other wins – this step can be performed by the MatchNSC (see the example in Section 4.6.1). In addition, some modifications to the procedure are necessary.

The notion of unequal entitlements was already discussed. To support this functionality, it is necessary that an objective specifying the 'equitability factor' EQF for the agreement can be set for the MediateNSC, which is defined as the ratio of the total points achieved by the buyer and the seller.

A sample objective could, for instance, specify the following ratio: $EQF = 1 + x \ (x \geq 0)$. In this example, the buyer is guaranteed 50% of the points assigned, but if the seller, perhaps due to competitive pressure, prefers to give even more points to the buyer, this can be specified dynamically with an x value greater than 0. If in this example x were set to 0.5, the buyer would receive three-fifths, the seller two-fifths of the settlement. It is important to notice that in this case of unequal entitlements, next to the obvious loss of equitability, the seller is not guaranteed to receive at least 50 points and therefore envy-freeness does not hold either.

One other useful, though uncritical, adaptation to the AW procedure is that the MediateNSC not only identifies the issue for the equitability adjustment but also calculates an alternative price (AP) adjustment, if applicable. The restriction to this approach is that if one agent 'won' only the *price* and the outcome of the procedure is that the other agent needs to transfer value back, an adjustment of the *price* cannot be made. If, on the other hand, AW determines *price* to be the issue for the adjustment because it is the SPR attribute, an alternative solution is not necessary. For this adaptation, *price*

has to be a mandatory issue for any agreement candidate pair. The Mediate-NSC also returns the total points achieved based on the SPR issue and the alternative price adjustment. The agents can then compare these two values and decide on one of the following two options:
- Accept the alternative price adjustment in order to achieve a simple but potentially inefficient solution.
- Negotiate the equitability adjustment for the SPR issue in order to achieve an efficient solution.

The motivation for introducing an alternative price solution is based on the hypothesis that, in most cases, agents will prefer a solution that might be slightly inefficient, but is easy to achieve. To decide on this trade-off, agents can assess the point distance to the efficient solution, the overall value of the transaction, and the complexity of the process to reach an agreement on the partition of the SPR issue.

Settling for the adjusted price prevents the agents from haggling over the fractional division of the SPR issue and also addresses the fact that this issue might not be divisible by nature (e.g. the feature of a product, such as the *CPU speed*). The adjustment of the price issue, however, can be easily computed. The alternative agreement based on a price giveback does not open up possibilities for strategic behaviour or manipulation in a sense that would allow agents to capitalise on the knowledge of which issue the adjustment will affect.

For the implementation of the MediateNSC, it would be a viable option to perform the adjustment for attributes other than *price* automatically as well. This is possible if the attribute value domain can be partitioned objectively and if intermediate values are acceptable for the agents. In practice, this would require meta-knowledge of the MediateNSC about attribute types. If this meta-knowledge is available, the MediateNSC could, instead of calculating a default price adjustment, calculate the most efficient adjustment for the set of objectively dividable attributes.

Finally, a requirement of the original AW procedure – assigning at least one point to an issue – can be skipped with a last adjustment. This requirement is necessary in order to avoid divisions by zero in the calculation of the SPR issue. In real eCommerce situations, however, assigning zero points to an issue might make sense in multilateral negotiations in which, for example, one buyer negotiates with several sellers. Why would the buyer want to assign zero points to an issue if this issue could be excluded from the mediation completely? Because, given a specific mediation situation with one seller, the buyer might not be interested at all in winning, for instance, the *guarantee* issue because the buyer trusts this particular seller and prefers spending all points available on other more important issues. With other sellers, however, a *guarantee* might be an important issue.

To deal with a zero point assignment for an issue, it can be assumed for the mediation that the issue, first, is awarded to the agent who gave it a non-zero assignment (if any), and, second has an infinitely high preference ratio and is therefore never selected for adjustment. In any case, no points can be transferred back to the losing agent who assigned zero points, because it seems to achieve no value at all by winning this issue and so decided to cede it to the other agent completely.

4.3.4 Results analysis

The results of the MediateNSC operation can be illustrated with an example. In a typical flight reservation scenario, the attributes for the preceding matchmaking operation could, for example, include the *destination*, the *date of departure*, and the *departure airport*. Potential constraints are the number of *stopovers* or the overall *duration* of the flight. A number of constraints could be tagged to be negotiable, such as *price, quality of the meal served*, or the *entertainment provided*. Let us assume that a seller (airline) is identified in the MatchNSC operation as an agreement candidate and that both sides accept mediation. The following table summarises example constraints and weights before the MediateNSC invocation.

Table 5. Flight reservation example

Issue	Buyer Constraint	Weight	Seller Constraint	Weight
Price	300	30	**350**	40
Meal	**Business**	40	Economy	25
Entertainment	**Included**	10	Extra	5
Magazines	**Included**	10	Extra	5
Drinks	Included	5	**Extra**	25
Points gained		60		65

The attributes marked bold in this table indicate which agent 'won' which issue. In this simple case, *price* is also the attribute with the SPR (40/30):

Price adjustment: $60 + 30x = 65 - 40x \rightarrow x = 5/70$
Final price: $350 - x(350-300) \approx 346.43$.

The final configuration of this deal comprises a *business meal, free video entertainment and magazines, alcoholic beverages at extra charge*, and a *price of $346*. On the basis of the adjustment, both agents gain ≈ 62.14 points. There is no other configuration for this deal that is more efficient for this buyer and seller according to their preferences.

What would be the mediation result if the equitability factor in this scenario were defined dynamically by the seller? Let us assume the seller defines $EQF = 3/2$, indicating willingness to make a larger concession in order to get the deal. The equitability factor before adjustment is $EQF' = 60/65 \approx 0.92$. To reach $EQF = 3/2$ the seller has to give back more of the *price* issue. The adjustment can then be computed as follows:

$$\frac{\text{Total points consumer}}{\text{Total points provider}} = \frac{60 + 30x}{65 - 40x} = \frac{3}{2}$$

Solving this equation results in $x = 5/12$ and an adjusted price of ≈ 329.17. If in this scenario the seller defined $EQF = 0.5$, there would be no price adjustment at all but an additional giveback from the buyer side.

5. NSC CANDIDATES

In this section additional NSC candidates are sketched to demonstrate the potential value and applications of the proposed component paradigm. All suggested candidates fulfil the necessary requirements defined for NSCs, but have not yet been evaluated from an efficiency perspective. For all candidates an outline of the external and internal view is presented, as well as the potential benefits of such an NSC. If available, existing solution procedures are named. The same is true for already existing systems or platforms providing similar functionalities.

5.1 BundleNSC

The decision task executed by a BundleNSC could comprise two dimensions in the space of accumulating demand or supply:
– Homogeneous bundling – for one transaction of objects of the same type.
– Heterogeneous bundling – for objects with different types.

In both dimensions of bundling, **total-offers** are opposed to a set of **part-offers** and the goal of the BundleNSC is to find a coalition of agents specifying part-offers who in total fulfil the requirements specified in the total offer. If there is more than one potential coalition, the optimal coalition has to be found (see below).

5.1.1 Outline

The solution procedure of the BundleNSC can be found in the field of coalition formation in game theory. A coalition can be defined as a set of self-interested agents that agree to cooperate to execute a task or achieve a goal [TsSy00]. A coalition is only viable if the increase in the set's total return from the aggregated transaction is greater than the costs of creating and maintaining such a coalition. The coalition is stable if no agent has an incentive to leave the set in order to achieve higher returns.

In general, the execution of the BundleNSC would consist of three steps [Sand00b]: structure generation, solving the optimisation problem (if applicable), and dividing the return of the transaction among the agents in the coalition. Regarding the generic NSC model and requirements, the BundleNSC would receive as inputs one total-offer and a set of part-offers. The output of a successful BundleNSC operation is then a result-set with suggested coalitions, represented as generated total-offers. These generated coalition offers might then be subject to subsequent enProcess steps (e.g. an auction). In addition, the BundleNSC might, depending on the objectives given, release intermediate information (e.g. the current price decrease achieved or the currently optimal combination). Other objectives of the BundleNSC could be used to specify its behaviour regarding typical issues in coalition formation such as the distribution of gains, costs, and risks [Tsve+01].

Heterogeneous bundling tries to find for one transaction one or more best combinations of objects of different types. The potential value of this second BundleNSC operation relates more to the cooperative than the competitive nature of negotiations, since through negotiated agreements, transactions might be executed that are not possible on the basis of fixed offers. A typical example is a combinatorial offer for a travel transaction, which includes the objects *flight*, *hotel*, and *rental car*. Given a set of competing offers for all the parts of the deal, the BundleNSC has to solve an optimisation problem considering, for instance, overall welfare maximisation.

Special consideration is necessary for the transaction *quantity* attribute. The quantity might not be fixed in the total-offer but variable. In this case, the agent specifying the total-offer may want to execute a transaction for the highest quantity of objects that can be bundled, and will suggest a price depending on the number of objects accumulated from the part-offers (the pricing strategy is often a predefined quantity/price function). However, if quantity is fixed, either for supply accumulation problems with large numbers of part offers, or, especially, for combinatorial offers requesting higher quantities of part objects, the optimisation problem can become computationally complex. The reason for this complexity is that the winner determination is NP-complete by reduction from the maximal weighted clique problem [Roth+98] – not all coalitions can be enumerated. In the area of combinatorial auctions several solutions have been discussed to address this problem: the iterative iBundle auction [PaUn00], the Generalized Vickrey Auction [VaMa94], or the tree search algorithm used for eMediator [Sand99]. The BundleNSC would need to implement one of these heuristics.

5.1.2 Benefits

The homogeneous bundling decision task is an NSC candidate because it relates to the notion of negotiation power. Power in negotiations can informally be defined as the ability to influence other agents in a way that contributes to the achievement of personal goals in a negotiation. In business negotiations the following sources of power[11] might be used [Lewi+97, 182ff.]:
- Resource control (money, time, critical services, or human capital).
- Personal power (attractiveness, emotion, integrity, persistence, and tenacity).
- Information power (ability to assemble information that supports a position, respect, or credibility).

Sources of power are applied in negotiations, for instance, to persuade or to put pressure on the other agent. Negotiation power is a relational concept. One agent tries to gain a power advantage in a certain area. Hence, homogeneous bundling leads to an increase of the resource controlled (in the case of a demand accumulation, the resource is the buyers' money) and therefore gives the members of the coalition more negotiation power. This power might be used, for instance, to achieve better prices.

In electronic markets bundling can be applied on a much larger scale and with much lower costs than in traditional markets, due to the cheap connectivity of the Internet [KaKo01]. The consequences are higher increases of negotiation power (resulting in potentially lower prices) and the possibility of using bundling also for low-value transactions. In general, superadditivity holds, meaning that increasing the size of the bundle is always beneficial. However, bundling has also costs, including the time needed and the communication necessary to form the bundle.

The alternative to using heterogeneous bundling is to run a number of independent negotiations. However, this requires the agent to deal with uncertainties (e.g. regarding how many objects will finally be transacted) and speculation on the behaviour of competitors (look-ahead, c.f. [Sand99]). The main benefit of the BundleNSC in the area of heterogeneous bundling is that it overcomes the need for look-ahead and the inefficiencies from uncertainty since it allows the expression of the dependencies between objects in bundles.

Generic homogeneous bundling services for electronic markets (often referred to as 'powerbuying', 'co-shopping', or 'pooling' solutions) have

---

[11] Two other sources of power are identified: legitimate power and one's location in the organisational structure. These sources are not relevant in the context of non-hierarchical market coordination.

already been introduced, for instance, by Emptoris [Empt01] (which uses the term 'collaborative sourcing') or MobShop [MobS01], which offers demand aggregation solutions for both buyers and sellers. Heterogeneous bundling solutions can be found in the area of combinatorial electronic auction support (see next section).

5.2 BidNSC

The static goal of the BidNSC is to execute a number of typical decision tasks in an auction. According to the electronic negotiation taxonomy introduced in Section 3.5, auctions are a special type of negotiation. All auctions are bilateral negotiations with multiple competing agents on one side and fixed rules. Beyond this commonality, specific auction protocols have been suggested for many other potential dimensions of the taxonomy (e.g. *single-/multi-attribute* or *forward/reverse*).

5.2.1 Outline

The design for a generic BidNSC can be driven from a process perspective, where auctions are characterised by a set of common tasks. The execution of these tasks is governed by the set of rules defined for the auction – the BidNSC would receive this set of rules as objectives and perform the bidding process accordingly. The potentially large number of objectives can be structured according to the enProcess execution tasks and the taxonomy categories introduced in Section 3.5.2.1, as illustrated with the following example:
- Roles:
  Open or closed admission of bidders.
- Offer specification:
  Number of attributes, their relation and the nature of the object(s).
- Offer submission:
  Single- or multi-sided bidding, event-based activity.
- Offer analysis:
  Ascending or descending price, threshold (reservation price).
- Offer matching:
  Clocked or continuous winner determination, defined or tie-breaking resolution.
- Offer allocation:
  Discriminatory or non-discriminatory distribution, mediated or open configuration.
- Offer acceptance:
  Binding or indicative commitment.

NSC candidates

- Information:
  Offer-restricted or free-form communication, private or public transparency.
- Strategy:
  Transaction- or access-based fees, punishing or rewarding arbitration.

The input for the BidNSC are offers, the output is the result-set with the winning bid(s). Typically one agent, the auctioneer, would define the rules for the auction, and the bidders have to agree to these rules in order to participate in the auction. In a multi-sided auction an intermediary, the third party governing the exchange, could determine the objectives. In this scenario, the clearing rules of the intermediary may define, for instance, that the BidNSC tries to find efficient, surplus-maximising allocations.

For one specific type of auction the BidNSC has to rely on a preceding ScoreNSC operation to execute the decision tasks in the auction process. If the auction constitutes a multi-attribute negotiation, the BidNSC requires a ScoreNSC operation to determine the multi-attribute utility value of a bid, which is necessary, for instance, to decide whether the bid is accepted and constitutes a new highest bid. Hence, the corresponding enScenario has to stipulate that offers are first scored by the ScoreNSC according to the auctioneer's criteria, and then submitted to the BidNSC. Combinatorial auctions, on the other hand, would not be supported by the suggested BidNSC, but could be executed through the BundleNSC.

5.2.2 Benefits

Auctions are currently the dominating type of negotiation in electronic markets. The main reason for this is that auctions especially benefit from the characteristics of electronic markets, as outlined with a number of arguments in Section 2.2.4. Hence, a number of advantages favour the use of electronic auctions as compared to traditional auctions. Electronic auctions are, for instance, virtual exchanges with low setup and transaction costs, which allow sellers to keep their reservation prices relatively high because unsold products do not incur return costs [Lee98].

Auction support for electronic markets is already in widespread use. Recent products from electronic market solution providers such as Ariba [Arib01] or Perfect [Perf01] can be customised with a variety of auction rules, supporting a range of negotiation types from simple price-based procurement scenarios to complex multi-attribute RFQ processes. The most flexible and most automated (but non-commercial) auction platform to date is the Michigan Auction Bot [Wurm+98], which is able to generate a wide range of electronic auction types on the basis of a set of parameters, which are structured in a way comparable to the suggestion in this section: receiving bids, clearing, and revealing intermediate information [Wurm+01].

5.3 ContractNSC

The static goal of the ContractNSC is to create an electronic contract on the basis of a set of signed offers. This creation process is mainly a transformation task, but depending on the objectives, the ContractNSC may also execute several decision tasks within the contract generation and enactment process (see below).

5.3.1 Outline

A contract is formed by an offer and its unequivocal acceptance; any proposed variation constitutes a new counteroffer. Offer and acceptance have to be communicated to the counterpart in order to become legally binding, which means that the message has "entered the sphere of influence of the receiver" [Gisl+99, 23ff.]. Depending on the enScenario design, a final contract might require that two or more compatible offer instances be found that are mutually signed by their originators with respect to the offer of the counterpart (one-sided contracting), or that one offer is signed by a number of agents (double-sided contracting). Finally a third option is that a trusted third party, such as a notary underwrites the contract [Lame+98]. The ContractNSC would receive signed offers (NSC precondition) and check the validity of the signatures and the associated authorisation.

If signed offers from all agents have been received and validated within the specified timeframe (NSC objective), the contract generation and enactment process is initiated. This time-constrained synchronisation helps to address the hold-up problem in electronic contracting (c.f. [Rung00, p.129]), where one agent tries to delay the signature as long as possible in order to find better deals, but thereby holds up the counterpart who had already committed.

The following tasks may be part of the subsequent contract generation and enactment process – the actual invocation of these tasks depends on the objectives defined for the ContractNSC operation:

- **Optimisation**
  For this decision task a number of contract optimisation technologies are suggested in [Sand00b]. Levelled commitment optimisation, as an example, allows unilateral decommitting of electronic contracts based on calculated penalties. Since it is as of today still difficult to enforce electronic contracts by law, an optimisation for unenforced contract execution creates an incentive to carry out the remaining exchange processes

within a transaction by splitting the deal into smaller chunks (with a sequencing algorithm). For bundled offers, a trivial part of the optimisation is the generation of a number of specific part-contracts for each of the agents contributing to the agreed-upon deal.

- **Standardisation**
 This transformation task performs a semantical and syntactical conversion of the accepted and signed offer(s) into a standard electronic contract format. Semantical transformation aspects include the use of standard terms and clauses (potentially provided by predefined contract templates, c.f. [Hoff99]), such as the terms defined in the INCOTERMS and ETERMS repositories (see for example [TaTh00] and Section 8.3.2.2). These standard terms can be referenced in electronic contracts. Complete agreed-upon contracts can also be deposited in these repositories. Syntactical transformation addresses conversions to standard electronic contract formats. Several standard formats such as UN/EDIFACT or ebXML have already been suggested (for an overview see [AnGr01]).

- **Validation**
 An electronic contract can not only be checked for valid signatures but also for compliance with industry practices, patterns, or trade standards within the transaction, agent, or object context (see [Rung00, 137ff.]). This validation can additionally comprise a check of the level of agreement, investigating, for instance, whether all negotiation issues are resolved or whether the submitted offers still specify agreement value ranges for certain attributes. Depending on the enScenario, it might be necessary to resolve all issues and ranges before it is possible to generate a contract. To support this, the ContractNSC can suggest default values.

- **Archiving**
 Especially from a legal perspective, it is essential that an electronic contract be archived in a secure manner, in order to prevent agents from performing an unauthorised modification of the contract [Gisl+99, 20ff.]. Security aspects relate to the confidentiality of the contract as well as to the tracing (audit trail) of the contract history for latter dispute resolution. This trace may start already with the initial offer specifications in the intention phase.

- **Enactment**
 For some transaction objects, especially services, the final contract can be used to set up the corresponding transaction execution infrastructure. This contract enactment process (see [Hoff+01]) could comprise activities such as configuring the service provisioning resources in the agent's organisation (e.g. creating application service providing accounts), and linking the infrastructures of the agents (e.g. by setting up virtual private networks and binding interfaces).

The output result-set of the ContractNSC is one or more generated electronic contracts, complemented, if desired and feasible, with a contract enactment infrastructure. In most cases, the generated contract will have to be accepted once more by the agents involved. If there is more than one generated contract, the agents will have to agree on one of the suggested alternatives.

A number of additional tasks related to the resulting electronic contracts might be executed in the settlement phase of the electronic transaction. Examples include contract monitoring and arbitration. Since this book focuses on the intention and agreement phase, these tasks are not considered for the proposed ContractNSC.

5.3.2 Benefits

The suggested ContractNSC constitutes the interface from the agreement to the settlement phase. Hence, its main benefit is that it enables consistent enMedia support for all phases of an electronic transaction, allowing one to avoid manual completion of an electronic intention and agreement phase, for example by filling out and signing traditional paper-based contracts. "An electronic contract is meant to be the link between different electronic commerce systems" [Gisl+99, p.20]. Through the consistent usage of electronic data exchange the overall transaction and coordination costs can be reduced and the time for transaction processing and contracting can be shortened.

But the ContractNSC may be more than just a bridge to the settlement phase. Through the execution of several decision tasks such as contract optimisation and validation, it also helps to increase the level of automation support for multi-attribute negotiation, and, by extending the functionality to the setup of the actual transaction execution infrastructure, it can enable new dynamic forms of business relationships.

Recently, electronic market solution providers have added support for electronic contracting. An example is the contract module within the Menerva MarketProcess solution [Mene01], which generates a draft contract and requires users to sign the contract electronically before it is exported to a hardcopy format, archived, and contract management tools (e.g. pricing calculators) are generated.

6. COMBINING NSC OPERATIONS

NSCs perform negotiation intermediation by supporting decision-making and communication in electronic negotiation processes. The basic offer communication between buyers and sellers can be enhanced with additional

Combining NSC operations 105

information for the agents' decision-making. On an offer-level this augmentation is done through offer result-codes (e.g., *matched* or *scored*) or offer element modification (e.g. determining agreement value ranges or suggesting fair agreement values). On a result-set level, intermediation is provided through meta-information such as an offer classification or the provision of an order for a set of offers.

In principle, it is possible to combine NSC operations arbitrarily in order to support electronic negotiations with a specific form of intermediation. The number and type of NSC operations may vary from enScenario to enScenario, depending on the rules specified for the enScenario.

6.1 Example MatchNSC/MediateNSC

The MediateNSC explicitly requires a preceding operation of the MatchNSC. Before dispute resolution can be applied, it is critical to determine the set of issues which define the conflict, and where both sides can accept that the other side wins – meaning that the final attribute value of this agent, transaction, or object attribute, equals the attribute value (domain) defined by a constraint in the offer of the winning agent. This definition of issues is the output of the MatchNSC operation: the disagreement spaces defined for the agreement candidates in the NAS.

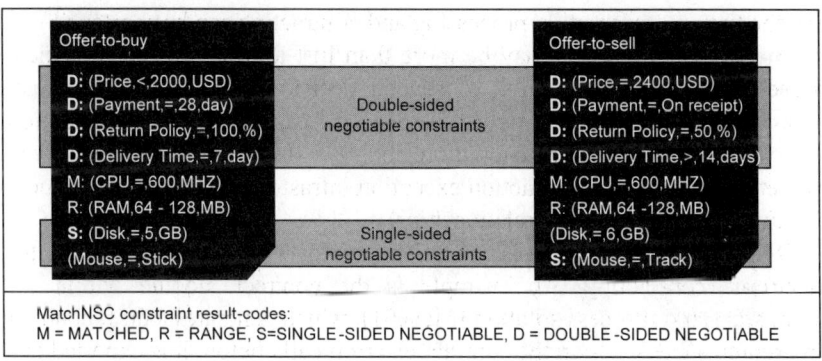

Figure 26. MatchNSC output example

For double-sided, multi-issue disagreement spaces with double-sided negotiable constraints (where both agents declared flexibility towards an issue, see Section 4.4.1.4), the MediateNSC is able to suggest an agreement that, by using the Adjusted Winner procedure, is efficient, equitable, and envy-free. For disagreement spaces with single-sided negotiable constraints this is not possible, because the outcome of the AW procedure for each issue might request either side to relax their constraint. But SNCs indicate flexibility on only one agent's side (in the given example, the notebook manufacturer simply might have no models with *stick pointer*).

Before the agreement candidate offers are subject to the MediateNSC operation, the agents have to assign importance ratings ranging from 0 to 100 to the four issues identified by the MatchNSC. For the DNCs in the example in *Figure 26*, the disagreement space determined by the MatchNSC and the associated importance ratings of the agents could be defined as follows:

Table 6. MediateNSC input example

Issue	Buyer Constraint	Weight	Seller Constraint	Weight
Price	< 2000 USD	60	2400 USD	10
Payment	28 days	30	On receipt	25
Return Policy	100%	5	50%	30
Delivery Time	7 days	5	> 14 days	35
Points gained		90		65

Given the values in the example, the AW procedure determines the suggested agreement attribute values initially to be *(Price,=,2000,USD)*, *(Payment,=,28,day)*, *(Return Policy,=,50,%)* and *(Delivery Time,=,14,days)*. This initial distribution is not equitable and envy-free since the buyer gained more points than the seller. Hence, an additional equitability adjustment is suggested on the issue with the smallest preference ratio, according to the following calculation:

Payment mode: $65 + 25x = 90 - 30x \rightarrow x = 5/11$
Final split: *17 days*
Points achieved: ≈ 76.36 *points*

The attribute with the SPR is the payment mode (*30/25*). A price alternative exists, so an additional solution can be suggested:

Price adjustment: $65 + 10x = 90 - 60x \rightarrow x = 5/14$
Final price: $2000 + x(2400-2000) \approx 2143$
Points achieved: ≈ 68.57 *points*

The difference of the alternative price solution from the efficient AW solution (in this example ≈ 7.79 *points*) is dependent on the difference of the price ratio to the smallest preference ratio. If the preferences of the buyer and seller towards the price are very diverse, the ratio might be high compared to the attribute with the SPR and, correspondingly, the distance to an effective solution is high as well.

It is up to the buyer and the seller whether to accept one of the suggested agreements. The benefit of this solution is that the procedure is fair (both agents have an interest in being honest) and long haggling processes are avoided. If the buyer and the seller accept this suggested agreement, it would be possible, for instance, to finalise the contract with a ContractNSC operation.

6.2 General interdependencies

Further interdependencies between negotiation support components can be identified. In general, NSCs are not 'aware' of the existence of other NSCs and therefore cannot, within their own execution state, trigger the execution of another NSC. This principle is important in order to guarantee loose coupling among the NSCs and to maximise the possibilities for NSC combination. However, the preconditions (required input offer structures) of some NSCs may demand, under specific objectives, the precedent operation of another NSC.

A first case of interdependency was already discussed in the previous example, in which the MediateNSC required a precedent operation of the MatchNSC. A second interdependency was identified for the BidNSC, which relies on a prior ScoreNSC operation for the support of multi-attribute auctions; the same holds for the BundleNSC in a multi-attribute case. For instance, in order to combine the best offers in a bundle, these offers must already have been scored. From the perspective of an agent, such a combination of operations in the enProcess can be transparent. The agent simply submits a bid to an auction run by the BidNSC, and does not need to know that this bid is evaluated first by the ScoreNSC. The designers and developers of electronic negotiations, though, have to respect these interdependencies in the enScenario design.

Although NSCs are independent, some operation sequences will recur in many enScenarios, because there are typical sequences of decisions in negotiations. To give an example, in most cases a MatchNSC operation will precede a ScoreNSC operation. This is because the scoring solution procedure requires bids with agreement value ranges specific to a pair of opposing offers, and the most efficient way to attain these is through a precedent MatchNSC operation. This sequence of NSC operations also reflects the nature of the sequential decision-making process in negotiations: first an agent needs to find potential transaction partners, then the offers of the candidates are evaluated in order to find the best offer. In many cases, a MatchNSC operation will also precede a BundleNSC operation, because before a part-offer can be assigned to a bundle, an agent usually needs to evaluate whether it complies with the constraints defined in the initiating offer.

For typical or necessary NSC operation sequences, Section 8.3.1.4 introduces the construct of negotiation support meta-components, which circumvents some of the restricting properties of NSCs. The recommendation of best practices for combinations of NSC operations from a general perspective is further investigated in Section 8.3.2.2.

7. SUMMARY

This chapter presents a general component paradigm for multi-attribute negotiation tasks. Instances of this paradigm, negotiation support components, encapsulate reusable solution procedures and can be almost arbitrarily combined in order to provide different means of negotiation intermediation. Concrete examples of NSCs, such as the MatchNSC, ScoreNSC, and MediateNSC were presented in detail and complemented with a set of additional NSC candidates. The overall set of NSCs presented here is an example and deliberately not intended to be complete. The reader may suggest other generalised solution procedures that support communication and/or decision-making in multi-attribute negotiations, can be packaged as an NSC, and may realise additional benefits in combination with other NSCs. For the presented NSCs, a number of extensions can be envisioned, which are discussed in Section 8.3.1, after a general evaluation of the proposed NSC solution procedures and a comparison to related work in Section 8.2.1.

Through the formalisation of negotiation support in this section, the original concept of negotiation intermediation in *Figure 11* can now be extended with the NSC paradigm and the NSCs defined, as illustrated in *Figure 27*.

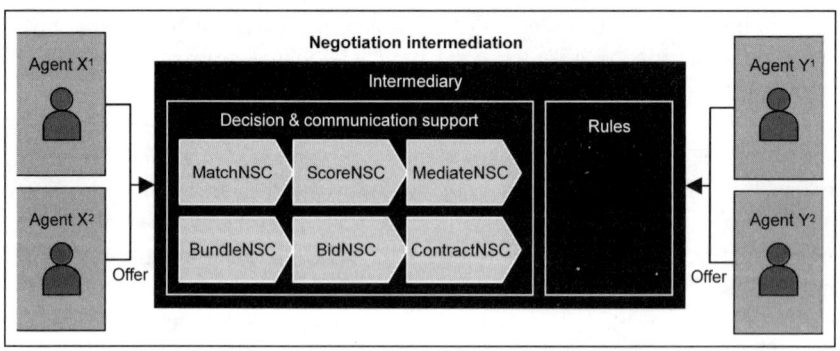

Figure 27. Negotiation intermediation with NSCs

To many decision-makers in eCommerce, it might be a novel experience to accept the decision made by an NSC, such as '*this is the best offer*' or '*with this agreement you meet in the middle*'. Hence, a lot of resistance can be

Summary

expected (see also the discussion of autonomous software agents in Section 2.2.2). On the other hand, eCommerce is becoming more and more complex, moving from single-attribute to multi-attribute negotiations, with potentially more and more partners from multiple countries and so forth. First studies show that decision-makers can hardly cope with the complexity of the eCommerce situations they are facing [Bich99b]. Hence, any means of support, such as the NSCs presented, can help negotiators to address this increasing complexity by automating some of the more structured and formalised decision tasks and allowing human agents to focus on critical and important tasks, for which no generalised solution procedures can be found.

Providing a set of NSCs is just one initial building block for symmetric multi-attribute negotiation intermediation systems that address the problems postulated for the research underlying this book. The solution procedures encapsulated in NSCs also have to be embedded in an enMedium system architecture, which supports an almost arbitrary and parameterised instantiation of NSCs, as well as to be considered in the design of an electronic negotiation. The enScenario design has to define the rules for combining NSC operations and for setting the objectives of these operations. Accordingly, the next chapter investigates how these rules, the empty box in *Figure 27*, can be specified.

Chapter 5

Electronic negotiation design
Specifying "what" and "how"

The second current problem identified in Section 2.3 for the domain of electronic negotiations describes a lack of comprehensive model representations for the design or discussion of electronic negotiation scenarios. As a solution to this problem, this chapter presents an approach for the design of multi-attribute negotiation intermediation scenarios in electronic markets that is based on and results in well-defined abstractions. These abstractions provide an extensive foundation for the implementation of electronic negotiation support. Overall, this chapter constitutes the second main contribution to the enMedia framework.

The design effort cannot be isolated from other activities necessary for the development of enMedia. Therefore, the discussion here is extended to interdependent activities in the analysis and the implementation phase. This chapter does not feature detailed design examples – these will be given in Section 7.2, which presents an application of the proposed design approach to exemplary enScenario cases is presented. Hence, the reader may decide to read this chapter and Section 7.2 in direct succession.

1. APPROACH

Referring back to the definitions introduced in Section 3.2, an electronic negotiation instance comprises an electronic negotiation scenario, which is executed within an electronic negotiation medium residing in a specific business domain. To agents, the enInstance will appear as one particular enMedium they can use for negotiating a deal. Hence, a design approach for electronic negotiations can be structured in a way analogous to the design of media in general, which encompasses three dimensions [Schm00]:

- The communication design provides the concepts for the logical space of the medium – syntactical and semantical representations of the agents, transactions, and objects.
- The organisation design describes the roles (structure) and protocols (behaviour) governing the agent interaction within the medium.
- The IT design addresses the technical architecture of the medium, its channels, components, and interfaces.

An additional element for the integration of the proposed design approach in the overall enMedia framework is the consideration of negotiation support component operations within the enProcess execution.

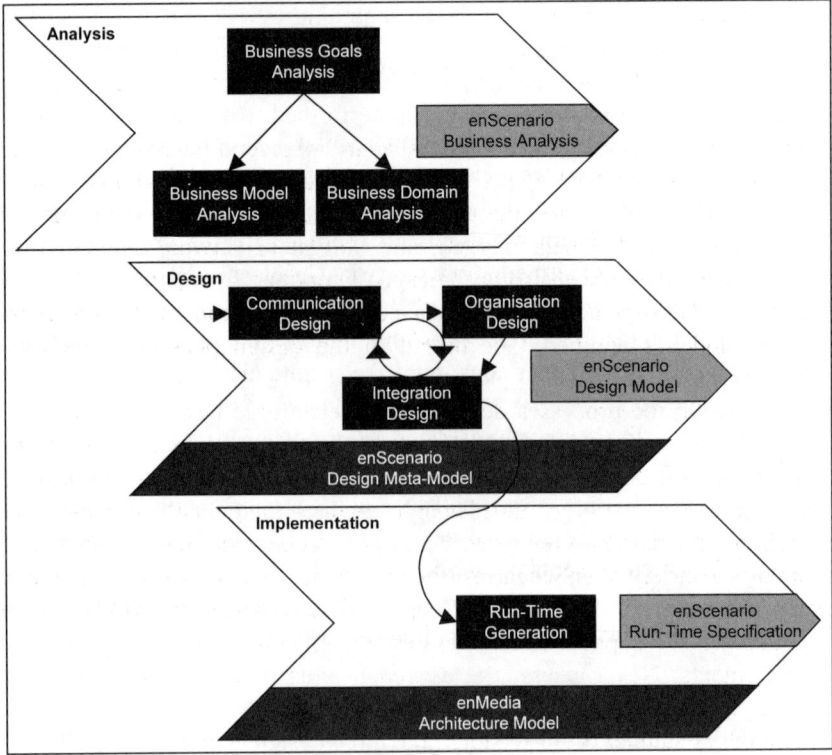

Figure 28. enMedia development action-model

In the enMedia framework design approach, the tasks and task interactions necessary for the development process are specified in the **development action-model** (DAM), which is illustrated in *Figure 28* (black areas represent tasks, lighter grey areas deliverables, and darker grey areas the meta-models underlying the tasks). The DAM defines an analysis phase in

Approach 113

which the business context of the electronic negotiation is analysed, in order to determine guidelines and recommendations for the design. In the design phase, all of the media design dimensions introduced above have to be specified. For this purpose the DAM prescribes how the communication and organisation design of an enScenario is performed, and how both design dimensions are integrated. The DAM also defines means to implement the design results in an enMedium system architecture. On the basis of this approach, the effort for the enMedium IT design and the implementation phase is reduced to the generation of enScenario run-time specifications, which can be deployed to one or more enMedia.

Figure 28 illustrates the sequence of actions in the DAM. The design phase starts with an initial enScenario communication design, which is based on the findings of the business context analysis and the enScenario design meta-model (DMM, see below), which underlies the whole design phase. Then the initial organisation design is performed, using the results of the communication design, the business analysis recommendations, and the constructs provided by the DMM for the organisation design. Finally, in the integration design activity, the results from the organisation and communication design are refined, merged, and validated. Having completed one design cycle, the enScenario designer may continue by alternating between these three design activities until a complete and consistent enScenario design model is attained. The output of the design phase is a validated enScenario design model.

Following the processes defined in the electronic negotiation reference model (*Figure 17*), the completed enScenario design model has to be implemented and deployed to the enMedium. The design approach assumes that the implementation and deployment environment is an enMedium system that is based on the generic enMedia architecture model and thereby supports a variety of enScenarios (the architecture model and an example for such a system are discussed in Chapter 6). The design approach requires certain generic support functionalities, which can be derived as implicit requirements. Nevertheless, the approach aims to be independent of the underlying enMedium system implementation.

In the remainder of this chapter, the three design activities, as well as the related run-time specification generation process in the implementation phase, are presented in detail. The analysis phase is outside the context defined by the identified research problems; therefore, only a high-level discussion is provided in the next section.

2. ANALYSIS

Every new enInstance will be situated in a specific business context, such as a market for *database services* or for the *wholesale distribution of computer notebooks*. Even before any development activity is started, a decision has to be made as to whether an electronic negotiation in this context makes sense or not. This decision process might assess, for instance, the range of expected benefits, such as a potential decrease in transaction costs (see Section 1.1.3), and will result in a set of goals defined for the creation and operation of the enInstance.

Next to the overall feasibility decision, the main objective for the analysis phase is to derive, on the basis of the business context, requirements and recommendations for the design phase. These requirements and recommendations should guide the actual design and implementation process, so that business goals, such as the realisation of a specific business model, can be achieved. The results of this analysis phase can be structured according to the taxonomy categorisation introduced in Section 3.5.1 as will be shown next.

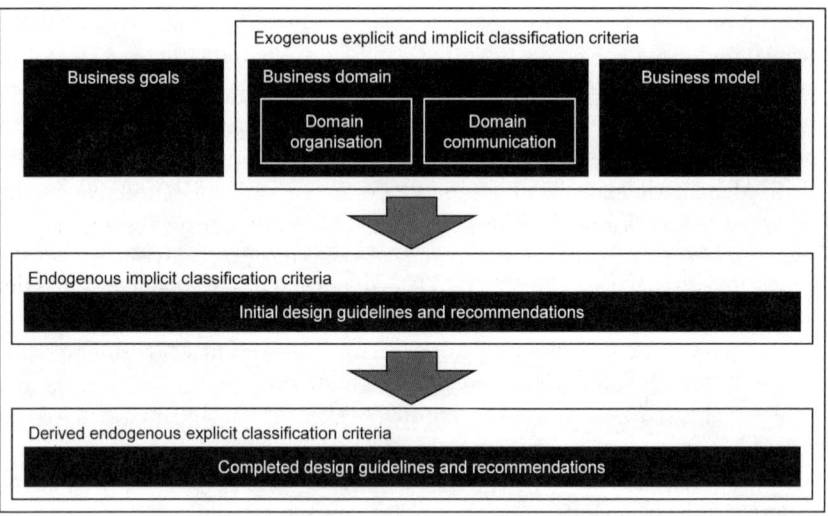

Figure 29. Business analysis approach

An enScenario analyst will typically try to identify distinct properties of the business context. Exogenous explicit and implicit classification criteria for the business domain and the business model represent one way of capturing the results of this assessment process (see *Figure 29*).

Analysis 115

For the enMedia framework design approach, it is also necessary to derive and separate analysis results that are specific to the organisation design and communication design. Business context characteristics such as the transaction value (e.g. high, low, or perishable), the available resources, the risk for the agents involved in this transaction, the agents' roles (their beliefs, desires, intentions…), as well as the customisability of the object of the transaction, could be investigated in order to select an appropriate organisation design for the electronic negotiation. For the communication design, the analysis needs to identify typical and necessary elements of the logical space, such as standard terms and conditions for transactions (e.g. *delivery_time*, *return_policy*) or common representation formats for the transaction objects in a certain business context (e.g. '*computer notebooks are always specified on the basis of CPU speed defined in MHz, whereas the mainboard memory size is defined in MB*').

Given business goals and a business domain/model classification, the analyst has to derive the guidelines and requirements for the design and implementation phase. Unfortunately, current theory in the field offers yet neither guidance nor a 'cookbook' to help an analyst select, for example, the 'right' auction type from the potentially high number of suggested auction types [Wurm01].

Assuming that a recommendation is found, these guidelines and requirements can initially be expressed with the set of endogenous implicit criteria suggested in Section 3.5.2.2. For instance, the analyst could come to the conclusion that the future enInstance has to guarantee efficiency and fairness to all participating agents in order to be successful and attractive in the business context. To achieve these properties, detailed design recommendations can be derived from the implicit criteria and can be specified on the basis of endogenous explicit classification criteria. To guarantee fairness, the analyst may recommend, for instance, that all sides during the offer submission be allowed to submit offers (*multiple-sides*) and, regarding the information revelation, that all sides have access to the same enProcess information (*public-transparency*).

Having these recommendations as input, an enScenario designer is empowered to define a complete enScenario model using the methodology and the constructs provided within the enMedia framework design approach. This is demonstrated in the subsequent sections.

3. DESIGN

The basis for all design activities is the **design meta-model** pictured in *Figure 30*, which introduces the principal entity types, as well as the relations among these types, for use in the organisation, communication, and integration design.

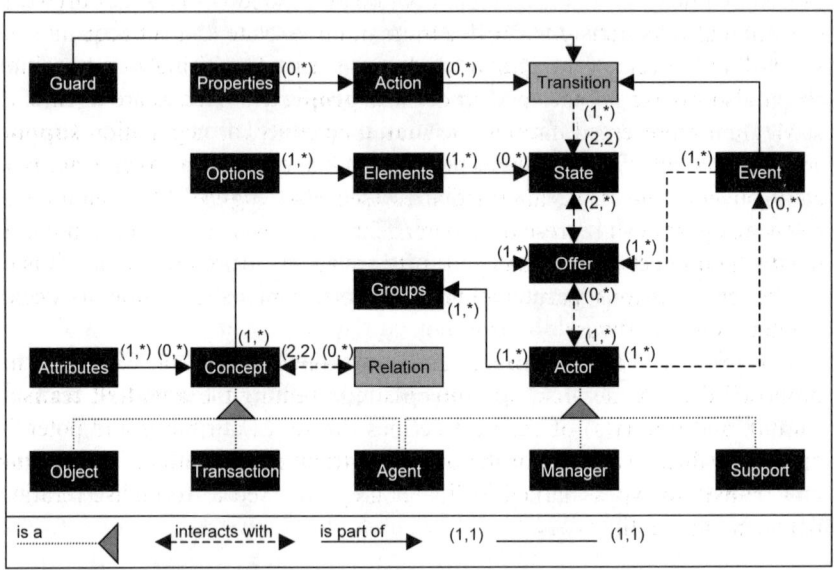

Figure 30. Design meta-model

This meta-model captures both structural and behavioural aspects of electronic negotiations. One graph of entity and relation instances constitutes one enScenario model. The DMM constrains and thereby supports the process of designing concrete models on a conceptual level. This process includes, with regard to the organisation design model, the specification of the structure (roles) and behaviour (protocols) of electronic negotiations with design artefacts that represent the functionality of an underlying enMedium. The DMM also provides the means to express communication models for the logical space of an electronic negotiation, that is, syntactical and semantical representations for the agents, transaction, and objects of the deals, which are supposed to be the subject of the electronic negotiation.

The concept of **state charts** is the underlying modelling paradigm for both the organisation and the communication design. The advantage of state charts is that they are commonly used in information systems design and are also part of the unified modelling language (UML, [Rumb+99]). Therefore it

Design 117

can be assumed that most designers are familiar with the methodology of state charts.

The basic semantics of the DMM can be summarised as follows: an **offer**[12] has two or more associated **states** with offer structure **elements** and notation **options**. **Actors** create, delete, or modify offers and cause **events**, which can trigger **transitions** between the states of an offer. One event is caused by one or more actors and might be associated with a set of offers. A transition always transfers an offer from an initial state to a subsequent state and will only occur if the **guard** condition is true. The 'firing' of a transition might also invoke an **action** with defined **properties**. Actors are **agents**, an enMedium represented through the **manager** entity, or negotiation **support** components, all of which might be part of an agent **group**. Agents are typically buyers, sellers, or intermediaries (see also *Figure 30*). Autonomous software agents can represent human agents. However, for the design phase, the distinction between human and software agents is not important – it is up to the organisations participating in an electronic negotiation to decide whether to use software agents or not.

An offer specifies **attributes** and constraints on attribute values of the proposed deal. A hierarchy of **concepts** representing the **agent(s)**, **transaction(s)**, and **object(s)** of the deal defines the set of attributes and potential attribute values available for the offer constraint specification. The **relation** and **transition** types marked in lighter grey are used to formalise relations between other entity types.

3.1 Communication design

Let us assume that a new electronic negotiation instance is being developed. One recommendation identified in the analysis phase might be that, owing to the nature of the transaction objects, price-focused coordination rules, such as those used in auction scenarios, are not applicable because an agreement between a seller and a buyer has to consider multiple attributes of the object (e.g. *price* and *quality*) as well as the terms and conditions of the transaction.

A critical factor for the efficiency of the future enProcesses and the success of the potential settlements is an a priori agreement among the negotiating agents about how the issues of a negotiation (agent, transaction, or object attributes) are represented as abstract concepts in the electronic negotiation and what this representation means to each of the negotiating agents. If, for instance, agent X offers a delivery date of *12/10/2002* for a worksta-

---

[12] In a deviation from the conventions of this book, the types of the DMM are introduced in this section in boldface for illustration purposes, although the types were either already defined in preceding sections or will be defined later, in the remainder of this book.

tion to agent *Y*, one potential conflict arises if this syntax is misinterpreted by *Y* as *October 12 2002* whereas *X* intended to offer *December 10 2002*. A semantic problem could occur if the meaning of this date to *X* is the point in time at which the product will leave the premises of *X*, whereas *Y* assumes that it is the date on which the workstation will arrive on the premises of *Y*. This problem is referred to as the ontology problem of electronic negotiations [Yoon+99].

To solve this problem the enMedia framework design approach proposes to perform a communication design for electronic negotiations that explicitly specifies the common syntax and semantics of the negotiating agents – that is, the logical space of the electronic negotiation – in an enScenario (see [Strö01b] for the following).

The central objects of the communication design are the offers exchanged in an enProcess. Offers are the primary means of communication in the intention and agreement phase (c.f. Section 3.2), and the only supported type of agent interaction in the design approach. Analogous to the formal model of Section 3.3, the communication design distinguishes between two types of offers that can be issued by agents: offers-to-buy (O2B) and offers-to-sell (O2S). The design of offer types is separated into the definition of offer context ontologies for the semantical aspects, and the specification of offer structure states, for the syntactical aspects of offer communication in an enProcess (see *Figure 31*).

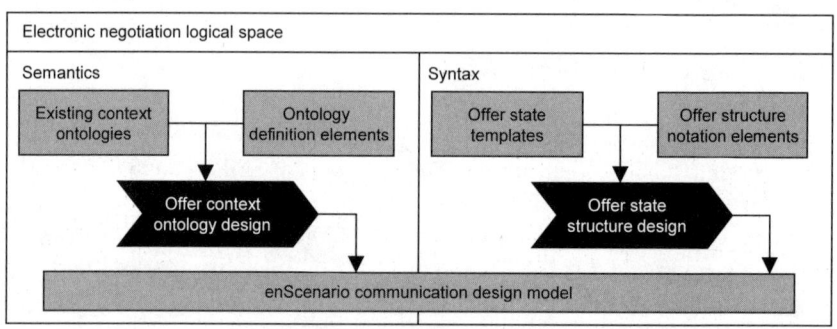

Figure 31. Communication design approach

3.1.1 Offer context ontology design

Ontologies are formally specified models of knowledge, which can be used to share semantics among a set of agents. An ontology defines the concepts describing a certain context and the relationships that hold between the concepts [CrPu99]. It can be represented as a hierarchy of concepts. Beam

Design 119

and Segev already suggested in [BeSe97] the use of ontologies for electronic negotiations as a means of ensuring that agents are referring to exactly the same context when offers are specified. This section describes how an ontology can be structured for the domain of electronic negotiations. Section 5.3.3.1 then demonstrates the integration of ontology models in the overall design approach.

The goal of commercial negotiations is to conduct one or more transactions between the agents involved in the enProcess. Referring back to Section 3.2, a transaction transfers the ownership of one or more objects (e.g. *goods* or *money*) from one agent to another and vice versa. The transaction, the object, and the agent(s) involved can be described with sets of attributes such as the *delivery date* of the transaction, the *colour* of the object, or the *location* of the agent. An attribute has a value or value domain such as *12/10/2002*, *green*, or *Switzerland*. It is therefore necessary for the design of the logical space of electronic negotiations to provide concepts with attributes and value domains for the representation of and reasoning about the agent, transactions, and object context. Why is it necessary to include concepts and attributes for the agent context? To give an example, let us assume a domain in which agents receive, perhaps through a third party, a certain recommendation or reputation level (e.g. *reputation=premium*) based on their transaction record. In an offer, an agent may then want to specify that only agents with a specific recommendation level are eligible to perform the proposed transaction. Agent attributes such as this, or the availability and accessibility of after-sale services provided by the agent, might also be negotiable.

Figure 32 (next page) illustrates an (incomplete) example of a hierarchy of concepts in the domain of *computer hardware*. The representation of ontology concept attributes in an offer follows the notation *context.attribute* (e.g. *transaction.delivery_date* or *seller.location*). A *notebook*, for instance, is a sub-concept of a *computer* and accordingly inherits the attributes of *computer*, which are in this example the *computer.CPU* clock-speed, the type of the *computer.media_drive* etc. *Notebooks* are also sub-concepts of *monitors*, thus inheriting another set of attributes (e.g. the *display resolution*). Attributes in the proposed ontology model have a certain type and can be constrained, thus allowing only specific attribute values (in the example, the *computer.CPU* clock-speed is constrained to the range above *300 MHz*). Relations between concepts complement the ontology (not shown in *Figure 32*). An example of such a relation is that the *CPU* of *notebooks* has to have *power management functions*. Through formal reasoning it is possible to infer new knowledge on the basis of given facts (such as relations) in the ontology. An agent could derive, for instance, that if a certain *CPU* is offered with *notebooks*, it must have *power management functions*.

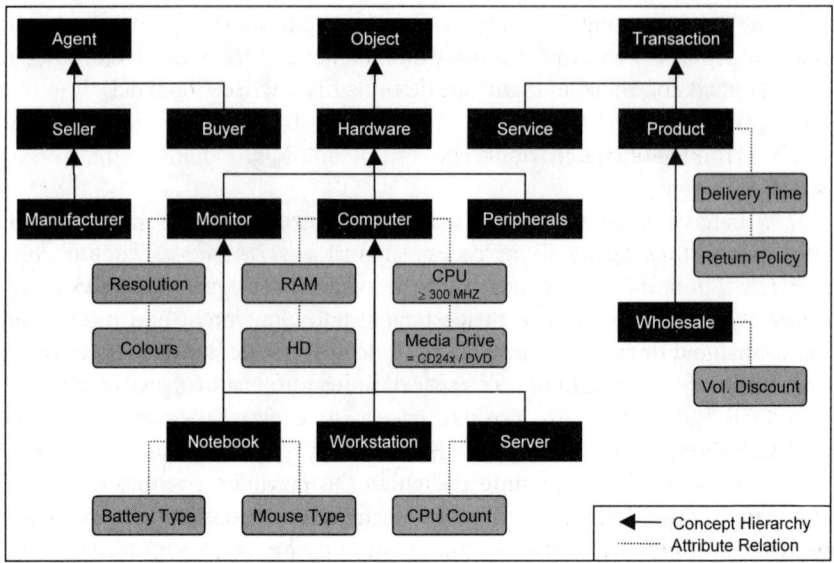

Figure 32. Offer context ontology example

In an offer instance, concepts from the agent, transaction, and object context can or must (depending on the design) be used to describe the proposed deal. In principle, multiple enScenarios can share elements of one context ontology. The ontology in the *computer hardware* example could also be applied in enScenarios designed for a similar context such as *computer software* or be further extended to cover *IT services* as well. However, if changes to the offer context ontology become necessary in one specific enScenario, the designers have to ensure that these changes do not affect other enScenarios sharing the same concepts in the offer context ontology design.

The effort to design and establish an offer context ontology for an electronic negotiation instance can be significant, as agents have to agree (in a social process) on a common terminology (c.f. [Benj+99]). In other words, before ontologies can be used in the intention and agreement phase, the agents have to negotiate on a meta-level the structure, meaning, and content of the context – their common language – and manifest the results in the ontology models developed or chosen for the intended enInstance. If, for instance, the agents agree a priori that, in general, products can be returned within three weeks, this agreement can be represented in the offer context ontology with an attribute *transaction.return_policy* constrained to a value of three weeks.

Design 121

When the offer context ontology is completed, the offers specified and issued in actual enProcesses can be validated against the specified ontology for semantical compliance, as will be demonstrated in Section 5.4.1.

3.1.2 Offer state structure design

From a behavioural perspective, an offer instance may assume different states of structure during an enProcess such as *advertisement*, *bid*, and *contract* (c.f. Section 3.2). Accordingly, the offer entity type in the DMM in *Figure 30* is associated with at least two states (an initial and a terminal state). The goal of the offer state design is to specify the possible states of an offer instance within an enProcess by defining offer structures for the primary O2B and O2S types[13]. To associate a state with an offer type in the design representation, the notation *OFFERTYPE.STATE* is used.

The basis for the offer state design in the enMedia framework design approach is a predefined set of **offer structure elements** with associated **notation options**. The elements and notation options represent a rich set of potential expressions in offer structures, which are derived from the formal electronic negotiation model in Section 3.3 and extended to incorporate as well the application of negotiation support components, e.g. the MatchNSC, MediateNSC, and ScoreNSC introduced in Section 4.4. The set of available offer structure elements and notation options is defined in *Table 7*.

Table 7. Offer state structure elements and notation options

Structure element	Notation option
Domains	Attributes, Values, Ranges, Dynamic
Constraints	Basic, Negotiable, Weighted, Supported[MatchNSC, MediateNSC]
Counters	None, n, Unbounded
Criteria	None, Basic, Weighted, Valued, Supported[ScoreNSC]
Signatures	None, Single, All
Timestamps	None, Start, End, Both

The notation options are ordered in the sense that a 'higher' option allows a richer (more expressive) notation, which is also more flexible because it always includes the options of 'lower' order. To give an example, formal model constructs such as dynamic domains (see Definition 10 in Chapter 3) are represented with the notation option **Dynamic** for the offer element **Domains**, which explicitly allows an agent to define the range of values for any attribute in an offer instance only if the agent has some knowledge about the particular counterpart or has accessed up-to-date external information. A

---

[13] Depending on the guidelines derived in the analysis phase, it could be sufficient to design state structures for only one offer type, because only instances of this offer type are required in the intended enProcess.

more restricted offer notation would disallow the Dynamic option and limit offer specifications to a definition of domain **Ranges**. Another example is the **Negotiable** value for the **Constraints** element (see Definition 20). It allows an agent to express in an offer a potential relaxation of a constraint in the electronic negotiation if, for instance, the agent is compensated for this sacrifice. A 'higher' option is to allow or require agents also to define weighted negotiable constraints to support potential third party intermediation.

To integrate the potential operation of NSCs without losing the generality of the design approach, a generic **Supported[]** notation option is defined that can be instantiated with proprietary NSC notation options for offers. This is necessary because NSCs might manipulate the structure of offer instances. The Supported[] notation option for the Constraints element in *Table 7* defines the values *MatchNSC* and *MediateNSC*. This means that through a corresponding MatchNSC or MediateNSC operation, a constraint could be matched or mediated and thus be marked on the offer notation level with the appropriate result-codes. For the MatchNSC the defined result-codes are (see the Appendix) *FAIL / MATCHED / RANGE / SINGLE-SIDED NEGOTIABLE / DOUBLE-SIDED NEGOTIABLE*.

The **Counter** element has been added to the offer structure elements in order to provide an enScenario designer with additional means for the specification of behavioural offer aspects in an enProcess. It allows specifically controlling the number of constraints an agent can modify in order to create a **counteroffer** given an offer of a counterpart. To control the complexity of the enProcess, agents often restrict their discussion to a small number of dimensions while fixing other issues (ceteris paribus, c.f. [LoMo97]). The number of potential counters can also be decreased during the enProcess, from offer state to offer state to ensure that the enProcess is converging.

Finally, the **Signatures** and **Timestamps** structure elements complete the offer notation specification. A typical characteristic of an offer is that it might be valid only for a certain period of time. This offer **validity** can be expressed with a **Start** and **End** date. A limited offer, for instance, will feature an End date. The inclusion of a commitment duration enables the design of a variety of enScenario models and is comparable to the approach undertaken in [Lee+00], which investigates an extension of the contract-net protocol with offers that feature zero-time, finite-time, or infinite-time commitments. Signatures are used to support various schemes of contracting such as binding offers or one-sided/double-sided contracting (see Section 4.5.3).

The specification of an offer state structure can be described as the task of choosing possible notation options for each offer structure element. Offers are created by actors, which can be agents, the enMedium itself, or NSCs. When the enScenario is executed, offer instances in a specific state, created

Design

or modified by actors, can be validated for syntactical correctness, i.e. compliance with the offer state structure design. This validation is analogous to the semantic validation for the offer ontology design.

Generic offer state templates can be provided as part of the design approach. For templates, the offer structure specification has to be performed on two levels: required offer notation options and possible offer notation options. Actors have to use required notation options and may use possible options in the offer specification. An *O2X.ADVERTISED* state, for instance, may be characterised by the offer state structure defined in *Table 8* (the '+' value in the 'Modifiable' column indicates that a 'higher' notation option may be chosen by the enScenario designer. The '-' value allows the designer to specify a more restricted offer structure).

Table 8. O2X.ADVERTISED state template

Structure element	Level	Notation option	Modifiable
Domains	Required	Attributes	+
	Possible	Dynamic	-
Constraints	Required	Basic	No
	Possible	Negotiable	-
Counters	Required	None	No
	Possible	None	No
Criteria	Required	None	+
	Possible	Values	-
Signatures	Required	None	+
	Possible	Single	-
Timestamps	Required	Start	No
	Possible	Both	-

In this template for the *O2X.ADVERTISED* state, *Signatures* are not required, but if a buyer or seller wants to make a binding advertisement, to which the counterpart merely needs to agree in order to perform the transaction, a signature from the originator of the advertisement can optionally be included. Another example in this template is the *Constraints* structure element. *Basic* constraints are required, but buyers or sellers might also indicate their willingness to negotiate certain constraints already in the *ADVERTISED* state of an offer. Finally, *Counters* are not allowed in this advertisement template, but could be added later, for example in a *BID* state.

Additional offer templates can be created for the pre- and post-NSC operation offer states. In many cases, the structure of an offer will change during an NSC operation (e.g. result-codes are manifested in the offer instance through marking). In addition, NSCs may require a specific offer instance structure (see the NSC preconditions defined Section 4.4). The MatchNSC, for instance, requires domains with values and will assign a result-code to the constraints, thereby changing the offer notation.

A set of offer-state templates is the starting point for the communication design. The enScenario designer can select states among the set of provided templates and, depending on the business analysis, apply refinements and adaptations to the offer structures, thus creating an initial sequence of offer states complemented with new states necessary for the specific enScenario case. Additional states might be discovered in the organisation and integration design (see below). For each additional offer state, the respective level of formality and structure has to be represented by allowing or disallowing offer structure notation options.

The offer state structure design implicitly defines a set of requirements for the enMedia architecture model in the implementation phase, in the sense that the syntax elements defined in the offer state structure design have to be supported by enMedia architectures and can be interpreted, for instance, by NSCs.

3.2 Organisation design

According to the DAM, the organisation design follows after an initial communication design. In addition to the ontology problem discussed in the previous section, which requires an a priori agreement of the negotiating agents about the structure of the logical space, another critical factor for the success of the latter enProcess is to address the agents' common understanding of the negotiation protocol and of their distinct roles. This initial agreement has to investigate a number of questions such as *'Should all attributes be negotiated at the same time, or one after another?'*, *'Can one agent counter an offer by including or requesting additional offer attributes (e.g. a guarantee)?'* or *'What happens if an offer is not signed within a certain timeframe?'* The organisation design model, which is the output of the organisation design activity presented in this section, is a representation of a settlement between negotiating agents on roles and protocols.

The foundation for the organisation design is an initial set of offer state structures that stem from the communication design. The goal for the organisation design is to complement these offer state structures with additional rules that constrain the conduct of an actor towards other actors when participating in an electronic negotiation (see also [Strö01a] for the following). Given the offer states, associated events, guards, transitions, and actions can be discovered. This results in the design of the roles and the protocol of the electronic negotiation. If the communication design defines state structures for both offer types, O2B and O2S, the organisation design also has to cover state transitions for both offer types. A **role** is defined as the set of all possible events an actor can raise. The **protocol**, represented by valid transitions

Design 125

between the offer states, ensures that all actors in an electronic negotiation coordinate meaningfully [PaCu01].

The organisation design also implicitly defines further requirements for the enMedia architecture model, as a certain set of actions, events, and guard semantics needs to be supported in order to express complete and consistent organisation design models.

3.2.1 Entity types and instances

Referring back to Section 5.3, the concept of state charts is the underlying modelling paradigm for both the organisation and the communication design. In this section the entity types available for the creation of state charts are specified. Basic entity types are defined in the DMM, but have to be further characterised to achieve the level of detail necessary for the transition to the implementation phase (see *Figure 33*).

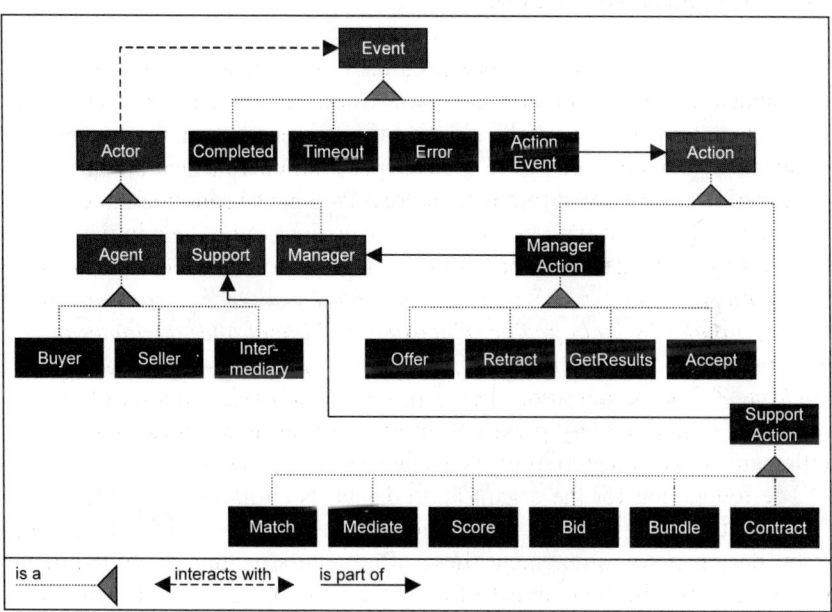

Figure 33. Extended organisation design meta-model

According to the DMM, actors may be agents, support components, or the enMedium represented by a manager system. A transition is triggered by an event and can cause an action with certain properties. Furthermore, actions are related to actors. The notation *ACTOR.ACTION* is used to represent this association.

For the organisation design, the support component actor type can be instantiated with the NSCs known to be available in the target enMedium system. Referring back to the NSCs introduced in Sections 4.4 and 4.5, the potential components and candidates in the context of this book are the MatchNSC, MediateNSC, ScoreNSC, BundleNSC, BidNSC, and ContractNSC. Accordingly, potential action instances are referred to as, for example, *SUPPORT.MATCH* or *SUPPORT.MEDIATE*.

In an organisation design model, NSC operations are represented as actions, which can be combined to provide a scenario-specific activation and configuration of decision-making and communication support. For example, the rules of an enScenario might define that the BundleNSC first be invoked to accumulate supply from several agents. Then the BidNSC may collect offers from suppliers, which the MatchNSC tests for compliance with the constraints specified in the bundle demand offer. If no matches can be found, the MediateNSC can still suggest an agreement. The ScoreNSC may compare several potential agreements on the basis of the preferences specified in the demand offer before the ContractNSC finalises the enProcess by generating a contract for the winning offer. Other enScenarios might require a completely different configuration and activation of negotiation support components. In principle, NSC operations can be combined arbitrarily in an organisation design model. However, the interdependencies and pre-/termination-conditions discussed in Section 4.6 have to be respected.

Table 9. enMedium manager operations

Manager operation	Explanation
Offer	This operation makes an offer instance available (active) in an enProcess and assigns a specific state to it.
Retract	An offer instance can be retracted from an enProcess with this operation. If the target property specifies an NSC instance, the offer instance is removed from the current set of target offers specified for this NSC instance.
Accept	With this operation the enMedium adds an agent signature attribute to an offer and renders all counters into real constraints (if applicable). The nature of the signature provided by the agent depends on the contracting mode chosen (e.g. a unique key, credentials, or a credit card number).
GetResults	This operation is used to retrieve the result-set from a current or past NSC operation.

In addition to the NSCs, the enMedium system also needs to make available basic operations, which can be represented as manager actions in the same way as NSC operations. For the organisation design, the basic operations defined in *Table 9* have to be provided by the enMedium system. These operations might be triggered by events raised by agents, support compo-

Design

nents, or the enMedium itself (e.g. time-bound events). Comparable to the generic interface defined for NSCs, manager operations have an initiating offer and a target, which can be instantiated through offer or NSC instances.

The configuration and activation of actions (NSC and manager operations) is specified through events, guards, actions, and properties.

If an offer is in a state where an operation is performed by an NSC and only an event caused by the NSC or the manager can trigger a transition, the state is denoted a **support-state** (e.g. *O2B.MATCHING, O2B.BIDDING*). As the set of NSCs is predefined, the number of corresponding support-states is limited. Non-support-states typically require an event raised by an agent (i.e. the enProcess is 'waiting' for the agent's decision). Hence, transitions from support-states to **agent-states** model the switch from automated enMedium processing to agent interaction, thus reflecting the sequential decision-making model for electronic negotiations in Figure *Figure 20*. In addition to the support-states, NSCs also define corresponding **precondition-states** and **termination-states** for the offer instances involved in the NSC operation, such as *O2B.READYMATCHING* and *O2B.MATCHED*, or *O2B.READYBIDDING* and *O2B.BID* (see *Figure 34*).

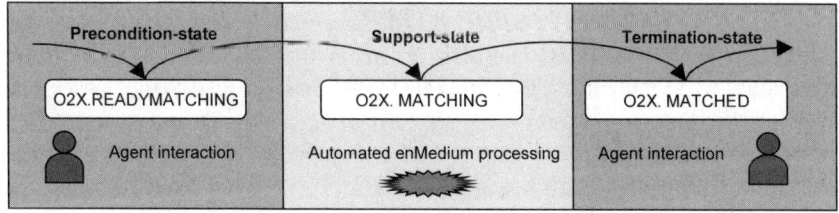

Figure 34. Types of offer states

Properties in the organisation design correspond to the objectives of actions such as the NSC operations. With property settings an NSC or manager operation can be customised at design- or run-time. An example for the second case of a run-time property value is the *HardMatching* property/objective defined for the MatchNSC. Depending on the recommendations for the enScenario, a value for this property can be set either at design-time or by agents during actual enProcesses. In the latter case, the agent needs to provide a value for this property before the MatchNSC operation is invoked. In the organisation design, a run-time property specification is indicated by a '*' property value.

The DMM specifies that events are associated with actors, and the corresponding notation is *ACTOR.EVENT*. Hence, an event can be further characterised by the actor causing the event to be an **agent-event**, **manager-event**, or **support-event** (comparable to the notion of internal and external events in UML). An event can be associated with one or more offers. If, for instance, an agent initiates a MatchNSC operation, this event (e.g. *BUYER.MATCH*) will be related to the initiating offer and a set of target offers.

It is not possible in the design approach to specify agent actions. Obviously, agents perform actions themselves (e.g. by signing an offer), but these actions are not represented in the design, because communication and decision-making tasks of agents are outside the defined scope of the negotiation intermediation approach (see Section 2.2.4).

NSCs (and all other actors) can raise the events **completed**, **timeout**, and **error** (for these and other design language elements, see the formal syntax specification in the next section). The COMPLETED event is used if the operation terminated successfully, that is if a winning bid was determined, whereas the TIMEOUT event indicates that the defined deadline for the operation was reached without successful termination, for instance because no offers were submitted. In addition, an agent might also cause, through inactivity, an *AGENT.TIMEOUT* event. Both agents and NSCs can raise **action-events**, which correspond to manager or NSC operations. For example, an agent can raise *AGENT.ACCEPT*, with the corresponding action *MANAGER.ACCEPT*, or *AGENT.MATCH*, which is associated with the action *SUPPORT.MATCH*. The **offer-event** is applicable if the NSC generates a new offer instance. The MatchNSC, for instance, generates new offer instances in the termination-state *OFFER.MATCHED* for every identified agreement candidate. Not all events that might be raised have to be used for the specification of transitions in a concrete organisation design model – a designer may choose to ignore events, for instance, simply because these events should not trigger a transition.

The DMM specifies that a transition fires if an event occurs that causes the guard condition of the transition to evaluate to 'true'. Guard conditions can assess and relate agent attributes, offer attributes, offer element resultcodes, and NSC result-set structures. The construction of guards is formalised in Definition 1 in the next section.

3.2.2 Design language

On the basis of the introduced entity types the language for the organisation design can be defined using a syntactic meta-language such as the Extended Backus-Naur Form (EBNF, [ISO96]). The EBNF specification in Definition 1 (next page) shows the syntactic structure of the organisation design language; that is, it shows which entity relations are valid combinations (sentences).

Definition 1. Organisation design language

```
<Relation> ::= ".";
<Number> ::=
   "0"|"1"|"2"|...|"9";
<Boolean> ::=
   "true"|"false";
<Operator> ::=
   "<"|"<="|"="|">="|">";
<Agent> ::=
   "BUYER"|"SELLER"|"INTERMEDIARY";
<Support> ::=
   "MATCH"|"MEDIATE"|"SCORE"|"BID"|"BUNDLE"|"CONTRACT";
<Actor> ::=
   <Agent>|<Support>|"MANAGER";
<Manager> ::=
   "OFFER"|"RETRACT"|"GETRESULTS"|"ACCEPT";
<Event> ::=
   "COMPLETED"|"TIMEOUT"|"ERROR";
<SupportAction> ::=
   "SUPPORT"<Relation><Support>;
<ManagerAction> ::=
   "MANAGER"<Relation><Manager>;
<ActorEvent> ::=
   <Agent><Relation>(<Support>|<Manager>|"TIMEOUT") |
   <Support><Relation>(<Event>|"OFFER") |
   "MANAGER"<Relation><Event>;
<Offer> ::=
   "O2B"|"O2C";
<Supported> ::=
   ("MATCH"|"MEDIAT"|"SCOR"|BIDD"|"BUNDL"|"CONTRACT")"ING";
<PreCondition> ::=
   "READY"<Supported>;
<Termination> ::=
   "MATCHED"|"MEDIATED"|"SCORED"|"BID"|"BUNDLED"|"CONTRACTED";
<OfferState> ::=
   <Offer><Relation>(<PreCondition>|<Supported>|<Termination>);
```

A valid actor event is *BUYER.OFFER* or *BID.COMPLETED*. An example for the correct syntax of an offer state is *O2B.READYMATCHING*. At run-time, an instantiation based on unique IDs occurs. A *BUYER* entity type might be replaced by a real buyer agent ID, e.g. *AG_007_B*, an offer type with a unique offer instance, e.g. *OF_DSP_ 003*, and the NSC entity type with a run-time instance such as *SUPPORT.BID:OF_DSP_003.AD-*

VERTISED:996055050984. (The rules of construction for NSC IDs will be presented in Section 6.2.2 and demonstrated in Section 7.2.)

For the syntax of guard conditions, the language specification in Definition 1 has to be extended to Definition 2. In this extended definition not all possible terminal symbols, e.g. for result-codes, are listed:

Definition 2. Extended organisation design language

```
<Set> ::=
  "MAS"|"DAS"|"NAS"|"SCORED"|"BUNDLED"|...
<ResultSet> ::=
  <Support><Relation>"RS"<Relation><Set>;
<Element> ::=
  "Match"|"Mediate"|"Score"|...
<OfferElement> ::=
  <Offer><Relation><Element>;
<ResultCode> ::=
  "Fail"|"Matched"|"Range"|"Score"|...
<Guard> ::=
  (["|"]<ResultSet>["|"]<Operator>(<Number>|<OfferElement>)) |
  (<Offer>"e("<ResultSet>")") |
  (<OfferElement><Operator>(<Number>|<Boolean>|<ResultCode>)) |
  (<OfferElement><Operator><OfferElement>) |
  (<ActorEvent>"("<OfferState>")"<Operator><Number>) |
  "!"<Guard>
```

The different types of guard conditions can be outlined on the basis of examples. If, for instance, the MatchNSC causes the event *MATCH.COMPLETED* and generates an associated result-set *RS*, which includes the set *MAS* of matching offers, the result-set *MATCH.RS.MAS* can be evaluated by the guard conditions of transitions connected to the support-state *O2X.MATCHING*. For $|MATCH.RS.MAS|=1$ (that is, the cardinality of the *MAS* result-set is 1) a guard condition of a transition to the state *O2X.CONTRACTING* could evaluate to 'true', while for $|MATCH.RS.MAS|>1$ a transition to the state *O2X.BIDDING* may fire. Guard conditions can also determine whether an offer instance is part of a result-set structure, by using the construct *O2B e(MATCH.RS.MAS)* ('e' stands for 'element of'). Another example is the comparison of offer attribute values such as *O2S.SCORE>O2B.RV*, which evaluates to 'true' if the score achieved by a target offer is higher than the reservation value of the initiating offer. On the basis of an enProcess history, conditions can also relate to agent behaviour. For instance, the condition *SELLER.OFFER (O2B.ADVERTISED)<1* verifies whether an agent has already submitted a bid for an offer instance in the *ADVERTISED* state. Finally, all types of conditions can be negated using the '!' ('NOT') operator.

Design 131

3.2.3 Design rationale

The goal for the organisation design is to specify, on the basis of the states defined in the communication design, valid state transitions for offer instances in an enProcess, thus creating a finite state machine (FSM) for offer instances of an offer type. An FSM can be defined through a tuple $\{I,O,Q,S,q_0,F\}$. 'I' is the input alphabet, 'O' the output alphabet, and 'Q' is a non-empty set of states with 'q_0' representing the initial state. 'S:Q x I → Q x O' is the function that assigns pairs of start states and input elements consecutive states with associated outputs, whereas 'F' stands for the set of terminal states. Offer type FSMs have an initial *START* state (which is not defined in the offer state structure design) and require at least one **terminal state**. Terminal states comprise the mandatory *END* state and additional **goal states**, which typically represent an offer state after a successfully completed enProcess. In terminal states no further transition can occur. If an offer instance is created (by an agent or the NSCs through the *MANAGER.OFFER* action) in a state that is not immediately preceded by the *START* state, a transition has to be defined from the *START* state to this advanced state (see *Figure 35*).

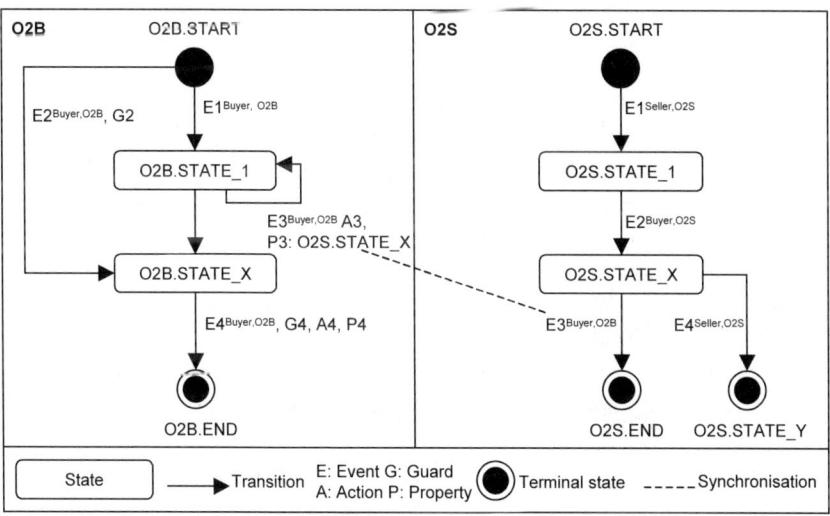

Figure 35. Organisation design state-chart semantics

An organisation design defines at least one transition from the *START* state to a terminal state. In one enScenario, transitions can be defined for the O2S type, the O2B type, or both. If transitions are defined for both offer types, two finite state machines are created and synchronisation might become necessary (see below). In some enScenarios it might be sufficient to use only one type of offer, in which case synchronisation is not necessary. An example of such an enScenario is one in which buyers can merely accept offers-to-sell without the need for creating an offer-to-buy. Events from buyer as well as seller agents may trigger transitions in both the O2B FSM and the O2S FSM.

The graphical notation for FSMs follows the UML conventions for state-chart diagrams [Rumb+99]. States are represented by rounded rectangles. The offer type related to a state is indicated with capital letters preceding the state identifier. Transitions are represented by arrows connecting states. Events (E), guards (G), actions (A), and properties (P) are specified as textual information next to the transition arrows.

In *Figure 35* two illustrative state charts for O2B and O2S FSMs are defined, which demonstrate the possible semantics of organisation design state charts. For further illustration, the notation for events is complemented with the originating actor and the FSM where the event is raised. The example shows that transitions can be designed with or without guards, actions, and properties, that a transition can have the same initial and subsequent state, and that one state chart may have several terminal states. A simple state-chart design example is illustrated in *Figure 36*.

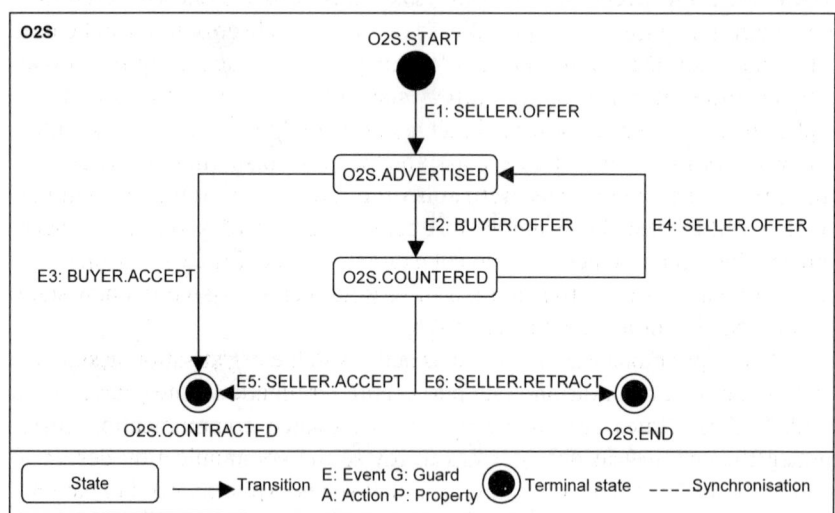

Figure 36. State-chart example

In this example only the events are specified – the full FSM definition can be found in Section 7.2.1.2. The example shows the FSM for offers-to-sell, which are created by sellers through the *SELLER.OFFER* event and

Design 133

assume the initial state *O2S.ADVERTISED*. In this state, buyers can either modify the offer (e.g. change the price), thereby triggering a transition to the *O2S.COUNTERED* state, or accept the offer, which will trigger a transition to the *O2S.CONTRACTED* state. The bilateral negotiation iterates if the seller decides to respond to the counteroffer, which changes the offer back to the *O2S.ADVERTISED* state.

Through **synchronisation**, events in the FSM for one offer type can be propagated to the corresponding FSM in the enScenario model. This means that an event that causes a transition for an O2B instance might also trigger a transition for an O2S instance. There are two ways to specify synchronisation in the organisation design; both are based on the action **target property**. Every action has a target property, which is used to define the target offers (e.g. the match candidates or the set of offers to score) for the NSC or manager operation. In case of a manager action, the target might also point to NSC instances, such as a current MatchNSC operation. An example for a *MANAGER.OFFER* action target in an O2B FSM could be *O2S.ADVERTISED* or *BID.ID* (which then at run-time is resolved to a specific NSC ID such as *SUPPORT.BID:OF_DSP_003.ADVERTISED:996055050984*).

If the target of an action is an offer in a certain state in the corresponding offer type FSM, this event will be propagated to the FSM and, through **event synchronisation** eventually lead to other transitions (as shown in the O2S state chart in *Figure 35*) A special case of event synchronisation can be used if the state defined for the target offer may not be reached by the corresponding offer instance at the current state of the overall enProcess; this applies mainly when the offer is in an agent-state. In this case, the execution will 'wait' for the offer instance to assume the target state (that is, the event is queued), and through **state synchronisation** the event handling is continued in both FSMs (see the example in Section 7.2.2.3) as soon as the agent updates the offer instance[14]. A typical example is an enProcess in which both negotiating agents have to sign their offer (and thereby assign it a new state) before a final contract can be generated.

If NSC operations are integrated as actions in the organisation design, the corresponding precondition-, support-, and termination-states have to be used. If these states are not defined in the related communication design model, the enScenario designer has to revise the communication design by adding these states. This does not mean that states explicitly need to have the name of the corresponding NSC state; they only need to have the same required offer state structure.

---

[14] It is not possible to replace state synchronisation with guard conditions, because guards are evaluated only once, when the corresponding transition event is raised, and therefore cannot 'wait' for an offer.

3.3 Integration design

The integration design follows the initial organisation design in the DAM. The bases for the integration design are the communication design model (offer context ontology and offer state structure design) and the organisation design model (offer state charts and FSM specification for the offer types). Three goals can be defined for the integration design activity in the DAM. The integration design
- further links the communication design model with the organisation design model,
- complements the enScenario design with security and transparency specifications,
- checks the unified enScenario design model for completeness and consistency.

These three goals are accomplished by three corresponding integration design tasks, which are outlined in the following sections.

3.3.1 Offer context assignment

The first activity of the integration design is to assign the offer types (and the related offer structure state designs) to the ontology concepts specified in the offer ontology context design. An offer type has to be associated with at least one agent, transaction, and object context. Multiple agent contexts might make sense if several agent types such as *distributors* or *outsourcers* participate in an enProcess and if their attributes might be referenced together in one offer. If a context concept (e.g. the *computer* concept in the object context in *Figure 32*) has sub-concepts (*workstation*, *notebook*, etc.), the offer can be issued for any of the sub-concepts as well.

The offer/ontology concept association guarantees that the content of offer instances can be validated not only syntactically on the basis of the offer state structure design, but also semantically with respect to the context specifications in the ontology. Hence, only concept attributes defined in the communication design model and assigned to the offer type in the integration design can be used for the offer specification. The offer context assignment in *Figure 37* (next page) extends the example in *Figure 32*. The *seller* concept in the agent context, the *notebook* concept in the object context, and the *wholesale* concept in the transaction context were assigned to an offer type *O2S.X*.

Hence, a seller constructing an offer instance for the type *O2S.X* can specify constraints in the object context only for attributes related to the *notebook* concept, such as *monitor.resolution*, *computer.CPU* or *notebook. -*

Design 135

battery_type. The offer context assignment defines the universe of discourse for offers.

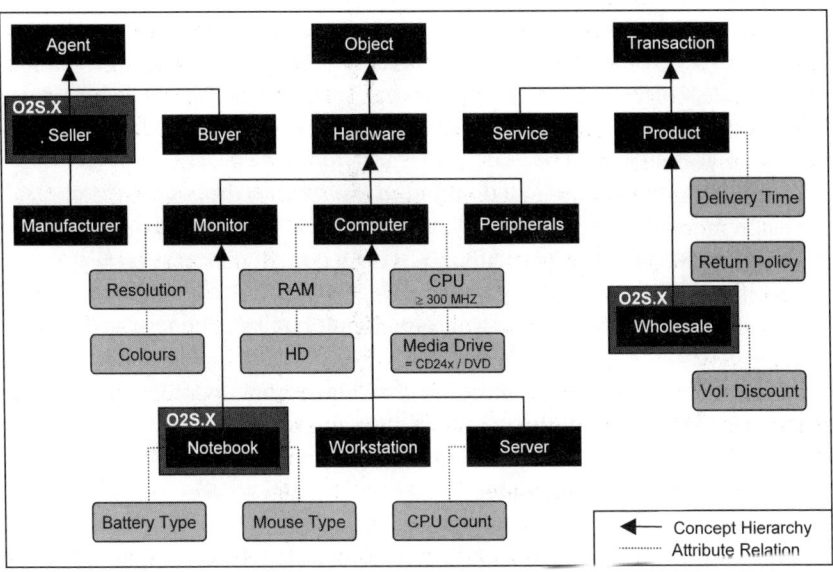

Figure 37. Offer context assignment example

3.3.1.1 Event and view authorisation

The second task in the integration design relates to security and transparency issues in electronic negotiations. The prerequisite for the following event and view authorisation activity (see below) is the creation of specific **agent groups**. Distinctive criteria for building groups might be agent attributes such as the *location* or *reputation*, as well as the level of authentication (anonymous versus registered). Once the enScenario is deployed, real agents using the enInstance have to be assigned to these agent groups by the enMedium administrator.

It is necessary for the completeness of the enScenario design that only specific agents, or agent groups, are authorised to raise a certain event in the organisation design. Through **event authorisation** one or more agent groups are assigned to each event. For every event, at least one agent group has to be authorised. As an example, an enScenario designer might decide to allow only registered and authenticated sellers to create initial offers through the *SELLER.OFFER* event, whereas buyer agents need no prior authentication in order create an offer with the *BUYER.OFFER* event. As another example, event authorisation enables a designer to make sure that sellers do not create false bids (shills) in an enProcess with auction character; this is done by prohibiting sellers from being part of the buyer group that is exclusively authorised to submit bids.

Event authorisation is complemented by **view authorisation**. This task enables a designer to specify which elements of an offer instance, if any, can be seen by different agent groups at run-time. As shown in [Thom89] or [PrLe75], the exchange of information is crucial in negotiations in order to achieve win-win solutions. The first study mentioned demonstrates, on the basis of experiments, that providing information to an opponent is not disadvantageous as might be thought, but rather can improve the overall performance of the negotiation dramatically. However, there are several levels of information revelation (see also the information classification category in *Table 3*) and a designer may decide, for example, that originators of an offer have to disclose only their evaluation criteria structure (including importance ratings), but not their complete utility function specification. Whether the information revealed by buyers and sellers in an enProcess is symmetric or asymmetric is also a design decision that has to be made in accordance with the recommendations of the analysis phase. By default, no agent has access to an offer of another agent unless a specific authorisation is defined, whereas the originator of an offer by default always has full access to the complete offer specification.

To provide an enScenario designer with means to specify the granularity of information revelation, the integration design allows the assignment of agent groups to offer state structure elements. The offer structure elements and notation options defined in *Table 7* are reused for the view authorisation.

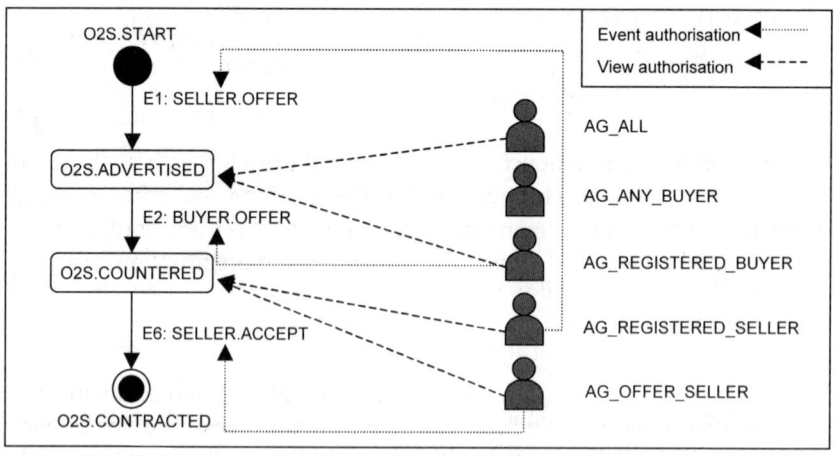

Figure 38. Event and view authorisation example

Design 137

This means that an agent group might be authorised to access (read) at run-time the basic constraints, as well as the attribute domain values and ranges, of an advertised offer instance, but not the indication of whether or not these constraints are negotiable from the originator's perspective. The set of authorisations of an agent group to access specific offer structure elements constitutes an **agent view** for an offer in a certain state. Different agent views can be specified for the different states of an offer type.

In *Figure 38* and the corresponding *Table 10*, an example for an event and view authorisation in an enScenario with O2S state definitions is given. The design specifies among other things, that any buyer in the enProcess can accept an O2S instance and thereby conclude the negotiation, but only registered buyers are able to create a counteroffer. In the *O2S.COUNTERED* state, only the seller who originated the initial O2S instance can accept, create a counteroffer, or retract. Hence, other sellers cannot accept a counteroffer created by a buyer for a specific seller. But other sellers can view the elements of the counteroffer, with the exception of the importance ratings of the buyer, which can only be inspected by the seller originating the offer.

Table 10. Event and view authorisation example

State	Transition event	Event authorisation
O2S.START	SELLER.OFFER	AG_REGISTERED_SELLER
O2S.ADVERTISED	BUYER.ACCEPT	AG_ANY_BUYER
	BUYER.OFFER	AG_REGISTERED_BUYER
O2S.COUNTERED	SELLER.OFFER	AG_OFFER_SELLER
	SELLER.ACCEPT	AG_OFFER_SELLER
	SELLER.RETRACT	AG_OFFER_SELLER

State	Offer structure element	View authorisation
O2S.ADVERTISED	Domains – Ranges	AG_ALL
	Constraints – Negotiable	AG_REGISTERED_BUYER
O2S.COUNTERED	Counters	AG_REGISTERED_SELLER
	Criteria – Weights	AG_OFFER_SELLER

The example also demonstrates why the authorisation activity is part of the integration design. The defined transition events and offer structure elements reused in the integration design specification are only available upon an initial completion of the communication and organisation design.

3.3.2 Model validation

The design of an enScenario model is finalised with a methodical validation of the unified enScenario design model for completeness and consistency, from both a structural and a behavioural point of view. To constitute a valid enScenario representation, the model has to comply with the following **test conditions**:

Table 11. enScenario model test conditions

#	Condition	Explanation
1	State usage consistency	Only the states defined in the communication design model are used in the organisation design model.
2	State usage completeness	Every state defined in the communication design model is incorporated in at least one transition definition in the organisation design model.
3	Guard expression consistency	Guard conditions of transitions evaluate only those offer structure elements or result-set attributes that are available in the initial offer state of the transition.
4	Action usage correctness	Only NSC and manager actions generally available in the enMedium architecture model are invoked through transitions, and only the objectives associated with these actions are specified as properties.
5	Valid component preconditions	If an NSC action is invoked by a transition, the initial offer state structure of the transition needs to comply with the precondition-state defined for the component.
6	Valid termination-states	The offer state structure defined as the succeeding offer state in a transition for the *SUPPORT.COMPLETED* event needs to comply with the termination-state defined for the NSC.
7	Offer creation completeness	If an NSC action is invoked, and its operation may create new offer instances, the corresponding *SUPPORT.OFFER* event has to be used for a transition from the *START* state to the specific termination-state of the NSC (e.g. *O2B.SCORED*).
8	Synchronisation completeness	If the target property of an action defines the offer type corresponding to the initiating offer type, the event of this transition has to be assigned as well to at least one transition in the corresponding offer type FSM (event synchronisation).
9	Component interdependency	Negotiation support component interdependencies have to be respected (e.g. a MatchNSC operation is a necessary predecessor of MediateNSC operation).
10	Intermediary agent-state	If the offer structure changes from one state to a succeeding state, and the structure change is not performed by an action, an intermediary agent-state has to be included in the organisation design model to allow an agent to update the offer.
11	Transition usage completeness	At least one terminal offer state is defined in the enScenario. All states can be reached. All transitions can fire.
12	Termination consistency	Only the *END* and the *CONTRACTED* state are terminal states in a FSM. All other states need to have at least one transition that can potentially fire for any FSM execution path.
13	Offer aliveness	The enScenario design has to avoid 'dead' offer instances – that is, offers that can assume for an unlimited time a non-terminal state. Through the usage of *TIMEOUT* events, continuity can be guaranteed.

Implementation 139

Test conditions 11 and 12 are based on the formal FSM foundation of the enScenario model. As a result of this, the final FSM specification can be tested for desirable protocol properties (see for example [Koni01]) such as quasi-aliveness, which requires that all transitions are, in principle, able to fire. Valid enScenario models can be passed on to the next development phase in the DAM, the implementation phase.

The model validation process could also be performed during the actual design, such as when new states or transitions are added. If one or more of the test conditions are violated, the enScenario model is invalid and has to be corrected accordingly.

4. IMPLEMENTATION

One guiding principle in the DAM is to minimise the effort of the enScenario implementation by generating run-time representations from design models. These imperative design representations have to be deployed to an enMedium, where the corresponding enScenario can be activated and executed (c.f. the illustration of the development and deployment process in Figure 6 in Chapter 3).

In this section, a generation process and a representation format for enScenario model run-time specifications is presented. The focus is on the communication design representation because this format has to be accessible to the negotiating agents for both local and remote construction of offer instances. This imposes several constraints on the representation because the offer construction might take place 'outside' the enMedium. This is not the case for the representation of the organisation design and the related integration design specifications, which are only used internally in the enMedium to control the enProcess execution and can be generated in an internal format.

4.1 Communication design representation

Communication design models, including the corresponding offer context assignment from the integration design, can be represented on the basis of XML Schema (see [Strö01b] for the following). In general, XML is a very suitable and customisable representation format for semi-structured data such as the contents of offers. XML schemata are used to specify classes of XML instance documents by describing the document structure in a much richer way than is possible on the basis of document type definitions (DTD) [ErSt99]. With the basic vocabulary and predefined structuring mechanisms of XML Schema, fine-grained constraints on XML documents can be defined, thus enabling rich automated validation. The primary advantages of using XML schemata, as compared to DTDs, are that it is possible to express hierarchies of data types and that schemata themselves are XML documents. Owing to their XML nature, schemata can be created in the same way, and with the same tools, as traditional XML documents. Hierarchies of types are critical for the generation process suggested in this book, because scenario-specific types are derived from a set of generic enMedia framework types.

As will be shown, a set of schemata can represent the logical space design of enScenarios at run-time. For each offer structure state definition in the enScenario design model, a customised schema is generated. If different offer context assignments are specified in the integration design for the same offer states, additional schemata have to be created. At run-time, agents may use these schemata to construct or update offer instances for the various offer states. *Figure 39* depicts an overview of the schema generation and customisation process, which is explained in the next sections.

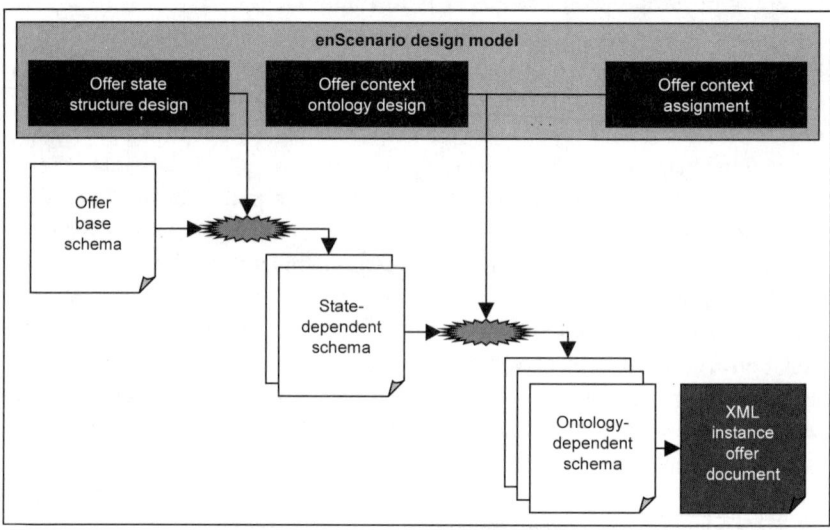

Figure 39. XML schema generation and customisation process

4.1.1 Offer base schema

The foundation for the generation and customisation process is a generic offer syntax specification defined in XML Schema, which is based on the formal electronic negotiation model developed in Section 3.3 and its extension in Section 4.4. All formal offer elements introduced in these formal definitions as well as the associated offer structure notation elements in *Table 7*, are rendered into a corresponding XML Schema specification – the

Implementation

offer base schema. In addition, potential manipulations of offer elements through NSC operations are reflected in the base schema (e.g. the marking of attributes with result-codes, see for example Section 4.4.1). The complete offer base schema can be found in the Appendix. The example in Code 1 shows a snippet of the offer base schema.

Code 1. Offer base schema snippet

```xml
...
<element name="CONTAINER" type="xen:CONTAINER">
  <unique name="AGENT_ID">
    <selector xpath="CONTAINER/AGENT"/> <field xpath="@ID"/>
  </unique>
</element>
<complexType name="CONTAINER" abstract="true" mixed="false">
  <sequence>
    <element name="AGENT" type="xen:AGENT"
      maxOccurs="unbounded"/>
    <element name="OFFER" type="xen:OFFER"
      maxOccurs="unbounded"/>
    <element ref="xen:AGENT_CONTEXT" maxOccurs="unbounded"/>
    <element ref="xen:TRANSACTION_CONTEXT"
      maxOccurs="unbounded"/>
    <element ref="xen:OBJECT_CONTEXT" maxOccurs="unbounded"/>
    <element ref="xen:CRITERIA" minOccurs="0"/>
  </sequence>
</complexType>
<complexType name="CONTEXT" abstract="true" mixed="false">
  <sequence>
    <element name="NAME" type="string"/>
    <element ref="xen:OFFER_CONSTRAINT" maxOccurs="unbounded"/>
    <element ref="xen:COUNTER_CONSTRAINT" minOccurs="0"
      maxOccurs="unbounded"/>
  </sequence>
  <attribute name="NUMBER" type="integer" use="optional"/>
</complexType>
...
```

The offer base schema defines fundamental constraints for offer instance documents such as 'an offer must have at least one unique agent ID'. Overall, the base schema declares all possible offer notations supported from a structural point of view. All types in the base schema are declared to be abstract (using the attribute setting *abstract="true"* in the type declaration). Abstract types cannot be used in conforming XML document instances.

Hence, all abstract types need to be redefined in subsequently customised schemata.

The main type used in the offer base schema is the *CONTAINER*. One *CONTAINER* can be defined by several agents (e.g. one buyer and one seller), comprise several offers, and may contain one or more constraint specifications for the agent, transaction, and object context. The *CONTEXT* type features one or more *OFFER_CONSTRAINTS* and an optional number of *COUNTER_CONSTRAINTS*. The *NUMBER* attribute can be used to indicate the number of transactions or the number of objects that are subject to the offer.

To generate a state- and ontology-dependent schema, additional constraints are derived from the communication design model, which lead to restrictions of the offer base schema. To restrict a schema, the following generic XML Schema mechanisms can be used in the generation and customisation process:
- Redefining types.
- Deriving types by extension or restriction.
- Changing attribute *use* from *optional* to *required*.
- Disallowing the use of attributes with *prohibited*.
- Assigning *fixed* values to attributes or elements.
- Setting elements to be required (the default is *minOccurs = 1*).
- Limiting the number of elements (*maxOccurs = x*).
- Deleting enumeration elements in simple types.

4.1.2 State-dependent customisation

Whereas the base schema defines a generic namespace (*www.enegotiation.ch* in the example), a new unique namespace is created for each enScenario. Hence, the first step in the generation and customisation process is to define this enScenario namespace.

For all states defined in the enScenario design model for an offer type, a corresponding **state-dependent schema** has to be generated that adds the state-specific offer notation to the namespace. This is done by importing all types defined in the offer base schema namespace and redefining state-specific types according to the notation options assigned to a specific state in the offer state structure design. The process can be illustrated using the example of the *O2X.ADVERTISED* state as defined in the template in *Table 8*. The generation process for this state example results in the *O2X.ADVERTISED* schema snippet for the namespace *www.enegotiation.ch/example* in Code 2.

Code 2. State-dependent schema snippet

```
<schema
    targetNamespace="http://www.enegotiation.ch/example"
    xmlns:example="http://www.enegotiation.ch/example"
    xmlns:xen="http://www.enegotiation.ch"
    xmlns="http://www.w3.org/2001/XMLSchema"
    elementFormDefault="qualified">
<import namespace="http://www.enegotiation.ch"/>
<complexType name="OFFER" mixed="false">
   <complexContent>
      <restriction base="xen:OFFER">
         <!-- Restriction applied - START required -->
         <attribute name="START" type="string" use="required"/>
      </restriction>
   </complexContent>
</complexType>
...
```

In Code 2, the use of the *START* attribute for the *OFFER* type is *required* by means of a restriction, corresponding to the structure element definition in the *O2X.ADVERTISED* template. Deriving by extension or restriction in XML Schema is comparable to the inheritance mechanism in object-oriented programming languages, in the sense that elements and attributes can be added or omitted and specifications of the super-type can be overwritten. The state-dependent schema redefines only those types for which the offer state structure design manifests specific notation options. For all other types, the definition in the offer base schema remains valid by default.

Another example is the restriction of the attribute domain structure. The attribute operator element specified in Definition 5 in Chapter 3 is reflected in the offer base schema as illustrated in the snippet in Code 3.

Code 3. Offer base schema snippet continued

```
...
<complexType name="ATTRIBUTE_DOMAIN" abstract="true" mixed="false">
   <sequence>
      <element name="NAME" type="string"/>
      <element ref="xen:OPERATOR" minOccurs="0"/>
      <element name="VALUE" minOccurs="0"use="fixed" value="*"/>
   </sequence>
</complexType>
<simpleType name="OPERATOR">
   <restriction base="string">
      <enumeration value="EQUAL"/> <enumeration value="UNEQUAL"/>
      <enumeration value="GREATER_THAN"/>
```

```
            <enumeration value="GREATER_OR_EQUAL"/>
            <enumeration value="LESS_THAN"/>
            <enumeration value="LESS_OR_EQUAL"/>
        </restriction>
    </simpleType>
...
```

If an offer state structure design does not allow attribute value ranges, all elements of the *OPERATOR* enumeration for a domain except the *EQUAL* operator have to be deleted. The notion of dynamic domains is also represented in Code 3 through the fixed *"*" VALUE*. The subsequent generation and customisation process adds further elements to the *VALUE* definition (see below), but through the state-dependent customisation, the specification of dynamic domains could also be disabled, simply by excluding the *value= "*"* clause.

The result of this first customisation step is the generation of a set of schemata, one for each offer state structure, which define an enScenario namespace and constrain XML instance documents from a syntactical perspective. Next, semantical constraints are added.

4.1.3 Ontology-dependent customisation

In this step, the ontology context assignment for the offer type, performed in the integration design, is manifested in all generated state-dependent offer schemata. An **ontology-dependent offer schema** is constructed on the basis of the syntactical notation from the state-dependent schema and the semantical concept specification from the offer context assignment. For each state-dependent offer schema, this ontology-dependent customisation has to be performed. The state-dependent offer schema is included (using the *include schemaLocation* directive in XML Schema) in a new ontology-dependent schema specification (which shares the namespace with the state-dependent schema). The offer base schema is also imported. An enScenario developer has two options for the ontology-dependent customisation:

- **Domain typing**
  For each attribute in the chosen ontology context, this option defines a new type as an extension to the *ATTRIBUTE_DOMAIN* type.
- **Context typing**
  This second option adds stronger semantics through additional extensions of the *CONTEXT* and the *CONSTRAINT* type and the definition of corresponding element substitution groups.

The trade-off between these two options is that domain typing does not guarantee structural integrity – it cannot be validated, for instance, whether an agent used all necessary attributes in the specification of an offer for a

Implementation 145

certain object context. Context typing, on the other hand, does provide a structure for the *CONTEXT* specification, but the elements introduced are proprietary to the schema, thus making parsing much more complicated, because every attribute is represented by a specific domain and constraint element[15]. The first example in Code 4 demonstrates domain typing for the *WORKSTATION.CPU* attribute, which is restricted to values greater than or equal to *300 MHZ* (see the definition of the *Computer* concept in *Figure 32*).

Code 4. Ontology-dependent schema example with domain typing

```
<schema
  targetNamespace="http://www.enegotiation.ch/example"
  xmlns:example="http://www.enegotiation.ch/example"
  xmlns:xen="http://www.enegotiation.ch"
  xmlns="http://www.w3.org/2001/XMLSchema"
  elementFormDefault="unqualified">
  <import namespace="http://www.enegotiation.ch"
    schemaLocation="enegotiation.xsd"/>
  <include schemaLocation="enegotiation_advertise_example.xsd"/>
  <complexType name="WORKSTATION.CPU" mixed="false"
    final="restriction">
    <complexContent mixed="false">
      <extension base="xen:ATTRIBUTE_DOMAIN">
        <sequence>
          <element name="VALUE">
            <simpleType>
              <restriction base="integer">
                <minInclusive value="300"/>
              </restriction>
            </simpleType>
          </element>
          <element name="UNIT">
            <simpleType>
              <restriction base="string">
                <enumeration value="MHZ"/>
              </restriction>
            </simpleType>
          </element>
...
```

---

[15] The distinction between domain and context typing is already reflected in the state-dependent customisation. For context typing, additional types from the offer base schema, such as *CONTEXT* and *ATTRIBUTE_DOMAIN*, are restricted. The *<NAME>* elements in these types are not needed, because specific named types such as *WORKSTATION.CPU* are created in the process of context typing.

Similarly, all other concept attributes from the chosen offer context ontology are defined as extensions to *ATTRIBUTE_DOMAIN* types in the state-dependent schema. Since the *ATTRIBUTE_DOMAIN* type is declared to be *abstract* in state-dependent schemata, only these new semantic domain types can be used for actual offer specifications. In addition, the ontology-dependent schema declares new types with *final= "restriction"*, which prevents further restrictions of these types in derived schemata, although extensions are still possible (e.g. if an agent needs to extend the MHz range or add GHz as another unit enumeration).

The second example illustrates context typing, in which additionally the *CONTEXT* and *CONSTRAINT* type are extended and complemented with corresponding element definitions. Code 5 demonstrates a customisation for the *CONTEXT* type with the derived type *WORKSTATION*, and also a customisation for the *CONSTRAINT* type with the derived type *CPU_CONSTRAINT*. The meaning of this example is as follows: the *WORKSTATION* type requires that a mandatory constraint be defined for the *CPU* attribute of a workstation. This *CPU_CONSTRAINT* can substitute for any valid occurrence of an offer constraint in an offer instance document. Furthermore, the *WORKSTATION.CPU* domain has to be used in this constraint.

Code 5. Ontology-dependent schema example with context typing

```
...
<complexType name="WORKSTATION" final="restriction" mixed="false">
    <complexContent mixed="false">
      <extension base="example:CONTEXT">
        <sequence>
          <element ref="example:CPU_CONSTRAINT"/>
          <element ref="example:HD_CONSTRAINT"/>
          ...
        </sequence>
      </extension>
    </complexContent>
</complexType>
<element name="CPU_CONSTRAINT" type="example:CPU_CONSTRAINT"
   substitutionGroup="xen:OFFER_CONSTRAINT"/>
<complexType name="CPU_CONSTRAINT" mixed="false">
   <complexContent mixed="false">
      <restriction base="xen:CONSTRAINT">
        <sequence>
          <element ref="example:WORKSTATION.CPU"/>
        </sequence>
        <attribute name="NEGOTIABLE" type="boolean"
          use="optional"/>
```

Implementation

```
      </restriction>
    </complexContent>
  </complexType>
  <element name="WORKSTATION.CPU" type="example:WORKSTATION.CPU"
    substitutionGroup="xen:ATTRIBUTE_DOMAIN"/>
  </complexType>
...
```

The example also explains how types from the base schema (denoted by the *xen:* namespace reference) and types from the state schema (such as *example:Context*) are combined to construct the ontology-dependent schema.

The final set of generated schemata can be deployed in the native XML Schema file format to the target enMedium system, as well as to the negotiating agents. Alternatively, the schema files can be hosted on a publicly available Web server and retrieved at run-time with URLs by both the agents and the enMedium system (see the prototype demonstration in Section 6.2.3.2).

4.1.4 XML instance document examples

With the completion of the final customisation step in the previous section, the set of ontology- and state-dependent schemata for an offer type is complete, ready for deployment, and can be used to construct and validate XML offer documents at run-time. To demonstrate the usage of the design representation, Code 6 features a snippet of an XML instance document that is compliant with the final ontology- and state-dependent schema in Code 4.

In this example, the attribute types are specified with the *xsi:type* assignment for the *ATTRIBUTE_DOMAIN* element. It can be seen that only standardised elements such as *OBJECT_CONTEXT* or *OFFER_CONSTRAINT* are used, thus simplifying the parsing of instance documents.

Code 6. XML instance document example with domain typing

```
<CONTAINER
    xmlns="http://www.enegotiation.ch/example"
    xmlns:xsi="http://www.w3.org/2001/XMLSchema"
    xsi:schemaLocation="http://www.enegotiation.ch/example">
    <OFFER ID="OF_007" TYPE="O2B" STATE="ADVERTISED"
        START="10.01.2001" SCENARIO="SC_EXAMPLE"
        CLASS="DISTRIBUTOR_WHOLESALE_WORKSTATION/>
    <OBJECT_CONTEXT NAME="WORKSTATION" NUMBER="10">
        <OFFER_CONSTRAINT>
            <ATTRIBUTE_DOMAIN xsi:type="WORKSTATION.CPU">
                <NAME>"WORKSTATION.CPU"</NAME>
```

```
          <OPERATOR>GREATER_THAN</OPERATOR>
          <VALUE>700</VALUE> <UNIT>MHZ</UNIT>
      </ATTRIBUTE_DOMAIN>
  </OFFER_CONSTRAINT>
...
```

However, there is no constraint in Code 6 that requires the usage of the *WORKSTATION.CPU* type in the offer. This missing level of structure validation can be achieved with context typing and is illustrated in the instance document example in Code 7.

Code 7. XML instance document example with context typing

```
<CONTAINER
  xmlns="http://www.enegotiation.ch/example"
  xmlns:xsi="http://www.w3.org/2001/XMLSchema"
  xsi:schemaLocation="http://www.enegotiation.ch/example>
  <OFFER ID="OF_007" TYPE="O2B" STATE="ADVERTISED"
    START="10.01.2001" SCENARIO="SC_EXAMPLE"
    CLASS="DISTRIBUTOR_WHOLESALE_WORKSTATION/>
  <OBJECT_CONTEXT NUMBER="10" xsi:type="WORKSTATION">
    <CPU_CONSTRAINT>
        <WORKSTATION.CPU>
          <OPERATOR>GREATER_THAN</OPERATOR>
          <VALUE>700</VALUE> <UNIT>MHZ</UNIT>
        </WORKSTATION.CPU>
    </CPU_CONSTRAINT>
    <OFFER_CONSTRAINT>
        <WORKSTATION.HD>
...
```

In the example in Code 7, the *xsi:type* specification is used to assign the restricted *WORKSTATION* type to the *OBJECT_CONTEXT* element, which requires that *CPU_CONSTRAINT* be used. The disadvantage of this added semantics is that an object specification may contain two different constraint types: customised constraints (e.g. *CPU_CONSTRAINT*) and generic *OFFER_CONSTRAINT* elements, which are used, for instance, to define additional binary constraints (see Definition 14 in Chapter 3).

4.2 Organisation design representation

As already argued, it is not necessary to provide an open or standardised representation format for the organisation design, since it is typically only used internally for the run-time processing in the enMedium system. Hence, a representation format can be chosen that is easy to generate and to interpret by enMedia architecture implementations.

The run-time representation suggested for the organisation design is an extended state-machine table. The generation of this table is straightforward: for every transition in the organisation design state charts, the initial state and the subsequent state, as well as the specifications for events, guard, action, and properties, are converted to row values in the table. This is demonstrated in *Table 12* for all transitions with the initial state *O2S.COUNTERED* from the example in *Figure 36*.

Table 12. State-machine table representation

State initial	Event	Gua.	Act.	Prop.	State new
O2S.COUNTERED	SELLER.OFFER	...	...	...	O2S.ADVERTISED
O2S.COUNTERED	SELLER.RETRACT	...	...	...	O2S.END
O2S.COUNTERED	SELLER.ACCEPT	...	...	...	O2S.CONTRACTED

This primary FSM table is complemented with additional tables, which directly map the event and view authorisation specification format introduced in *Table 10*. For the actual execution, the enMedium administrator has to replace the symbolic design-time agent groups in these tables with actual run-time agent groups defined for the enMedium system. Finally, depending on the enMedium implementation, a multitude of formats such as delimited ASCII or Integrated Exchange Format can be chosen to deploy the generated tables and import the encoded run-time specification.

5. SUMMARY

This chapter presents a design approach for electronic negotiations that is based on several interdependent abstractions and structured according to a development action-model (DAM) and a design meta-model (DMM).

The proposed design approach defines a language for the expression of enScenarios that captures aspects of the communication in an electronic negotiation ('what is negotiated') as well as aspects related to the way these negotiations are executed ('how is the negotiation organised'). The language for the organisation design allows the specification of rules governing the intermediated offer exchange of agents and the execution of actions supporting this exchange. The language for the communication design defines syntactical and semantical rules represented through offer structure elements, i.e. building blocks, and the means to combine these elements in an offer instance. The communication and the organisation design are not separated but integrated activities, which eventually lead to one unified enScenario design model. This resulting enScenario model has to be complemented with security and transparency specifications, and can be validated for completeness and correctness.

Regarding all the design, validation, and generation activities necessary to create and further use the model of an electronic negotiation, the question arises whether this significant effort is justified? A critical discussion and evaluation of the design approach can be found in Section 8.2.2, but one main advantage of this conceptual process is already obvious in this chapter – the design model is not only an abstract representation of an electronic negotiation, but can also be rendered into an imperative representation format, which is reused for the implementation of enMedium systems. Furthermore, through the availability of an imperative representation format, the effort in the implementation phase is largely reduced (e.g. to the development of user interfaces), since these representations can be deployed and instantiated natively in enMedium systems, if the underlying architecture supports the design language and its corresponding representations.

Beyond the concrete development advantage of a model representation, the transparency of an enScenario design to the negotiating agents has to be considered a key success factor [KaKo01]. Given the enScenario design model, agents can evaluate the rules specified and thereby understand what happens or will happen within the corresponding enProcess, e.g. what rights and obligations they have. Furthermore, a model helps agents to come to an agreement about the negotiation they are going to perform – the enScenario design model itself may become the object of a negotiation with offers and counteroffers.

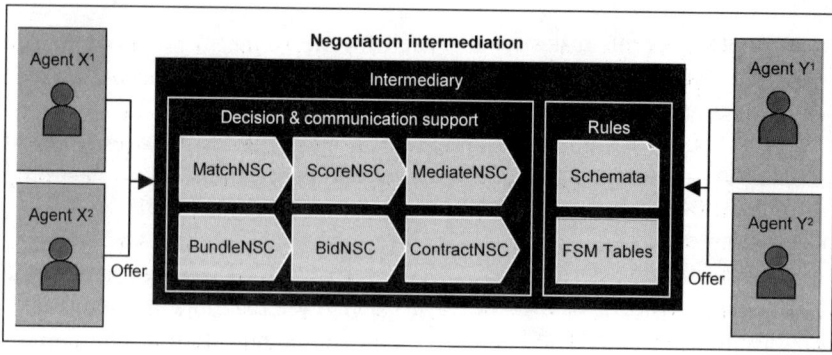

Figure 40. Negotiation intermediation with run-time specifications

On the basis of a set of negotiation support components such as the ones suggested in the previous chapter, and the design approach proposed in this chapter, two of the current problems in the domain of multi-attribute negotiations to be addressed by this book were already discussed: insufficient

Summary 151

support for decision tasks and the lack of comprehensive models. The solution manifested in the design approach complements the design and implementation framework for symmetric multi-attribute negotiation intermediation, which is the main proposition of this book (see *Figure 40*). This enMedia framework will be further extended in the next chapter, where the missing solution for the third problem is conceptualised: an enMedia architecture model.

Chapter 6

Electronic negotiation architecture
An application framework for electronic Silkroads

The contribution of this chapter is two-fold. First, an architecture model for symmetric multi-attribute negotiation intermediation systems in electronic markets is developed which completes the enMedia framework proposed in this book. Implementations of this model, enMedium systems, should be able to support a broad range of electronic negotiation scenarios, thereby addressing the third current problem identified in Section 2.3 – the lack of a flexible media architecture model for electronic negotiations. Second, a prototype implementation of the suggested architecture model, SILKROAD, is presented, which also provides tools for the enMedia framework design approach and shells for negotiation support components.

The following understanding of information systems, architectures, and architecture models underlies this chapter. The structure (e.g. the components, their interfaces and relations) and behaviour (e.g. the component interaction) of an information system are defined through its **architecture**. An architecture specifies rules for the implementation of an information **system** such as an enMedium. In keeping with the general notion of an architecture (such as is used for buildings), the goals of an architecture are (c.f. [FoBa01]) to ensure that an information system fulfils its requirements (utilitas), is robust regarding modifications (firmitas), and possesses beauty (venustas) – the third goal meaning that the structure is clear and understandable. An **architecture model** is an abstract representation and/or generalisation of one or more architecture specifications. Different enMedia (systems) with slightly varying architectures – for instance on different platforms – might be implemented on the basis of the same architecture model.

1. ARCHITECTURE MODEL

The generic enMedia architecture model needs to fulfil the requirements identified during the preceding development of the enMedia framework building blocks. The proposed solution does so by following the paradigm of application frameworks (see below). It is not the only possible architecture model design resulting from the requirements, but represents one potential incarnation – many other designs achieving the same goals may be possible.

The architecture model design is conceptual and semi-formal – a detailed design of an enMedium system architecture is presented later through the prototype implementation.

1.1 Requirements

Throughout the development of the enMedia framework design approach in Chapter 5, a number of implicit requirements for a compatible enMedia architecture model (which 'speaks the design language') were identified. These requirements comprise the ability to do the following:
- to host a number of enScenario design models and corresponding run-time specifications, and to control the execution of concurrent enProcesses for these enScenarios.
- to provide basic enMedium management actions such as receiving or retracting offer instances (see *Table 9*).
- to maintain and modify a state for each offer instance in an enProcess according to a FSM specification for the offer type of this instance.
- to validate offer instances towards the syntactical and semantical constraints as defined in the offer state structure design for the offer type and the corresponding offer context assignment.
- to interpret events raised by actors for one offer instance, including the evaluation of guards and the invocation of manager or support actions (such as a matchmaking operation) with the associated properties.
- to generate events (e.g. if an offer expires) and to propagate events raised for one offer instance to the event interpretation mechanism for offer instances of the corresponding offer type FSM.
- to validate the authorisation of actors and especially agents to raise events or to view certain elements of an offer instance.

These requirements are complemented by implicit requirements, which can be derived from the functionality necessary for the integration of NSCs, such as the specification of the external view and behaviour of NSCs (see Section 4.3). Since enMedium systems have to provide a run-time environment for NSCs, the architecture model also needs to support the

Architecture model 155

- creation of multiple and concurrently existing NSCs (of the same or different types).
- setting of the initiating offer, the target offers, and the objectives for a new NSC instance.
- invocation of the NSC operation and runtime handling (e.g. error interpretation).
- handling of events and offers that are generated during the NSC execution.
- retrieval of the results of the NSC operation and the termination or passivation of the NSC.

A third source of requirements is the facilitation of the deployment process proposed in the referential development and deployment process in *Figure 17*. The enMedia architecture model needs to anticipate interfaces to the functionalities necessary for the tasks (e.g. 'activation' and 'inspection') and roles (e.g. 'administrator'), identified for this process.

The enMedia architecture model proposed in this chapter reflects the three principal sources of requirements described above, but also strives for additional goals such as high reusability, as will be outlined in the next section.

1.2 Rationale

"There is not a single best negotiation protocol for all negotiation situations" [Bich01, p.82]. Because different negotiation rules are appropriate in different situations, any generic architecture has to support a range of rules [Wurm+98]. For that reason, the key goal for the enMedia architecture model is to support an open range of enScenarios, which specify the protocols/rules for various negotiation situations.

This intended flexibility is achievable through the identification of a set of abstract, reusable architecture components, which can be combined and customised to build enMedium systems for specific enScenarios. The architecture model proposed in this book represents the highest common abstraction level for the potential enScenario types that might result from the enMedia framework design approach.

Achieving flexibility through reuse and customisability is a goal also pursued by application frameworks. An **application framework** provides the semi-complete skeleton of an application – a specific application is an instantiation of the framework completed through customisation [Faya+99]. The enMedia architecture model follows this application framework approach[16]. A concrete **enMedium system** is an implementation of the archi-

---

[16] Alternatives to an application framework approach are discussed in Section 8.2.3.

tecture model – the system's architecture complies with the architecture model. Since the architecture model has an application framework character, its implementation, the enMedium system itself, represents a semi-complete skeleton. An **enMedium server** is a physical copy of such an enMedium system architecture skeleton, which may feature all or only selected architecture components and may run multiple enInstances. These enInstances are instantiations of the enMedium system architecture skeleton, customised according to an enScenario model.

Overall, these relations result in several electronic negotiation architecture and system layers as illustrated in *Figure 41*. The enMedia architecture model is defined on a conceptual layer, whereas enMedium systems (or skeletons) are situated on the implementation layer. On a physical layer sit real servers, each of which may host several enInstances on a logical layer.

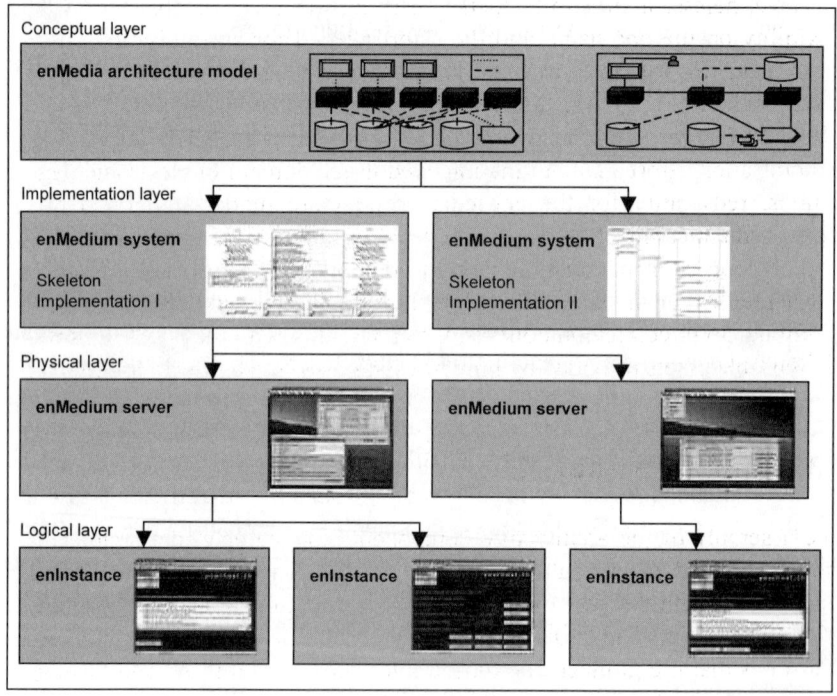

Figure 41. Architecture and system layers

An enScenario developer has to complement the customised skeleton instantiation with scenario-specific application logic, such as the user interface, which cannot be expressed through an enScenario model. The amount of unique code required for the implementation of an enScenario is propor-

Architecture model 157

tional to its specific features. The paradigm of application frameworks also comprises **inversion of control** – the skeleton invokes the execution of scenario-specific application logic whereas the overall application flow control resides within the generic system architecture and cannot be changed by the developer.

A goal for the architecture model is to minimise the amount of unique code. For this reason, an enMedium system should not only provide the reuse of code, but also the reuse of design. An enScenario developer can benefit from the effort spent on the decomposition of an enMedium system into a set of reusable components with well-defined and standardised interfaces. This decomposition and standardisation makes it possible to mix and combine the components depending on the requirements identified for the enScenario.

Nevertheless, a trade-off exists regarding the level of abstraction and flexibility on the one hand, and the effort needed for customisation on the other hand. In principle, extreme abstraction can lead to the provision of basic components on the level of programming-language types, such as *string* or *integer*, thus achieving high flexibility but also requiring high customisation efforts. Due to the intended usage domain of electronic negotiations, reusability for the enMedia architecture model is defined on a higher semantical level, that is, on the level of functional components.

The concept of negotiation support components was already introduced in Chapter 4. For the enMedia architecture model, the next section presents additional architecture components, which together with the NSCs constitute the reusable assets provided by implementations of the enMedia architecture model.

1.3 Model structure

The assembly of the architecture components for the enMedia architecture model is based on a mapping of the required functionalities to different components with the goal of achieving loose coupling and strong coherence within the model. The high-level architecture design presented in *Figure 42* illustrates that the number of exposed interfaces is minimised and that only one pair of architecture components is mutually dependent: the agent manager and the execution manager have to know each other's interfaces.

The enMedia architecture model distinguishes adapters, architecture components, support components, and data repositories. Adapters are the only means to communicate externally with an enMedium system. For design-time support, a **design adapter** is provided that allows an enScenario designer to create and store enScenario models in the **design-time model repository** (DR), using functionalities of the **design manager** (DM). For the deployment process, the design manager will generate run-time specifications and store them in the **run-time specification repository** (RR). An enScenario administrator will use the **management adapter** to activate/deactivate enScenarios but also to create agents and agent groups in the **enMedium repository** (MR) in order to assign them to specific enScenario roles. The enMedium repository also contains status information for enScenarios (e.g. 'activated' or 'instantiated') as well as run-time data, such as the current state of offers within an enProcess or an offer event trace.

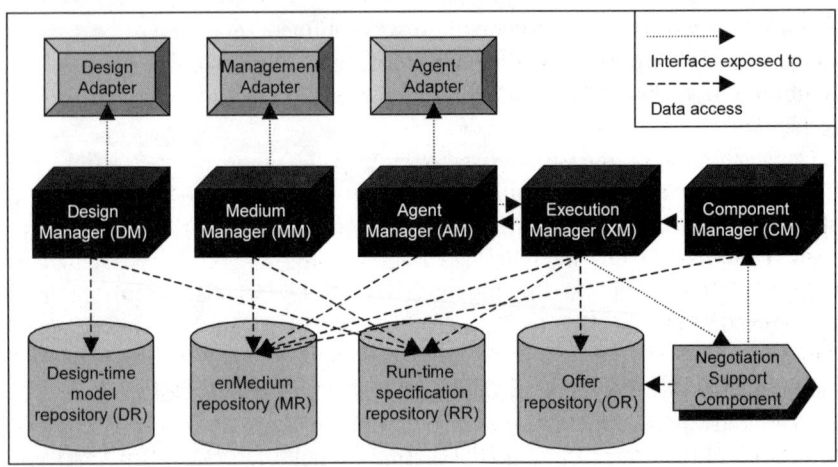

Figure 42. enMedia architecture model components

The actual execution of enProcesses is controlled by the **execution manager** (XM). This architecture component receives offers and/or events for specific offers, validates these offer and event combinations for correctness with respect to the run-time specifications, and potentially invokes actions if a transition fires. The XM itself behaves as a state machine with a finite number of states, no memory, and an input alphabet consisting of events. Its internal state transition function is defined through the FSM specification for the offer type associated with the event. The output alphabet comprises the potential action specifications.

Valid offers and the offer history are stored in the **offer repository** (OR). Events and offers are passed to the execution manager via the **agent manager** (AM), which provides the **agent adapter** to agents. The agent manager models a facade pattern [Gamm+95] for the run-time functionality of the system – it exposes a unified interface with all methods available to agents, and thereby decouples adapters from the system, but realises no functionality itself except the authentication of agents and the resolution of pseudonyms

Architecture model

for agents (to enable anonymous requests). Through the agent manager an agent can raise an event (such as submitting an offer or inquiring about the results of an action), which is then forwarded to the execution manager. An agent may also receive notifications (e.g. if an offer times out). Notifications are generated by the execution manager and passed via the agent manager to the agent adapter. The execution manager also implements manager actions (e.g. accepting an offer, see *Table 9*). Actions associated with NSC operations are relayed to the **component manager** (CM), which invokes analogous to the mediator pattern the corresponding NSC – NSCs are not aware of each other but only interface with the component manager. NSCs have access only to the offer repository and to the execution manager interface in order to raise events, e.g. to indicate errors or a successful termination.

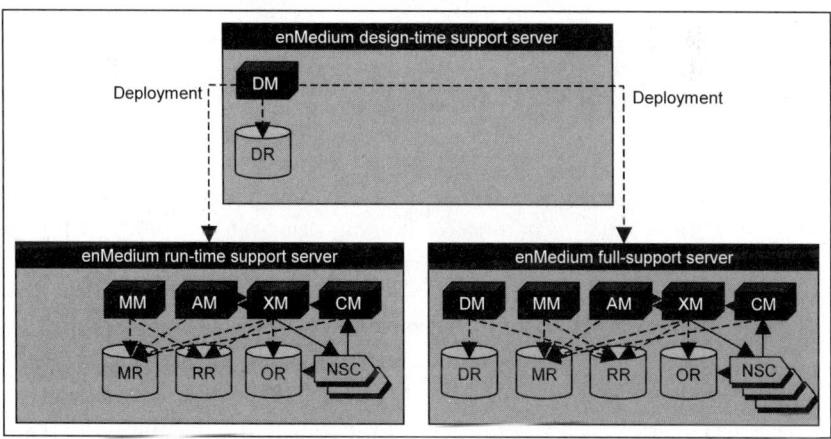

Figure 43. Functional architecture component distribution

The proposed architecture model also allows for **functional component distribution**. Through the deployment process, system functionality for the design-time (e.g. enScenario modelling) can be separated from run-time support functionality. It is possible to run an enMedium server with copies of only the design manager and the design-time model repository. Generated enScenario model representations can then be deployed to federated enMedium servers which are dedicated to providing run-time support only and therefore do not feature the design manager and the design-time model repository (see *Figure 43*). In addition, NSCs can be distributed across enMedium servers. Depending on the enScenarios supported, one enInstance might require, for instance, the BidNSC, whereas another needs only the MatchNSC.

NSCs in this architecture model correspond to **plug-in mechanisms** (c.f. [Tu+01]). The number of available NSCs, as well as their functionality, is unknown at system compilation-time, but all NSCs share the same well-known public interface and cooperation pattern (protocol). On the basis of this combination of interface and pattern, together with the imperative action specification in the FSM, NSCs can cooperate at run-time with other system components.

Event processing is the only trigger of run-time processing in the enMedia architecture model. Hence, the structure of the model is complemented with a generic **enMedia event signature**. An event must contain information about the actor raising it, the offer it is initiated for, and its actual event ID (for example *BUYER.ACCEPT*, see Definition 1 in Chapter 5). Furthermore, the event may specify objects (e.g. the target offers for an NSC operation) and a set of parameters (e.g. the objectives for an NSC operation).

1.4 Model behaviour

Whereas the previous section focused on the structural elements of the enMedia architecture model, this section discusses behavioural aspects. In the architecture model, a number of guiding principles are defined for the component interaction during run-time processing:

- **Stateless and stateful components**
  There is no need for any of the architecture components to retain the conversational state or interaction context. Run-time processing within the architecture is triggered only through events for associated offers. Because the static FSM definition is available in the run-time specification repository and the current offer state persists as an attribute of the offer instance (see the offer examples in Section 5.4.1.4), processing of single events is possible without regard to preceding or subsequent events – the state of a component needs to be retained only for the duration of the invocation. In contrast, NSCs may respond to several events (e.g. the addition of target offers or an inquiry of results) during the NSC operation, and therefore have to be stateful. Specific agent adapters, such as those that have to provide a user with a conversational context, might also be stateful.
- **Asynchronous action invocation**
  If an event raised by an agent leads to the execution of an action, no immediate feedback on the result of this action can be returned to the agent, as the operation of NSCs may require an undetermined amount of time. The event processing in the execution manager may be completed but the invoked action (e.g. the scoring operation) could still be running. Therefore all actions receive a unique ID, which allows the retrieval of the

result of the action through consecutive events at a later point in time. The execution manger returns only the success of the event processing (e.g. whether the event was valid and the agent authorised) and associated information such as the new offer state and an action ID (if applicable).

- **Imperative dynamic composition**
For the offer type of every offer instance associated with an event an imperative FSM specification is available at run-time. All run-time architecture component interaction is dependent on these FSM specifications – that is, the run-time interaction is dynamically composed. The execution manager interprets the FSM, retrieves the action and property specification of the transition that fires, and tries to invoke this action. Depending on the type of the action (support or manager) this might involve an operation unknown to the execution manager – namely, an NSC operation. In this case the invocation is relayed to the component manager, which tries to find the NSC based on the configuration stored in the enMedium repository, binds to the NSC interface, and executes the NSC.

Adhering to these principles, the behaviour of an enMedium system at run-time can be outlined with several main use cases (see *Figure 44* and *Figure 45* below). The first use case in *Figure 44* illustrates the submission of an offer with an event to an enInstance. Through the agent adapter the agent raises an *AGENT.OFFER* event (1). The agent manager passes the corresponding offer on to the execution manager (2). The first internal operation of the execution manager is to check the offer for syntactical and semantical correctness. This requires reading the appropriate state- and ontology-dependent offer schema from the run-time specification repository (3). Evaluating the event information in combination with the enScenario type of the enInstance and the state of the offer submitted, the execution manager queries the run-time specification repository for the appropriate FSM specification (4). If a valid transition is found for this event, the execution manager checks through the enMedium repository whether the agent is authorised to submit an offer (5), i.e. whether the agent belongs to the group authorised to raise this event. If that is the case, the action related to the transition, *MANAGER.OFFER*, is initiated. This action stores the offer in the offer repository (6). Upon success, the execution manager will update the state of the offer in the enMedium repository (7), for example to *O2X.AD-VERTISED*. After this final run-time processing step, all involved architecture component instances can be destroyed, since it is unnecessary to keep the conversational state. The agent can inquire about the success of this action through a subsequent *AGENT.GETRESULTS* event for the same offer. The execution manager responds to this request by returning the result-set and result-codes of the last action (8) (9).

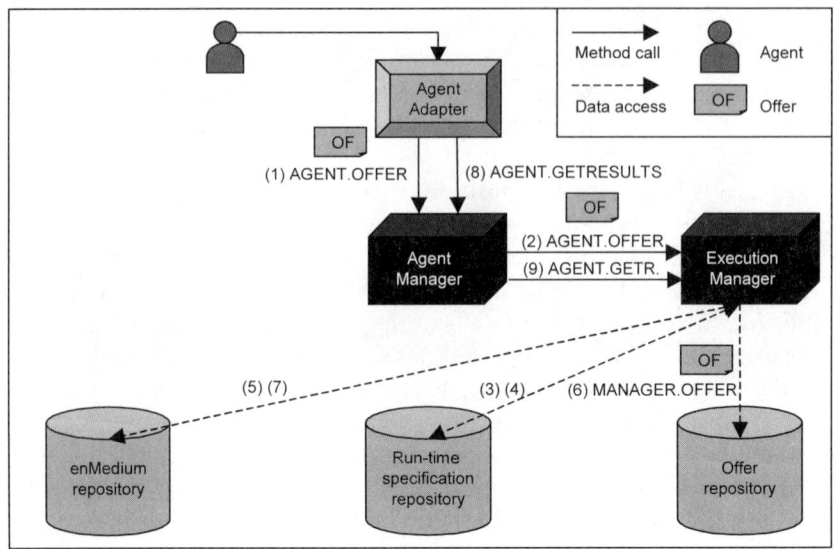

Figure 44. Offer submission run-time use case

Since event processing is the only 'write' action possible at run-time, the implementation of transactional properties (ACID: atomicity, consistency, isolation, and durability, [HaRe83]) for the event processing in the execution manager guarantees transaction consistency. For the first use case above, the transactional context has to include the writing of a new offer instance to the offer repository and the corresponding update of the offer state in the enMedium repository.

The second use case (see *Figure 45*, next page) demonstrates how NSCs are invoked at run-time. The agent raises an *AGENT.MATCH* event, which includes a specification of the initiating offer (e.g. *O2X.ADVERTISED*) and the target offers (1). In accordance with the preceding use case, the execution manager will look up the FSM specification and verify that the agent is authorised to invoke a matchmaking operation (3) (4). Let us assume that the agent has this right and the FSM specifies a transition from the current state of the initiating offer to the state *O2X.MATCHING* with an associated action *SUPPORT.MATCH*. The execution manager will then generate a new action ID and forward the action specification, including its properties, to the component manager (5). Next, the state of the initiating offer can be updated in the enMedium repository (6). The action specification is also written to the event log in the enMedium repository. This last step can be done in parallel with the component manager execution, since the event processing is complete from the execution manager's point of view. The subsequent NSC operation is invoked asynchronously.

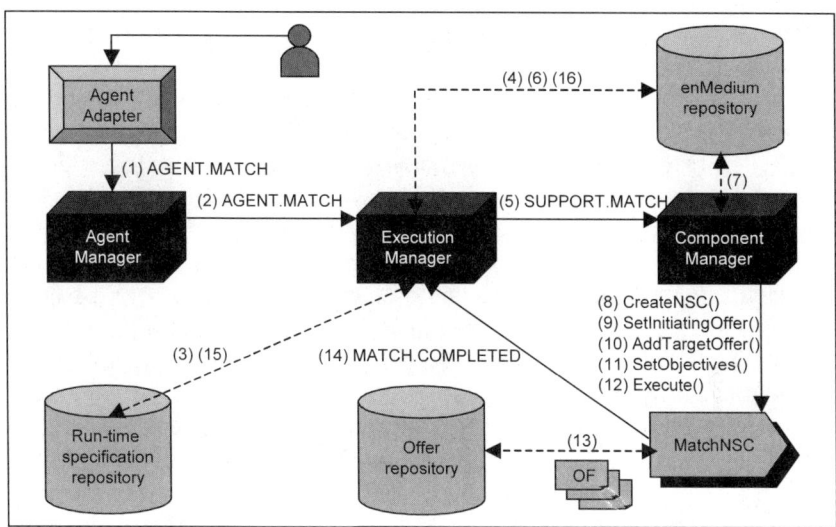

Figure 45. NSC invocation run-time use case

To execute the matchmaking operation, the component manager first verifies the existence of the MatchNSC in the enMedium repository (7) and loads a reference to the corresponding interface. Then a number of public NSC methods have to be called (see *Table 4*) in order to create a MatchNSC instance with the new action ID and to invoke the MatchNSC operation (8) (9) (10) (11) (12). As part of the operation of the MatchNSC, the support component will read the initiating and the target offers from the offer repository (13). Once the matchmaking operation is completed, the MatchNSC raises a *MATCH.COMPLETED* event through the system-internal execution manager interface (14). As for any other event, the execution manager then tries to find a corresponding transition in the state *O2X.MATCHING* (15) for this event in the FSM specification associated with the offer. In case of a successful MatchNSC operation, the new offer state that is written to the enMedium repository (16) is *O2X.MATCHED*.

If the agent wants to inquire about the results of the MatchNSC operation after the completion of the *AGENT.MATCH* event processing (e.g. during or after the MatchNSC operation) a subsequent *AGENT.GETRESULTS* event needs to be raised that specifies the unique action ID as object. Not shown in *Figure 45* are extensions of the use case such as an additional notification of the agent, which might be generated for a change in the initiating offer's state, and the potential creation of new offer instances through the Match-NSC operation.

An NSC instance may also retrieve a target offer with dynamic attribute domains (see Definition 10 in Chapter 3). In this use case, the originator of the offer will be requested to update this offer. Only updated offer instances in which dynamic domains are replaced with concrete attribute values can and will be evaluated in the NSC operation. To give an example, the Match-NSC might read a target offer for notebooks in which the domain for the attribute *memory_upgrade_price* is defined to be dynamic, because the manufacturer wants to base the price calculation on the latest market price for memory chips. In this case, the enMedium system sends a notification to the manufacturer indicating that this offer instance is subject to a matchmaking operation and requires an update for the *memory_upgrade_price* attribute. Unless the manufacturer completes the offer instance with the calculated price, it will not be matched.

These use cases complement the conceptual layer of the enMedia framework architecture model for symmetric multi-attribute intermediation. As a result of the specified model structure and behaviour, the means to interface with an enInstance at run-time, from an agent's perspective, are solely offers and events. In the next section, this restricted agent interface to an enMedium system, as well as other outcomes of the proposed architecture model, will be demonstrated on the basis of an example architecture model implementation – the SILKROAD prototype.

2. SILKROAD

The SILKROAD prototype is an implementation of the enMedia framework. SILKROAD is an enMedium system that complies with the architecture model proposed in the preceding section, but also includes shells for the NSCs introduced in Chapter 4 and tools for the design of enScenario models following the design approach suggested in Chapter 5. The prototype was developed during the author's research at IBM's Zurich Research Laboratory in order to refine the conceptual models on the implementation level, to prove that the propositions of this book are practical, and to justify the claims postulated to solve the current problems identified in the domain of electronic negotiations. It is just one possible implementation for the enMedia framework, and while this prototype focuses on a basic proof of concept, other implementations might emphasise, for instance, performance issues or usability and therefore have a different implementation focus.

The Silk Road itself was an ancient trade route that led across Central Asia's desert to Persia, Byzantium, and Rome. Along this road negotiations

SilkRoad 165

of all kinds took place (e.g. camel auctions or bargaining for spices at bazaars). Using the "Silk Road" as a metaphor, the SILKROAD prototype enables the creation of virtual silk roads, where a similar variety of negotiations can be conducted electronically.

To demonstrate the different technical aspects of the implementation, the discussion of the SILKROAD system architecture is separated into a technical architecture view, which illustrates the building blocks of the system infrastructure, and a logical application architecture view.

2.1 Technical architecture

The technical architecture of the SILKROAD prototype is a three-tier architecture based on the Java 2 Enterprise Edition (J2EE). The J2EE application model (see [Kass00]) provides the benefits of native scalability for multi-tier applications and 'write once, run anywhere' cross-platform portability without the need for recompilation or source code modification. The pre-packaged software building blocks used for the three tiers of SILKROAD are illustrated in *Figure 46*.

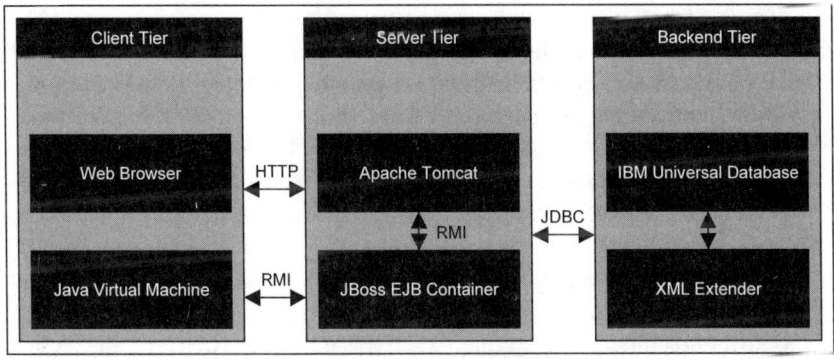

Figure 46. Three-tier technical architecture

For the presentation functionality in the **client tier** a standard Java Virtual Machine (JVM) or a Web browser is used. In the **server tier**, two open source packages are integrated for the processing of presentation and application logic: an Apache Tomcat Web server with a Java Server Pages (JSP) servlet engine and a JBoss Enterprise JavaBeans (EJB) container. Web browsers communicate via HTTP through the Tomcat Web server with the EJB container. The JVM can directly access the EJB container with Remote Method Invocation (RMI). The **backend tier** comprises IBM's Universal Database (UDB) for the storage of data tables and the associated XML extender for native persistence of XML documents. The server tier connects to the backend tier via JDBC. Through the JBoss implementation of the EJB data source mechanism, database connections can be pooled.

These building blocks have to be installed and configured as infrastructure on the target platform before the components of the SILKROAD system can be deployed. From a physical distribution perspective, all infrastructure building blocks except the combination of UDB and the XML extender (see *Figure 46*) may reside on different computers. The server tier together with the backend tier comprises an enMedium server (see *Figure 43*). The system components of the SILKROAD prototype have the following technical representations:

- **J2EE client application classes**
  The design and the management adapter are realised as J2EE client applications that use Java Swing classes for the presentation functionality. The design and management adapter application comprises the remote interfaces necessary to connect to the JBoss EJB container that hosts the design manager and medium manager components. For the lookup of these components on a specific enMedium server, the Java Naming and Directory Interface (JNDI) is used in combination with the directory service provided by the JBoss container.
- **Java Server Pages and JavaBeans**
  Java Server Pages and JavaBeans are used for the agent adapter. Through the JSP technology, stateful agent sessions can be handled. In addition, dynamic Web pages for the presentation of enProcess information to the agents can be generated in a straightforward manner. These JSPs reside on the Apache Tomcat Server. Run-time interaction with the agent manager is provided through a JavaBean, which is created in the Apache Tomcat server for every agent session and which relays agent events and result-sets between the Web server and the EJB container. JSPs simply write and read data from properties of the JavaBean, whereas methods from the agent manager are called through a bean listener, which monitors changes in the bean state (see Appendix D). Through this design, the presentation functionality of the agent adapter is completely decoupled from the application functionality in the server tier. The only requirement for an agent adapter implementation is to access the set() and get() methods of the JavaBean.
- **Enterprise JavaBeans**
  The application functionality is represented with different types of EJBs (see below), which are located in the JBoss EJB container and have a unique reference in its JNDI directory. The EJB container provides life cycle management for EJBs, which means that at run-time they are created, instantiated, or destroyed by the container in order to achieve

scalable and fault-tolerant behaviour without the necessity for specific consideration of these system quality issues by the developer.
- **Data model**
  The backend tier is defined through a relational data model, which specifies and relates a number of database tables (see the Appendix). These tables are used to provide configuration, design-time, and run-time information, such as information on the available NSCs, the FSM specifications for the supported enScenarios, or the agent accounts of an enMedium server.

For deployment, the JSPs and related resource files of the agent adapter are bundled to a Web Application aRchive (WAR), which has to be installed on the Web server. The EJBs and associated helper classes are enclosed in Java ARchives (JAR) and injected into the EJB container. Also part of these JARs are deployment descriptors for the beans, which contain declarative deployment information such as the name of data sources or the log level. The compiled classes for the J2EE client application are also packaged as a JAR and can be downloaded and run on any computer with a standard JVM. Not every enMedium server will necessarily include a J2EE client application JAR for download, as this JAR can be distributed from one server to arbitrary locations and can, on the basis of a given URL, connect to any enMedium server available on the network through TCP/IP.

In summary, the following steps are necessary to set up a SILKROAD enMedium server with one enInstance:
- Installation of the technical architecture building blocks on the target platform.
- Deployment of the system components to the technical infrastructure installation.
- Configuration of the enMedium server (e.g. account creation, NSC registration, etc.).
- Deployment of the enScenario run-time specification to the enMedium server.
- Activation of the enScenario on the enMedium server.

Through the enScenario deployment process, organisation and integration design specification tables (*XSR_ORGANISATION_TRANSITIONS* and *XSR_INTEGRATION_EVENTS*, see the Appendix) are populated. The XML schemata generated for the communication design are made accessible through the Web server. XML schemata are referenced with a URI in XML instance documents[17].

---

[17] An XML parser typically tries to read the XML schema for an XML document by resolving the specified *xsi:schemaLocation* reference, which requires a Web server to supply the XML schema document if a URL is referenced.

2.2 Application architecture

Whereas the preceding section focuses on the technical construction of the SILKROAD prototype, this section provides a discussion of the logical prototype structure. Since a complete account of the prototype structure is not the goal of this book, the discussion is focused on a number of key elements that demonstrate how the defined enMedia architecture model structure and behaviour are reflected in SILKROAD.

SILKROAD is implemented as an object-oriented system based completely on the Java language. To support potential functional component distribution (c.f. *Figure 43*), the SILKROAD source code classes are logically separated into four Java packages: *com.ibm.silkroad.design* for classes that implement the generation process for run-time specifications (see Section 5.4.1) as well as the methods necessary to manipulate design models, *com.ibm.silkroad.support* for the NSC shells, *com.ibm.silkroad.interfaces* for the adapters, and the main *com.ibm.silkroad.architecture* package with the run-time processing functionality.

All components in the enMedia architecture model, except the adapters, are represented as Enterprise JavaBeans (see [DeMi+00] for details regarding the specifications of EJB types). The design manager, medium manager, agent manager, and execution manager are implemented as **stateless session beans** (in compliance with the first guiding principle in Section 6.4). These types of beans exist for only one single method invocation and are then destroyed by the EJB container. The component manager is represented as a **message-driven bean**, which subscribes to a certain message topic in order to receive messages with action specifications from the execution manager. This construction is necessary in order to achieve asynchronous action invocation. The event processing in the execution manager can terminate after the generation and publishing of the message, and is therefore decoupled from the consecutive invocation of an NSC operation by the component manager. The message contains the specification of the NSC action including its properties. It is unpacked and interpreted by the component manager, which creates the corresponding NSC.

NSCs are **entity beans** with bean-managed persistence. Persistence is necessary for NSCs since an NSC operation might consume an undetermined amount of time and since its results have to be available after the completion of the operation. To achieve this persistence, two tables are created for every type of NSC in the enMedium repository: *XSR_MEDIUM_NSC_PARAMETERS* and *XSR_MEDIUM_NSC_RESULTS*. In case of a termination or re-creation of an NSC instance, the state of the bean is written to or read from these tables. Entity beans require a primary key, which in SILKROAD is represented in the *SilkSupportPK* class (see *Figure 47* for the following) and constructed in the following way: *action ID* + *":"* + *initiating offer ID* + *":"* + *target offer IDs* + *":"* + *timestamp*.

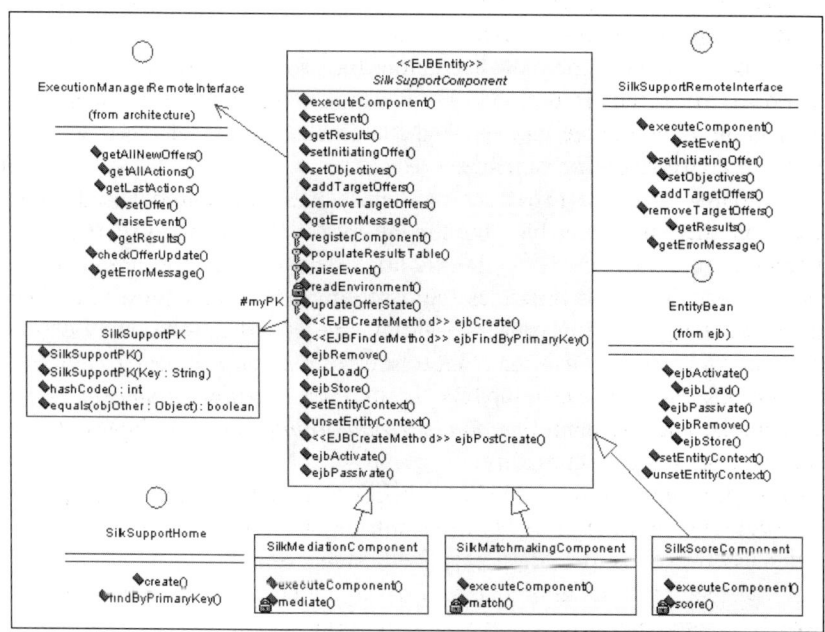

Figure 47. Support package UML class diagram

An example is *SUPPORT.MATCH:OF_X.ADVERTISED:OF_Y.ADVERTISED:100226236401*. After the NSC instantiation, this key is generated and inserted into the system table *XSR_MEDIUM_COMPONENTS*, thus enabling the later retrieval of the NSC instance by the generic Entity Bean *findByPrimaryKey()* method. This method is part of the *SilkSupportHome* interface, which is implemented by all NSCs. In addition, all NSCs are derived from the abstract super class *SilkSupportComponent* and also share the same remote interface *SilkSupportRemoteInterface*. The only method that is overwritten in NSCs is *executeComponent()*. Through this design, the implementation effort for new NSCs can be focused on the solution procedure, since the standard external behaviour is completely inherited from the superclass. Furthermore, the usage of one remote interface for all NSCs allows the component manager to create and invoke arbitrary NSC types. The component manager simply looks up the JNDI name for an action ID (specified in the message from the execution manager) in the system configuration table *XSR_MEDIUM_ACTIONS* and uses the standard interfaces *SilkSupportHome* and *SilkSupportRemoteInterface* to create and invoke the NSC instance. The *SilkSupportRemoteInterface* defines exactly the methods defined in the generic NSC interface in *Table 4*.

The EJBs are complemented by a number of helper classes. The *Silk Event* class provides a standard encapsulation for all types of events that might be raised by agents, NSCs, or the execution manager. It is defined according to the enMedia event signature introduced in Section 6.1.3. A serialisation of this class can be used for passing events between arbitrary system components – for example, events from clients sent through JSPs, or the text messages sent by the execution manager to the component manager. An event may include values for the *AGENT, EVENT, OFFER, OBJECT* (Vector), and *PARAMETERS* (Hashtable) class attributes. Similarly, a seria-lisable *SilkResults* class is used as standard interface to the results of an NSC operation. Internally this class is structured as a table model with the columns *OFFER_ID, RESULT_CODE, ELEMENT, ELEMENT_CODE,* and *ELEMENT_RESULT,* thus mapping the output structure defined for NSCs. Finally, the *OfferManager* and *OfferManipulator* helper classes in the *com.ibm.silkroad.architecture* package provide functionalities for manipulating XML instance documents. These classes use the Apache Xerces parser [Xerc01] to validate XML offers at run-time for compliance with the offer state schema or to update offers (e.g. if the state changes).

2.3 Tool support

SILKROAD provides a number of tools to support enScenario designers, and developers, as well as enMedium administrators, analysts, and providers. These tools are packaged into a J2EE client application that realises the functionality of the design and management adapter. The user interface of the client application, after a successful connection to an enMedium server, is illustrated in *Figure 48* (next page).

The menu structure maps the enScenario development and deployment tasks defined in *Figure 17*. The second menu item, entitled 'Design', links to tools supporting the organisation and communication design of enScenarios. Through the 'Deploy' menu, run-time specifications can be generated and deployed to enMedium servers. An enScenario developer is then able to test activated enScenarios (e.g. by submitting sample offers) on this enMedium server using several functions in the 'Test' menu, while the enScenario administrator may use the 'Manage' menu to, for instance, activate and deactivate enScenarios or to define agent authorisations and assignments. Finally, primitive enProcess analysis data, such as statistics regarding the number of active offers, is provided by the 'Analyse' menu functionalities.

SilkRoad   171

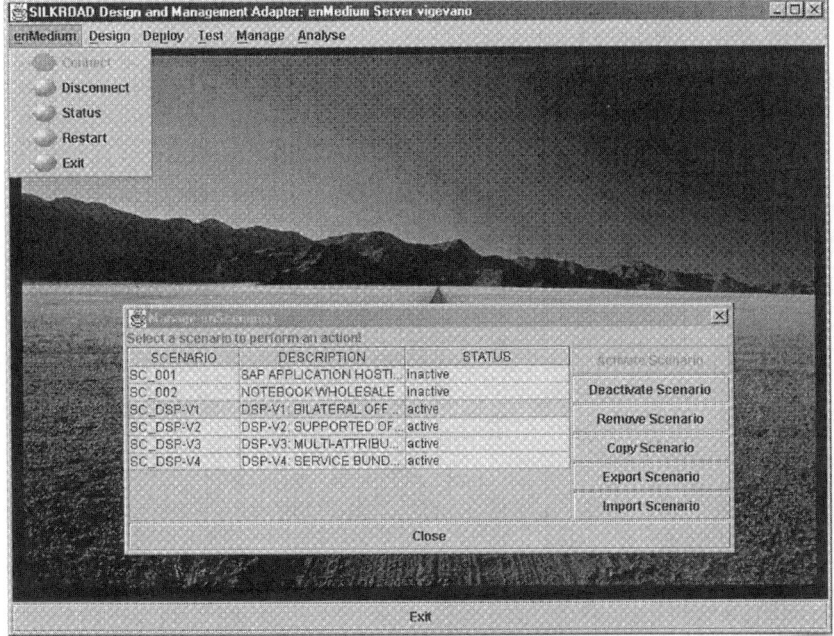

Figure 48. SILKROAD client application user interface

Figure 48 illustrates the client application user interface for a typical task of the enScenario administrator, the activation of enScenarios on a particular enMedium server. In the following sections the main support functionalities of the client application for the enScenario development and deployment process are further outlined.

2.3.1 Development

The enScenario design is supported through the enScenario designer window. This window has four panels that represent the different views and activities of the enMedia framework design approach. When the designer selects a different panel, the state of the enScenario model is updated and synchronised across all views.

The first panel, the enScenario overview, displays the enScenario ID and description, shows a graphical state-chart representation of the FSM specification (if available), and allows switching from the O2B to the O2S offer type or vice versa (see *Figure 49*).

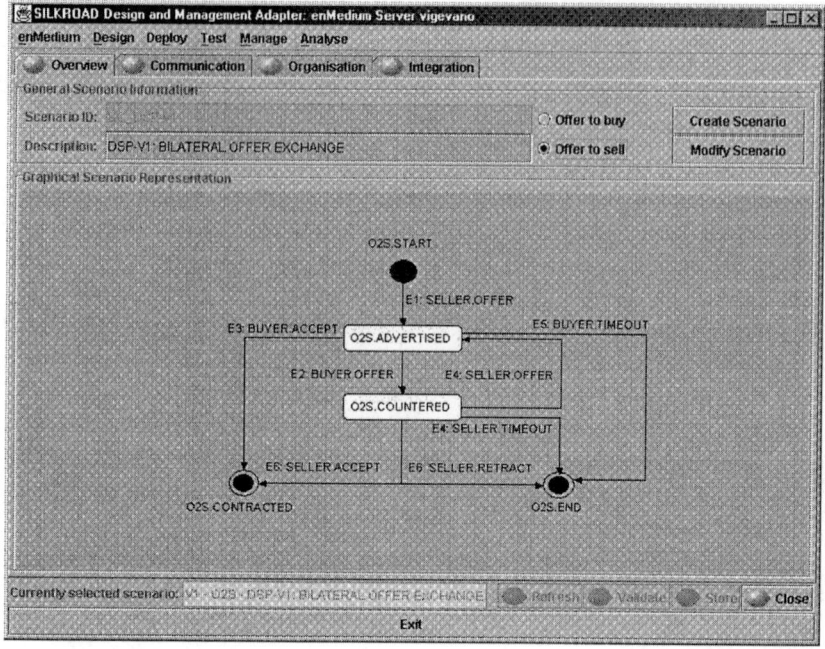

Figure 49. enScenario designer window in the SILKROAD client

The communication design panel in the designer window is shown in *Figure 50* (next page) for the example enScenario model already introduced in Section 5.3.2.3. In the communication design panel, new states for the current enScenario model can be created by either selecting a state template or entering a new state definition. States already included are listed with the defined notation options in the main table in *Figure 50*. These listed offer state structures are editable as well. In the communication design table the column headers correspond to the offer structure elements in *Table 7*.

The designed set of offer states has to be used in the organisation design panel to model the transitions of offers in the enScenario. This is illustrated in *Figure 51* (next page). The *TransitionEditor* dialog window presents the enScenario designer with the available states, events, and actions supported by the enMedium as well as a with table to define, depending on the chosen action, the properties associated with an action. The events and actions available in the *TransitionEditor* dialog window depend on the configuration of the target enMedium server, that is, on the NSCs available or the actions provided by the execution manager.

SilkRoad 173

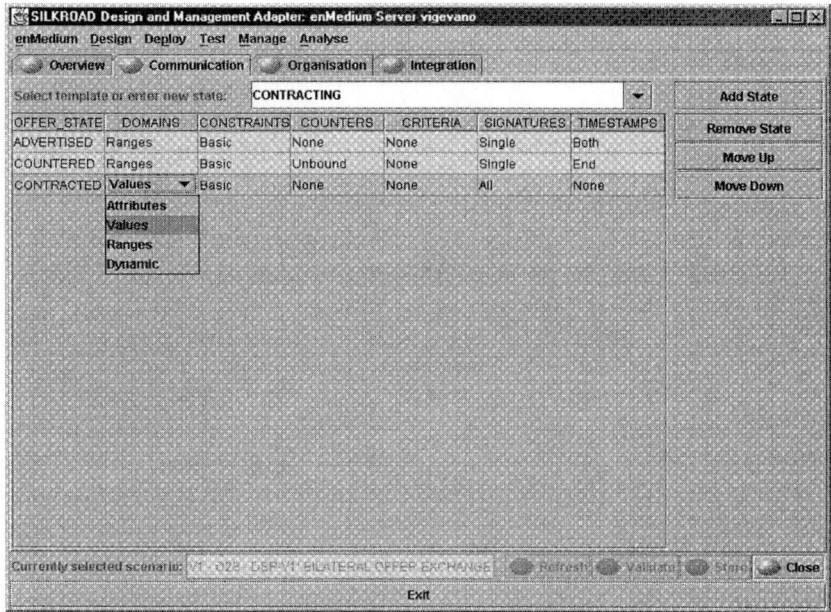

Figure 50. Communication design with SILKROAD

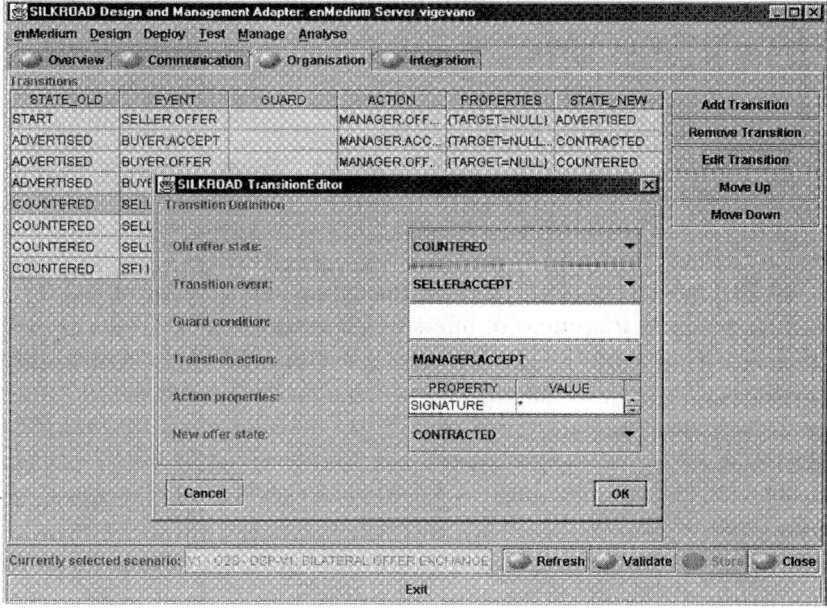

Figure 51. Organisation design with SILKROAD

The integration panel in *Figure 52* provides the interface for the integration design activities: event authorisation, view authorisation, and offer context assignment. The SILKROAD client application ensures that before a new or modified enScenario model can be saved to the design repository, it has to be validated against the test conditions defined in *Table 11*. This test procedure is triggered through the 'Validate' button in the enScenario designer window.

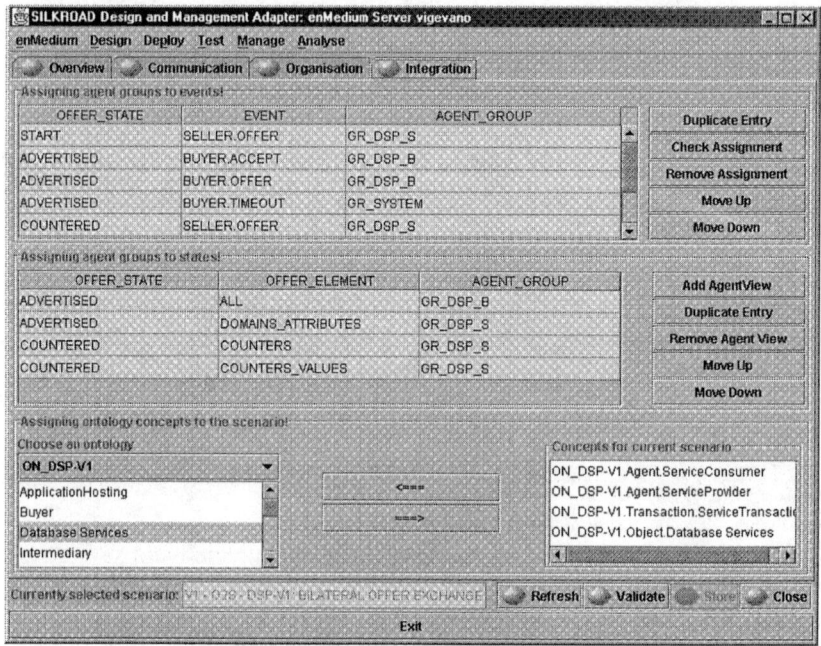

Figure 52. Integration design with SILKROAD

SILKROAD's tool support for the enMedia framework design approach is completed with the ontology designer window (see *Figure 53*, next page), which assists in the construction of offer context ontologies. In the offer context assignment user interface of the integration panel, concepts from ontology models can be selected and assigned to the current offer type. As depicted in *Figure 52*, the assignment interface also displays the root context of the selected concept, such as *agent.service_provider*, or *object.database_services*.

SilkRoad 175

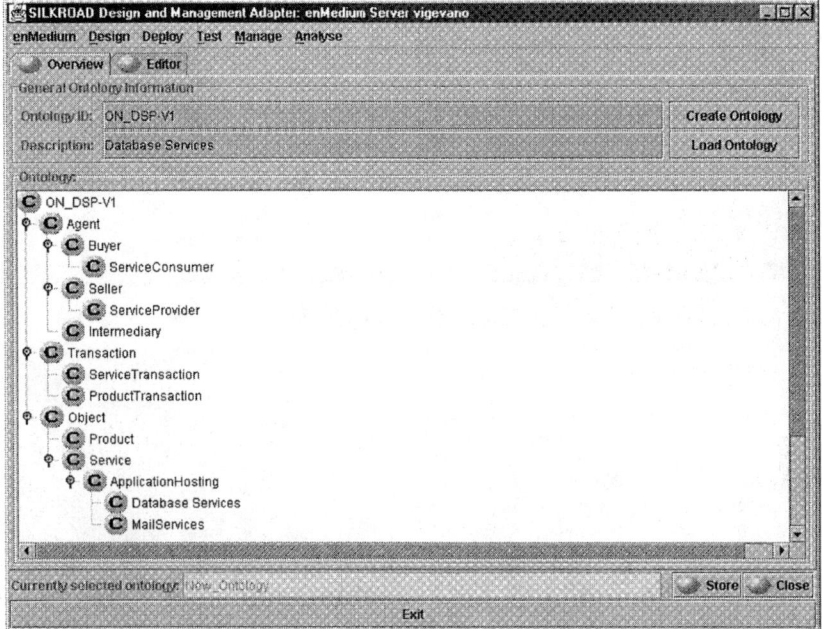

Figure 53. Ontology design with SILKROAD

2.3.2 Deployment

Once an enScenario model has been successfully validated and saved, run-time specifications for this enScenario model can be generated. Within the generation and customisation process the *DesignManager* class creates a state- and ontology-dependent offer schema for every offer state and for every offer type, and then stores the generated XML schemata in the *XSR_RUNTIME_SCHEMATA* table. If the generation process terminates without errors, the enScenario developer can deploy the generated run-time specifications to remote enMedium servers by using a simple FTP upload functionality.

The success of the deployment operation is dependent on an initial verification of the target enMedium server NSC configuration. The deployment process has to check whether all NSCs used in the enScenario model are available on the target enMedium server, because the functional component distribution defined in the architecture model (see *Figure 43*) supports enMedium servers that host only selected NSC plug-ins. If all NSCs required by the enScenario model are available, the upload process is initiated.

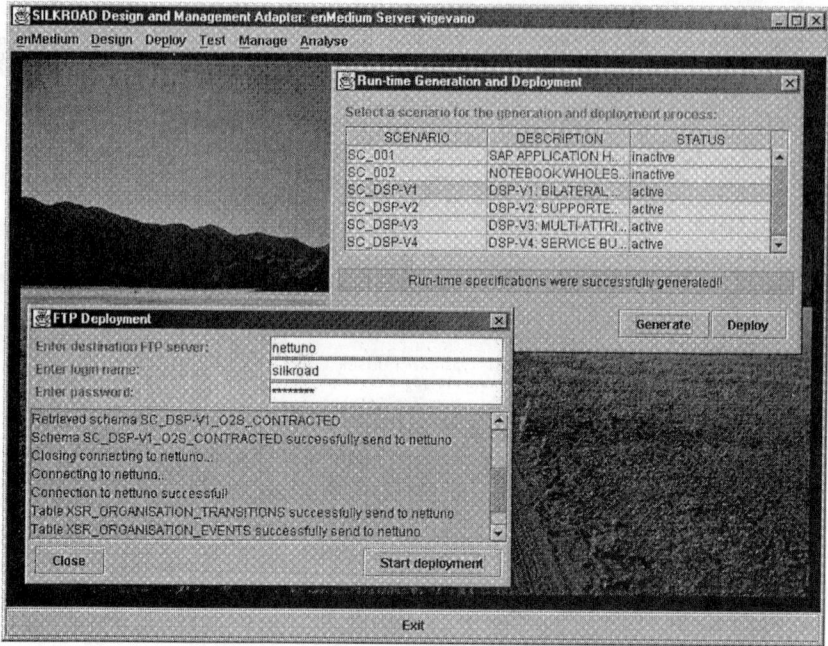

Figure 54. Generation and deployment of run-time specifications

The FTP upload is illustrated in *Figure 54*, where specifications for the enScenario model *SC_DSP_V1* are generated and deployed to a server with the name *nettuno*. The tables for the organisation design, e.g. *XSR_OR-GANISATION_TRANSITIONS*, are converted into delimited ASCII files and also transferred to the enMedium server, where the file statements can be imported into the run-time repository.

Schemata such as *SC_DSP_V1_O2S_CONTRACTED* are transferred as XML schema files to a standard *silkschema* directory on the enMedium server. Successfully deployed XML schemata can then be accessed, for reasons such as the validation of offer instances, with standardised URLs pointing to the deployment directory, as illustrated in the example in *Figure 55* (next page) for the *nettuno* server (see Section 5.4.1 for details regarding the XML specification).

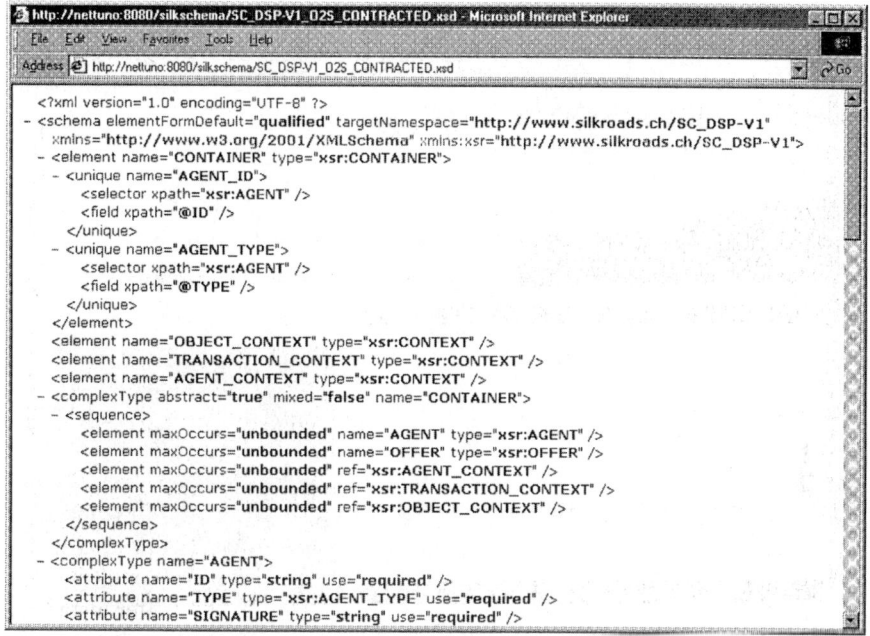

Figure 55. Retrieval of generated XML schemata

2.4 Run-time processing

The main task of a SILKROAD enMedium server at run-time is to receive offers, to interpret events for offers in order to execute the associated actions (if appropriate), and to manage the state of concurrent enProcesses by updating offer states. The run-time data for offers is stored in the *XSR_OFFER_INSTANCES* and *XSR_MEDIUM_CURRENT_STATE* tables in the offer and medium repository. Because active offer instances in an enProcess might be overwritten, all new or modified offer instances are always logged to the *XSR_OFFER_HISTORY* table in order to keep a trace or audit trail.

At run-time, an offer always has a unique **offer root** and a derived unique **offer ID**. An **offer session** is defined as a thread of offer instances associated with one offer root. The offer root for new offer sessions is derived from new offers, which are not related (e.g. as a counteroffer) to any other active offer in the enInstance. Consecutive offer instances in this offer session (enProcess thread) may represent different states of the offer root or a specific configuration of the original offer for another offer/agent (an example is given in Section 7.2.1.4). During the enProcess, new offer instances in this session might be created by the originator of the root offer, other agents, or

NSC operations (c.f. Section 5.3.2.3). These offer session instances can exist concurrently in the enProcess.

The syntax of an offer ID can be specified in EBNF as an extension to Definition 1 and Definition 2 in Chapter 5 as follows:

Definition 1. Offer ID

```
<Letter> ::=
    "A"|"B"|"C"|...|"Z";
<ID> ::=
    [{<Letter>}"_"]{<Number>}[<Letter>];
<OfferRoot>
    "OF_"<ID>
<AgentID> ::=
    "AG_"<ID>;
<OfferID> ::=
    <OfferRoot><Relation><OfferState><Relation>(<OfferID>|<AgentID>);
```

According to this definition an offer ID consists of the following elements: offer root, offer state, and offer identity extension. Let us assume an initial offer has the ID *OF_X_001.ADVERTISED*. The corresponding offer root and name of the offer session is *OF_X_001*. Consecutive offer instances in this enProcess thread might be *OF_X_001.ADVERTISED.AG_A* (agent extension) and *OF_X_001.MATCHED.OF_Y_007* (offer extension). An offer session can be terminated if one or more offer instances reach a successful terminal state (e.g. *OF_X_001.CONTRACTED*), or if all instances in the session are retracted by the execution manager (e.g. in case of a timeout) to a terminal state. In this case the execution manager will, depending on the design specification, either archive the offer instance or delete them from the offer repository and purges the entry from the *XSR_MEDIUM_CURRENT_STATE* table.

The agent adapter dynamically generates an interface for manipulating current or creating new offer instances through a Web browser. All agent actions require a prior login. The provided ID and password are used to authenticate the agent and to retrieve the group membership defined for this agent in the enMedium server. On the basis of group memberships, the execution manager searches for active enInstances in which at least one of the agent's groups is authorised to raise an *AGENT.OFFER* event in the technical *O2X.START* state. If one or more such transitions can be found, *SilkRoadLogin.jsp* will display these options as illustrated in the example in *Figure 56*[18] (next page).

---

[18] The user interface in this example already refers to the *yourhost.ch* scenario presented in Section 7.2.

SilkRoad 179

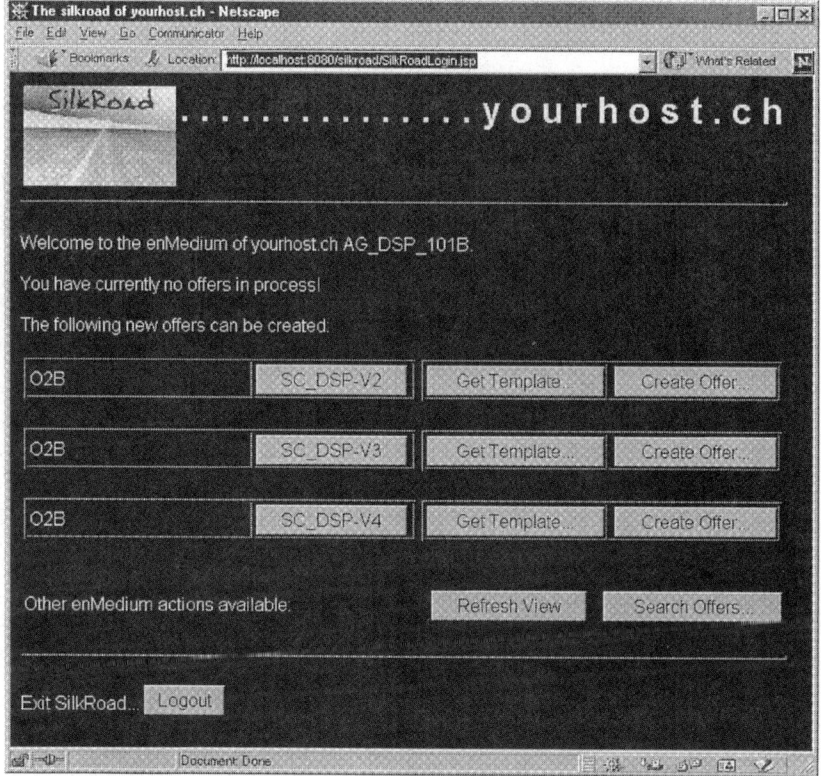

Figure 56. SilkRoadLogin.jsp run-time example

Clicking on the name of the enScenario ID in this JSP (e.g. the *SC_DSP_V2* button) leads to *SilkGetScenario.jsp*, which displays a brief summary of the enScenario design specification. If an agent is interested in creating an offer for this enInstance, SILKROAD can, through *SilkGetTemplate.jsp* provide an offer template (from the *XSR_RUNTIME_TEMPLATES* table), which is compliant with the first state structure defined in this enScenario (e.g. *O2B.ADVERTISED*) and already customised for this agent. To do this, the *OfferManipulator* class inserts, for example, the ID and type of the agent. This template (see the example in *Figure 57*) can be modified remotely in order to edit, for instance, constraints or evaluation criteria. At any time, the agent may check this new offer instance for compatibility with the offer state structure and ontology context specified in the enScenario design model by running a validating parser on the XML document. This parser can access the deployed state- and ontology-dependent XML schema through the *xsi:schemaLocation* URL pointing to the SILKROAD enMedium Web server (see Section 6.2.1).

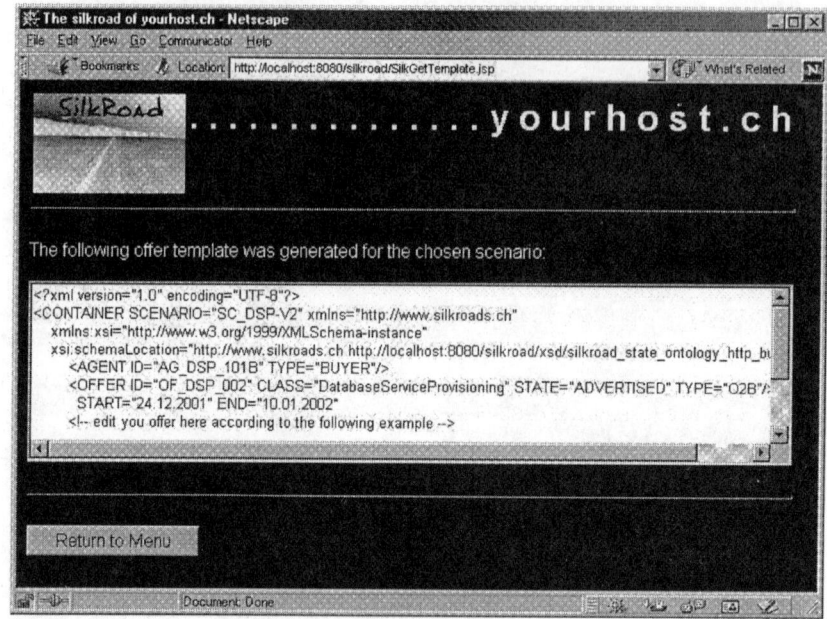

Figure 57. SilkGetTemplate.jsp run-time example

Once the specification of the offer instance is complete, the agent can submit this offer by clicking on 'Create Offer...' in the interface shown in *Figure 56*. *SilkSetOffer.jsp* then uploads the offer file via the *SilkJSPBean* class to the SILKROAD enMedium server. The subsequent event processing performed by the execution manager can be illustrated with a sample extract from an enMedium server log.

```
1535969 INFO    SilkJSPBeanListener - action = SET_OFFER
1535969 INFO    SilkJSPBeanListener - created event:
 [AG_DSP_101B AG_DSP_101B.OFFER_OF_DSP_002.START null null]
1535979 DEBUG   AgentManager - setOffer()...
1535979 DEBUG   ExecutionManager  - setOffer()...
1536239 INFO    OfferManager - Offer validation successful!
1536700 DEBUG   OfferManager - setOffer()...
1537341 DEBUG   ExecutionManager - raiseEvent()
1537511 DEBUG   ExecutionManager - event type = BUYER.OFFER
1537521 DEBUG   ExecutionManager - checkAuthorisation()...
```

SilkRoad

```
1537521 DEBUG ExecutionManager - SQL statement:
 select AGENT_GROUP from XSR_INTEGRATION_EVENTS where SCENARIO =
 'SC_DSP-V2' and OFFER_TYPE = 'O2B' and OFFER_STATE = 'START' and
 EVENT = 'BUYER.OFFER'
1537561 DEBUG ExecutionManager - SQL statement:
 select GROUP_ID from XSR_MEDIUM_GROUPS_AGENTS where AGENT_ID =
 'AG_DSP_101B'
1537591 INFO  ExecutionManager - Agent is authorised!
1537591 DEBUG ExecutionManager - getNextState()...
1537601 DEBUG ExecutionManager - SQL statement:
 select  GUARD,OFFER_STATE_NEW  from  XSR_ORGANISATION_TRANSITIONS
 where SCENARIO = 'SC_DSP-V2' and OFFER_STATE_OLD = 'START' and
 OFFER_TYPE = 'O2B' and EVENT = 'BUYER.OFFER'
1537631 DEBUG ExecutionManager - evaluateGuard()...
1537637 INFO  ExecutionManager - Guard evaluation is successful!
1537638 DEBUG ExecutionManager - invokeAction()...
1537641 DEBUG ExecutionManager - SQL statement:
 select ACTION,PROPERTIES from XSR_ORGANISATION_TRANSITIONS where
 SCENARIO = 'SC_DSP-V2' and OFFER_STATE_OLD = 'START' and OFFER_
 TYPE = 'O2B' and EVENT = 'BUYER.OFFER' and GUARD = ''
1537691 DEBUG ExecutionManager - got: {MANAGER.OFFER={TARGET=NULL}}
1537701 INFO  ExecutionManager - next state = ADVERTISED
1537701 INFO  ExecutionManager - next action = MANAGER.OFFER
1537701 DEBUG ExecutionManager - executeAction()...
1537712 INFO  ExecutionManager - new state = OF_XYZ.ADVERTISED
1538493 DEBUG ExecutionManager - SQL statement:
 update XSR_MEDIUM_CURRENT_STATE set OFFER_ID =
 'OF_DSP_002.ADVERTISED' where OFFER_ID = 'OF_DSP_002.START'
1538513 DEBUG ExecutionManager - SQL statement:
 insert into XSR_MEDIUM_HISTORY values('SC_DSP-V2','OF_DSP_002',
 'AG_DSP_101B','[AG_DSP_101B MANAGER.OFFER OF_DSP_002.START null
 {TARGET=NULL}]','MANAGER.OFFER','OF_DSP_002.ADVERTISED','2001-10-
 10 08:07:27.634')
1538613 INFO  ExecutionManager - raiseEvent() completed!
```

In this example the *SilkJSPBeanListener*, detects a change in the *SilkJSP Bean*, forwards the new offer to the agent manager, and creates an *AG_DSP_101B.OFFER* event for the technical offer state *OF_DSP_002. START*. After receiving the event, the agent manager first passes the offer to the execution manager helper classes (offer manager) where the offer is validated against its schema and stored in the offer repository (lines marked in milliseconds 1535969 to 1536700). Then the agent manager raises the new event for the execution manager. The execution manager transforms this event into a generic *BUYER.OFFER* event and checks whether the agent is authorised to raise this event (milliseconds 1537341 to 1537591). If this is the case, the FSM specification for this enScenario is retrieved through the *getNextState()* method in order to determine a valid transition (milliseconds 1537591 to 1537637). The execution manager also invokes the action for a valid transition, *MANAGER.OFFER*, and in this case also performs the action because it is not an NSC operation (milliseconds 1537638 to 1537701). Finally, the new offer state after the transition, *OF_DSP_002.AD-VERTISED*, is determined and reflected in the medium repository (milliseconds 1537712 to 1538613).

Once an offer is submitted and active in the enProcess, it will appear in the **offer in-tray** of the originating agent (c.f. *Figure 70*). In the case that the offer is created as a response (counteroffer) to an existing offer instance, it will also be added to the in-tray of the counterpart. For offers in the in-tray the agent has, in principle, two options:
- to raise new events for this offer instance (e.g. to initiate a MatchNSC operation),
- to wait for other agents to raise an event for this offer (e.g. by scoring or matching it).

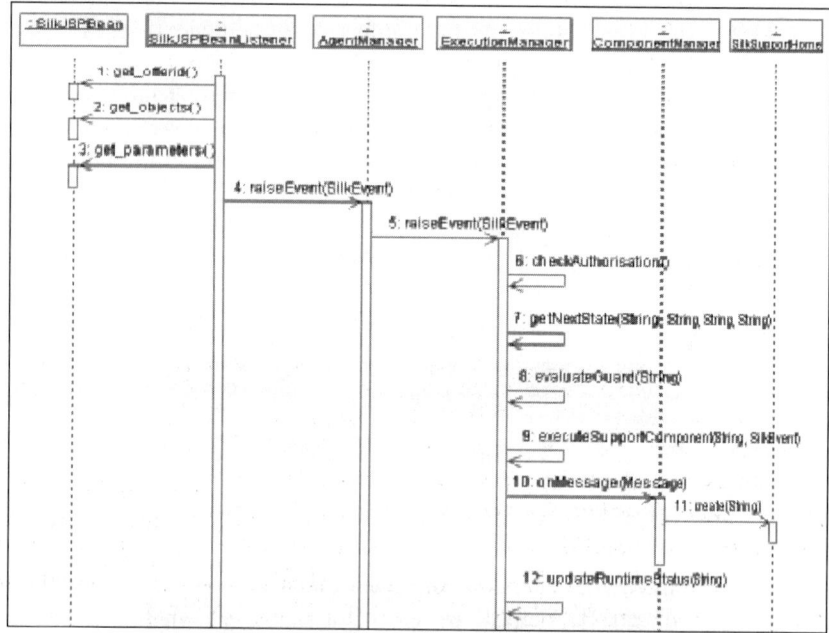

Figure 58. Run-time processing UML sequence diagram

Summary

In the second case, new offer instances for this offer root (such as *OF_DSP_002.MATCHED.OF_DSP_007*) might appear in the offer in-tray in *SilkRoadLogin.jsp*. In addition, an agent always has the option to search for offers from other agents and to raise events for these offers (e.g. to counteroffer). More extensive examples of the run-time behaviour functionality of the SILKROAD prototype are illustrated in the enScenario cases in Section 7.2.

Standard event processing without offer submission is executed in a similar way. This is illustrated for the example of an NSC invocation in the UML sequence diagram in *Figure 58* (previous page). The sequence of actions follows the run-time processing use case defined in Section 6.1.4. The execution manager method *executeSupportComponent()* is called, which sends a message object to the component manager bean, where subsequently the NSC is created using the *SilkSupportHome* interface (c.f. *Figure 47*).

3. SUMMARY

This chapter proposed an architecture model for enMedia that comprised both a structure definition with loosely coupled architecture components and a behaviour definition for the run-time processing based on use cases.

This architecture model strives for high flexibility and reusability through an incorporation of application framework techniques. Referring back to the sequential decision-making model (see *Figure 20*), an enMedium system compliant with the proposed architecture model, can, from an agent's perspective, provide decision-making support (through NSC operations) and communication support (through the intermediation and control of agent interactions).

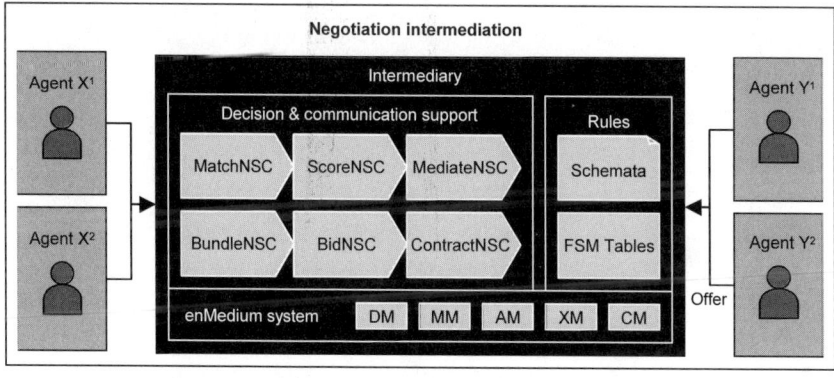

Figure 59. Complete enMedia framework negotiation intermediation

This architecture model complements the core proposition of this book, the enMedia framework for symmetric multi-attribute negotiation intermediation in electronic markets, as illustrated in *Figure 59* (previous page).

Furthermore, this chapter presents an implementation of the enMedia architecture model – the SILKROAD enMedia framework prototype – which also provides support for the design approach of the enMedia framework. The goal for the development of this prototype was to study the problems related to electronic negotiation architecture flexibility (e.g. the inherent tradeoffs) as well as the usability of the proposed design methodology, because through its tool support, SILKROAD facilitates the application of the design approach to a large number of cases.

The prototype implementation represents a proof of concept and first verification for the solution approaches suggested in this book to address the current problems in the domain of electronic negotiations. The SILKROAD enMedia framework prototype demonstrates that an electronic negotiation architecture can be flexible and adaptable in such a way that a broad variety of enScenarios, with potentially new or unknown sets of rules, can be supported in a standardised and generic manner by enMedium systems compliant with the architecture model. The prototype also illustrates how the support functionality provided by the enMedium system is defined solely through the enScenario model, and how corresponding run-time enProcesses incorporate the intended decision-making and communication support.

A more extensive discussion of the suggested architecture model is available in Section 8.2.3. The proof of concept achieved through SILKROAD will be further extended in the next chapter, where the propositions of this book are applied to realistic enScenario cases on the basis of the prototype tools.

Chapter 7
Application
The case of yourhost.ch

This chapter serves two major purposes. First of all it outlines general usage domains for the enMedia framework that has been presented in this book. The second purpose is to demonstrate in detail the application of the enMedia framework and its prototype implementation, SILKROAD, through a sequence of electronic negotiation scenario cases. In these cases, specific emphasis is set on an extensive application of the design approach conceptualised in Chapter 5.

On the basis of this chapter, the reader should be enabled to discuss a new enScenario or to analyse an existing one, to decide whether employing the enMedia framework could be beneficial, and, if this is the case, to design and implement the enScenario, using, for instance, the SILKROAD framework prototype.

1. POTENTIAL USAGE

The proposition of this book are three core elements for the development of symmetric multi-attribute negotiation intermediation systems: electronic negotiation support components, a design approach, and an architecture model. These elements are integrated into one design and implementation framework, the enMedia framework.

The primary question regarding the potential usage is whether the enMedia framework is targeted at specific business domains or at specific types of scenarios as opposed to being generally applicable. This is not the intention. The requirements for the conceptualisation of the framework are derived and generalised from abstract enScenario cases. Whereas most NSS are focused on specific types of scenarios (bilateral or multilateral, single-attribute or multi-attribute) and developed on a case-by-case basis [Hols+91], the presented framework is not designed to have such inherent limitations, since flexibility was one of the primary requirements driving its design. On the basis of the examples presented in this chapter, the reader may decide whether or not the price for this flexibility is tediousness. In practice it might also turn out that some business domains or scenario types are more suited for the application of the enMedia framework, whereas others may be more difficult to represent.

Without an extensive practical evaluation, guidelines for the usage can only be very generic. Explicit assumptions underlying the enMedia framework are discussed in Section 8.1. Considering especially the necessary steps to design and implement an enScenario, the most general usage guideline is that the more often an enScenario is instantiated and corresponding enProcesses are executed successfully, the easier it is to achieve amortisation and to justify the design and implementation effort.

In the following sections, general usage domains for the enMedia framework in the context of electronic markets are outlined.

1.1 Online buying/selling

One potential usage domain for the enMedia framework is to assist eCommerce buying or selling activities. A seller, for instance, might offer potential buyers the opportunity to negotiate the attributes of non-standard or high-value transactions (e.g. special imports) on the basis of an enMedium system. This enMedium can feature an enScenario that utilises the BundleNSC to support buyers in accumulating demand, and the MediateNSC to suggest fair agreements if the initial offers of the buyer coalition and the seller do not match. Through the use of the MediateNSC the seller may avoid long haggling processes.

In another example, a buyer could use the BidNSC to execute a multi-attribute procurement scenario and the ScoreNSC to evaluate incoming bids. The advantages for either buyer or seller to use the enMedium for the execution of enProcesses are, in principle, outlined in Section 1.1.3, e.g. the avoidance of price comparisons or the increased number of potential negotiation partners.

1.2 Electronic market intermediation

An intermediary hosting an EM can apply the suggested NSCs to extend the market support to transaction types and objects that are not suited for simple enScenarios but require the execution of several interdependent decision-making and communication tasks, such as the resolution of configuration options or the coordination of bundling efforts. Successful enScenarios have the potential to increase the EM trading volume if, for instance, the design chosen fosters win-win solutions for buyers and sellers. With regard to the trading volume, the architecture model bears various possibilities for revenue collection. For instance, the intermediary could charge per 'offer in process', per NSC execution, or per generated contract.

The intermediary might also benefit especially from the usage of the design approach, as it supports the discussion of scenarios with the participants and stakeholders of the EM on a conceptual level. "The parameters of a negotiation process are themselves negotiable" [KeNo99, p.11], and the transparency of both the enProcess as well as the functionality of the support mechanisms is critical to attain the trust of the EM participants (c.f. [HoLo98]). If a meta-level agreement among the stakeholders on the critical issues of 'what is subject to the negotiation' and 'how the negotiation is organised' is reached, the enMedia development process allows the design decisions to be directly used in the implementation of the enScenario. Furthermore, the flexibility of the enScenario design and of the underlying architecture model should enable the intermediary to develop incrementally efficient models that are very specific to the business context.

1.3 Dynamic outsourcing

A virtual organisation demands dynamic, loosely-coupled relationships with business partners on a short-term basis. Virtual organisations transfer the performance of non-strategic services, usually handled by internal resources, to external providers. The final state of the traditional outsourcing process is an outsourcing relationship (usually formalised in a contract) with one consumer and one provider organisation. In contrast to this, dynamic outsourcing is an ongoing process that involves a set of provider organisations competing in an EM [Strö00d]. At the moment of the service request, the consumer organisation chooses one provider among the open set of providers (which providers can dynamically join) to perform the service.

Next to a standardisation of outsourcing services, speed and low costs of coordination are critical factors for achieving this flexibility. For instance, a logistics provider could, using the enMedia framework, set up an enMedium system with an enScenario that incorporates the BidNSC and an offer context ontology for insurance providers. A corresponding enInstance is created every time the provider needs to find insurance for a specific load. Using the enMedium, the logistics provider can, in principle, always buy the current best insurance offer on the market, avoiding long-term contracts, which might over time become inefficient due to changing market competition or capacity. For other domains of dynamic business relationships (e.g. subcontractors for airfreight), the logistics provider may use different enScenario models hosted by the same enMedium. An additional advantage of reusing an existing enScenario is that the logistics provider, on the basis of the experience gained from enProcesses in the past, is able to fine-tune the parameters of the enScenario (e.g. the preferences structure used, the initial offer structure, or the time constraints).

1.4 Negotiation service provisioning

Let us assume a negotiation service provider (NSP) offers outsourcing of eCommerce negotiation processes. Instead of implementing enScenarios themselves and running these in proprietary negotiation systems, buyers, sellers, or intermediaries can support the agreement phase of their electronic transactions by using the services of the NSP. The NSP may support its customers already in the design phase of electronic negotiations, but the functional distribution capabilities of the enMedia architecture model also allow parties to create their enScenario design models locally and to deploy only the generated run-time specifications to enMedium servers run by the NSP. With additional means of encryption for the run-time specifications, the 'local design approach' might be suitable, for instance, in cases where the enScenario design is confidential.

To enable a profitable NSP operation, a standardisation of the services provided and low setup/customisation costs are necessary. Whereas the enMedia framework design approach with its run-time specification generation process could lead to low setup costs, the reusability and modularity of the NSC and architecture components contributes also to the standardisation of NSP services. In addition, the NSP can run a multitude of enScenarios on the basis of one enMedium server, thus benefiting from economies of scale (e.g. regarding maintenance efforts).

But the business model of an NSP can benefit in yet another way from the application of the enMedia framework. Running a large number of enProcesses may allow the derivation of an enScenario reference model (c.f. Section 8.3.2.2) that features best-practice communication and organisation designs, which can be used to recommend enScenario design models for specific business contexts.

2. SCENARIO CASES

After the introduction of potential usage domains in the previous section, this section demonstrates the application of the enMedia framework to more detailed cases – real negotiation scenarios, which are modelled and imple-

Scenario cases 189

mented with the methodology, tools, and techniques presented in this book. One real world application domain, *database service provisioning*, is used throughout the cases. The complexity of the cases is increasing. The first example illustrates a simple bilateral enScenario based on iterative offer exchange with no NSC involvement, i.e. only communication support. The second case adds intermediating NSC operations to support the enProcess. Multilateral negotiations on the basis of advanced organisation design techniques are the focus of the third example. Finally, bundling in negotiations for heterogeneous objects is introduced in the fourth case.

The presented enScenarios do not aim for completeness. The goal of this section is to demonstrate by example the usage of NSCs, the potential dimensions of communication and organisation design, and the capabilities of the suggested architecture model[19]. Step by step, from case to case, all of the different elements of the design approach are applied. The cases also demonstrate the typical flow of tasks defined by the enMedia development action-model (see Section 5.1).

For the following cases, let us assume *yourhost.ch* is an intermediary running an electronic market for application service provisioning (ASP). *Yourhost.ch* wants to add an additional market segment for *database service provisioning* (DSP). Sellers in this segment offer to host databases for buyers and to provide them with means to access the databases with various levels of service quality. The EM created by *yourhost.ch* is an implementation of the enMedia architecture model, namely a SILKROAD installation, and therefore constitutes an enMedium. This enMedium system is distributed to one design-time and one run-time support server (see Section 6.1.3). *Yourhost.ch* employs enScenario analysts, designers, developers, and enMedium administrators, who use the approach of the enMedia framework and the tools provided by SILKROAD to create new, or to adapt and extend existing, enScenarios[20].

---

[19] For the design of the scenario cases, the NSC candidates (BundleNSC, BidNSC, and ContractNSC) are used, although the interfaces and solution procedures are not fully specified in this book. However, the SILKROAD framework prototype provides sample implementations (shells) for these NSCs in order to simulate a complete enMedium server.

[20] The figures/tables complementing the following enScenario case demonstrations are all screenshots from the SILKROAD prototype, and therefore not always complete; for instance, owing to space restrictions they show some column values only in abbreviations. If specific design elements are discussed in the cases, the corresponding specifications are highlighted in the figures or tables by a black frame.

2.1 Bilateral offer exchange: DSP-V1 case

To start its business in the DSP segment, yourhost.ch asks those current market participants (e.g. Internet service providers) who also offer DSP to participate in a trial enInstance. The associated enScenario, code-named DSP-V1, simply models the traditional way of negotiating through an iterative and bilateral exchange of offers and counteroffers. The initial benefit yourhost.ch can propose to its customers is, that using this enInstance, this exchange is faster, much more structured than with traditional (e.g. letters) or non-structured (e.g. emails) means of offer exchange, and also more secure if encryption is used.

2.1.1 Communication design

The first design task in the development action-model is the definition of an offer context ontology. As *yourhost.ch* already runs enInstances for other application-hosting segments, the main concepts needed for the *DSP* offer context ontology are already defined in an offer context ontology for related enScenarios: *ServiceProvider* and *ServiceConsumer* in the agent context, *ApplicationHosting* in the object context, and *ServiceTransaction* in the transaction context. For the *DSP* scenario an additional *DatabaseServices* concept is included in the object context. An extract of concepts from the *DSP-V1* ontology model is shown in *Figure 60*.

Figure 60. DSP offer context ontology

The attributes of the lowest-level concepts of the *yourhost.ch DSP-V1* offer context ontology are listed in *Table 13* ('inh.' stands for 'inherited', meaning that this attribute is defined for one of the super-concepts in the hierarchy). It can be seen that most attributes for the selected concepts are inherited from super-concepts. It is necessary though, to define some attributes specific to the *DSP* domain, such as the *database_space* or the *interface_type*. The *interface_type* attribute demonstrates how the value domain can be constrained in order to control the types of offers, as well as the associated offer language that will be accepted when the enScenario is instantiated. If, for instance, *yourhost.ch* prefers to deal with offers specifying multiple database interface types, an alternative definition of the *interface_type* value domain (slot-constraint) may use the notion of min- and max-cardinality (c.f. [Fens+00]).

Table 13. Attributes in the *DSP* offer context ontology

Concept	Attribute	Constraint
DatabaseServices	software_manufacturer(inh.)	one_of(IBM, Microsoft, Oracle)
	software_version(inh.)	string
	mean_availability(inh.)	range integer in %
	backup_frequency(inh.)	range time
	recovery_time(inh.)	time
	database_space	range integer in GB
	interface_type	one_of(JDBC, ODBC, SQLNet)
ServiceProvider	location(inh.)	string
	turnaround(inh.)	int in CHF
	reputation(inh.)	one_of(High, Medium, Low)
	support_type	one_of(OnSite, Online, CallCenter)
ServiceTransaction	price(inh.)	range float in CHF
	execution_date(inh.)	time
	payment_mode	one_of(PerTime, PerUsage)
	penalty	string
	duration	range time
	expiration	range time

Following the development action-model, the next step for the enScenario designers of *yourhost.ch* is to define the offer states for the offer types in the enScenario model. The result of this task is shown in *Figure 61* for the O2S type.

OFFER_STATE	DOMAINS	CONSTRAINTS	COUNTERS	CRITERIA	SIGNATURES	TIMESTAMPS
ADVERTISED	Ranges	Basic	None	None	Single	Both
COUNTERED	Ranges	Basic	Unbound	None	Single	End
CONTRACTED	Values	Basic	None	None	All	None

Figure 61. O2S states in DSP-V1

The *O2S.ADVERTISED* state design requires the originator of the offer, the seller, to provide a signature for the offer, so that a buyer can simply accept it in order create a binding contract. The *O2S.COUNTERED* definition is slightly different. It requires only an *End* timestamp to define when the counteroffer expires, and it allows an unbound number of counters. A buyer might want to make a counteroffer with different value domains for attributes such as *transaction.price*, *object.database_space*, and *agent.support_type*. The *O2S.CONTRACTED* state is defined through additional changes in the offer structure: signatures of the seller and the buyer are now required for the offer, no timestamps for the validity period can be defined, the offer attribute value domains have to be narrowed to singe values, and no counter constraints are allowed since this offer is agreed upon by both sides.

The sequence and structure of the states already indicates the intended enProcess. The protocol for this enProcess has to be defined in the complementary organisation design.

2.1.2 Organisation Design

The states defined in the communication design are used in the specification of the offer state transitions. The FSM for this enScenario model is similar to the organisation design example presented in the state chart in *Figure 36*. The detailed definition of the transitions for the O2S type is illustrated in *Figure 62*.

STATE_OLD	EVENT	ACTION	PROPERTIES	STATE_NEW
START	SELLER.OFFER	MANAGER.OFFER	(TARGET=NULL)	ADVERTISED
ADVERTISED	BUYER.ACCEPT	MANAGER.ACCEPT	(TARGET=NULL,SIGNATURE=*)	CONTRACTED
ADVERTISED	BUYER.OFFER	MANAGER.OFFER	(TARGET=NULL)	COUNTERED
ADVERTISED	BUYER.TIMEOUT			END
COUNTERED	SELLER.ACCEPT	MANAGER.ACCEPT	(TARGET=NULL,SIGNATURE=*)	CONTRACTED
COUNTERED	SELLER.OFFER	MANAGER.OFFER	(TARGET=NULL)	ADVERTISED
COUNTERED	SELLER.RETRACT	MANAGER.RETRACT	(TARGET=NULL,ARCHIVE=FALSE)	END
COUNTERED	SELLER.TIMEOUT			END

Figure 62. O2S transitions in DSP-V1[21]

The first event a seller can raise is *SELLER.OFFER*, which invokes the action *MANAGER.OFFER* with no specific target object, as well as a transition to the state *O2S.ADVERTISED*. In this state, any authorised buyer can either accept the offer or counter the offer by submitting a modified O2S instance. For the *MANAGER.ACCEPT* action, the value of the additional

---

[21] Guards are not specified for *DSP-V1* and therefore the column is omitted in the table. The TARGET property is also not used in this enScenario model and so is set to 'NULL' for all actions.

Scenario cases 193

SIGNATURE property has to be provided by the buyer at run-time (indicated by a '*' value, see also Section 5.3.2.1). If no event is raised by a buyer for this offer instance by the time the expiration timestamp is reached, the execution manager raises a *BUYER.TIMEOUT* event and the offer moves to the technical *O2S.END* state. If the offer is countered, the seller has three options: to accept the counteroffer, to advertise a modified offer, or to retract the offer. If the seller chooses to modify the *O2S.COUNTERED* instance, the countered constraints are internally rendered back into 'standard' constraints, because they are defined by the original author of the offer. In the case of *SELLER.RETRACT*, the *ARCHIVE* property has already been set at design-time to 'false' – at run-time this cannot be changed. Again, the counteroffer automatically shifts to the state *O2S.END* if the seller does not invoke any action for this offer instance within the period of counteroffer validity.

The number of state transitions in actual enProcesses is not bounded by enScenario rules. The enProcess will proceed until one agent accepts an offer, the seller retracts the offer, or the offer expires (an example offer session and thread is demonstrated in the run-time section of this case). Double-sided contracting is used in this example. Through the *MANAGER.ACCEPT* action, a signature from the buyer is added to an O2S instance, which already features a signature of the seller, thus resulting in an *O2S.CONTRACTED* offer instance with both signatures.

Following a recommendation of the analysis phase, the enScenario designers choose an asymmetric scenario. It is always the seller who initiates an enProcess by advertising an offer, whereas buyers can only react to these advertisements through counteroffers. In a fully symmetric scenario, the enScenario designers would simply mirror the complete state and transition definition for the O2B and exchange the agents raising the events (the event causing a transition from *O2B.START* to *O2B.ADVERTISED* would be *BUYER.OFFER*).

2.1.3 Integration Design

The first step in the integration design is the offer context assignment, which in this case comprises two concepts for the agent context, *ServiceConsumer* and *ServiceProvider*, complemented by the *ServiceTransaction* and *DatabaseServices* concepts.

The next task for the enScenario designers is to authorise agent groups to raise events in the FSM. Two design groups are defined, *GR_DSP_B* for the buyers, and *GR_DSP_S* for the sellers. Furthermore, the technical *GR_SYSTEM* group needs to be integrated because *TIMEOUT* events are not raised by the agents, but rather created automatically by the execution manager, which also requires a corresponding authorisation. In this enScenario, the assignment of agent groups to events is trivial (see *Figure 63*).

OFFER_STATE	EVENT	AGENT_GROUP
START	SELLER.OFFER	GR_DSP_S
ADVERTISED	BUYER.ACCEPT	GR_DSP_B
ADVERTISED	BUYER.OFFER	GR_DSP_B
ADVERTISED	BUYER.TIMEOUT	GR_SYSTEM
COUNTERED	SELLER.OFFER	GR_DSP_S

Figure 63. Event authorisation in DSP-V1

The same is true for the view authorisation specification in the integration design. Both groups are authorised to view all offer elements of advertised opposing offers. Access to counteroffers is restricted, though, to the seller originating the initial offer.

Before the run-time specifications can be generated, the enScenario model resulting from the integration design needs to be validated. The SILKROAD framework prototype can support this check for completeness and consistency with an automated procedure that tests the model with the conditions specified in *Table 11*. The enScenario design model presented in this case does not violate any of the test conditions, and thus the run-time specifications can be generated on the *yourhost.ch* design-time support server and exported to the *yourhost.ch* run-time support server.

2.1.4 Run-time behaviour

After the generation of the run-time specifications for the *DSP-V1* enScenario model, the administrators of the *yourhost.ch* run-time support server can activate the new *DSP-V1* instance. If after this activation an agent *AG_DSP_101S*, who may belong to the run-time group corresponding to *GR_DSP_S*, logs in, the agent adapter of the enMedium server will provide this agent with the possibility to create an offer within the *DSP-V1* scenario.

Once a new offer, for example *OF_DSP_001*, is created, it will assume the state *OF_DSP_001.ADVERTISED*. In this state, the seller has no further actions available. Another agent, *AG_DSP_201B*, who may have the role of a buyer in *GR_DSP_B*, can now search for offers, select offer *OF_DSP_001.ADVERTISED*, and raise one of the events *BUYER.ACCEPT* or *BUYER.OFFER*, as shown in the agent adapter user interface in *Figure 64* (next page). The agent adapter dynamically generates a button for each possible event. Since buyer agents are not authorised to raise the *BUYER.TIMEOUT* event, it is not presented as one of the options in the agent interface. If the buyer chooses to counter, the new state of the offer is *OF_DSP_001.COUNTERED.AG_DSP_201B* (the extension meaning that this offer is

Scenario cases

countered by *AG_DSP_201B*). If the seller reacts with a counteroffer, the state becomes *OF_DSP_001.ADVERTISED.AG_DSP_201B*.

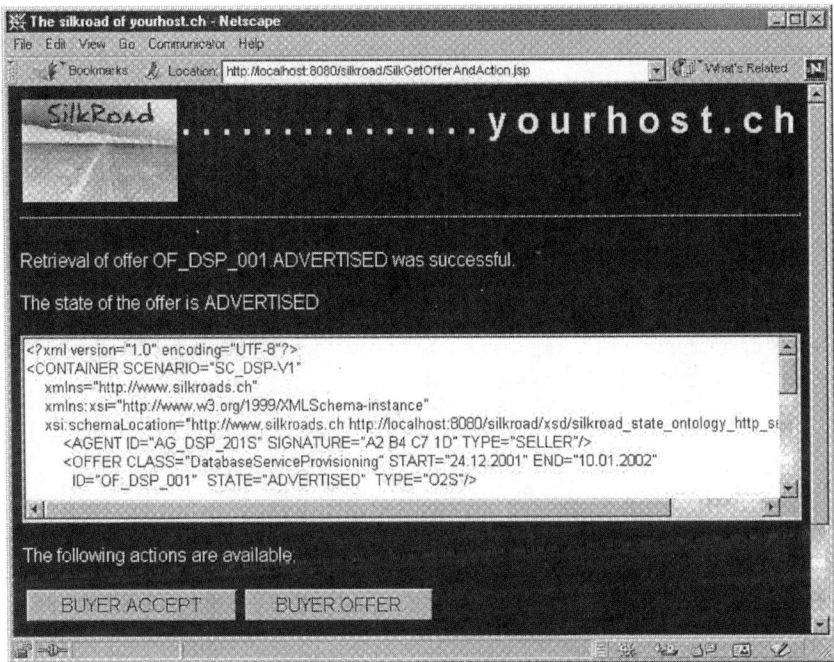

Figure 64. Prototype interface for buyer agents in DSP-V1

Finally, if one agent decides to accept the offer, the agent has to enter its signature and the transaction is completed. *Table 14* demonstrates a complete offer session (or enProcess thread) for one seller with two buyers and an example discussion on the transaction attributes *price* and *duration*.

Table 14. Offer session example

Offer ID	Originator	Constraint
OF_DSP_001.ADVERTISED	AG_DSP_101S	(Price,=,2000,CHF) (Duration,=,1,year)
OF_DSP_001.COUNTERED.AG_DSP_201B	AG_DSP_201B	(Price,=,**1600**,CHF) (Duration,=,1,year)
OF_DSP_001.COUNTERED.AG_DSP_301B	AG_DSP_301B	(Price,=,**1400**,CHF) (Duration,=,1,year)
OF_DSP_001A.ADVERTISED.AG_DSP_201B	AG_DSP_101S	(Price,=,**1800**,CHF) (Duration,=,**2**,year)
OF_DSP_001B.ADVERTISED.AG_DSP_201B	AG_DSP_101S	(Price,=,**1600**,CHF) (Duration,=,**3**,year)

Offer ID	Originator	Constraint
OF_DSP_001A.COUNTERED.AG_DSP_201B	AG_DSP_201B	(Price,=,**1700**,CHF) (Duration,=,2,year)
OF_DSP_001A.ADVERTISED.AG_DSP_201B	AG_DSP_101S	(Price,=,**1750**,CHF) (Duration,=,2,year)
OF_DSP_001A.CONTRACTED.AG_DSP_201B	AG_DSP_201B	(Price,=,1750,CHF) (Duration,=,2,year)

In this example the seller, *AG_DSP_101S*, receives two counteroffers. *AG_DSP_101S* ignores the counteroffer from *AG_DSP_301B* because the suggested price of *1400 CHF* is by far not in the original intention space. For the other counteroffer, *AG_DSP_101S* proposes logrolling on price and duration by creating two new offer instances (identified through an additional letter after the offer root ID) advertised to *AG_DSP_201B*. Again, the buyer counters one of these instances. The seller considers the price of *1700 CHF* in the counteroffer too low and replies with a slightly modified offer, thus overwriting the original instance of *OF_DSP_001A.ADVERTISED.AG_DSP_201B*. Note that the offer history is still logged by SILKROAD. Finally, the buyer decides to accept this counteroffer by signing *OF_DSP_001A.ADVERTISED.AG_DSP_201B*, and the enProcess thread is completed.

2.2 Supported offer exchange: DSP-V2 case

Yourhost.ch continues to analyse the market for service provisioning. It seems that owing to varying service quality, buyers typically assess several attributes of an offer (e.g. agent.support_type and transaction. payment_mode) within the enProcess in order to compare an offer with other competing offers. Furthermore, as the provider is location-independent and the service delivery requires only electronic interaction, the number of potential providers in the DSP scenario is already quite large and growing continuously. Regarding the enactment of the service provisioning, the enScenario analysts of yourhost.ch learn, that most service providers run highly configurable and scalable server farms. They agree that it might be feasible to automate the process of setting up the provisioning of a service to a large degree, if a standard electronic contract format were available that defined core parameters of the service functionality and quality.

As a result of this analysis, yourhost.ch identifies the MatchNSC, ScoreNSC, and ContractNSC as promising support components for the intermediation of DSP negotiation processes. Hence, a DSP-V2 scenario is developed, which, through automation support for several decision tasks, gives customers of yourhost.ch the potential to execute an enProcess much more efficiently than in DSP-V1.

Scenario cases 197

2.2.1 Communication Design

Assuming that the current users were satisfied with the expressiveness of the semantic offer language defined by the offer context concepts chosen in *DSP-V1*, no updates to the offer context ontology are necessary and it can be reused for *DSP-V2*. The main focus of the communication design activity for *DSP-V2* is the new offer state definitions necessary to support the application of NSCs.

Based on the symmetric version of *DSP-V1*, in which buyers can also submit offers, the extensions of *DSP-V2* consist of the following additional support and termination-states used for both the O2B and the O2S FSM specification: *MATCHING, MATCHED, SCORING, SCORED,* and *CONTRACTING*. SILKROAD provides templates for all these states (see *Figure 65*). The offer structure for *O2B.ADVERTISED* needs to be changed, as this state requires not only a signature from the buyer, but also a definition of evaluation criteria – in this case utility functions, which will be used for the ScoreNSC operation (see below). In addition, The *O2B.COUNTERED* state is further constrained to allow for only one counter constraint.

OFFER_STATE	DOMAINS	CONSTRAINTS	COUNTERS	CRITERIA	SIGNATURES	TIMESTAMPS
ADVERTISED	Ranges	Basic	None	Valued	Single	Both
COUNTERED	Ranges	Basic	1	Valued	Single	End
MATCHING	Ranges	Basic	None	Valued	Single	Both
MATCHED	Values	Matched	None	Valued	Single	Both
SCORING	Values	Matched	None	Valued	Single	Both
SCORED	Values	Matched	None	Scored	Single	Both
CONTRACTING	Values	Matched	None	None	Single	Both
CONTRACTED	Values	Basic	None	None	All	None

Figure 65. O2B states in DSP-V2

2.2.2 Organisation Design

The transitions for the O2B are shown in the offer state chart in *Figure 66* (next page) and the corresponding transitions table in *Figure 67*. After advertising an offer, the buyer can raise the *BUYER.MATCH* event, which causes a *SUPPORT.MATCH* action. This action corresponds to an operation of the MatchNSC. The target property of this action defines offers in the *O2S.ADVERTISED* state – O2S instances in this state will be matched with the O2B instance of the buyer. If the target specifies an offer of a different type (in this case O2S), an event synchronisation occurs – the transition raises an event in the O2S FSM (c.f. Section 5.3.2.2). The consecutive support-state for the O2B is *O2B.MATCHING*.

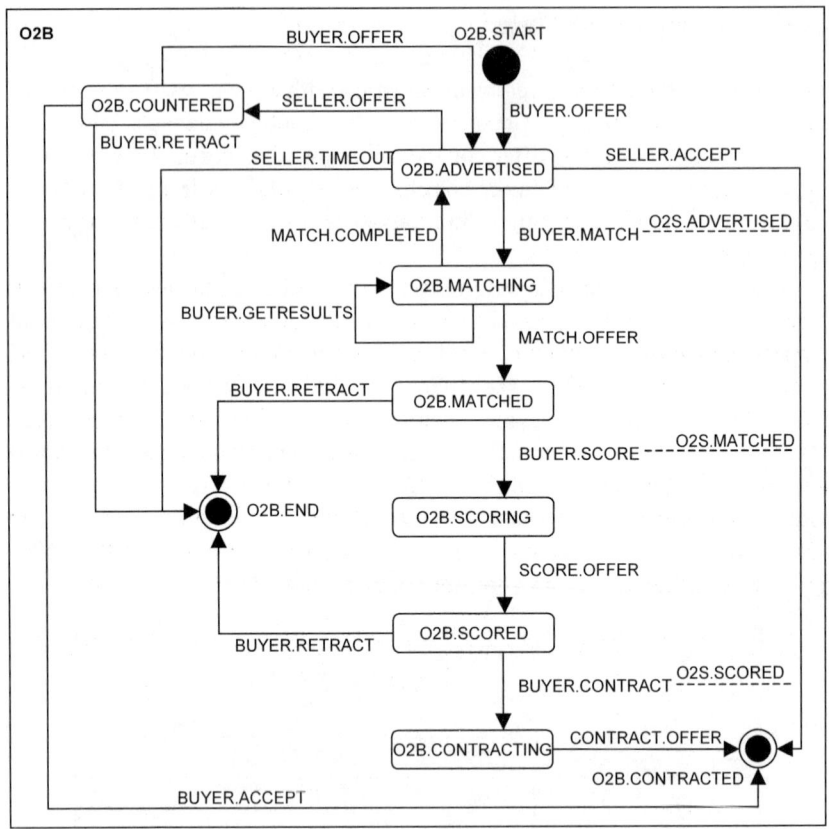

Figure 66. O2B state chart for DSP-V2

The buyer can, during the MatchNSC operation, inquire about the current result-set by raising the *BUYER.GETRESULTS* event (new agreement candidates might complement the result-set if sellers complete offers with dynamic domains). The target property of this action specifies the operation ID of the MatchNSC operation. When the MatchNSC signals *MATCH.COMPLETED* (depending, for instance, on the *TIME_RESTRICTION* objective property), the initial offer instance changes back to the state *O2B.ADVERTISED*. Whenever a successful match is found by the MatchNSC, a *MATCH.OFFER* event generates through the associated *MANAGER.OFFER* action a new offer instance for the agreement candidate in the *O2B.MATCHED* state – NSC operations may generate new offer instances for every pair of initiating

Scenario cases

and target offers[22]. If the initiating offer is an O2B instance and the target offer is an O2S instance, both, the buyer and the seller receive new generated offer instances (see the example in the run-time section for this scenario case).

The definition of a transition for the initiating offer is not always necessary and can be omitted if the old offer instance is not used anymore (as is the case in the ScoreNSC and ContractNSC operation in this enScenario). In this MatchNSC operation example, the agent may proceed with the enProcess using the new offer instances, but maintains the original offer instance as an advertisement to other potential agreement candidates.

For a new offer instance in the *O2B.MATCHED* state, the buyer has two options – the offer can be retracted or scored. The target of the *SUPPORT.SCORE* action is the corresponding new offer instance in the *O2S.MATCHED* state (indicated also with the event synchronisation connection in *Figure 66*). By using the ScoreNSC operation, this offer will be scored based on the evaluation criteria defined in the original offer advertised, which are still part of the offer structure in *O2B.MATCHED*. It is also possible to execute the scoring procedure for multiple offers. To support this functionality, the designers of *yourhost.ch* could add a transition with the event *BUYER.SCORE* in the state *O2B.ADVERTISED* and define a corresponding target of, for instance, *O2S.ADVERTISED.X*

STATE_OLD	EVENT	ACTION	PROPERTIES	STATE_NEW
START	BUYER.OFFER	MANAGER.OFFER	{TARGET=NULL}	ADVERTISED
ADVERTISED	BUYER.MATCH	SUPPORT.MATCH	{TARGET=O2S.ADVERTI...	MATCHING
MATCHING	BUYER.GETRESULTS	MANAGER.GETRESU...	{TARGET=MATCH.ID}	MATCHING
MATCHING	MATCH.COMPLETED			ADVERTISED
MATCHING	MATCH.OFFER	MANAGER.OFFER	{TARGET=NULL}	MATCHED
MATCHED	BUYER.RETRACT	MANAGER.RETRACT	{TARGET=NULL,ARCHIV...	END
MATCHED	BUYER.SCORE	SUPPORT.SCORE	{TARGET=O2S.MATCHE...	SCORING
SCORING	SCORE.OFFER	MANAGER.OFFER	{TARGET=NULL}	SCORED
SCORED	BUYER.RETRACT	MANAGER.RETRACT	{TARGET=NULL,ARCHIV...	END
SCORED	BUYER.CONTRACT	SUPPORT.CONTRACT	{TARGET=O2S.SCORED...	CONTRACTING
CONTRACTING	CONTRACT.OFFER	MANAGER.OFFER	{TARGET=NULL}	CONTRACTED
ADVERTISED	SELLER.ACCEPT	MANAGER.ACCEPT	{TARGET=NULL,SIGNAT...	CONTRACTED
ADVERTISED	SELLER.OFFER	MANAGER.OFFER	{TARGET=NULL}	COUNTERED
ADVERTISED	SELLER.TIMEOUT			END
COUNTERED	BUYER.ACCEPT	MANAGER.ACCEPT	{TARGET=NULL,SIGNAT...	CONTRACTED
COUNTERED	BUYER.OFFER	MANAGER.OFFER	{TARGET=NULL}	ADVERTISED
COUNTERED	BUYER.RETRACT	MANAGER.RETRACT	{TARGET=NULL,ARCHIV...	END
COUNTERED	BUYER.TIMEOUT			END

Figure 67. O2B transitions in DSP-V2

---

[22] The associated transition from the START state to the new offer instance with the termination-state of the NSC operation is omitted in this and the following examples, for reasons of simplicity.

Once the ScoreNSC operation is completed, the offer transitions changes to the state *O2B.SCORED*, in which the buyer can still retract the offer (e.g. if the score achieved is unsatisfactory) or alternatively initiate a ContractNSC operation.

STATE_OLD	EVENT	...	ACTION	PROPERTIES	STATE_NEW
START	SELLER.OFFER		MANAGER.OFFER	(TARGET=NULL)	ADVERTISED
ADVERTISED	BUYER.MATCH				MATCHING
MATCHING	MATCH.OFFER				MATCHED
MATCHING	MATCH.COMPLETED				ADVERTISED
MATCHED	BUYER.ACCEPT				CONTRACTED
MATCHED	BUYER.SCORE				SCORING
SCORING	SCORE.OFFER				SCORED
SCORED	BUYER.CONTRACT				CONTRACTING
CONTRACTING	CONTRACT.OFFER				CONTRACTED
ADVERTISED	BUYER.ACCEPT		MANAGER.ACCEPT	(TARGET=NULL,SIGNATUR...	CONTRACTED
ADVERTISED	BUYER.OFFER		MANAGER.OFFER	(TARGET=NULL)	COUNTERED
ADVERTISED	BUYER.TIMEOUT				END
COUNTERED	SELLER.ACCEPT		MANAGER.ACCEPT	(TARGET=NULL,SIGNATUR...	CONTRACTED
COUNTERED	SELLER.OFFER		MANAGER.OFFER	(TARGET=NULL)	ADVERTISED
COUNTERED	SELLER.RETRACT		MANAGER.RETRACT	(TARGET=NULL,ARCHIVE=...	END
COUNTERED	SELLER.TIMEOUT				END

Figure 68. O2S transitions in DSP-V2

The example of the O2S FSM specification (see *Figure 68*) illustrates that the *CONTRACT.COMPLETED* event is ignored, i.e. no transition is defined for this event. Therefore no offer instance will remain in the state *O2S.SCORED* for the entire enProcess (unless the buyer never raises *BUYER.CONTRACT*). The same is true for *SCORE.COMPLETED*. If an enScenario designer wanted to give sellers the opportunity to inspect their matches at some later stage in the enProcess, *SCORE.COMPLETED* could be used to restore the original *O2S.MATCHED* offer instance after the completion of the ScoreNSC operation. It would make sense in many cases to empower sellers as well to score an agreement candidate offer based on the seller's evaluation criteria before this offer might be signed. To enable this functionality, a transition with the event *SELLER.SCORE* and a corresponding *SUPPORT.SCORE* operation could be added in the state *O2S.MATCHED*. The event *BUYER.SCORE* would then be ignored in the O2S FSM and synchronisation would take place via the common state *X.SCORED*.

2.2.3 Integration Design

A new element in the integration design for *DSP-V2* is the use of the design-time agent group *GR_SUPPORT*, which represents the NSCs installed in the enMedium run-time support server of *yourhost.ch*. If an event, such as

MATCH.OFFER or *MATCH.COMPLETED*, is raised by an NSC, this event, like an agent event, also requires an authorisation, since the execution manager does not distinguish the type of the actor while testing compliance of an event with the transition definition. The SILKROAD design adapter automatically adds *GR_SUPPORT* entries for events raised by NSCs to the event authorisation table.

Using the model validation functionality of the enMedium design-time support server, the enScenario designers of *yourhost.ch* identify an 'intermediary agent-state' violation (see Condition 10 in *Table 11*). The state *O2S.CONTRACTED* requires the signature of the seller, which is not the case for the preceding states. However, based on the current scenario definition, sellers do not have the possibility of complementing their offer instances with a signature. To reach model consistency, a new state, *O2S.READY-CONTRACTING*, has to be added to the communication design, and two corresponding transitions for this state have to complement the organisation design (see *Figure 69*).

STATE_OLD	EVENT	ACTION	PROPERTIES	STATE_NEW
START	SELLER.OFFER	MANAGER.OFFER	{TARGET=NU...	ADVERTISED
ADVERTISED	BUYER.MATCH			MATCHING
MATCHING	MATCH.OFFER			MATCHED
MATCHING	MATCH.COMPLETED			ADVERTISED
MATCHED	BUYER.ACCEPT			CONTRACTED
MATCHED	BUYER.SCORE			SCORING
SCORING	SCORE.OFFER			SCORED
SCORED	SELLER.OFFER	MANAGER.OFFER	{TARGET=NU...	READYCONTRACTING
READYCONTRACTING	BUYER.CONTRACT			CONTRACTING
CONTRACTING	CONTRACT.OFFER			CONTRACTED
ADVERTISED	BUYER.ACCEPT	MANAGER.ACCEPT	{TARGET=NU...	CONTRACTED
ADVERTISED	BUYER.OFFER	MANAGER.OFFER	{TARGET=NU...	COUNTERED
ADVERTISED	BUYER.TIMEOUT			END
COUNTERED	SELLER.ACCEPT	MANAGER.ACCEPT	{TARGET=NU...	CONTRACTED
COUNTERED	SELLER.OFFER	MANAGER.OFFER	{TARGET=NU...	ADVERTISED
COUNTERED	SELLER.RETRACT	MANAGER.RETRACT	{TARGET=NU...	END
COUNTERED	SELLER.TIMEOUT			END

Figure 69. Corrected O2S transitions in DSP-V2

To complete the patch, the target of the *SUPPORT.CONTRACT* action initiated by *BUYER.CONTRACT* in the O2B FSM has to change from *O2S.SCORED* to *O2S.READYCONTRACTING*. At this state of the enProcess, the agreement candidate offer instance generated by the ScoreNSC for the seller could not already be in this state, because the seller has not yet submitted a modified offer instance containing his/her signature (see *Figure 68*). As soon as this is the case, a state synchronisation occurs: the Contract-NSC will retrieve the updated offer from the seller, which changes the state to *O2S.CONTRACTING* by the *BUYER.CONTRACT* event without further action (as the action was caused already by the event of the buyer in the O2B FSM). This design technique reflects another approach to synchronise transitions in the O2B and O2S FSM. After correcting this enScenario design model error, the model validation procedure identifies no additional errors and the run-time specifications can be generated and exported.

The two different modes of contracting are illustrated in this example. Whereas a *MANAGER.ACCEPT* action requires a signature as a property, this is not the case for the *SUPPORT.CONTRACT* action. For the Contract-NSC the signature has to be part of the offer instance. The properties of an NSC are always objectives, not inputs (see Section 4.2). In addition to the original double-sided contracting from *DSP-V1*, which is still represented in *DSP-V2* (the seller can accept an advertised offer of the buyer, which already contains a signature, c.f. *Figure 67*), this enScenario also demonstrates one-sided contracting. Each agent signs its agreement candidate offer instance (i.e. the seller signs an O2S instance in the state *O2S.SCORED.O2B*) 'towards' the offer of the counterpart, but there is no offer with two signatures until the ContractNSC generates it.

2.2.4 Run-time behaviour

The run-time behaviour constrained by the rules of *DSP-V2* is demonstrated with the lifecycle of offer instances belonging to the same offer root (a sample offer session). In continuation of the previous example, *AG_DSP_101B* might create an *OF_DSP_002* for the *DSP-V2* scenario. In the state *OF_DSP_002.ADVERTISED* the buyer decides to invoke the MatchNSC by raising *AGENT.MATCH* through the agent adapter. As soon as the MatchNSC operation is finished, the offer will shift to *OF_DSP_002.MATCHING*.

Let us assume that there are several O2S instances advertised and that the MatchNSC is able to discover successful matches with two sellers: *OF_DSP_102.ADVERTISED* and *OF_DSP_104.ADVERTISED*.

AG_DSP_101B will, upon completion of the MatchNSC operation, view in the in-tray three offer instances associated with the offer root *OF_DSP_002* for this offer session (see the agent adapter example in *Figure 70*): the initiating offer *OF_DSP_002.ADVERTISED*, *OF_DSP_002.MATCHED.OF_DSP_102*, and *OF_DSP_002.MATCHED.OF_DSP_104*. The counterpart sellers will also receive offer instances created by the MatchNSC operation in their in-trays, for example *OF_DSP_102.MATCHED.OF_DSP_002*.

Scenario cases 203

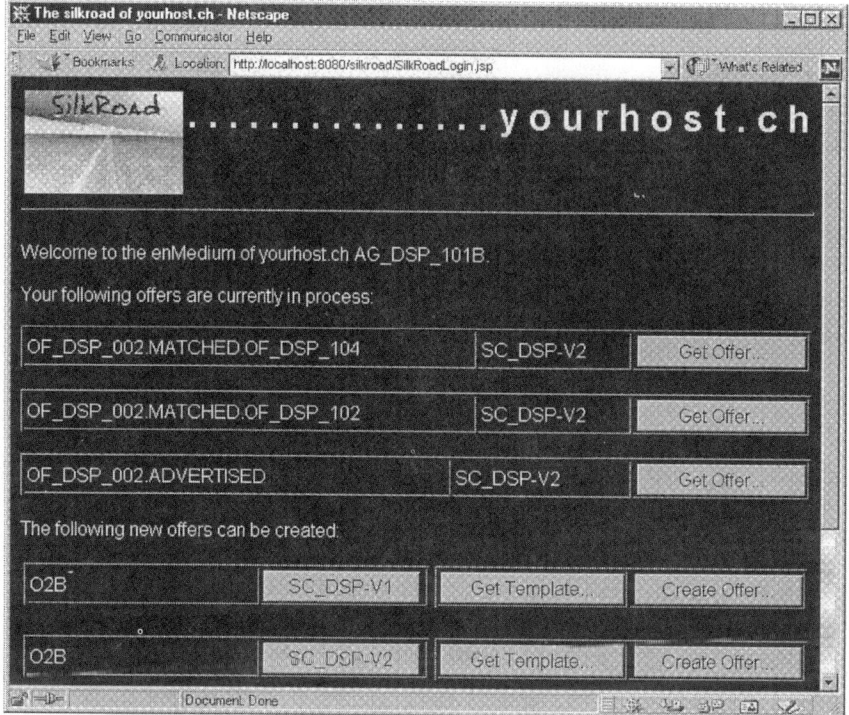

Figure 70. Prototype interface in-tray example for DSP-V2

If the buyer proceeds by invoking a ScoreNSC operation with *TARGET= OF_DSP_102.MATCHED.OF_DSP_002*, the offer instances of the sellers change owing to the synchronisation with the ScoreNSC support-state, which in this case is *OF_DSP_102.SCORING.OF_DSP_002*. Once the offer is scored, a new instance is generated, such as *OF_DSP_102.SCORED. OF_DSP_002*, to which the seller can add a signature. When the offer is re-submitted it assumes the pre-condition state *OF_DSP_102.READYCON-TRACTING.OF_DSP_002*. If the buyer has already raised *BUYER.SCORE*, the ContractNSC retrieves the offer immediately and the final contracted offer instances for each agent (since double-sided contracting is used) are available after the *CONTRACT.OFFER* event.

2.3 Multi-attribute auction: DSP-V3 case

The ongoing analysis of the business domain and the potential business models in the Yourhost.ch example reveals that the market for database services, due to its high transparency, is very competitive. Offers are to a large degree comparable, since all of them are based on the dominating database software solutions from IBM, Microsoft, and Oracle. The enScenario analysts of yourhost.ch therefore decide to add another scenario, DSP-V3, which exploits the competitive nature and high standardisation of the market segment in favour of the service consumers. Elements of this enScenario are comparable to the concept of a multi-attribute auction with the following key characteristics (see Section 3.5.2.1): bilateral-participation, multiple-agents, single-round, single-stage, multiple-attributes, independent-relation, multiple-objects, multiple-sides, ascending-value, and anonymous-identity. Furthermore, the MediateNSC is used as an alternative method of finding agreements.

2.3.1 Communication design

The complete offer state structure design for *DSP-V3* is reflected in *Figure 71*. The table illustrates the dynamic nature of the offer structure within an enProcess defined by this enScenario.

OFFER_STATE	DOMAINS	CONSTRAINTS	COUNTERS	CRITERIA	SIGNATURES	TIMESTAMPS
ADVERTISED	Dynamic	Negotiable	None	Valued	Single	End
BIDDING	Dynamic	Negotiable	None	Valued	Single	End
BID	Ranges	Negotiable	None	Valued	Single	End
MATCHING	Ranges	Negotiable	None	Valued	Single	End
MATCHED	Ranges	Matched	None	Valued	Single	End
SCORING	Ranges	Matched	None	Valued	Single	End
READYMEDIATING	Ranges	Weighted	None	Scored	Single	End
MEDIATING	Ranges	Weighted	None	Scored	Single	End
MEDIATED	Values	Mediated	None	Scored	Single	End
CONTRACTING	Values	Mediated	None	None	Single	End
CONTRACTED	Values	Basic	None	None	Single	End

Figure 71. O2B states in DSP-V3

The *Domains* structure element, for instance, first allows the specification of *Dynamic* value domains. Later, starting with the *O2B.BID* state, only *Ranges* can be specified, before through an operation of the MediateNSC narrows these ranges to *Values* for the final contract. Another example is the setup of the notation options for the *Constraints* structure element. Initially, *Negotiable* constraints are required, but after a MatchNSC operation these constraints have to be updated with importance ratings to become *Weighted* constraints, before a MediateNSC operation renders these expressions into *Mediated* constraints.

2.3.2 Organisation design

The organisation design for the *DSP-V3* model makes use of two organisation design techniques that have not been used in the cases presented so far: automated component invocation and guard conditions.

STATE_OLD	EVENT	GUARD	ACTION	PROPERTIES	STATE_NEW
START	BUYER.OFFER		MANAGER.OFFER	{TARGET=NULL}	ADVERTISED
ADVERTISED	BUYER.BID		SUPPORT.BID	{TARGET=NULL,TIMEOUT...}	BIDDING
ADVERTISED	BUYER.MATCH		SUPPORT.MATCH	{TARGET=O2S.ADVERTIS...}	MATCHING
ADVERTISED	MANAGER.COMPLETED		SUPPORT.SCORE	{TARGET=O2S.READYSC...}	SCORING
SCORING	SCORE.COMPLETED				ADVERTISED
MATCHING	MATCH.OFFER		MANAGER.OFFER	{TARGET=NULL}	MATCHED
MATCHED	BUYER.CONTRACT	e(MATCH.RS.MAS)	SUPPORT.CONTRACT	{TARGET=O2S.MATCHED,...}	CONTRACTING
MATCHED	BUYER.OFFER	e(MATCH.RS.NAS)	MANAGER.OFFER	{TARGET=NULL}	READYMEDIATING
READYMEDIATING	SELLER.MEDIATE				MEDIATING
READYMEDIATING	BUYER.MEDIATE		SUPPORT.MEDIATE	{TARGET=O2S.READYME...}	MEDIATING
MEDIATING	MEDIATE.OFFER		MANAGER.OFFER	{TARGET=NULL}	MEDIATED
MEDIATED	BUYER.RETRACT		MANAGER.RETRACT	{TARGET=NULL,ARCHIVE...}	END
MEDIATED	BUYER.CONTRACT		SUPPORT.CONTRACT	{TARGET=O2S.MEDIATED...}	CONTRACTING
BIDDING	BUYER.GETRESULTS		MANAGER.GETRESULTS	{TARGET=BID.ID}	BIDDING
BIDDING	SELLER.GETRESULTS				BIDDING
BIDDING	BID.TIMEOUT				ADVERTISED
BIDDING	BID.OFFER		MANAGER.OFFER	{TARGET=NULL}	BID
BID	BUYER.CONTRACT		SUPPORT.CONTRACT	{TARGET=O2S.BID,OPTIM...}	CONTRACTING
BID	BUYER.RETRACT		MANAGER.RETRACT	{TARGET=NULL,ARCHIVE...}	END
CONTRACTING	CONTRACT.OFFER		MANAGER.OFFER	{TARGET=NULL}	CONTRACTED

Figure 72. O2B transitions in DSP-V3

Figure 72 shows the transitions for the O2B. A first decision point for the buyer is the state *O2B.ADVERTISED*. In this state, either the BidNSC or the MatchNSC can be invoked. Through the *BUYER.BID* event, the BidNSC executes a bidding session and may receive bids from sellers, which are generated through the *SCORE.OFFER* event in the O2S FSM (see below). In the O2S FSM, a *MANAGER.COMPLETED* event is raised by default, after the successful storage of the O2S instance of a seller in the *MANAGER.OFFER* action. This event is passed to the O2B FSM because of the event synchronisation (the *MANAGER.OFFER* action in the O2S FSM has O2B.ADVERTISED defined as target, see *Figure 73*). The propagated *MANAGER.COMPLETED* event is used in the O2B FSM to invoke automatically a ScoreNSC operation for the seller's offer based on the buyer's *O2B.AD-VERTISED* instance.

The expiration of the bidding session is determined through the objective properties defined for the BidNSC operation. Let us assume that the properties are defined as indicated in *Table 15*. A value of '*' indicates that this objective has to be set at run-time by the agent invoking the action. In this case the buyer might either specify a fixed timeframe for the bidding session or define a clear-timing rule, which could be based, for instance, on a period of inactivity. Upon successful completion of the operation (i.e. there was at least one accepted bid), the BidNSC will create the winning offer instance for the buyer and the seller who issued the winning offer, and the contracting process can be initiated. If there was no winning bid, the BidNSC raises *BID.TIMEOUT* and the O2B instance transitions back to the state *O2B.ADVERTISED*, giving the buyer the opportunity to restart the bidding session with modified objectives and/or a modified offer (e.g. with different evaluation criteria). During the bidding process both the buyer and sellers can inquire with *AGENT.GETRESULTS* about the status of the auction, namely the result-set specifying the current winning offer and the other (anonymous) quotes.

Table 15. SUPPORT.BID action property definition in DSP-V3

Action	Objective property	Value
SUPPORT.BID (BidNSC)	TARGET	NULL
	TIMEOUT	*
	DOMINANCE	BEAT_QUOTE
	CLEAR_TIMING	*
	QUOTE_INFORMATION	ANONYMOUS

A complete enProcess would be executed if the buyer raised *BUYER.MATCH* in the *O2B.ADVERTISED* state and the MatchNSC were able to find successful matches. In the event that the MatchNSC identifies negotiable agreements, the buyer has the option to submit a modified *O2B.MATCHED* instance with weights assigned to the negotiable constraints, and to initiate a MediateNSC operation for this agreement candidate offer. The same option is modelled for the seller. Thus, two alternative events may lead to *O2B.MEDIATING – BUYER.MEDIATE* or *SELLER.MEDIATE*. The corresponding *SUPPORT.MEDIATE* action is always associated with the source event, not the synchronised event. The result of the MatchNSC operation is evaluated with the guard condition $e(MATCH.RS.MAS)$. This condition evaluates whether the *O2B.MATCHED* instance is part of the matching agreement set that is specified in the result-set of the MatchNSC operation. If this condition evaluates to 'true', the transition to *O2B.CONTRACTING* is activated.

Guards are also used in the transition definitions for the O2S in *Figure 73*. At the start of the enProcess, the seller already has two options: to generally advertise an O2S, or to submit an offer specifically towards the advertised offer of a buyer. The guard condition defined for the second option checks (via the enProcess run-time history in the enMedium server) whether the agent has already submitted an offer to this *O2B.ADVERTISED* instance or not. The design specifies that the agent can only submit one offer

Scenario cases

to the O2B. If the seller already made an offer, this guard condition will evaluate to 'false', the transition will not fire, and the seller will receive a corresponding error message. If it fires, the offer changes to the state *O2S.READYSCORING*. In this state, the automated component invocation defined through the *MANAGER.COMPLETED* event in the O2B FSM starts the ScoreNSC operation and sets the O2S instance to the state *O2S.SCORING*.

STATE_OLD	EVENT	GUARD	ACTION	PROPERTIES	STATE_NEW
START	SELLER.OFFER		MANAGER.OFFER	{TARGET=NULL}	ADVERTISED
START	SELLER.OFFER	AG.OFFER(O2B.ADVERTISED)<1	MANAGER.OFFER	{TARGET=O2B.ADVERTISED}	READYSCORING
ADVERTISED	BUYER.MATCH				MATCHING
MATCHING	MATCH.OFFER		MANAGER.OFFER	{TARGET=NULL}	MATCHED
MATCHED	BUYER.CONTRACT				CONTRACTING
MATCHED	SELLER.OFFER	e(MATCH.RS.NAS)	MANAGER.OFFER	{TARGET=NULL}	READYMEDIATING
READYMEDIATING	SELLER.MEDIATE		SUPPORT.MEDIATE	{TARGET=O2B.READYMEDI...	MEDIATING
READYMEDIATING	BUYER.MEDIATE				MEDIATING
MEDIATING	MEDIATE.OFFER		MANAGER.OFFER	{TARGET=NULL}	MEDIATED
MEDIATED	SELLER.RETRACT		MANAGER.RETRACT	{TARGET=NULL,ARCHIVE=...	END
MEDIATED	BUYER.CONTRACT				CONTRACTING
READYSCORING	MANAGER.COMPLETED				SCORING
SCORING	SCORE.OFFER	O2S.SCORE<O2B.RV	MANAGER.OFFER	{TARGET=NULL}	REJECTED
SCORING	SCORE.OFFER	O2S.SCORE>=O2B.RV	MANAGER.OFFER	{TARGET=BID.ID}	BIDDING
BIDDING	SELLER.GETRESULTS		MANAGER.GETRESULTS	{TARGET=BID.ID}	BIDDING
BIDDING	BID.TIMEOUT				REJECTED
BIDDING	BID.OFFER		MANAGER.OFFER	{TARGET=NULL}	BID
BID	BUYER.CONTRACT				CONTRACTING
CONTRACTING	CONTRACT.OFFER		MANAGER.OFFER	{TARGET=NULL}	CONTRACTED

Figure 73. O2S transitions in DSP-V3

Two other transitions are also dependent on the evaluation of guard conditions that compare the score calculated for the O2S in the ScoreNSC operation to the reservation value defined in the *O2B.BIDDING* instance. Based on this conditional branching, a higher score for an offer instance activates a transition with a *MANAGER.OFFER* action and a target defined to be the operation ID of the BidNSC for the *O2B.BIDDING* instance. A lower score leads to the state *O2S.REJECTED*. If the bidding session terminates, the seller with the winning bid receives the generated offer through the *BID.OFFER* action. Sellers with unsuccessful bids receive a *BID.TIMEOUT* event from the BidNSC.

The buyer can voluntarily initiate the contracting process for the winning bid, whereas the seller has no further choice – the offer is already binding. The same is true for the *O2S.MEDIATED* state. This enScenario model example illustrates how the protocol design might influence the strategies of agents. The seller can only submit one bid, and this bid cannot be retracted if it is a winning bid. This rule should induce sellers to bid their truthful valuation for the database service contract without considering potential competitor moves. The enScenario design also prevents them from examining extensively the competitive situation. Fairness arguments might urge *yourhost.ch* to force the buyer, too, to accept the winning bid without the possibility to retract. This additional rule can also be expressed within *DSP-V3* – since the O2B instance already features a signature, the *BUYER.CONTRACT* and *BUYER.RETRACT* events in the O2B FSM can be removed. With the *MANAGER.COMPLETED* event in the state *O2B.BID*, it is then possible to start the ContractNSC operation automatically.

2.3.3 Integration design

To reflect the sealed-bid nature of the auction design chosen by *yourhost.ch*, sellers submit their offers to the BidNSC in an anonymous way with pseudonyms (generated by the agent manager, as described in Section 6.1.3). Thus, the group *GR_DSP_S_ANONYMOUS*, which contains the pseudonyms assigned to sellers, has to be authorised in the integration design to raise certain events, such as the *SELLER.OFFER* event (see *Figure 74*).

OFFER_STATE	EVENT	AGENT_GROUP
START	SELLER.OFFER	GR_DSP_S_ANONYMOUS
BIDDING	SELLER.GETRESULTS	GR_DSP_S_ANONYMOUS
REJECTED	SELLER.RETRACT	GR_DSP_S_ANONYMOUS
ADVERTISED	BUYER.MATCH	GR_DSP_B
MATCHED	BUYER.CONTRACT	GR_DSP_B

Figure 74. O2S event authorisation for sample states in DSP-V3

The validation of the enScenario model by the design adapter of the *yourhost.ch* design-time support server exposes a 'termination consistency' violation (see Condition 12 in *Table 11*). *O2S.REJECTED* is a terminal state in the O2S FSM – no transition is defined from this state to another state. However, only the *END* and the *CONTRACTED* state can be used as terminal states (that is, offers in the *END* state will be archived automatically by the execution manager). Therefore an additional transition with the *SELLER.RETRACT* event has to be added to the *O2S.REJECTED* state (see *Figure 75* next page). An alternative solution is to allow sellers to re-submit a rejected offer with modifications. In this case, the guard conditions for the *O2S.SCORING* state would also have to change in order to allow more than one bid from one seller for one O2B instance. Furthermore, a number of missing *TIMEOUT* events are detected, which leads to the addition of auxiliary transitions (c.f. Section 7.2.4.3).

Scenario cases

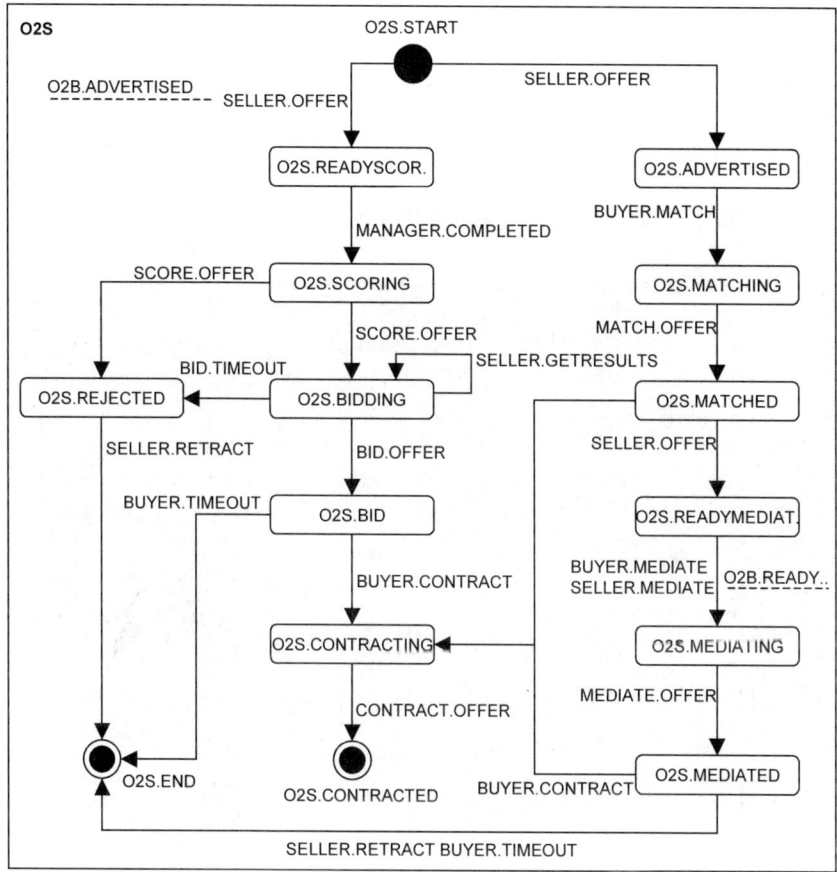

Figure 75. Corrected O2S state chart for DSP-V3

2.3.4 Run-time behaviour

The illustration of a sample run-time enProcess for *DSP-V3* in this section is focused on the auction elements of the enScenario model, because the resulting enProcess differs significantly from the run-time behaviour in the previous enScenario cases.

After submitting the initial offer (e.g. *OF_DSP_003*), *AG_DSP_101B*, the buyer agent, can raise *BUYER.BID* and determine two properties for the corresponding action, *TIMEOUT* and *CLEAR_TIMING*, because these objectives have a '*' value assigned in *Table 15*. This is illustrated in the agent adapter screenshot in *Figure 76* (next page). The *SilkPerformAction.jsp* of SILKROAD generates an input field for every property in the transition specification that has a '*' value. The example given dictates that the auction finish on January 10 2002, or earlier if a 24 hours period of inactivity occurs. Using these objectives, the component manager creates a BidNSC with the operation ID determined by the execution manager, such as *SUPPORT.BID: OF_DSP_003.ADVERTISED:996055050984* (the suffix number is a time-stamp representation in milliseconds).

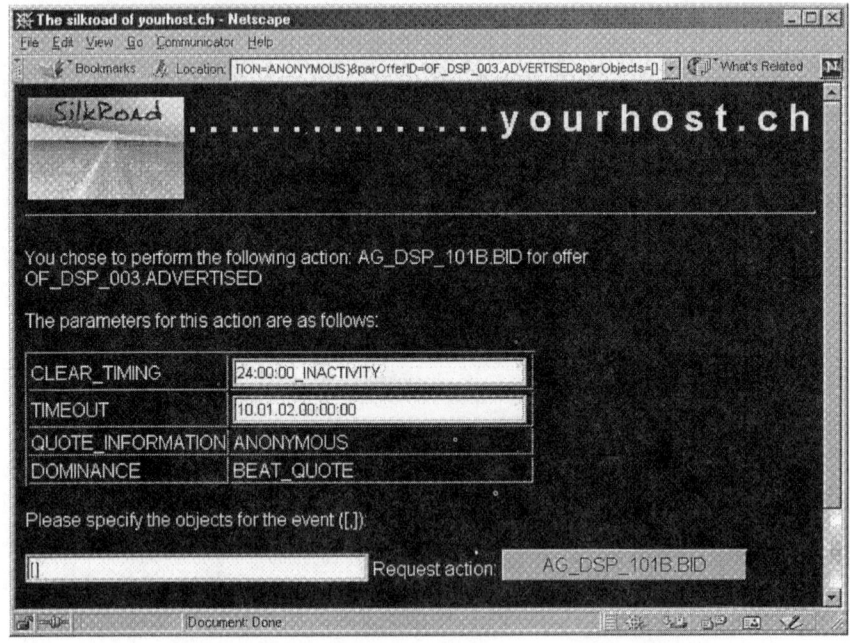

Figure 76. Prototype interface for raising AGENT.BID in DSP-V3

Sellers searching for offers might find OF_DSP_003.ADVERTISED and decide to submit an O2S instance, e.g. *OF_DSP_103*. This O2S instance will be scored automatically on the basis of the evaluation criteria defined by *AG_DSP_101B*. If the score achieved is *0.86* and the reservation value in *OF_DSP_003* is defined to be *0.85*, then the transition to the state *OF_DSP_103. BIDDING* fires and the offer is submitted to the BidNSC, e.g. *SUPPORT.BID:OF_DSP_003.ADVERTISED:996055050984*.

If the consecutive bidding session determines *OF_DSP_103* to be the winning bid (that is, if no other seller agent submits an offer with a higher score), this bid is represented in a new offer instance generated by the BidNSC: *OF_DSP_003.BID.OF_DSP_103*. If *OF_DSP_103* is not the winner, the offer, upon termination of the bidding session, assumes the state *OF_DSP_003.REJECTED*.

Scenario cases 211

2.4 Service bundling: DSP-V4 case

Suppose that according to a survey of yourhost.ch, the ASP market is growing, not only with respect to the number of participants and the volume of the deals, but also regarding the range of applications offered for hosting. In response to this situation, yourhost.ch wants to give its customers the opportunity to execute enProcesses for heterogeneous bundles of services, including, for example, not only database services but also office productivity or enterprise resource planning applications. Hence, a new DSP-V4 enScenario project is initiated with the goal of allowing buyers to specify bundles of services, in which they are interested and sellers to bid for parts of these bundles or for complete bundles.

2.4.1 Communication design

The ontology initially developed for *DSP-V1* has been gradually extended by the enScenario designers with new concept specifications whenever a new segment of application-hosting has been added to the market offering of *yourhost.ch*. As a result of this, the extended offer context ontology shown in *Figure 77* is available for the communication design of the new *DSP-V4* scenario.

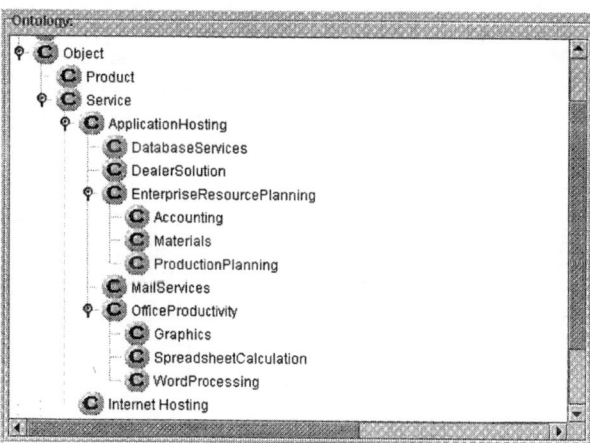

Figure 77. Offer context ontology for DSP-V4

On the basis of this ontology model, a bundle offer might, depending on the offer context assignment, contain constraints for different types of services within one sub-concept group, e.g. *Accounting, Materials,* and *Produc-*

tionPlanning, or across several non-hierarchically related concepts, e.g. *WordProcessing* and *MailServices*.

2.4.2 Organisation design

To enable bundling in the enProcess, a BundleNSC operation needs to be incorporated in the *DSP-V4* enScenario model. *Figure 78* presents the set of transitions defined for the O2B FSM by the enScenario designers of *your-host.ch*.

STATE_OLD	EVENT	GUARD	ACTION	PROPERTIES	STATE_NEW
START	BUYER.OFFER		MANAGER.OFFER	{TARGET=NULL}	ADVERTISED
ADVERTISED	BUYER.BUNDLE		SUPPORT.BUNDLE	{TARGET=NULL,HOM...	BUNDLING
BUNDLING	BUNDLE.COMPLETED				BUNDLED
BUNDLED	BUYER.GETRESULTS		MANAGER.GETRESULTS	{TARGET=BUNDLE.ID}	BUNDLED
BUNDLED	BUYER.ACCEPT		MANAGER.ACCEPT	{TARGET=O2S.READY...	CONTRACTED
BUNDLED	BUYER.RETRACT		MANAGER.RETRACT	{TARGET=NULL,ARC...	END
BUNDLED	BUYER.OFFER	BUNDLE.RS.BUNDLED>1	MANAGER.OFFER	{TARGET=NULL}	READYSCORING
READYSCORING	BUYER.SCORE		SUPPORT.SCORE	{TARGET=*,TOPCUT=...	SCORING
SCORING	SCORE.COMPLETED				SCORED
SCORED	BUYER.GETRESULTS		MANAGER.GETRESULTS	{TARGET=SCORE.ID}	SCORED
SCORED	BUYER.ACCEPT		MANAGER.ACCEPT	{TARGET=O2S.SCOR...	CONTRACTED
SCORED	BUYER.RETRACT		MANAGER.RETRACT	{TARGET=NULL,ARC...	END
SCORED	BUYER.BUNDLE	SCORE.RS.SCORED=0	SUPPORT.BUNDLE	{TARGET=NULL,HOM...	BUNDLING
SCORED	BUYER.OFFER		MANAGER.OFFER	{TARGET=NULL}	READYSCORING

Figure 78. O2B transitions in DSP-V4

In contrast to the previous enScenario models, no new offer instances are generated in the O2B FSM but instead the initiating offer instance assumes different states in one offer session, such as *O2B.BUNDLED*, *O2B.SCORED*, and *O2B.CONTRACTED*. Through the *MANAGER.GETRESULTS* action with an NSC.ID target type, the buyer agent can inquire about the results of both NSC operations, bundling and scoring. If, for example, O2S instances were generated through the BundleNSC operation, the buyer learns about these offers in the result-set of the corresponding BundleNSC instance. Upon invocation, the BundleNSC may receive part-offers from sellers and will try to combine these to satisfy the requirements specified in the O2B instance. If a combination can be found, a corresponding total-offer is generated from the part-offers, specifying the coalition of seller agents contributing part-offers.

Upon completion of the BundleNSC operation, when the offer instance is in the *O2B.BUNDLED* state, the buyer can either accept one of the generated total-offers or launch a multilateral ScoreNSC operation. This action requires submitting a modified offer with evaluation criteria and is only possible if there is more than one total-offer (this is expressed as the guard

Scenario cases 213

condition *BUNDLE.RS.BUNDLED>1* for the transition to *O2B.READYSCO-RING*). Which total-offers are scored, as well as the *MINIMUM_SCORE* objective property, can be defined by the buyer at run-time (see the '*' value for the *TARGET* property of the *SUPPORT.SCORE* operation).

In the consecutive *O2B.SCORED* state, the buyer has options such as inspecting the results of the ScoreNSC operation, accepting a scored O2S instance, or retracting the O2B instance. Furthermore, the BundleNSC operation can be restarted in the case that no O2S instance was successfully scored, that is, no instance received a score above the user-defined minimum score (the corresponding guard condition is defined as *SCORE.RS. SCORED=0*). The O2B instance can also be re-submitted to the state *O2B.REA-DYSCORING* in order to change the evaluation criteria and to repeat the ScoreNSC operation.

STATE_OLD	EVENT	GUARD	ACTION	PROPERTIES	STATE_NEW
START	SELLER.OFFER		MANAGER.OFFER	(TARGET=BUNDLE.ID)	BUNDLING
BUNDLING	SELLER.GETRESULTS		MANAGER.GETRESULTS	(TARGET=BUNDLE.ID)	BUNDLING
BUNDLING	BUNDLE.OFFER		MANAGER.OFFER	(TARGET=NULL)	BUNDLED
BUNDLING	SELLER.RETRACT		MANAGER.RETRACT	(TARGET=BUNDLE.ID...)	END
BUNDLING	BUNDLE.COMPLETED	!e(BUNDLE.RS.BUNDLED)			REJECTED
BUNDLED	SELLER.OFFER		MANAGER.OFFER	(TARGET=NULL)	READYCONTRACTING
READYCONTRACTING	BUYER.SCORE				SCORING
SCORING	SCORE.COMPLETED	!e(SCORE.RS.SCORED)			REJECTED
SCORING	SCORE.OFFER		MANAGER.OFFER	(TARGET=NULL)	SCORED
SCORED	SELLER.GETRESULTS		MANAGER.GETRESULTS	(TARGET=SCORE.ID)	SCORED
SCORED	BUYER.ACCEPT				CONTRACTED
REJECTED	SELLER.RETRACT		MANAGER.RETRACT	(TARGET=NULL,ARC...)	END
REJECTED	SELLER.OFFER		MANAGER.OFFER	(TARGET=BUNDLE.ID)	BUNDLING

Figure 79. O2S transitions in DSP-V4

In the O2S FSM for *DSP-V4* in *Figure 79*, another type of guard condition is used. If the BundleNSC operation raises the *BUNDLE.COMPLETED* event, the condition *!e(BUNDLE.RS.BUNDLED)* holds 'true' if the O2S instance is not part of a generated coalition. In this case, the new state for the offer is *O2S.REJECTED*. In this state the seller can either modify or retract the offer. For the *SCORE.COMPLETED* event, a similar guard condition is used that evaluates to 'true' if the O2S instance did not receive a score higher than the minimum score defined by the buyer.

2.4.3 Integration design

The O2S event authorisation for *DSP-V4* in *Figure 80* (next page) reflects the change from anonymous offers to authenticated offers.

OFFER_STATE	EVENT	AGENT_GROUP
START	SELLER.OFFER	GR_DSP_S_ANONYMOUS
BUNDLING	SELLER.RETRACT	GR_DSP_S_ANONYMOUS
BUNDLING	SELLER.GETRESULTS	GR_DSP_S_ANONYMOUS
BUNDLED	SELLER.OFFER	GR_DSP_S
READYCONTRACTING	BUYER.SCORE	GR_DSP_B

Figure 80. O2S event authorisation in DSP-V4

Whereas sellers in the group *GR_DSP_S_ANONYMOUS* can submit offers to the BundleNSC, further action for a successfully bundled offer requires an authenticated offer instance in the *O2S.READYCONTRACTING* state (see *Figure 79*), which can only be submitted by agents in the *GR_DSP_S* group.

Especially for the enScenario design of *DSP-V4*, it is important to define views on offer states, since no new offers are created in the O2B FSM and the buyer therefore needs specific authorisation to inspect O2S instances. By default, an offer instance can only be viewed by its originator, unless a view authorisation is specified in the integration design. The level of confidentiality can be controlled via the offer elements exposed. *Figure 81* illustrates samples of the view authorisation specified for the O2B type.

OFFER_STATE	OFFER_ELEMENT	AGENT_GROUP
ADVERTISED	ALL	GR_DSP_S_ANONYMOUS
BUNDLING	ALL	GR_DSP_S_ANONYMOUS
SCORED	CRITERIA	GR_DSP_S
SCORED	CRITERIA_VALUES	GR_DSP_S

Figure 81. O2B view authorisation in DSP-V4

In the *O2B.ADVERTISED* state, potential sellers need to be authorised to inspect the offer, in order to create a corresponding part- or total-offer. Accordingly, all offer elements can be viewed by the seller group *GR_DSP_S_ANONYMOUS*. The same is true for the state *O2B.BUNDLNG*, because sellers need to find out whether the BundleNSC is already operating. It is not necessary to specify a view for an instance in the *O2B.BUNDLED* state, since sellers have access to their complementary *O2S.BUNDLED* instances. Buyers will not be able to view the O2B instances of other buyers in any state. For offer instances in the *O2B.SCORED* state, only the criteria and the importance ratings (weights) defined by the buyer can be viewed by authenticated sellers, because this information is likely to be valuable for the sellers in order to improve their offer ranking in a potential repetition of the BundleNSC operation.

For the O2S, the view design chosen in the sample in *Figure 82* is slightly different, because offers are advertised anonymously and sellers are authenticated only when their offers are part of a successful bundle. As long as the O2S instance is in the state *O2S.BUNDLING*, other sellers can view the constraint values, which is important because coordination among sellers might be necessary in order to build successful bundles. The first time a buyer can view an O2S instance, its constraint values, and the timestamps defining its validity, is when the instance is in the state *O2S.BUNDLED*. The same is true for other sellers with successful part-offers. Finally, only the buyer who originated the complementary O2B instance can inspect the scores achieved by an O2S instance. Still, the overall ranking information is available to sellers via the *MANAGER.GETRESULTS* operation for the ScoreNSC.

OFFER_STATE	OFFER_ELEMENT	AGENT_GROUP
BUNDLING	DOMAINS_VALUES	GR_DSP_S_ANONYMOUS
BUNDLING	TIMESTAMPS	GR_DSP_S_ANONYMOUS
BUNDLED	DOMAINS_VALUES	GR_DSP_B
BUNDLED	DOMAINS_VALUES	GR_DSP_S
BUNDLED	TIMESTAMPS	GR_DSP_B
SCORED	CRITERIA_SCORED	GR_OFFER_BUYER

Figure 82. O2S view authorisation in DSP-V4

As long as the O2S instance is in the state *O2S.BUNDLING*, other sellers can view the constraint values, which is important because coordination among sellers might be necessary in order to build successful bundles. The first time a buyer can view an O2S instance, its constraint values, and the timestamps defining its validity, is when the instance is in the state *O2S.BUNDLED*. The same is true for other sellers with successful part-offers. Finally, only the buyer who originated the complementary O2B instance can inspect the scores achieved by an O2S instance. Still, the overall ranking information is available to sellers via the *MAN-AGER.GETRESULTS* operation for the ScoreNSC.

The model validation process for the resulting *DSP-V4* enScenario model uncovers an 'offer aliveness' violation (see Condition 13 in *Table 11*) because of missing *TIMEOUT* events. In the *O2B.BUNDLED* state, for instance, no *BUYER.TIMEOUT* event is defined. At run-time, this inconsistency could result in 'dead' offer instances in the *O2B.BUNDLED* state. A violation of the same type is discovered for the ScoreNSC operation. If sellers never update their offer instances to the state *O2S.READY-CONTRACTING*, the ScoreNSC will raise a *SCORE.TIMEOUT* event, which has to be incorporated into the organisation design for the O2B type – otherwise O2B offer instances will reside continually in the state *O2B.SCORING*, from which no further transition is possible. As soon as the enScenario designers complete *DSP-V4* with the necessary *TIMEOUT* events, the enScenario model is consistent and can be deployed.

2.4.4 Run-time behaviour

To demonstrate the run-time behaviour specified through *DSP-V4*, let us assume that *AG_DSP_101B* advertises an offer instance *OF_DSP_004* and thereby declares interest in a bundle of two application services: *Accounting* and *WordProcessing*. This event leads to a non-optimising BundleNSC operation with the objective of generating as many total-offers as possible within the timeframe specified by *AG_DSP_101B*. In the case of a successful BundleNSC operation, the transition associated with *BUNDLE. COMPLETED* changes the state of the O2B instance to *O2B.BUNDLED*. Now, *AG_DSP_101B* may inspect the result of the BundleNSC operation by raising *BUYER.GETRESULTS*.

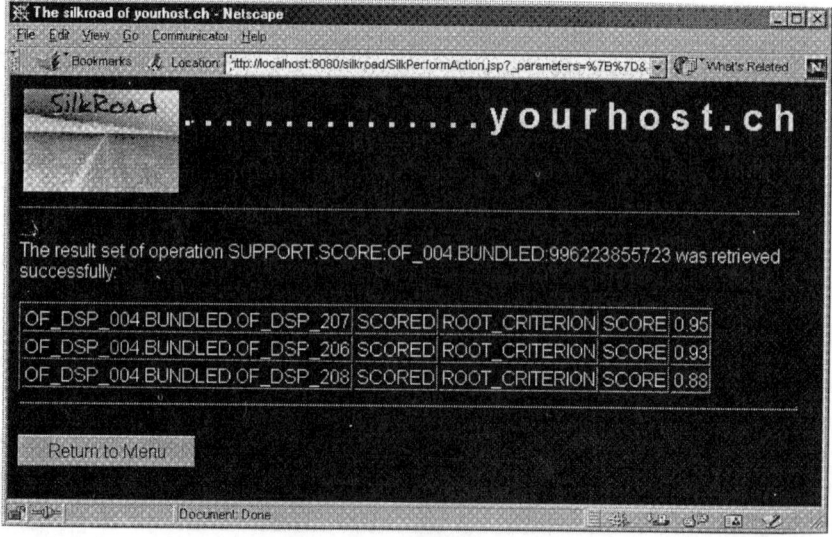

Figure 83. Prototype interface for reading result-sets

The result-set, exemplified in *Figure 83*, contains three potential bundles, two of them representing a coalition of sellers, and one offer from one seller for both services. All sellers use pseudonyms. The corresponding total-offers with new offer IDs were generated by the BundleNSC through *BUNDLE. OFFER*: *OF_DSP_004.BUNDLED.OF_DSP_206*, *OF_DSP_004.BUNDLED.OF_DSP_207*, and *OF_DSP_004.BUNDLED.OF_DSP_208*.

Summary 217

Upon completion of the BundleNSC operation in this example, a number of unsuccessful part-offers from sellers were switched to the state *O2S.RE-JECTED* because they violated constraints in the O2B instance. Sellers who contributed part-offers to successful total-offers can view these newly generated offer instances (including the other part-offers in the bundle) in their in-tray. Checking the enScenario design at run-time, the sellers with agreement candidate offers learn that they have to modify the generated offer by adding authentication information to their part-offer.

AG_DSP_101B is not sure which offer returns the best value and so decides to run the ScoreNSC on all three generated offers. This requires completing the offer instance with evaluation criteria. However, *AG_DSP_101B* chooses not to provide a minimum score objective, since the number of agreement candidates is small, and it is not necessary to reject any of the total-offers automatically. Otherwise, this would happen through the O2S transition with the guard condition *!e(BUNDLE.RS.BUNDLED)*. The ScoreNSC returns the best score for *OF_DSP_004.BUNDLED. OF_DSP_207*. Still, *AG_DSP_101B* is not sure whether this result truly reflects his/her preferences for this transaction. To gain more confidence, *AG_DSP_101B* first checks *O2S.SCORED* instances in its in-tray for the scores assigned to specific criteria (which is possible because the *GR_OFFER_BUYER* is authorised to view these scores, see *Figure 82*). The agent then submits a modified O2B instance with modified criteria importance values and repeats the ScoreNSC operation. Again, *OF_DSP_004.BUNDLED. OF_DSP_207* achieves the highest score, and after this confirmation, *AG_DSP_101B* accepts the total-offer.

3. SUMMARY

This chapter outlines various forms of using the enMedia framework – on a very abstract level by means of potential usage domains, and on a detailed level with the discussion of realistic enScenario cases. The goal is to designate 'where' and 'how' the enMedia framework can be applied. However, the application and expressiveness of the framework is not limited to either the suggested usage domains or the presented cases. The reader may have various other usage domains and enScenarios already in mind.

This chapter also demonstrates the run-time behaviour of the SILKROAD framework prototype and thereby illustrates how the design of enScenarios is reflected in corresponding enProcesses, as well as how the run-time processing adapts depending on the generated run-time specification. Referring back to the preceding chapter, the SILKROAD enMedia framework prototype constitutes a first validation of the propositions presented in this book. This chapter represents a second warrant as it demonstrates the actual application of the theoretical elements of this book to constructed, but practically relevant electronic market cases. However, maximum evidence can only be achieved if the suggested solution approaches are evaluated on a wider scope in real world electronic negotiation scenarios.

Another goal pursued with the scenario cases is a practical demonstration of the design approach application. By evaluating the developed cases, it should become apparent that the design of enScenarios can become very complex and requires detailed knowledge of the design approach. The structure, restrictions, and guidelines imposed by the development action-model and the design meta-model, as well as the formalised model validation procedure, cannot replace a certain level of proficiency and experience. Still, if the design is consistent and matches the requirements, most of the work for the implementation is done – what remains is basically the effort needed to provide specific agent adapters, such as user interfaces. And even if the first design is not the best design, the enMedia framework is well suited to pursue an iterative refinement process. Alternatively, the import of a proven enScenario model from another business domain can serve as an initial starting point.

The next chapter continues the evaluation of the enMedia framework on a theoretical level, but also discusses a number of potential extensions. One suggestion in particular, the addition of Negotiation Support Meta-Components, may reduce the complexity of the enScenario design significantly, because meta-components would allow a designer to enclose a typical collaboration of multiple NSCs (such as the NSC interoperation necessary for a multi-attribute auction case) and to provide it to fellow designers as a reusable artefact.

Chapter 8

Evaluation, exploration, and conclusion
The art and science of negotiating

In this final chapter, the solution approaches suggested in this book are evaluated with regard to the initial problems identified in the domain of electronic negotiations. This includes a discussion of related efforts and of future work that can be based on the foundation provided by this book.

To evaluate the propositions of this book several approaches are possible. One could use the endogenous implicit evaluation criteria defined in Section 3.5.2.2, such as efficiency or fairness, to examine the properties of electronic negotiations that are designed and implemented on the basis of the enMedia framework. However, such properties are subject to the specific enScenario design considerations and therefore not in the sphere of influence of this book. Nevertheless, these criteria could be applied to evaluate the negotiation support components suggested, since NSCs comply to some extent with the notion of mechanisms in economics. This investigation is undertaken in Section 8.2.1. Evidence for the correctness and completeness of the enMedia framework design approach can only be gathered empirically through its application to constructed or real world cases. A first effort in this direction was performed in Section 7.2 and is complemented in Section 8.2.2 with additional theoretical arguments. Finally, it is possible to evaluate the enMedia architecture model on the basis of the SILKROAD framework prototype. This discussion, which is undertaken in Section 8.2.3, is based on general information system properties such as the flexibility and scalability of the architecture, as well as the usability of the tools provided by SILKROAD.

Usability may also serve as a criterion for the enMedia framework design approach, and it could be evaluated on the basis of an empirical study, but a reasonable study would require users who are not only negotiators familiar with electronic media, but electronic negotiation designers. However, subjects who are competent in the design of multi-attribute negotiation intermediation in electronic markets are difficult to find, because state-of-the-art commercial platforms capture neither the different views of the design activity nor many aspects of the symmetry and intermediation support enabled through the enMedia framework.

Readers less interested in a critical discussion of the solution approaches suggested in this book but more curious about a general outlook for electronic negotiations, may skip Sections 8.1 and 8.2 completely and move on to Section 8.3, which scripts various exciting areas of future research.

1. INTENDED SCOPE AND ASSUMPTIONS

The primary goal defined for this book was to investigate design and implementation support for symmetric negotiation intermediation in electronic markets. In particular, the focus was set on multi-attribute negotiations, an area in which three main questions can be identified:
- Which decision tasks in multi-attribute negotiations can be performed through intermediating enMedia?
- How can enScenarios be represented and discussed holistically within a design approach so that it is possible to derive and develop enMedia on the basis of these design models?
- What are the elements of a flexible enMedia architecture model that is able to support an open range of enScenarios?

This book presents distinct solution approaches as answers to each of these questions. Together, these solution approaches constitute the integrated enMedia framework, which can be used to design and implement electronic markets with multi-attribute negotiation intermediation. Before it is possible to evaluate the solution approaches in detail, the scope of the enMedia framework has to be specified explicitly. For this purpose, the following types of electronic negotiations are declared to be outside the intended scope of the enMedia framework:
- Negotiations with fully automated agent decision-making that require the design and/or implementation of negotiation strategies and tactics, such as negotiations based on autonomous software agents.
- Automated negotiations with severe time constraints, i.e. for the resolution of resource allocation problems in real-time.
- Electronic negotiations with communication beyond the exchange of structured offers, i.e. with support for free-form messages such as questions or enquiries.

Intended scope and assumptions 221

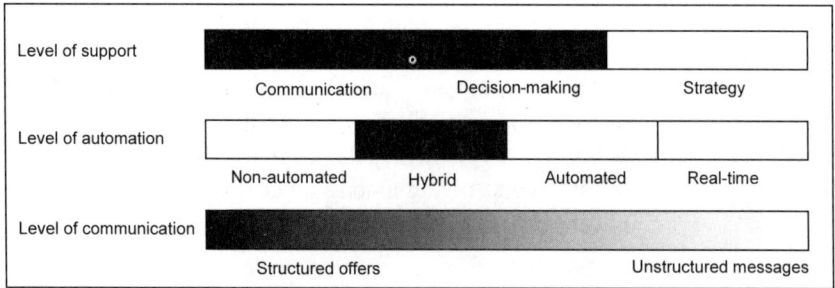

Figure 84. Intended scope of the enMedia framework

These disclaimers are summarised in *Figure 84*. The dark areas are in the focus of the enMedia framework. Nevertheless, the enMedia framework offers many conceptual and technical interfaces that are available to extend its scope towards the areas that are currently not covered, as will be discussed in the remainder of this chapter. Next to the scope defined in *Figure 84*, the following assumptions underlie the enMedia framework:

- The enMedia framework is used within a context in which the issues of a negotiation can be described on the basis of attributes for agents, transactions, or objects. This is the case in most commercial negotiations, for example.
- The potential attributes (the communication aspects) of the electronic negotiation have to be known a priori, before an actual negotiation is executed, so that the common logical space of the agents can be expressed with the formalisms provided by the framework.
- The same applies to the behaviour of the agents involved in the process. The actions they can in principle take (not necessarily the sequence), as well as all their possible reactions to events have to be prior knowledge.
- Typically more than one attribute should become the subject of the negotiation. It is possible to design and implement single-attribute negotiations such as typical auction formats with the proposed enMedia framework, but in general these types of negotiations can be developed and supported in a much simpler and more efficient way.
- The agents negotiating in the designated context trust an intermediary to the extent that they are willing to submit offers (potentially disclosing private information such as evaluation criteria) to the intermediary, and to accept decisions made by the intermediary on their behalf.

The first and the second assumption are also known as the **closed-world assumption** (see for example [Hust94]). If the closed world assumption and the other assumptions outlined above hold for a specific business context and the intended electronic negotiation scenario, the enMedia framework is principally applicable.

On the basis of this discussion, the water management conflict described in [Kilg+99], or examples of political disputes such as the Camp David negotiations illustrated in [BrTa99], clearly do not fall in the area of application for the enMedia framework, owing among other things to the unknown dimensions of the logical space at the beginning of the negotiation.

2. SOLUTION APPROACHES REVISITED

In this section, the evaluation of the enMedia framework moves from the level of its general scope and assumptions to a detailed discussion of the solution approaches suggested. The structure of this discussion follows the sequence of introduction within this book.

2.1 Electronic negotiation support

With the paradigm of negotiation support components a general concept for the encapsulation and reuse of negotiation support functionality was introduced in Chapter 4. NSCs share the same interface and external behaviour. On the basis of this abstraction, NSCs are able to cooperate at run-time as plug-ins in the enMedia architecture and can be integrated in the specification of an enScenario model at design-time. Through the combination and customisation of the existing NSCs enScenarios of almost arbitrary nature may be supported. Through the introduction of new NSCs it is possible to extend the scope of the enMedia framework support in a structured way. The set of NSCs proposed in Chapter 4 is an initial suggestion. If additional solution procedures for decision tasks in multi-attribute negotiations are discovered, the NSC paradigm defines necessary and sufficient conditions to examine whether these procedures are NSC candidates. The NSC paradigm also provides a framework for the dynamic provision of these new formalisms in an enMedium system. In the following sections, the solution procedures suggested in Section 4.4 are critically reviewed and compared with related work.

2.1.1 MatchNSC

The MatchNSC complements genuine constraint satisfaction solving with constraint relaxation analysis to discover not only matching pairs of offers within an electronic market, but also potential agreements that require additional negotiations. It classifies agreement candidates in three sets: matching agreements, distribution agreements, and negotiation agreements. For the third set, the area of conflict between a buyer and a seller is defined by the disagreement space. This disagreement space comprises the negotiation issues, the boundaries of these issues, and the areas of compromise. By means of an analysis of this conflict information, the complexity of a consecutive negotiation for the agreement candidates can be assessed. Hence, the potential enProcess is pre-structured and may in most cases be reduced to the essential discussion of the already identified negotiation issues.

The preference specification required for the MatchNSC operation enables agents to control their level of compromise in a transparent and dynamic way. Depending, for instance, on the current market situation and the feedback from previous matchmaking operations, negotiable constraints can be activated and de-activated in the initiating offer, thus resulting in more or fewer agreement candidates discovered. Furthermore, the detailed agreement and disagreement space analysis provides the agents with additional information that can be used on a case-by-case basis to decide whether constraints are relaxed regarding the operative set of negotiation issues for a specific counterpart's offer.

The MatchNSC is based on the matchmaking concepts developed for the ViMP project [FiHo98]. The core of it can be considered as a non-distributed version of the ViMP trader. In [Iwai00] and [Rama+99] similar matchmaking systems are suggested, but the use of matchmaking for the preparation and support of negotiation processes is not discussed. On the other hand, negotiation support systems have to date focused on core bilateral or multilateral agreement processes such as conflict resolution, but have not addressed the phase typically preceding a negotiation in electronic markets, namely the selection of the most promising agreement candidates.

In addition to the application of matchmaking to electronic negotiation situations, novel to the MatchNSC solution procedure is that in order to identify spaces of agreement and disagreement, constraint satisfaction based on symmetric preferences is augmented with symmetric indications of offer flexibility. Typical multi-agent systems (e.g. [Will+00]) also rely on CSP approaches to resolve conflicts, but require complete utility function specifications for the resolution and have no means to express potential compromises. On the other hand, NSS such as Sardine [MoMa00] deal with notions of flexibility, but not in a symmetric way – only the buyer can indicate flexibility.

2.1.2 ScoreNSC

The hierarchical evaluation procedure of the ScoreNSC was originally suggested in [Stol00] with the concept of the scoring tree. On the basis of a subjective hierarchical composition of evaluation criteria, the ScoreNSC is able to automatically parse a set of offers and to determine utility values for each criterion and an aggregated score for each offer. These scores may provide the foundation for subsequent decisions of an agent in the enProcess (e.g. *'Which offer should be chosen for a counterproposal?'*) as well as the input for consecutive NSC operations such as a multi-attribute auction operation of the BidNSC. "The essence of decision analysis is to break complicated decisions down into small pieces that you can deal with individually and then recombine logically" [Bich99a, p.7].

For its operation, the ScoreNSC requires a complete specification of evaluation criteria in order to determine the best offer(s). However, the specification of utility functions can be very complex and error-prone (see for example [KrDu80]). It can be shown that human agents tend to be inconsistent in their specification of criteria as well as in their final choices. Furthermore, the application of MAUT in the ScoreNSC operation imposes severe restrictions on the decision problem (such as the independence of issues) and requires a clear structure of the decision problem (the number of attributes has to be known and all values for the attributes have to be in an expected range, see Section 8.1).

Unfortunately, these are conditions that many real world negotiation problems will not fulfil [RaSh97]. For instance, in the area of financial services, it is increasingly common to bundle and customise products (e.g. life insurance, pension plans, and funds management) to the specific needs of the buyer. In such a scenario, offers with interdependent attributes, unexpected options, and incomparable structure are very likely. Often high scores for all attributes might be worth more than the sum of the values obtained from the individual utilities. To some extent, these interdependencies can be reflected with multiplicative utility functions (see [KeRa76, 232ff.] for a detailed discussion). In addition, it cannot be assumed that preferences are constant in a negotiation process. Pressures (e.g. time constraints) or new knowledge can alter these preferences at any time [KeSz86].

Hence, in most cases, human decision makers will have to review the results of the ScoreNSC operation. But this review can be based on a result-set of offers that already has a defined order and utilities associated not only on an aggregated level, but also on a single criterion or attribute level. Upon inspection of these results, the agent may, in an iterative scoring process, refine the evaluation criteria and restart the ScoreNSC operation, until confidence in the results is reached. Structured approaches such as a sensitivity analysis (see for example [Klei95]) can guide this iterative process.

Finally, the evaluation criteria defined and refined for a certain negotiation problem, could, in principle, be reused for other comparable negotiation situations. Results of previous ScoreNSC operations can be reviewed on the

Solution approaches revisited 225

basis of the results achieved in the eventual transaction executions, enabling an iterative scoring process over a number of enProcess executions. The more such evaluation criteria are used in comparable negotiation situations, the better they should reflect the intentions and preferences of the decision maker (see also the proposed Score NSC extension in Section 8.3.1.2).

Is the ScoreNSC a 'true' negotiation support component? In principle, the ScoreNSC also supports agreement processes without actual negotiations (see the definitions in Section 3.2). On the basis of the scores an agent can simply accept the best offer ('hit and take') and the enProcess ends without a real negotiation taking place. However, as long as there is more than one offer to consider from the perspective of one agent (e.g. in a context of multiple, parallel bilateral negotiations), a process involving a comparison and decision among the set of competing offers has to be part of any type of negotiation, and therefore the ScoreNSC is an essential support component.

MAUT evaluation approaches such as the one incorporated into the ScoreNSC are used in the majority of multi-agent negotiation systems and NSS to date (see for example [Arpi+00], [BaLo00], or [GuMa98a]). Considering the restrictions and shortcomings of the MAUT representation (see above), it is surprising that no alternative approach for the representation of the preferences of human negotiators has yet found widespread acceptance.

2.1.3 MediateNSC

The adjusted winner procedure is central to the proposed MediateNSC, and thus many of the benefits of AW identified in [BrTa99] are preserved: agreements can be equitable, efficient, and envy-free. The procedure is fair and both agents have an interest in being honest. As Brams and Taylor prove, misrepresenting true preferences can lead to disastrous outcomes. Correspondingly, the procedure forces agents to reveal preferences (and not bargaining positions) and to accept the consequences of their choices, which is one of the requirements of the NSC paradigm. There is no necessity for the agents to specify utility functions. It is sufficient to distribute importance weights. Though distributing weights may also be challenging in real life situations, this task is certainly less demanding than the complete specification of utility functions.

Other procedures that can be used for fair division include 'balanced alternation' and 'proportional allocation'. AW is the only procedure that is efficient, envy-free and equitable. Nevertheless it does not fulfil a fourth condition – inducing the parties to be truthful in announcing their preferences. Proportional allocation can provide a default settlement if the application of AW is vulnerable to false announcements. However, Brams and Taylor state in [BrTa96, p.67] that "... this safeguard will hardly ever be necessary". In addition, agreements on the basis of proportional allocation are not efficient allocations and require all issues to be partitioned. As a result of this, AW is the most promising foundation to choose for the MediateNSC. In summary, the main benefits of the MediateNSC operation are:

- Long haggling processes are avoided. Depending on the agreement suggested (especially with regard to the determined adjustment issue), the enProcess is often very simple. In cases where the initial assignment returns an equal total of points to both agents, no adjustment is necessary. The next simple option is to agree on the alternative price. If the agents do not agree on this option, the enProcess is still reduced to the discussion of a single issue where the relative adjustment is already fixed.
- Sellers have an incentive to compromise – otherwise they will not be selected for the MediateNSC operation and accordingly will not be an agreement candidate for the execution of the transaction. Although their reservation values were not met in the preceding MatchNSC operation, sellers can still achieve a win-win solution with a high utility in the subsequent negotiation.
- There is a high potential for automation, especially from a seller's perspective. A seller could rely on fixed-point assignments on a relative scale (e.g. *'warranty is always twice as important as payment'*) and a set of rules (e.g. *'refuse negotiation if the buyer offer specifies four years of warranty'*) to reduce the level of human intervention.
- Compared to price menus in configuration catalogues, from which the buyer can choose an attribute value within a certain range (e.g. the amount of *RAM* in a *notebook*), it is possible, based on a MediateNSC operation and mutual concessions, to find agreements outside the intention space originally defined by the constraints in the offers.

One question regarding the mandatory price issue needs to be considered: is *price* an independent issue in the sense of AW? Normally, the price is calculated on the basis of the deal configuration (e.g. as output of a cost function) and therefore might be deemed dependent. Whereas the original offer price could be based on a cost function, the price in an enProcess with MediateNSC operation is not dependent on other attribute values, but on the assignment of points to fixed attribute values. Dependency would only exist if the combination of winning *price* and, for instance, *delivery time* results in a greater or smaller value than the sum of the points assigned to these issues (e.g. because the longer timeframe and higher price allows a service to be outsourced and still return a surplus).

For the application of the adjusted winner procedure in an electronic market and negotiation setting, it is critical to further investigate the requirements manifested in the conditions identified in Section 4.4.3.1. The second condition, mirroring utility functions, will be discussed in Section 8.3.1.3. The first condition, binding offers, is a general problem in the domain of electronic negotiations. If it is possible for buyers to explore (e.g. anonymously with a software agent) the intention space of a seller before actually submitting their offer to the enInstance, any negotiation is reduced to a trial-and-error optimisation process. This can be illustrated with the Priceline air travel ticket auctions [Pric01]. In order to 'name your price', the recommended strategy is to perform a market analysis of current flight prices prior to bidding, because any flight bid accepted by an airline has to be purchased. The risk is that the offer submitted is 'too high' and the buyer could have made a better deal without having used Priceline. To decrease this risk, the buyer might submit a sequence of bids with initially very low but increasing prices to Priceline in order to incrementally discover the cheapest offer available.

There are several ways to circumvent this strategy. One alternative is to charge for bids or search requests. The other is to restrict the options available to buyers for changing failed O2B instances. In the airline ticket case, buyers could, for example, be restricted to changing only the number of *stopovers* or the *duration* but not the *price*. Both suggested alternatives require authentication of the buyers. In the Priceline example this happens on the basis of a credit card number. In the enMedia design approach, enScenario rules can prevent sellers from retracting their offer. As an example, the enScenario design can specify that it is sufficient for the buyer to accept an O2S instance in order to reach an agreement for the execution of the transaction (see the *DSP-V1* case in Section 7.2.1).

Regarding the nature of negotiations and especially of integrative negotiations, several restrictions of the MediateNSC have to be discussed.

In general, the MediateNSC operation is restricted to situations in which agents are willing to communicate confidentially their preference structure at least to a third party. Nevertheless, the preferences revealed for the MediateNSC operation are not communicated to the counterpart, although this is supposed to be a necessary condition in order to achieve 'true' integrative negotiations. Exchanged preferences can be used to learn more about the interests of the other agent and to modify an offer accordingly. An integrative negotiation process could also involve the inclusion of additional issues or different attribute values that were originally not defined or advertised, in order to achieve real win-win solutions. Although real win-win solutions might be missed, the main advantage of the proposed MediateNSC operation is that it requires only one single and unproblematic input from the agents to come up with a resolution.

Another issue is the necessity for the agents to accept at least some extreme offer positions expressed by the counterpart. The negotiating agents might see this in a negative way, because it eliminates the 'softer' approach of intermediate solutions ('meeting halfway'). However, the overall utility of the agreement is guaranteed to be maximised with AW, and therefore it is rational for an agent to trust the solution procedure.

A restriction of the adaptation chosen is the potential loss of the efficiency in cases where the price is not the attribute with the SPR, but is nevertheless accepted by the negotiating agents for the settlement. However, prior research indicates that the efficiency of a solution is not a critical decision factor for negotiating agents and that they often refuse to move from their bargained solution to a more efficient solution if this is suggested by some form of intermediation (see for example [KeMa98]).

Another potential problem related to the suggested MediateNSC is that agents will miss the opportunity to exert pressure on the counterpart in the negotiation process in order to, for instance, force a compromise. Bargainers tend to believe in their ability to achieve good results on the basis of superior negotiation power or skills [Lewi+97, 179ff.]. Why should they agree to execute a solution procedure that guarantees fair shares to everybody? In case of the MediateNSC, they should, because the agents can quickly achieve an agreement that, in most cases, is better than no agreement at all.

Regarding related work, one similar solution procedure based on flexible and symmetric constraints expressed in a formal contract language was suggested in [Reev+00]. This solution procedure requires an iteration of interactions and automatically generates an appropriate negotiation mechanism (an auction) for the conflict resolution, thereby resulting in executable contracts. In comparison, the MediateNSC represents a formalisation of a single decision task without the need for iteration. In addition, the MediateNSC solution procedure is only loosely coupled with other support functionalities and can be executed in a number of different enScenarios.

2.2 Electronic negotiation design

The approach for the design of electronic negotiations presented in Chapter 5 is structured according to a development action-model. This model covers elements of the analysis phase, a methodology for the design phase that separates aspects of the organisation and the communication design, and a proposed transition to the implementation phase based on the generation of run-time specifications for the design model in an imperative format.

The main goal of the proposed design approach is to structure the problem domain of electronic negotiation design through a number of techniques:
- The enScenario designer is supported with a design meta-model that defines the potential model dimensions.

Solution approaches revisited 229

- The resulting design models can be checked for completeness and consistency on the basis of model validation test conditions.
- The graphical notation used in the design approach allows for the communication of modelling aspects to non-technical stakeholders and the discussion of design issues on a conceptual level.

If all involved parties agree to the enScenario design model, the likelihood that actual enProcesses following the rules in this model will succeed is certainly increased.

Furthermore, the design approach explicitly integrates the use of NSCs and implicitly defines requirements for an enMedia architecture model that can instantiate a variety of enScenarios on the basis of the generated run-time specifications. However, the design approach is independent from the implementation platform chosen for an enMedium system, and can also be used for a proprietary electronic negotiation implementation.

Due to the generation of run-time specifications, the overall implementation effort for an enMedium system is greatly reduced. This property allows for an iterative development approach where a representation is generated and tested multiple times in order to refine the original design (see the discussion of a round-trip engineering approach in Section 8.3.2.1). A 'heavier' implementation phase would certainly limit the number of feasible iterations. If a later evaluation of the enProcess execution at run-time by the enMedium analyst leads to changes in the design model, the necessary implementation effort is simply the task of re-generating the run-time specifications. An additional benefit of the mechanistic generation process is that the decisions made in the design model are guaranteed to propagate to the enScenario implementation. It is, in principle, impossible for an implementation to contradict the rules specified in the design, which may happen in a programming-based approach, perhaps simply because rules are forgotten or misinterpreted.

The primary question for the evaluation of the proposed design approach proposed is whether the languages defined are complete in the sense that it is possible to express (in sufficient detail) logical spaces as well as roles and protocols for a variety of potential enScenarios in a multitude of business contexts. This question can only be answered after a significant number of practical scenarios have been modelled with the proposed approach, and the results have been evaluated. A first attempt in this direction is made with the scenario cases in Section 7.2.

In general, the languages defined through the design approach are not static but can easily be extended if, for instance, the expressiveness is insufficient for the requirements of a specific negotiation scenario. New offer structure elements might be necessary for the offer state structure design, and additional actions may have to be integrated in the offer transition specification. The proposed design approach provides the overall structure and foundation for the inclusion of new design elements. The foundation and global paradigm of the design approach is basically the idea of specifying FSM representations for offers-to-sell and offers-to-buy, as well as providing different means to complement and integrate these specifications.

One typical system design methodology is missing in the suggested approach – a process of stepwise abstraction or top-down refinement (see for example [FeSi93, p.309]). In this method, designers begin with a conceptual system model, which is then incrementally refined with more and more technical details until a detailed design for the model implementation is available. The proposed design approach allows designers to iterate through the communication, organisation, and integration design activities, thereby potentially starting with a very simple model, which becomes more detailed with each iteration. But the same modelling constructs and rules are used throughout the design activity. In Section 8.3.4 an extension to address this lack of refinement is discussed. In the following sections, the respective communication and organisation design approaches are investigated in more detail.

2.2.1 Communication design

Referring back to the initial claims, an evaluation of the presented communication design approach has to treat two interrelated questions:
- Can the ontology problem of electronic negotiations (c.f. Section 5.3.1) be addressed by the proposed solution?
- Is XML Schema a useful representation format for expressing and validating the communication design at run-time?

The results of the explicit communication design within the enMedia framework design approach are an offer ontology representation for the agent, transaction, and object contexts, and offer state structure specifications for offer instances associated with these contexts. To achieve a common understanding of the issues that are subject to the negotiation, these design deliverables can be specified in a joint process with all parties involved in the later use of the enScenario.

Once the communication design has been mutually accepted, it can be turned into a run-time specification, thus enabling the checking of offer instances in an enProcess for semantical and syntactical correctness with respect to the original design. Assuming that both the communication design and the generation of the run-time specification are complete and correct, the ontology problem cannot occur during actual enProcesses because violations of the agreed-upon logical space would be detected. This is true at least for the agents of parties originally involved in the design process. Accordingly, the admission of new agents to an enInstance requires, in principle, an acknowledgement of the logical space defined for the enInstance.

Whether the run-time representation is complete and correct depends largely on the mechanisms provided by XML Schema in association with the defined customisation and generation process. Various suggestions (see for example [CrPu99]) have been made to move from proprietary ontology formalisms (KL-ONE, KIF, or frame logic) towards more standardised and widely used representation mechanisms such as UML or XML document type definitions (DTDs). The latter approach was chosen in [ErSt99]. The authors point out that it appears to be more appropriate to transform ontologies into XML Schema than into DTDs, mainly because of the ability to define type hierarchies. A process for the stepwise translation of an ontology to XML Schema is proposed in [Klei+00]. In comparison to this method, communication design specifications in the enMedia framework do not represent a complete ontology in a schema but only the set of concepts assigned to a specific offer type.

Regarding completeness, the status of the current representation is still insufficient. On the basis of domain typing, the relation of attributes to concepts is lost if multiple concepts are represented in one state- and ontology-dependent schema. This might be the case if an agent intends to issue a combinatorial offer for several types of objects (e.g. *notebooks* and *servers*). Related to this problem is also the fact that multiple inheritance cannot be represented in XML Schema. This is one of the shortcomings of the current representation, which could be addressed in future work.

Beyond the completeness and correctness necessary to tackle the ontology problem, the use of XML Schema provides an additional advantage. Since XML Schema is a W3C standard, powerful and widely distributed tools such as the Xerces parser can be used to create or validate XML documents that adhere to this standard. Hence, agents can easily interface with enMedium systems by simply submitting XML documents. These documents can be edited, administered, and validated remotely according to the internal processes of the agent's organisation. Though this creates a distributed and decentralised system of negotiating agents, common integrity rules are defined centrally by the intermediating enMedium system through the published logical space schemata.

As stated above, the communication design is restricted to the specification of offer types. Unstructured communication beyond offers, for example with free-form messages, is not in the scope of the current approach. To support such additional means of interaction, semi-structured offers could be introduced that may include free-form messages but still relate terms in the messages to an ontology context. This is demonstrated, for instance, in the DOC.COM system [ScQu01].

2.2.2 Organisation design

The main task of the organisation design is the modelling of offer state charts and the specification of corresponding FSMs, which are complemented within the integration design with event and view authorisation specifications. Offer state charts are not a proprietary construct of this design approach but rather adhere to the notion of state charts in UML. Hence, an enScenario designer can also create state charts with tools supporting the general UML notation, and still focus on the specific semantics necessary for the enMedia framework organisation design, such as the specification of target properties for actions.

From a high-level perspective, the language for the enMedia framework organisation design consists of a set of primitive actions ('match', 'score', etc.) that can, adhering to a certain grammar, be combined to form sentences (e.g. 'bundle – match – mediate – score'). The language defined also covers the specification of conditions for the triggering of these actions by events. Regarding its flexibility, this language can be extended to cover additional words (actions). But basic restrictions have to be respected. Specific types of guard conditions that may, for instance, evaluate dynamic domain knowledge (e.g. current market prices) are not supported, because this imposes additional demands on the run-time interpretation capabilities provided by an enMedium system. A customisation of the design approach would make such custom extensions possible, but then the advantage of generality is lost and additional requirements have to be defined for implementations of the enMedia framework.

Work related to the organisation design approach presented in this book can be found in the COSMOS project [Lame+98] and the TEM effort [Beny+00]. COSMOS supports the design of electronic negotiations with models on the basis of rules [KuLa00]. Rules describe, for instance, the protocol of a marketplace with conditions, trigger, and activation elements. Agents are modelled using state diagrams in which, again, rules define the state transitions. The support for rules also allows capturing negotiation strategy formalisms for autonomous software agents. The generation of these strategies is based on genetic algorithms, thus enabling completely automated negotiations. In contrast to this, the design approach proposed in this book does not aim to cover automated negotiations and accordingly, its language does not provide means to design or represent negotiation strategies. Another main distinction is that the state charts used in this book capture the transition of offer states, not of agent states (see below).

For TEM, Benyoucef and Keller evaluated several modelling paradigms with regard to their application in the domain of electronic negotiations, and they came to the conclusion that UML state charts with event-condition-

Solution approaches revisited 233

action specifications are the most appropriate to use [BeKe00]. The presented design approach also relies on state charts, but in TEM what is modelled is the state of a negotiation (e.g. 'taking bids' or 'clearing') – not the state of offers. The same is true for the negotiation models presented by Kumar and Feldman [KuFe98]. Modelling offer states has several advantages. Due to its real representation as an offer instance, an offer is more tangible from the perspective of a negotiator than an abstract protocol or the inner states of an agent. Still, a protocol is implicitly defined through offer state transitions. In addition, the validation of actual negotiations for compliance with the design can be performed on the level of offer instances, which also provide an inherent persistence of the state of an enProcess. Finally, the states of different types of offers (O2B and O2S) in one enScenario need to be considered in the organisation design in order to support the symmetry of buyers and sellers – meaning that the roles of buyers and sellers are not distinguished regarding the available semantics. For enMedium systems supporting the design language, the paradigm of offer state modelling is also advantageous since it enables simple implementations of transactional guarantees and the use of stateless components (see Section 6.1.4).

Paurobally and Cunningham [PaCu01] also use state charts to implicitly define negotiation protocols, but they add an additional logic layer for a more explicit representation that allows checking coherently for errors and enables autonomous software agents to derive possible negotiation paths, in the sense of a strategy. This is an interesting extension of the FSM representation in this work, which could be further investigated, especially because the cases presented by the authors (bilateral negotiation, auction, etc.) can be expressed in a similar way with the organisation design proposed in this book.

In contrast to all of the discussed related work, the FSMs modelled in the enMedia framework design approach are integrated with other complementary design elements, in order to achieve a comprehensive, abstract specification of an electronic negotiation, including the customisation and configuration of NSC operations, in one enScenario model.

2.3 Electronic negotiation architecture

An enMedia architecture model that fulfils the requirements identified through the development of the enMedia framework and aims primarily at flexibility and reusability is presented in Section 6.1. An enMedium system is an implementation of this architecture model. Arbitrary types of enScenarios developed with the enMedia framework design approach can be activated and executed in an enMedium system that is compliant with the architecture model, because its architecture components are able to interpret generated run-time specifications of enScenario design models and to adapt the run-time behaviour accordingly. Owing to the fact that a large variety of enScenarios can be modelled with the design approach, and that these models can be interpreted by implementations of the architecture model, the property of flexibility for the architecture model is guaranteed.

A part of this flexibility is also structural flexibility. Through the plug-in mechanism for NSCs and the functional architecture distribution possibilities, the composition of the architecture model can be adapted depending on the specific requirements of the deployed enScenarios (e.g. whether a MediateNSC is required or not) and the organisation of the development process.

The enScenario cases demonstrate how an implementation of this architecture model, namely the SILKROAD prototype, achieves the intended flexibility of supporting a variety of different enScenario design models with no need for unique implementation code. SILKROAD enMedium systems customise their run-time processing solely depending on imperative run-time specifications and declarative enMedium configurations (e.g. agent authorisations). Furthermore, the JSP agent adapter prototype of the SILKROAD framework prototype can generate a primitive generic user interface on the basis of a given run-time specification, thus removing the necessity for scenario-specific implementation effort at all.

Are there alternatives to an application framework approach for building systems that combine flexibility and reusability? One alternative solution would be to package the reusable functionalities and especially the solution procedures proposed in Chapter 4 in a common negotiation support library with a corresponding application programming interface. This approach, however, is not able to capture the reuse of code in combination with the reuse of design, since a library does not specify, for example, the decomposition of a system into coherent elements. Another alternative would be to define, instead of an interpreter solution, a more formal language for enScenario models and an associated compiler, so that executable code for a complete system can be generated. Nevertheless, the disadvantage of this approach is that the subsequent customisation of this system for specific requirements is much more complex on the basis of generated code than on the basis of an application framework with predefined customisation points and standardised, open interfaces.

Beyond flexibility and reusability, the architecture model can also be evaluated from a theoretical perspective with respect to additional measures of quality for information systems (see for example [Kan95]):

- **Completeness and correctness:**
  The architecture model represents an abstract application framework. Hence, its completeness and correctness with respect to the requirements has to be evaluated for enInstances in a real enMedium system. If all requirements identified in the analysis are respected in the design of an enScenario, the enInstance based on the imperative run-time specification generated for the enScenario design model is necessarily complete and correct and results in the intended behaviour.
- **Scalability and efficiency:**
  The scalability of the architecture model is supported by the possibilities for component distribution and the suggested usage of stateless architecture components. Inherent in the nature of an application framework approach is a loss of efficiency because the composition of an enMedium system and its run-time processing is not 'hardwired' or pre-compiled but dynamically established on the basis of run-time specifications.
- **Reliability:**
  A foundation for the reliability of an enMedium system is already laid out in the architecture model. If the event processing is implemented with transactional properties, the architecture model provides a large degree of failure robustness, since offer states are persistent in the offer instance documents and no context or state has to be propagated from event to event. These ACID properties also guarantee concurrency robustness, because offer instances can be locked exclusively for the execution of one event transaction.
- **Maintenance:**
  Ease of maintenance is achieved through the application framework approach, which opens up the possibility to change enInstances simply by modifying the design model and re-generating the run-time specification. For maintenance purposes an up-to-date and complete specification of the enScenario rules is always available in the design-time and run-time repository.

Other quality properties such as the security, portability, or tracing capability of the enMedia architecture model can only be evaluated for a particular implementation. The SILKROAD framework prototype, for instance, is portable to all major operating system platforms due to its compliance with the J2EE model.

3. FUTURE WORK

Reviewing the results of the research underlying this book and the proposed solutions, a number of areas for future work can be identified that (a) address limitations of the current approach, (b) extend the scope of the support provided, or (c) build upon the foundation provided by the enMedia framework in order to explore new possibilities in the field of electronic negotiation research and practice.

This section elaborates on these areas of future work. First, extensions of the negotiation support components and related augmentations of the architecture model are discussed. Then areas of future research for the design approach are investigated, before a technical vision for the SILKROAD framework prototype is presented. At last, the complete enMedia framework approach constitutes the foundation for possible further exploration.

3.1 Support extensions

A number of extensions can be envisioned to enhance the support provided by the suggested NSCs. Not all of these extensions suit the notion of an NSC; some require the introduction of additional architecture model component types, for example to represent the interest of third parties or for the support of the decision-making of a single agent.

3.1.1 MatchNSC

From a matchmaking perspective, a first extension becomes feasible if a constraint cannot only be tagged as negotiable, but is also complemented by a certain **value domain probability** (distribution). In supply chain scenarios, it is often the case that, for example, a delivery time of *10 days* can be guaranteed only with a probability of *90%* and in *10%* of the cases, delivery is delayed. Matching with respect to such probabilities could be incorporated into the MatchNSC, resulting, for instance, in distribution agreement candidates with an associated cumulative level of uncertainty.

Beyond the scope of an internal MatchNSC extension, interesting opportunities arise if the MatchNSC operation is initiated centrally, comparable to the clearing process in an exchange. The current solution approach assumes that one agent always triggers matchmaking for one initiating offer. Through central invocation, sets of agreement candidates with alternative initiating offers could be considered. This totality of matches allows introducing market optimisation measures such as the maximisation of the overall welfare, as well as imposing competitive pressure on the agents of the initiating offers. For instance, the measure of the overall success of the MatchNSC operation could be based on the level of conflict, defined as either the total number of matchmaking conflicts or the total of buyer/seller utility disparities.

To centrally initiate a MatchNSC operation, an additional architecture component, a **market manager**, becomes necessary in the enMedia architecture model. Similar to other actors, this market manager would submit offers and raise events (e.g. periodically) to execute actions. This allows controlling the enProcess from a market perspective and enables enMedia framework support for scenarios such as a continuous double auction (see for example [Teic+98]).

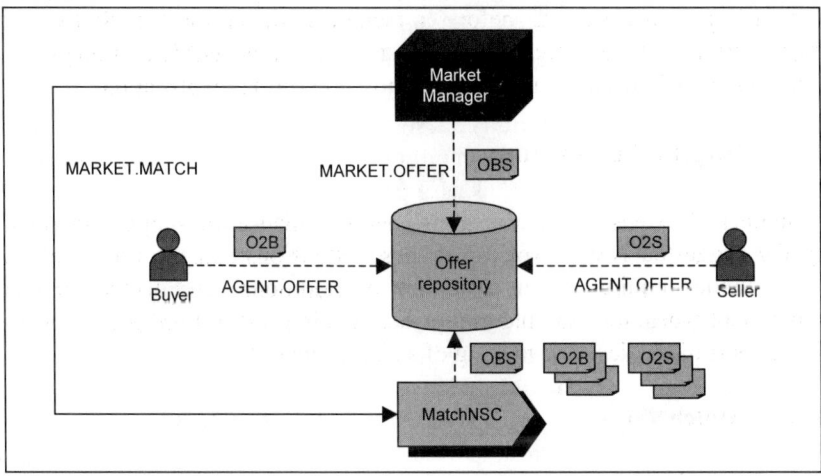

Figure 85. Three-way-NSC-operation architecture model extension

To enable the design of an enScenario with a market manager role, a third extension of the MatchNSC is required. The MatchNSC may match not only offers of agents with the role 'buyer' or 'seller', but also offers from third parties. The offers of third parties (e.g. from the market manager), could define constraints on the other agents' attributes (e.g. *'match only buyers older than 18 and sellers with a location in Switzerland'*), as well as on attributes of complementary offer types. To keep the symmetry of the overall approach, the attributes of this third party agent role might also be subject to constraints specified by the other agents, such as (*intermediary.fee,<,100,USD*). The resulting **three-way-NSC-operation** (see *Figure 85*) can also be exploited to support specific requirements of enMedium providers (e.g. legal access restrictions), and might prove to be useful for the other NSCs introduced as well.

From a design perspective, the introduction of the market manager component would require a new offer type, an **offer-to-buy-and-sell** (OBS, e.g. for *notebook* transactions). In a continuous double auction enScenario, for instance, the market manager could then assume the role of the third party and advertise OBS instances, which in a consecutive *OBS.BIDDING* state may become the target of *BUYER.OFFER* or *SELLER.OFFER* actions, if buyers or sellers submit bids to this auction.

3.1.2 ScoreNSC

To address the problems of inconsistent and error-prone evaluation criteria specifications (see Section 8.2.1.2), an incremental procedure of preference specification and scoring could be used. Evaluation criteria can be derived in a number of ways, such as by asking the agent questions and interpreting the answers. The foundation for this question and answering process would be a set of rules that deduce evaluation utility functions from a buyer's answers to needs-oriented questions. Let us assume a buying agent is questioned about whether the intended use of the desired *notebook* is for *Internet* or for *games*. Depending on the choice of the agent, the importance for a *graphics performance* criterion and a *networking options* criterion can be adjusted. This could be done with the following sample rule: '*if the purpose is for games than the importance of the graphics performance criterion is high*.' Using such an **incremental preference elicitation** process, needs and objectives of the agent can be mapped implicitly to the formal expressions of utility functions. An interesting problem is to ask the right number and appropriate sequence of questions. One solution is to optimise the decision-tree representing the interview structure on the basis of an estimation of the expected 'revenue' for the next question (see [StSt01a] for details).

The solution procedures to support such an interviewing process can be automated. However, since interviewing is not an intermediating task that receives inputs from several agents, this procedure cannot be part of the ScoreNSC, but has to be conducted by a **decision-support component** (DSC). A DSC is private to one agent and precedes the execution of the ScoreNSC. In the case of interviewing this would be a QuestionDSC. The DSC type constitutes a new architecture model component that resides between the actual agent and the agent adapter as illustrated in *Figure 86* (next page).

The same is true for additional assistance provided by a **repository of previously used evaluation criteria and scoring trees**. Instead of defining new evaluation criteria for every new enProcess participation, already applied and potentially refined criteria could be re-used. Similar to case-based reasoning systems (see for example [Leak96]), a CaseDSC can try to find comparable evaluation situations and, if successful, suggest a corresponding evaluation structure.

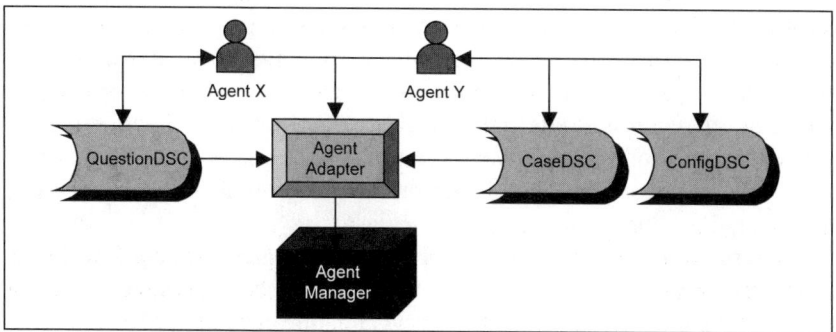

Figure 86. Decision support component architecture model extension

Finally, a DSC might also assist an agent in resolving **offer configuration** problems. An offer instance might feature options and dependencies (c.f. Section 3.3.1) and at some state in the enProcess an agent typically has to choose the desired configuration of this offer instance, thereby determining the final price. On the basis of the constraint specification in the offer instance, a ConfigDSC could present these options to the agent and generate a modified offer instance that reflects the configuration chosen by the agent.

3.1.3 MediateNSC

The second condition necessary for the application of the MediateNSC (c.f. Section 4.4.3.1) demanded vertically mirrored utility functions with identical boundaries. An extension of the MediateNSC solution procedure could require that agents also specify **utility function boundaries** for the negotiable constraints. If an asymmetry is discovered during the MediateNSC operation, a compensation can be calculated, for example on the basis of linear default utility functions. This approach can be illustrated with the sample MediateNSC result in *Table 16*:

Table 16. MediateNSC compensation example

Issue	Buyer Utility		Constraint	Buyer Weight	Seller Weight	Constraint
1	$U(X) = 1$	$U(Y) = 0$	Option X	**30**	25	Option Y
2	$U(0) = 0$	$U(40) = 1$	40	20	**45**	20
3	$U(3) = 1$	$U(2) = 0$	3	**50**	30	2
Points gained				80	45	

If in this case according to the utility function of the buyer, losing issue *2* results in an attribute value of *20*, which still returns a utility of *0.5*, the buyer will not score *zero* but *10* points, increasing the overall total to *90* points. As a result of this, the giveback of the buyer for a fair agreement has to increase. To discourage strategic behaviour, additional means for the elicitation of truthful utility functions have to complement this compensation approach. An alternative is that the enMedium provider supplies default utility functions for a given business context.

To further adapt the AW solution procedure to multilateral enScenarios, an interesting improvement is to increase the competitive pressure in enProcesses based on the MediateNSC. If the MediateNSC posts feedback on the ranking (the number of points achieved) of the suggested agreement as compared to other agreements, sellers, for instance, might be willing to perform the adjustment more in favour of the buyer – or to concede issues they initially won.

Another extension for the MediateNSC operation is to reveal information regarding the best alternative to a negotiated agreement (BATNA). This **BATNA** could either constitute the 'best' offer among the set of offers that did not match in the preceding MatchNSC operation, or the 'best' mediated agreement with another seller if, for example, one buyer is involved in a set of bilateral parallel negotiations. As an additional output of the MatchNSC operation, the BATNA could be used as input for an agent's decision whether or not to opt for mediation with a certain counterpart.

3.1.4 Negotiation support meta-components

The application of the design approach in Chapter 7 illustrates that an enScenario model can become quite complex and may require many intermediate offer states and multiple NSC invocations with additional pre-condition states. One reason for this complexity lies within the NSC paradigm and the corresponding architecture model design – NSCs are plug-ins and not aware of each other (c.f. Section 6.1.3). With this design, dependencies are avoided, reusability is enhanced, and flexible means of functional component distribution are supported.

However, complex application cases, such as the multi-attribute auction scenario illustrated in Section 7.2.3, often specify partial FSMs in which offers are automatically passed from one NSC to the other. An example is that offer instances are scored upon submission through the agent and then automatically passed to a bidding session (see the transition in *Figure 73* from *O2S.SCORING* to *O2S.BIDDING*). Through such automated NSC interactions, intermediate offer instances are generated that agents never inspect (and therefore such offers need no persistent storage). These NSC collaborations could be enclosed in **Negotiation Support Meta-Components** (NSMC) that define a fixed flow of offer states, state transitions, and NSC invocations. NSMCs could be incorporated into enScenario models in the same way as standard NSCs, assuming that the external behaviour is identical – that is, assuming they receive initiating and target offers as well as objectives (which might be passed on to the incorporated NSC actions) and produce offers and a result-set structure. Note that for the sake of compatibility with the component paradigm, the operation of NSMCs never has to be interrupted, for example to receive additional agent inputs.

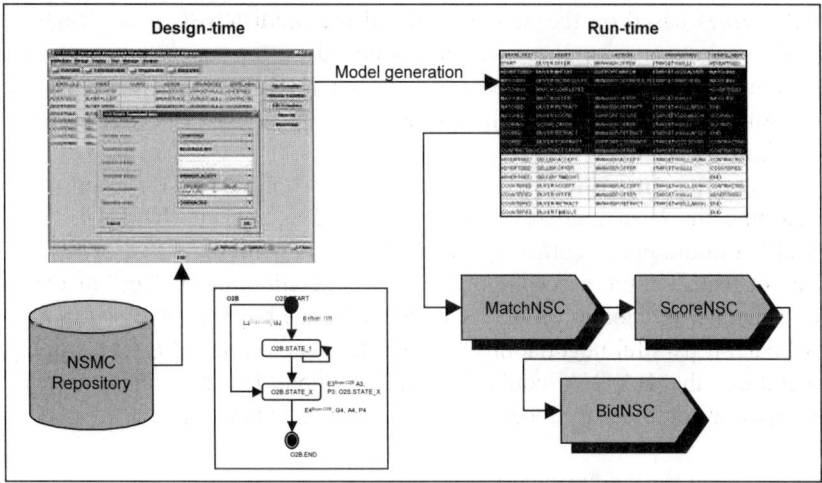

Figure 87. Negotiation support meta-component extension

This requirement is the major design restriction for the definition of NSMCs. From a technical perspective, the incorporation of NSMCs into the enMedia framework would require, next to a persistent storage of NSMCs with internal partial FSM specifications (FSM 'chunks' in an NSMC repository), an extension to the enScenario model generation and deployment process. In this extended process, the offer state transition specifications also have to be parsed. If an NSMC support-state were specified in a transition, the internal FSM specification would have to be retrieved and included in the existing enScenario model FSM, resulting in an expanded FSM specification. Hence, NSMCs exist only at design-time and need not be deployed, but rather are resolved to expanded FSM specifications at run-time as illustrated in *Figure 87.* This resolution has to be performed before the verification of the enMedium server configuration in the deployment process (Section 6.2.3.2), in order to guarantee that all NSCs implicitly invoked through the NSMC expansion are available on the target platform.

An alternative resolution method is to allow nested FSMs. With this technique, the FSM specifications of an NSMC could be referenced in the main enScenario model FSM, and it would be possible to propagate events back and forth between the main and the nested FSM without the need for partial FSM inclusion in the generation and deployment process.

At run-time, NSMC-internal intermediate offer states can be represented by virtual offers (in memory), which is beneficial from a scalability point of view but requires an additional objective (e.g. *OFFER_OUTPUT = VIRTUAL*) for the incorporated NSC invocations. The notion of NSMCs is also a useful construct to represent general NSC interdependencies (see Section 4.6) in a 'hard-coded' way, as long as the specified NSC cooperation requires no intermediate agent input. Finally, NSMCs can represent fully automated negotiation patterns – this idea is further investigated below under the subject of reference models.

3.2 Design extensions

Next to an incorporation of new design entities such as the OBS type and the NSMCs introduced above, future research in the area of electronic negotiation design on the basis of the enMedia framework can also address novel uses for enScenario design models.

3.2.1 Model simulations

The current status of the enMedia framework supports checking of enScenario models for completeness and correctness by means of the test conditions defined in *Table 11*. However, this model validation does not provide any feedback about the expected run-time properties of the resulting enProcesses, especially regarding the potential behaviour of agents participating in these enProcesses.

Through the FSM compatibility of the offer state charts, a foundation for simulated approximation of enProcesses is already provided. A protocol specified through organisation design FSMs can be simulated with tools such as a Petri Net simulator [Koni01]. The missing pieces for this run-time approximation are agent models that represent agent communication and decision-making in the enProcess. Agent models can also be specified with FSMs (see for example [KuLa00]). Hence, for a complete enProcess run-time approximation, the interdependencies of interlinked protocol and agent FSMs can be studied using one simulation paradigm.

Future work 243

The simulation of enProcesses allows an enScenario designer or analyst to preview the properties of future enProcesses and to verify whether design guidelines and recommendations from the analysis phase are reflected in the enScenario model. If this is not the case and adjustments are necessary, the enScenario model can be refined iteratively in a round-trip engineering process as illustrated in *Figure 88*.

It should be feasible to structure the simulation results on the basis of the endogenous implicit classification criteria of the taxonomy introduced in Section 3.5.2.2 (e.g. efficiency or convergence). Given a comprehensive model simulation capability, the enMedia framework may grow into a platform for experimental economics (see for example [Bich99b]) that allows experimenting with a broad range of market rules and mechanism designs.

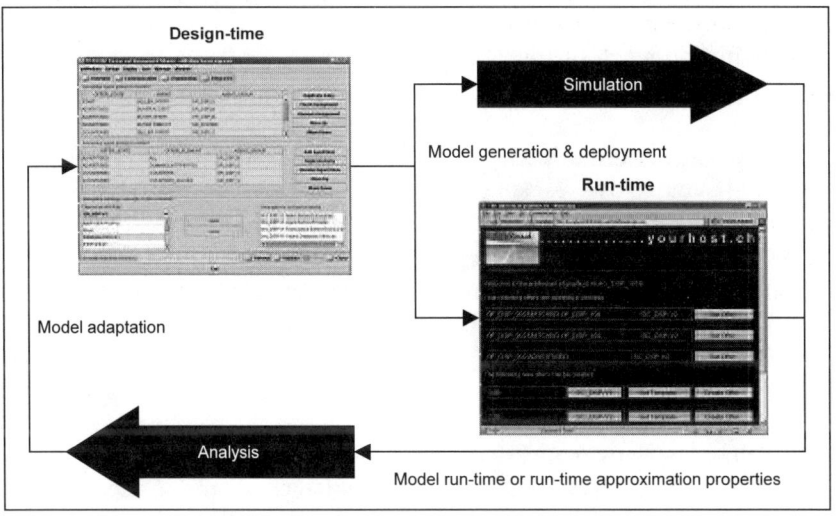

Figure 88. Round-trip engineering of enScenario models

3.2.2 Reference models

The fourth usage domain for the enMedia framework in Section 7.1.4 discussed the role of a negotiation service provider who offers outsourcing of negotiation processes in electronic markets. After a certain period of operation, this NSP may have supported many different enScenarios and may have acquired a large number of corresponding enProcess logs. By means of mining, this historical data could allow the derivation of reusable organisation and communication patterns.

A **communication pattern** might suggest, for example, that offers for the business context of *database service provisioning* usually comprise certain attributes such as the definition of a *support contract* (e.g. *24×7*) or the *pricing scheme* (e.g. *fixed rate* or *volume-priced*). Another promising foundation for the definition of communication patterns are the INCO-TERMS and ETERMS repositories [TaTh00]. These collections of standard commercial terms aim at avoiding the friction resulting from the diversity of semantic and legal interpretation of terms in international commerce. For use in a reference model, INCOTERMS or ETERMS could be represented in generic offer context ontologies that define, for instance, the terms in standard concepts for transaction attributes such as *packaging*, *delivery points*, or *transits*.

Similarly, an **organisation pattern** may recommend that the efficiency of agreements in the domain of *database services* can benefit from a short phase of bidding with a set of potential service providers selected on the basis of an initial offer scoring operation. This pattern might be suggested because in the past, the standardisation of *database services* allowed in many cases a large number of providers to quote, thus stimulating strong market competition.

These patterns can be compared to proven idioms used for the design of software [Gamm+95] – except that in this case the design relates to rules in enScenarios. Eventually the NSP is empowered to develop an enScenario reference model, featuring best-practice communication and organisation designs, which are available through a design repository (c.f. [Lomu+01]). Whereas the development action-model and the design meta-model specify 'how' to model electronic negotiations, a reference model can specify 'what' to model. Complementing the code reuse of NSCs, a reference model offers the possibility to further extend the design reuse offered by the enMedia framework. In the case that the organisation pattern is at least partially automated and requires no further agent interaction, negotiation support meta-components (see Section 8.3.1.4) can represent the pattern in enScenario design models.

If this abstraction is feasible, the enMedia framework, which is currently focused on the design and implementation of electronic negotiations, may also comprise a reference model for electronic negotiations. To recommend the 'best' enScenario in the analysis phase, reference model patterns can be matched with design guidelines and recommendations identified for the business context.

3.2.3 Dynamic models

The closed-world assumption is one of the primary restrictions for the usage of the enMedia framework: the attributes that may become the issues of an electronic negotiation, as well as the potential events (decisions or actions) of the agents participating in an enProcess, have to be known at design-time.

To allow agents the introduction of new attributes or new attribute domains during an enProcess requires either a change to the enScenario communication design representation at run-time or the provision of structures in the representation that can be extended without jeopardising the means for the syntactical and semantical validation of offer instances. XML Schema offers the ability to extend the ontology in a dynamic way through the control options for the schema derivation process. Let us assume, that an agent has the possibility to sell computers with new features that are not reflected in the ontology model assigned to the current enScenario, such as a *DVD writer* in *Figure 32*. By modifying the offer state schema, the agent can extend the context specification with a derived *media drive* type that also includes an enumeration for the *DVD write* option.

This extension functionality enables the communication design to be adapted dynamically, but requires that an offer instance be submitted together with the derived offer state schema. Consequently, a component in the architecture model would have to determine changes to the offer context ontology underlying the enScenario, and to update the corresponding centrally located run-time specification so that other agents and the NSCs can interpret this offer instance as well. Some enScenarios might require an approval of all counterparts for dynamic extensions of the logical space. One promising approach to support this approval process is the application of game-theoretic voting procedures (see for example [Davi97, 163ff.]).

Much simpler is the incorporation of unknown attributes at run-time, if offer instances are extended with a non-validated structure element that allows agents to add free content such as a suggestion of new negotiation issues or comments. XML Schema allows restraining elements explicitly from validation. The disadvantage inherent in this approach is a potential loss of integrity and general interpretation capability (c.f. the discussion of free-form messages in Section 8.2.2.1).

Whereas it is possible to define dynamically the communication specification of the logical space at run-time, this is very difficult to do for organisation aspects. The reason is that during the enProcess execution, multiple concurrent offer instances might possess different offer states. If the FSM specification is modified at run-time, the states of all current offer instances in enProcesses for this enScenario have to be checked for compliance with the altered FSM specification. This test has to determine whether the state of the offer instance is still a valid and reachable state in the modified FSM, and whether this state has potentially active transitions.

Another level of dynamism that also incorporates organisation design aspects can be envisioned for enScenario specifications. Budimir and

Gomber suggested the notion of a dynamic market model, in which a unique negotiation scenario can be specified for the requirements of each individual transaction [BuGo99].

The enMedia framework already provides a foundation for the support of such a dynamic market model through the automated generation of run-time specifications. An agent could use the design adapter to create an enScenario model for the intended transaction, and generate the corresponding run-time specification (see steps 1-4 in the run-time processing use case for a dynamic market model in *Figure 89* below). Then an offer instance referencing this enScenario model could be submitted through the agent adapter (steps 5-8). Since in the dynamic market model every transaction may refer to its proprietary enScenario rules, two levels of agreement are necessary to perform a transaction.

First the agents need to agree on the enScenario design, then on the actual issues of the negotiation. The first level of agreement requires transparent access for agents to the enScenario model at run-time. In addition, the MatchNSC could support this two-level agreement process by matching also agent constraints towards enScenario specifications (steps 9-12).

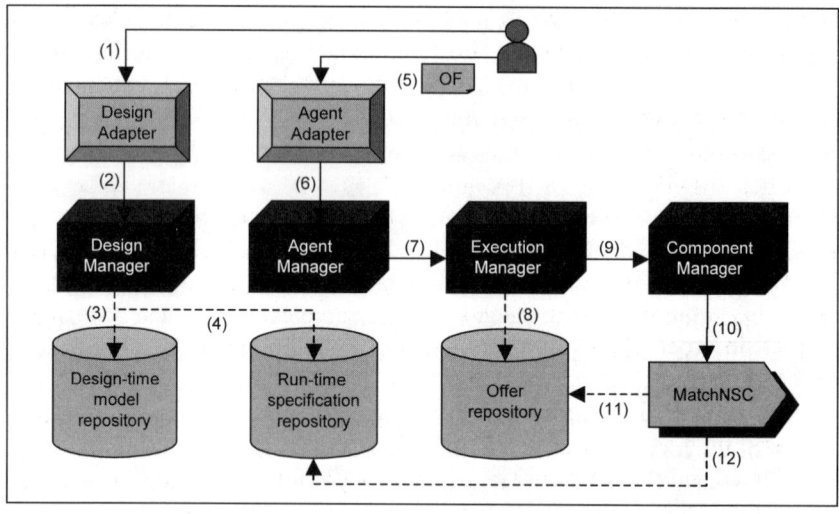

Figure 89. Run-time processing for dynamic enScenario models

Beyond the conceptual level in the architecture model, several extensions are necessary in the SILKROAD prototype in order to provide acceptable usability for the support of a dynamic market model. These extensions and other, more technical, issues are discussed in the next section.

3.3 SILKROAD extensions

The SILKROAD enMedia framework prototype is an implementation of the enMedia architecture model and the tools necessary to support the associated development approach. Future work for the prototype can be targeted at its completeness, such as with regard to the implementation of NSC solution procedures and objectives. This section, however, focuses more on potential extensions.

For the support of a dynamic market model (see the preceding section) it would be necessary to offer to the agent in addition to the design adapter client application, a **JSP design adapter**, because buyers and sellers might be reluctant to download and install the SILKROAD administration client JAR. Furthermore, the construction of enScenario models in the administration client requires a certain level of technical proficiency (see the discussion in Section 7.3). To reduce the design complexity, a design adapter for agents could support a high-level prescriptive classification of intended enScenarios, based for instance on implicit and explicit endogenous classification criteria from the taxonomy. This higher-level design language issue is further discussed in the next section. In the design manager, the desired enScenario classification then has to be rendered, perhaps based on rules, into a corresponding detailed enScenario design model. A serialised format of the enScenario classification may also be used for the two-level matchmaking process in the dynamic market model.

Section 8.2.2.1 already elaborated how the parties involved in an enProcess may benefit from the possibility of interacting with the enMedium server at run-time through XML offer instance documents, which can be created and modified outside the enMedium server (remotely). However, this is not the case for the activation or reception of events for an offer instance, since this requires calling methods, for example through the JSP agent adapter. In order to provide agents with complete lightweight accessibility, the agent adapter could be extended to offer a **Web service interface**. The invocation of Web services [WebS01] and the reception of execution results are based on XML messages and therefore constitute natural candidates for an adapter interface extension of the SILKROAD framework prototype. JBoss, the technical building block underlying SILKROAD servers, already supports the Web services specification through a SOAP (Simple Object Access Protocol, [SOAP01]) module, and thus it is not necessary to change the internal EJB architecture.

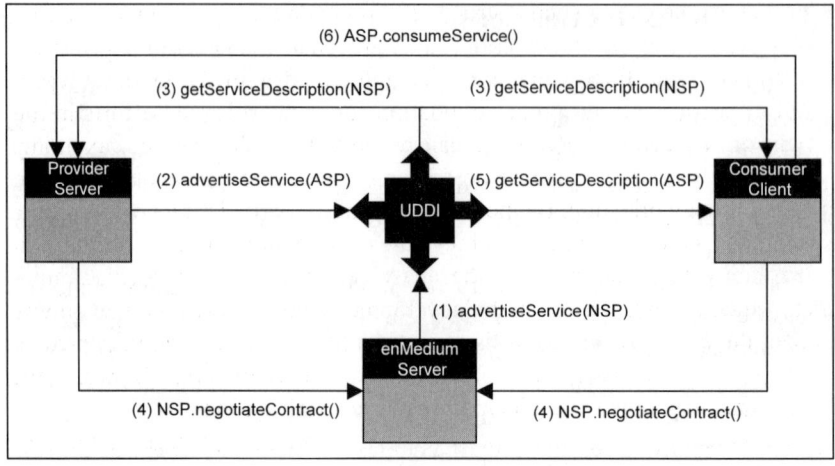

Figure 90. UDDI and Web services prototype extension

Furthermore, an enMedium server could advertise its Web services through UDDI (Universal Description, Discovery and Integration) directories. This option especially suits the application domain of a negotiation service provider. An NSP might advertise, for example, an enMedium Web service to host electronic negotiations in the business context of *database services* (see *Figure 90* for the following), including the discovery of potential database service providers through a matchmaking operation (1). In this scenario, interested service consumers can find the enMedium Web service in the UDDI directory, download the WSDL (Web Service Description Language) specification of the service interface (3), create compliant offers and event messages, and use the exposed Web services to negotiate with potential service providers (4). If the service providers in the application-hosting domain also advertise Web services in UDDI (2), it is possible to dynamically establish the execution of an agreed-upon service provisioning relationship on the basis of the contract specification (see steps (5) and (6) in *Figure 90*, as well as Section 4.5.3).

3.4 Further exploration of the enMedia framework

As a whole, the enMedia framework can be seen as a contribution to an emerging **electronic negotiation engineering discipline**. Engineering bears the promises of measurable quality and methodological approaches. The goal for an electronic negotiation engineering discipline is to provide a structured approach for the development of electronic negotiations that does not rely on the art or the skill of individual developers. The enMedia framework already

Future work

supports to some extent such a structured approach through a consistent methodology, well-defined abstractions, and a mechanistic generation process.

If the enMedia framework is further integrated with the taxonomy presented in Section 3.5, an initial foundation for standardisation efforts in the domain of electronic negotiations can be provided. Whereas the taxonomy supports the classification of a broad range of electronic negotiations, the enMedia framework supports the development of a broad range of electronic negotiations. One possibility to achieve the desired integration is the addition of taxonomy-based support for the analysis phase in the enMedia framework, which is currently not in the development scope. Relying on taxonomy criteria, the output of the analysis phase would have a declarative representation (e.g. *'the negotiation scenario has to be double-sided'*), while the subsequent design phase results in imperative specifications.

This potential integration opens up the opportunity to explore the language aspects of the enMedia framework on a wider scale. A complete **electronic negotiation engineering language stack** could evolve, as illustrated in *Figure 91*.

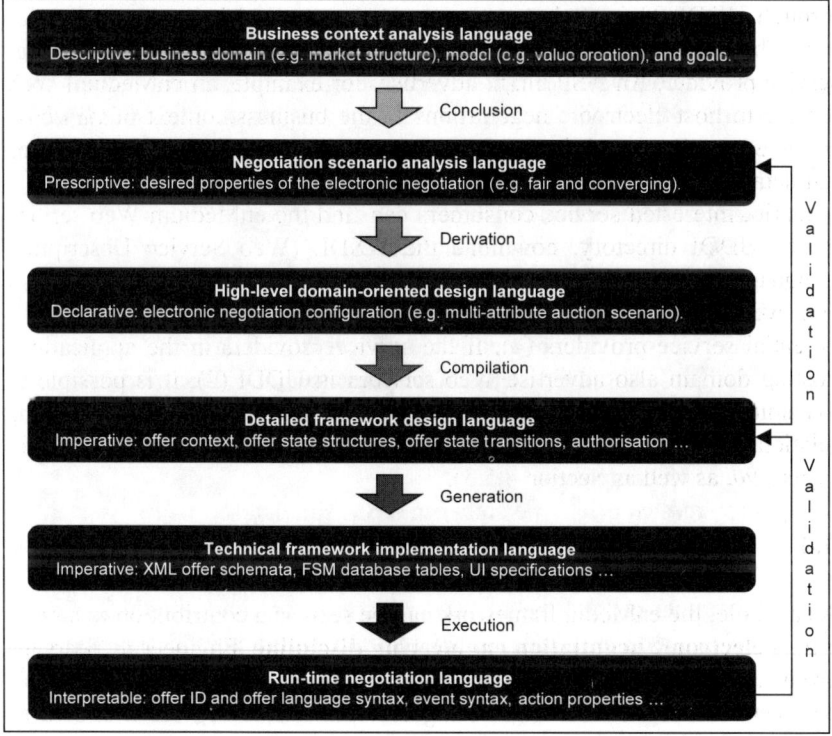

Figure 91. Electronic negotiation engineering language stack

The transitions from layer to layer in this language stack are characterised by an increasing formality and therefore would require a decreasing amount of intervention. Whereas the derivation of desired electronic negotiation properties from a business context analysis will probably require a certain level of creative skill from the analyst, the generation of imperative run-time specifications from design models is straightforward and can be automated as illustrated in this book. Thus, a step-wise abstraction process (of which the current lack in the enMedia framework was discussed above) can be supported through this language stack with additional levels of cross-layer validation; the detailed imperative design, for instance, can be validated on the basis of the prescriptive properties defined for the intended electronic negotiation.

Starting points for the high-level domain-oriented design language in this stack are the concept of negotiation support meta-components and the related notion of negotiation patterns (see above). NSMCs can represent pre-configured building blocks that support a high-level functional design approach, and are compiled into low-level specifications during the model generation and deployment process. Assuming feasibility of the NSMC proposal as well as of the suggested simulation (see Section 8.3.2.1), reference model (see Section 8.3.2.2), and overall language stack construction, all elements of a complete domain-oriented design environment (DODE) could be provided in the enMedia framework. Following the definition of [Fisc98], a DODE comprises components that can be mapped to elements of the enMedia framework as follows:

- a palette of domain building blocks
  > the elements of the design meta-model,
- an argumentative hypermedia system for the design rationale
  > derived from the theoretical foundation of the design approach,
- a catalogue consisting of a collection of pre-stored designs
  > the NSMCs and the patterns in the suggested reference model,
- a specification component
  > the SILKROAD design client, including model validation rules, and
- a simulation component
  > the suggested offer type and agent FSM simulator.

Typical DODE functionalities, such as critiquing a design on the basis of design constraints, are already supported to some extent by the current enMedia framework by the model validation test conditions (c.f. Section 5.3.3.3). In general, a DODE should assist an evolutionary design approach, and is intended to facilitate communication about the evolving system with the stakeholders – goals also defined for the enMedia framework. Hence, the enMedia framework has, in principle, all the elements it needs to become a DODE for the domain of electronic negotiations.

The resulting common multi-layered language stack for electronic negotiation engineering and execution would also enable software agents, for instance, to participate in a number of different electronic negotiations, for example with different rules (protocols), and to adapt their behaviour according to the declarative configuration provided for a particular negotiation (see for example [Tu+01]). Eventually an **electronic negotiation directory service** could be established that supports structured searching based on the criteria defined in the taxonomy, and which also allows downloading a machine-readable format of an enInstance classification, i.e. the corresponding enScenario run-time specification. This representation could be used, for example, to automatically generate a software agent for this enScenario and bind it to the interfaces of the enInstance, or to check whether the configuration/strategy of an existing agent is suitable for the defined enScenario rules.

4. SUMMARY

The notion of a negotiation in the widest sense stands for conflict and/or cooperation [Crot92], for the process of joint solution search [Sebe92], for coordination through managing interdependencies [Pars+98], or for the determination and/or creation of value [Kers+00] – phenomena that are inherent in almost all forms of communication and interaction between humans or organisations. In principle, nearly every communication could be regarded as a negotiation, and negotiations as a coordination mechanism may be applied in a wide variety of cases ranging from very structured situations, such as task or resource allocation problems, to completely open situations, e.g. political conflicts. Depending on the standpoint of the reader, the usage domain, and the negotiation situation of interest, it might be possible to use the solution approaches presented in this book sometimes unswervingly, sometimes only through additional adaptation. Nevertheless, insights into the domain of electronic negotiations can be gained from this book independent of the characteristics of the application domain.

This universality may be one of its primary strengths. Because negotiations are often fuzzy, complex, ill-structured, and subject to great uncertainties, it does not make sense to search for the most optimal (or efficient, fair, secure, fast, etc.) and situation-specific solution. It seems to be almost impossible to reflect all interdependencies, and users of negotiation support systems often struggle to accept the most efficient solutions anyway (see for example [KeMa98]). That is why, through the construction of one holistic picture for the various dimensions (support, design, and architecture) of electronic negotiation development, the enMedia framework proposed in this book generally aims more at breadth than at depth.

With the enMedia design and implementation framework for symmetric multi-attribute negotiation intermediation in electronic markets, this book addressed major problems in the domain of eCommerce negotiations, and thereby introduced several novel concepts:

- The encapsulation of solution procedures for decision-making and communication support in the paradigm of reusable negotiation support components, including the conception of new approaches for discovering disagreement spaces and the suggestion of fair agreements in this context.
- An explicit and integrated design of the rules of an electronic negotiation, capturing the syntax and semantics of the subject of the negotiation, as well as the roles and protocols of the negotiation process on the basis of finite-state-machine specifications for offer types and a generated run-time specification using open standards.
- The modelling and implementation of an electronic negotiation architecture as an application framework, with reusable components that dynamically cooperate at run-time according to specifications generated from design models.

These novel concepts are integrated into one holistic view on the development of electronic negotiations that leads from formal, theoretical definition aspects to detailed, practical application issues. Through the implementation of the different elements of this view in the SILKROAD prototype and the subsequent diligence in testing the results in realistic electronic negotiation scenario cases, this book demonstrates that the initial problems identified in today's electronic negotiation practice can indeed be solved, using knowledge and techniques from multiple disciplines such as computer science, economics, game theory, and information systems.

Today, one can often notice, that 'strategy follows technology' in eCommerce practice. This is because either the current technology limitations impose restrictions on the business model, or ventures simply want to use new exciting technology in order to be 'on top of the market'. Through flexible negotiation support technologies with a broad scope, such as demonstrated with the enMedia framework and SILKROAD, this chain could be turned around, and sound electronic market strategies could again drive the underlying technology. This is important, because the specific nature of electronic markets, i.e. their transparency, obviously will lead to more competition and cooperation among their players – and as a result of this also to more negotiations.

To some extent, this is a vicious cycle: new electronic market technologies, including the examples suggested in this book, are necessary to respond to a growing demand for advanced eCommerce infrastructures – but these

Summary

technologies are also the initial reason for this demand, since they enable new ways of electronic interaction and coordination.

The final question to discuss is whether the technologies proposed in this book, namely the elements of the enMedia framework, really have prospects to have an impact on the real world of eCommerce. Like any other form of electronic negotiation media, the suggested framework faces the issues of user trust and acceptance. An early study outlined in [Shef92] showed that information transfer in negotiations via electronic media was perceived as less efficient by users than traditional face-to-face negotiations. Another investigation concluded that only 18% of users would accept negotiation by computers [Rung98]. Users often fear that effective relationship building for long-term cooperation is not possible through electronic negotiation media, that rigid positions are encouraged, or that the inherent equalisation of status may contradict cultural values (see the discussion of social aspects in Section 2.2.4.1).

But the times are changing. More and more electronic media, email for instance, are used for business communication, and managers get used to non-face-to-face interaction. A very recent study already concludes that the lack of context and non-verbal cues in electronic negotiations can be compensated with more meta communicative speech acts [Ulji+01]. Furthermore, the 'noise' of negotiations (e.g. threats or bluffing) would vanish if structured negotiation support, such as the intermediation provided by an enMedium, were introduced in electronic markets.

It can be expected that many humans who feel uncomfortable with this emotional side of negotiations would welcome an orientation towards facts and more rationality. The experiment described in [LiDo00] showed that a significant portion of the subjects purchased from a store with bargaining agents although this meant paying higher prices, and although the switching costs to a shop with classified ads and lower prices were virtually zero. Either the subjects were irrational or the software agents offered something more than bargaining for prices – fun maybe? Why not, since negotiations are games by nature, electronic negotiations in eCommerce may become the equivalent to online games in the entertainment industry. Thus, to be successful, the enMedia framework, just like many other novel means and visions of eCommerce, also requires to some extent a different style of interaction, with different attitudes, strategies, and rituals. If such a new style of negotiating electronically were established, and if one day somebody ran a Turing test for electronic negotiations, the jurors would certainly have a difficult time to distinguish human agents from software agents in rather structured negotiations with, for instance, a fixed number of attributes. In less rigid settings though, this distinction will become less difficult because it can be assumed that complex problems, such as the creativity necessary to 'enlarge the pie', will remain 'hard' for a long time.

The vision of this book is the establishment of an electronic negotiation engineering discipline with artefacts such as reference models, domain-oriented design environments on the basis of a multi-layered language stack, and electronic negotiation directory services. As of today, the participation in, as well as the development of, electronic negotiations is still considered to be more an art than a science. The view of negotiations as an art is based on their creative, unpredictable nature and the need for the participants' imagination and skills. In contrast, the scientific perspective of an electronic negotiation focuses on understanding its elements and their relationships, explaining why it works, and describing the electronic negotiation in a structured and abstracted way that allows it to be repeated.

This book strives – through the development of sound engineering principles – towards to emphasise the science of electronic negotiations, but leaves humans the freedom to add the art. Referring back to the introductory quotation: it is better to pursue complementarity, not substitution.

Appendix
Technicalities

This appendix provides more technical background for rather abstract theoretical concepts introduced in this book, such as NSCs. Furthermore, specific details and examples for the SILKROAD prototype implementation are given. A table with the acronyms used in this book is available at the end of this appendix.

1. NSC INTERFACE DEFINITIONS

The following three tables provide abstract interface definitions for the NSCs presented in Chapter 4. The description uses common data types in analogy to, for example, the CORBA interface definition language IDL.

Table 17. MatchNSC interface

Group	Element	Definition
OfferInput	InitiatingOffer	Preconditions: constraints in the initiating offer have to define attribute values.
	TargetOffers	Preconditions: constraints in the target offers have to define attribute values. If no target offers are specified, the MatchNSC will search for all offers of the same deal type in a designated state.
Objectives	TimeRestriction	TIMESTAMP The search of the MatchNSC for target offers of the same deal type is limited by the time restriction. In addition, for offers with dynamic constraints, this objective defines the time the NSC waits for these offers to be completed.
	NullConstraints	BOOLEAN True: null constraints do not create a match conflict. If specified, the value range from the opposing offer constitutes the solution.
	HardMatching	BOOLEAN True: only the sets MAS and DAS are returned – 'false' will only return different results if soft constraints are specified.
	OfferViolationFeedback	BOOLEAN True: ranges of disagreement for constraint violations are disclosed.
	SetViolationFeedback	BOOLEAN True: constraint violation statistics for all match candidates with regard to the number of violations per constraint are returned.
	MaxConstraintViolations	NUMERIC Offers with more than n violated constraints will not be returned as successful matches if HardMatching = false.
	Friends	VECTOR Limits the search of matching offers (in case no target offers are specified) to offers from agents specified in this list.
OfferOutput	Generated agreement candidate offers. Result-set with pointers to and classification of agreement candidates.	The inclusion of agreement candidates (MAS, DAS, NAS) is dependent on the objectives set. Offers within the sets might be modified with resolved attribute values and marked constraints. Result-codes for offers: FAIL/MATCH/DISTRIBUTE/NEGOTIATE Result-codes for constraints: FAIL/MATCHED/RANGE/SNC/DNC

Appendix

Table 18. ScoreNSC interface

Group	Element	Definition
OfferInput	InitiatingOffer	Preconditions: the initiating offer specification includes the evaluation criteria (utility functions, weights, etc.) for the scoring operation.
	TargetOffers	Preconditions: constraints in the target offers have to define attribute values.
Objectives	TimeRestriction	TIMESTAMP This parameter defines the length of time the ScoreNSC will wait for offers to be submitted in the target state or for offers with dynamic constraints to be completed.
	TopCut	NUMERIC The number of 'best' offers which should be identified by the ScoreNSC.
	MinimumScore	NUMERIC The score a target offer needs to achieve in order to be returned among the 'best' offers.
	DefaultScore	NUMERIC If an offer does not specify constraints for a certain attribute, the offer scores zero utility for this constraint but is still scored. If a value is defined (e.g. *0.5*), this value is used in the scoring operation instead of zero utility.
	MandatoryScore	STRING At least one offer for each deal attribute defined in an abstract set in the target offer is part of the result-set (a common example is 'one offer per agent'). This objective requires building classes of offers according to the defined attribute, and returning the best offer within these classes. Overrides the TopCut objective.
OfferOutput	Scored offers.	Result-codes for offers:
	Result-set with pointers to and classification of scored offers.	FAIL/SCORED/SCORE Result-codes for criteria: FAIL/SCORED/SCORE

Table 19. MediateNSC interface

Group	Element	Definition
OfferInput	InitiatingOffer	Preconditions: the offer needs to belong to the NAS of a preceding MatchNSC operation – thus featuring matched or negotiable constraints. The initiating offer and the target offer are instances of the same matched offer instance (agreement candidate) but have to be complemented with importance ratings by the agents before the MediateNSC operation.
	TargetOffers	See above
Objectives	EquitabilityFactor	NUMERIC The equitability factor EQF (0.0 – 1.0) determines 'where' the agents meet. The default value is *0.5*, which results in fair, efficient, and envy-free solutions.
	TimeRestriction	TIMESTAMP The MediateNSC is typically invoked by the first agent who updated the matched offer with importance ratings. The NSC then tries to retrieve the target offers. As some target offers might not have assumed the designated state yet (because the agent is not updating), the TimeRestriction objective defines the waiting period for the MediateNSC.
	ResolutionProcedure	String The conflict resolution procedure to be used: Adjusted Winner, Proportional Allocation, etc.
	EfficiencyFeedback	BOOLEAN True: the number of points achieved is returned with the result-set.
OfferOutput	Mediated offers. Result-set with pointers to and classification of mediated offers.	Offers with suggested attribute values for all negotiation issues. Result-codes for offers: FAIL/MEDIATED/POINTS_ACHIEVED Result-codes for constraints: ORIGINATOR/COUNTERPART/ADJUSTED

Appendix 259

2. SILKROAD DATA MODEL

In *Figure 92* the main entities in the SILKROAD data model are defined using the notation of the structured entity relationship model [FeSi93, 101ff.]. In this model, existential dependencies between object types are visualised through a hierarchical graph structure.

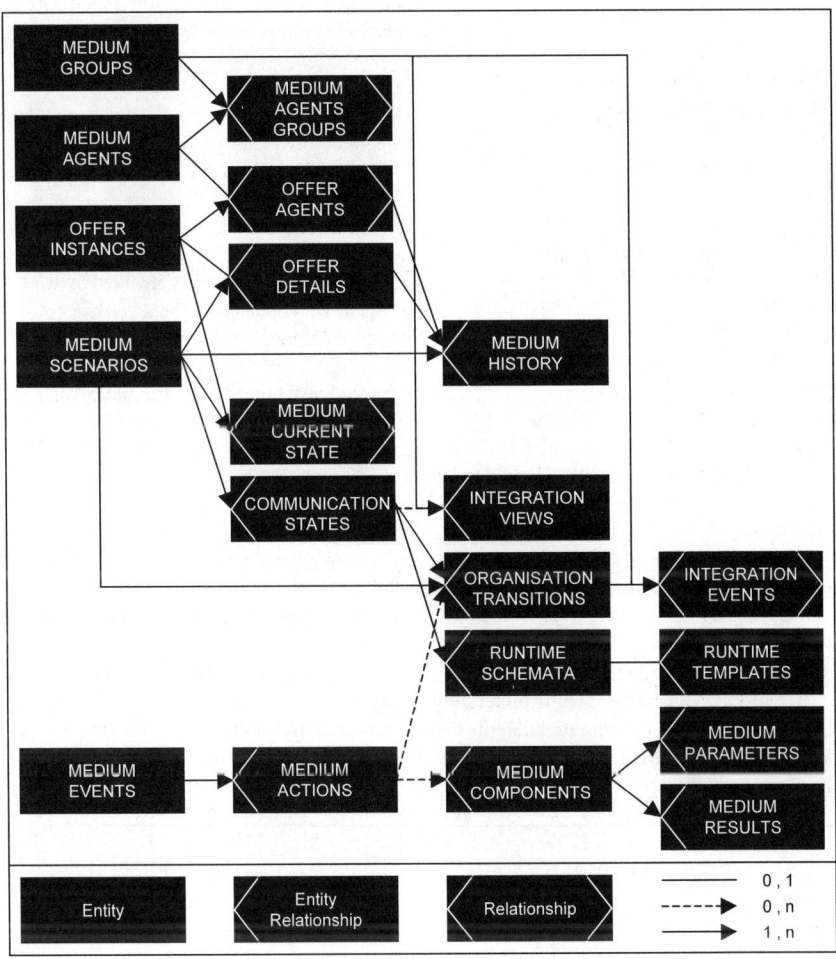

Figure 92. SILKROAD data model

For types in this data model, the following tables list the corresponding relations as SQL table definitions with sample contents. The tables are grouped according to their association with the architecture model repositories introduced in *Figure 42*. No distinction is made between foreign keys and primary keys. The "integer SEQ_ID" column is used in some table definitions to keep the order of the entries for the user interface in the J2EE client application.

Table 20. Relations in the enMedium repository

enMedium repository entities	Sample content
XSR_MEDIUM_SCENARIOS (configuration)	
SCENARIO_ID varchar(20) not null, DESCRIPTION varchar(200), STATUS varchar(20), primary key (SCENARIO_ID)	"SC_DSP-V1", "BILATERAL OFFER EXCHANGE", "active"
XSR_MEDIUM_EVENTS (configuration)	
EVENT_ID varchar(40) not null, TYPE varchar(10) not null, ACTION_ID varchar(20), primary key (EVENT_ID, TYPE)	"MATCH", "AGENT", "SUPPORT.MATCH"
XSR_MEDIUM_ACTIONS (configuration)	
ACTION_ID varchar(20) not null, ACTION_TYPE varchar(20), PROPERTIES varchar(200), JNDINAME varchar(40), EXECUTION_STATE varchar(40), SUCCESS_STATE varchar(40), primary key (ACTION_ID)	"SUPPORT.MATCH", "SUPPORT", "{TARGET=O2X, TIMEOUT=DATE,…} ", "mySilkMatchNSC", "MATCHING", "MATCHED"
XSR_MEDIUM_AGENTS (configuration)	
AGENT_ID varchar(20) not null, MAIL varchar(100), URL varchar(100), JNDINAME varchar(40), primary key(AGENT_ID)	"AG_DSP", "AG_DSP@ASP", "", "myAG_DSP"
XSR_MEDIUM_GROUPS (configuration)	
GROUP_ID varchar(20) not null, GROUP_TYPE varchar(20) not null, GROUP_DESCRIPTION varchar(100), primary key(GROUP_ID)	"GR_SUPPORT", "SUPPORT", "Negotiation Support Components"
XSR_MEDIUM_GROUPS_AGENTS (configuration)	
GROUP_ID varchar(20) not null, AGENT_ID varchar(20) not null, primary key (GROUP_ID, AGENT_ID)	"GR_SUPPORT", "MatchNSC"
XSR_MEDIUM_COMPONENTS (run-time)	
COMPONENT_ID varchar(200) not null, COMPONENT_TYPE varchar(20), ACTION_ID varchar(20), primary key (COMPONENT_ID)	"SUPPORT.MATCH:OF_DSP_1. ADVERTISED:1004546014939", "MATCH_NSC", "SUPPORT-.MATCH"
XSR_MEDIUM_X_NSC_PARAMETERS (run-time)	
COMPONENT_ID varchar(200) not null, PARAMETER_SET varchar(20, PARAMETER_KEY varchar(60) not null, PARAMETER_VALUE varchar(60), primary key (COMPONENT_ID, PARAMETER_KEY)	"SUPPORT.MATCH:OF_DSP_1. ADVERTISED:1004546014939", "OBJECTIVE", "HARD", "FALSE"

Appendix

enMedium repository entities	Sample content
XSR_MEDIUM_X_NSC_RESULTS (run-time)	
COMPONENT_ID varchar(200) not null, OFFER_ID varchar(60) not null, RESULT_CODE varchar(20), ELEMENT varchar(60) not null, ELEMENT_CODE varchar(60), ELEMENT_RESULT varchar(60), primary key (COMPONENT_ID, OFFER_ID, ELEMENT)	"SUPPORT.MATCH:OF_DSP_1.ADVERTISED:1004546014939", "OF_DSP_1", "MATCHED", "PRICE", "NEGOTIABLE", "450-300"
XSR_MEDIUM_CURRENT_STATE (run-time)	
SCENARIO_ID varchar(20) not null, OFFER_ID varchar(60) not null, primary key(SCENARIO_ID, OFFER_ID)	"SC_DSP-V1", "OF_DSP_1.ADVERTISED"
XSR_MEDIUM_HISTORY (run-time)	
SCENARIO_ID varchar(20) not null, OFFER_ROOT varchar(20) not null, AGENT_ID varchar(20), EVENT varchar(200), ACTION varchar(160), OFFER_ID_NEW varchar(60), TIME timestamp, primary key (SCENARIO_ID, OFFER_ROOT, TIME)	"SC_DSP-V1", "OF_DSP_1", "AG_DSP", "[AG_DSP SUPPORT.MATCH OF_DSP_1.ADVERTISED null {TARGET= NULL}]", "SUPPORT.-MATCH:OF_DSP_1.-ADVERTISED:1004546014939", "OF_DSP_1.MATCHING", "2001-10-31 17:33:45.965"

Table 21. Relations in the offer repository

Offer repository entities	Sample content
XSR_OFFER_INSTANCES	
OFFER_ID varchar(40) not null, OFFER db2xml.xmlvarchar, primary key (OFFER_ID)	"OF_DSP_1.ADVERTISED", "?xml version="1.0" encoding…"
XSR_OFFER_DETAILS (XML Extender populated side table)	
OFFER_STATE" type="varchar(40)" path="/CONTAINER/OFFER/@STATE" OFFER_TYPE" type="varchar(20)" path="/CONTAINER/OFFER/@TYPE" OFFER_CLASS" type="varchar(40)" path="/CONTAINER/OFFER/@CLASS" "SCENARIO" type="varchar(20)" path="/CONTAINER/OFFER/@SCENARIO_ID"	"ADVERTISED", "O2B", "DSP", "SC_DSP-V1"
XSR_OFFER_AGENTS(XML Extender populated side table)	
"AGENT_ID" type="varchar(20)" path="/CONTAINER/AGENT/@ID" "AGENT_TYPE" type="varchar(20)" path="/CONTAINER/AGENT/@TYPE"	"AG_DSP", "BUYER"
XSR_OFFER_HISTORY	
OFFER_ID varchar(40) not null, MODIFIED timestamp, "AGENT_ID" type="varchar(20)", OFFER db2xml.xmlvarchar, primary key (OFFER_ID, MODIFIED)	"OF_DSP_1.ADVERTISED", "2001-10-31 18:40:16.965", "AG_DSP", "?xml version="1.0" encoding…"

Table 22. Relations in the in the run-time specification repository

Run-time specification repository entities	Sample content
XSR_RUNTIME_TRANSITIONS	
same as XSR_ORGANISATION_TRANSITIONS	
XSR_RUNTIME_EVENTS	
same as XSR_INTEGRATION_TRANSITIONS	
XSR_RUNTIME_VIEWS	
same as XSR_INTEGRATION_VIEWS	
XSR_RUNTIME_SCHEMATA	
SCHEMA_ID varchar(100) not null, SCENARIO_ID varchar(20) not null, OFFER_TYPE varchar(20) not null, OFFER_STATE varchar(20) not null, OFFER_SCHEMA db2xml.xmlclob not logged, primary key (SCHEMA_ID)	"SC_DSP-V1_O2S_ADVERTISED", "SC_DSP-V1", "O2S", "ADVERTISED", "<?xml version="1.0" encoding="UTF-8"?> <schema elementForm...
XSR_RUNTIME_TEMPLATES	
SCHEMA_ID varchar(100) not null, SCENARIO_ID varchar(20) not null, OFFER_STATE varchar(60) not null, SCHEMA_URL varchar(80) not null, OFFER_TEMPLATE db2xml.xmlclob not logged, primary key (SCHEMA_ID)	"SC_DSP-V1_O2S_ADVERTISED", "SC_DSP-V1", "ADVERTISED", "http://nettuno:8080/silkschema/SC_DSP-V1_O2S_ADVERTISED.xsd", "<?xml...

Table 23. Relations in the in the design-time model repository.

Design-time model repository entities	Sample content
XSR_COMMUNICATION_STATES	
SCENARIO_ID varchar(20) not null, OFFER_TYPE varchar(20) not null, SEQ_ID integer not null, OFFER_STATE varchar(60) not null, DOMAINS varchar(20), CONSTRAINTS varchar(20), COUNTERS varchar(20), CRITERIA varchar(20), SIGNATURES varchar(20), TIMESTAMPS varchar(20), SCHEMA_ID varchar(100), primary key (SCENARIO_ID, OFFER_TYPE, OFFER_STATE)	"SC_DSP-V1", "O2S", 0, "ADVERTISED", "Ranges", "Basic", "None", "None", "Single", "Both", "SC_DSP-V1_O2S_ADVERTISED.xsd"
XSR_ORGANISATION_TRANSITIONS	
SCENARIO_ID varchar(20) not null, OFFER_TYPE varchar(20) not null, SEQ_ID integer not null, OFFER_STATE_OLD varchar(60) not null, EVENT varchar(20) not null, GUARD varchar(80), ACTION varchar(20), PROPERTIES varchar(200), OFFER_STATE_NEW varchar(60), primary key (SCENARIO_ID, OFFER_TYPE, OFFER_STATE_OLD, EVENT)	"SC_DSP-V1", "O2S", 0, "START", "SELLER.OFFER", "MANAGER.OFFER", "{TARGET=NULL}", "ADVERTISED"

Appendix

Design-time model repository entities	Sample content
XSR_INTEGRATION_EVENTS	
SCENARIO_ID varchar(20) not null, OFFER_TYPE varchar(20) not null, SEQ_ID integer not null, OFFER_STATE varchar(60) not null, EVENT varchar(20) not null, AGENT_GROUP varchar(20) not null, primary key (SCENARIO_ID, OFFER_TYPE, OFFER_STATE, EVENT, AGENT_GROUP)	"SC_DSP-V1", "O2S", 0, "START", "SELLER.OFFER", "GR_DSP_S"
XSR_INTEGRATION_VIEWS	
SCENARIO_ID varchar(20) not null, OFFER_TYPE varchar(20) not null, SEQ_ID integer not null, OFFER_STATE varchar(60) not null, OFFER_ELEMENT varchar(20) not null, AGENT_GROUP varchar(20), primary key (SCENARIO_ID, OFFER_-TYPE, OFFER_STATE, OFFER_ELEMENT, AGENT_GROUP)	"SC_DSP-V1", "O2S", 0, "ADVERTISED", "ALL", "GR_DSP_B"
XSR_INTEGRATION_CONTEXTS	
SCENARIO_ID varchar(20) not null, OFFER_TYPE varchar(20) not null, SEQ_ID integer not null, ONTOLOGY_ID varchar(20) not null, CONCEPT varchar(40) not null, primary key (SCENARIO_ID, OFFER_TYPE, ONTOLOGY_ID, CONCEPT)	"SC_DSP-V1", "O2S", 0, "ON_DSP-V1", "Database Services"

3. SAMPLE SCENARIO CASE SPECIFICATION

This section features the database table entries for a complete enScenario model specification. The example is the second case from Section 7.2.2, *DPS-V2*:

XSR_COMMUNICATION_STATES

"SC_DSP-V2","O2B",0,"ADVERTISED","Ranges","Basic","None","Valued","Single","Both",""
"SC_DSP-V2","O2B",1,"COUNTERED","Ranges","Basic","1","Valued","Single","End",""
"SC_DSP-V2","O2B",2,"MATCHING","Ranges","Basic","None","Valued","Single","Both",""
"SC_DSP-V2","O2B",3,"MATCHED","Values","Matched","None","Valued","Single","Both",""
"SC_DSP-V2","O2B",4,"SCORING","Values","Matched","None","Valued","Single","Both",""
"SC_DSP-V2","O2B",5,"SCORED","Values","Matched","None","Scored","Single","Both",""
"SC_DSP-V2","O2B",6,"CONTRACTING","Values","Matched","None","None","Single","Both",""
"SC_DSP-V2","O2B",7,"CONTRACTED","Values","Basic","None","None","All","None",""
"SC_DSP-V2","O2S",0,"ADVERTISED","Dynamic","Basic","None","None","None","None",""
"SC_DSP-V2","O2S",1,"COUNTERED","Ranges","Basic","1","None","None","End",""
"SC_DSP-V2","O2S",2,"MATCHING","Ranges","Basic","None","None","None","None",""
"SC_DSP-V2","O2S",3,"MATCHED","Values","Basic","None","None","None","None",""
"SC_DSP-V2","O2S",4,"SCORING","Values","Basic","None","None","None","None",""
"SC_DSP-V2","O2S",5,"SCORED","Values","Basic","None","None","None","None",""
"SC_DSP-V2","O2S",6,"READYCONTRACTING","Values","Basic","None","None","Single","None",""
"SC_DSP-V2","O2S",7,"CONTRACTING","Values","Basic","None","None","Single","None",""
"SC_DSP-V2","O2S",8,"CONTRACTED","Values","Basic","None","None","All","None",""

XSR_ORGANISATION_TRANSITIONS
```
"SC_DSP-V2","O2B",0,"START","BUYER.OFFER","","MANAGER.OFFER",
 "{TARGET=NULL}","ADVERTISED"
"SC_DSP-V2","O2B",1,"ADVERTISED","BUYER.MATCH","","SUPPORT.MATCH",
 "{TARGET=O2S.ADVERTISED,TIMEOUT=*,NULL=TRUE,HARD=FALSE,FRIENDS=
 NULL,OFFER_VIOLATION=FALSE,SET_VIOLATION=FALSE,MAX_VIOLATION=
 NULL}","MATCHING"
"SC_DSP-V2","O2B",2,"MATCHING","BUYER.GETRESULTS","",
 "MANAGER.GETRESULTS","{TARGET=MATCH.ID}","MATCHING"
"SC_DSP-V2","O2B",3,"MATCHING","MATCH.COMPLETED","","","",
 "ADVERTISED"
"SC_DSP-V2","O2B",4,"MATCHING","MATCH.OFFER","","MANAGER.OFFER",
 "{TARGET=NULL}","MATCHED"
"SC_DSP-V2","O2B",5,"MATCHED","BUYER.RETRACT","","MANAGER.RETRACT",
 "{TARGET=NULL,ARCHIVE=BOOLEAN}","END"
"SC_DSP-V2","O2B",6,"MATCHED","BUYER.SCORE","","SUPPORT.SCORE",
 "{TARGET=O2S.MATCHED, TIMEOUT=*,TOPCUT=5,MINIMUM=NULL,DEFAULT=0.5,
 MANDATORY=NULL}","SCORING"
"SC_DSP-V2","O2B",7,"SCORING","SCORE.OFFER","","MANAGER.OFFER",
 "{TARGET=NULL}","SCORED"
"SC_DSP-V2","O2B",8,"SCORED","BUYER.RETRACT","","MANAGER.RETRACT",
 "{TARGET=NULL,ARCHIVE=TRUE}","END"
"SC_DSP-V2","O2B",9,"SCORED","BUYER.CONTRACT","",
 "SUPPORT.CONTRACT",
 "{TARGET=O2S.READYCONTRACTING,TIMEOUT=*,OPTIMISE=FALSE}",
 "CONTRACTING"
"SC_DSP-V2","O2B",10,"CONTRACTING","CONTRACT.OFFER","",
 "MANAGER.OFFER","{TARGET=NULL}","CONTRACTED"
"SC_DSP-V2","O2B",11,"ADVERTISED","SELLER.ACCEPT","",
 "MANAGER.ACCEPT","{TARGET=NULL,SIGNATURE=STRING}","CONTRACTED"
"SC_DSP-V2","O2B",12,"ADVERTISED","SELLER.OFFER","",
 "MANAGER.OFFER","{TARGET=NULL}","COUNTERED"
"SC_DSP-V2","O2B",13,"ADVERTISED","SELLER.TIMEOUT","","","","END"
"SC_DSP-V2","O2B",14,"COUNTERED","BUYER.ACCEPT","",
 "MANAGER.ACCEPT","{TARGET=NULL,SIGNATURE=*}","CONTRACTED"
"SC_DSP-V2","O2B",15,"COUNTERED","BUYER.OFFER","","MANAGER.OFFER",
 "{TARGET=NULL}","ADVERTISED"
"SC_DSP-V2","O2B",16,"COUNTERED","BUYER.RETRACT","",
 "MANAGER.RETRACT","{TARGET=NULL,ARCHIVE=TRUE}","END"
"SC_DSP-V2","O2B",17,"COUNTERED","BUYER.TIMEOUT","","","","END"
"SC_DSP-V2","O2S",0,"START","SELLER.OFFER","","MANAGER.OFFER",
 "{TARGET=NULL}","ADVERTISED"
```

```
"SC_DSP-V2","O2S",1,"ADVERTISED","BUYER.MATCH","","","","MATCHING"
"SC_DSP-V2","O2S",2,"MATCHING","MATCH.OFFER","","","","MATCHED"
"SC_DSP-V2","O2S",3,"MATCHING","MATCH.COMPLETED","","","",
 "ADVERTISED"
"SC_DSP-V2","O2S",4,"MATCHED","BUYER.ACCEPT","","","","CONTRACTED"
"SC_DSP-V2","O2S",5,"MATCHED","BUYER.SCORE","","","","SCORING"
"SC_DSP-V2","O2S",6,"SCORING","SCORE.OFFER","","","","SCORED"
"SC_DSP-V2","O2S",7,"SCORED","SELLER.OFFER","","MANAGER.OFFER",
 "{TARGET=NULL}","READYCONTRACTING"
"SC_DSP-V2","O2S",8,"READYCONTRACTING","BUYER.CONTRACT","","","",
 "CONTRACTING"
"SC_DSP-V2","O2S",9,"CONTRACTING","CONTRACT.OFFER","","","",
 "CONTRACTED"
"SC_DSP-V2","O2S",10,"ADVERTISED","BUYER.ACCEPT","",
 "MANAGER.ACCEPT", "{TARGET=NULL,SIGNATURE=*}","CONTRACTED"
"SC_DSP-V2","O2S",11,"ADVERTISED","BUYER.OFFER","","MANAGER.OFFER",
 "{TARGET=NULL}","COUNTERED"
"SC_DSP-V2","O2S",12,"ADVERTISED","BUYER.TIMEOUT","","","","END"
"SC_DSP-V2","O2S",13,"COUNTERED","SELLER.ACCEPT","",
 "MANAGER.ACCEPT", "{TARGET=NULL,SIGNATURE=*}","CONTRACTED"
"SC_DSP-V2","O2S",14,"COUNTERED","SELLER.OFFER","","MANAGER.OFFER",
 "{TARGET=NULL}","ADVERTISED"
"SC_DSP-V2","O2S",15,"COUNTERED","SELLER.RETRACT","",
 "MANAGER.RETRACT","{TARGET=NULL,ARCHIVE=TRUE}","END"
"SC_DSP-V2","O2S",16,"COUNTERED","SELLER.TIMEOUT","","","","END"
```

XSR_INTEGRATION_EVENTS
```
"SC_DSP-V2","O2B",0,"START","BUYER.OFFER","GR_DSP_B"
"SC_DSP-V2","O2B",1,"ADVERTISED","BUYER.MATCH","GR_DSP_B"
"SC_DSP-V2","O2B",2,"ADVERTISED","SELLER.ACCEPT","GR_DSP_S"
"SC_DSP-V2","O2B",3,"ADVERTISED","SELLER.OFFER","GR_DSP_S"
"SC_DSP-V2","O2B",4,"ADVERTISED","SELLER.TIMEOUT","GR_SUPPORT"
"SC_DSP-V2","O2B",5,"COUNTERED","BUYER.RETRACT","GR_DSP_B"
"SC_DSP-V2","O2B",6,"COUNTERED","BUYER.ACCEPT","GR_DSP_B"
"SC_DSP-V2","O2B",7,"COUNTERED","BUYER.OFFER","GR_DSP_B"
"SC_DSP-V2","O2B",8,"COUNTERED","BUYER.TIMEOUT","GR_SUPPORT"
"SC_DSP-V2","O2B",9,"MATCHING","MATCH.OFFER","GR_SUPPORT"
"SC_DSP-V2","O2B",10,"MATCHING","MATCH.COMPLETED","GR_SUPPORT"
"SC_DSP-V2","O2B",11,"MATCHING","BUYER.GETRESULTS","GR_DSP_B"
"SC_DSP-V2","O2B",12,"MATCHED","BUYER.SCORE","GR_DSP_B"
"SC_DSP-V2","O2B",13,"MATCHED","BUYER.RETRACT","GR_DSP_B"
"SC_DSP-V2","O2B",14,"SCORING","SCORE.OFFER","GR_SUPPORT"
```

Appendix

```
"SC_DSP-V2","O2B",15,"SCORED","BUYER.RETRACT","GR_DSP_B"
"SC_DSP-V2","O2B",16,"SCORED","BUYER.CONTRACT","GR_DSP_B"
"SC_DSP-V2","O2B",17,"CONTRACTING","CONTRACT.OFFER","GR_SUPPORT"
"SC_DSP-V2","O2S",0,"START","SELLER.OFFER","GR_DSP_S"
"SC_DSP-V2","O2S",1,"ADVERTISED","BUYER.ACCEPT","GR_DSP_B"
"SC_DSP-V2","O2S",2,"ADVERTISED","BUYER.OFFER","GR_DSP_B"
"SC_DSP-V2","O2S",3,"ADVERTISED","BUYER.MATCH","GR_DSP_B"
"SC_DSP-V2","O2S",4,"ADVERTISED","BUYER.TIMEOUT","GR_SUPPORT"
"SC_DSP-V2","O2S",5,"COUNTERED","SELLER.OFFER","GR_DSP_S"
"SC_DSP-V2","O2S",6,"COUNTERED","SELLER.RETRACT","GR_DSP_S"
"SC_DSP-V2","O2S",7,"COUNTERED","SELLER.ACCEPT","GR_DSP_S"
"SC_DSP-V2","O2S",8,"COUNTERED","SELLER.TIMEOUT","GR_SUPPORT"
"SC_DSP-V2","O2S",9,"MATCHING","MATCH.COMPLETED","GR_SUPPORT"
"SC_DSP-V2","O2S",10,"MATCHING","MATCH.OFFER","GR_SUPPORT"
"SC_DSP-V2","O2S",11,"MATCHED","BUYER.ACCEPT","GR_DSP_B"
"SC_DSP-V2","O2S",12,"MATCHED","BUYER.SCORE","GR_DSP_B"
"SC_DSP-V2","O2S",13,"SCORING","SCORE.OFFER","GR_SUPPORT"
"SC_DSP-V2","O2S",14,"SCORED","SELLER.OFFER","GR_DSP_S"
"SC_DSP-V2","O2S",15,"READYCONTRACTING","BUYER.CONTRACT","GR_DSP_B"
"SC_DSP-V2","O2S",16,"CONTRACTING","CONTRACT.OFFER","GR_SUPPORT"
```

XSR_INTEGRATION_VIEWS

```
"SC_DSP-V2","O2B",0,"ADVERTISED","DOMAINS_RANGES","GR_DSP_S"
"SC_DSP-V2","O2B",1,"COUNTERED","COUNTERS_VALUES","GR_DSP_S"
"SC_DSP-V2","O2B",2,"MATCHED","CONSTRAINTS_MATCHED","GR_DSP_S"
"SC_DSP-V2","O2B",3,"MATCHED","DOMAINS_VALUES","GR_DSP_S"
"SC_DSP-V2","O2B",4,"MATCHED","CRITERIA_VALUES","GR_DSP_S"
"SC_DSP-V2","O2B",5,"SCORED","CRITERIA_SCORED","GR_DSP_S"
"SC_DSP-V2","O2S",0,"ADVERTISED","ALL","GR_DSP_B"
"SC_DSP-V2","O2S",1,"ADVERTISED","DOMAINS_ATTRIBUTES","GR_DSP_S"
"SC_DSP-V2","O2S",2,"COUNTERED","COUNTERS","GR_DSP_B"
```

XSR_INTEGRATION_CONTEXTS

```
"SC_DSP-V2","O2B",0,"ON_DSP-V1","DatabaseServices"
"SC_DSP-V2","O2B",1,"ON_DSP-V1","ServiceTransaction"
"SC_DSP-V2","O2B",2,"ON_DSP-V1","ServiceConsumer"
"SC_DSP-V2","O2B",3,"ON_DSP-V1","ServiceProvider"
"SC_DSP-V2","O2S",0,"ON_DSP-V1","DatabaseServices"
"SC_DSP-V2","O2S",1,"ON_DSP-V1","ServiceConsumer"
"SC_DSP-V2","O2S",2,"ON_DSP-V1","ServiceProvider"
"SC_DSP-V2","O2S",3,"ON_DSP-V1","ServiceTransaction"
```

4. JSP AGENT ADAPTER CLASSES

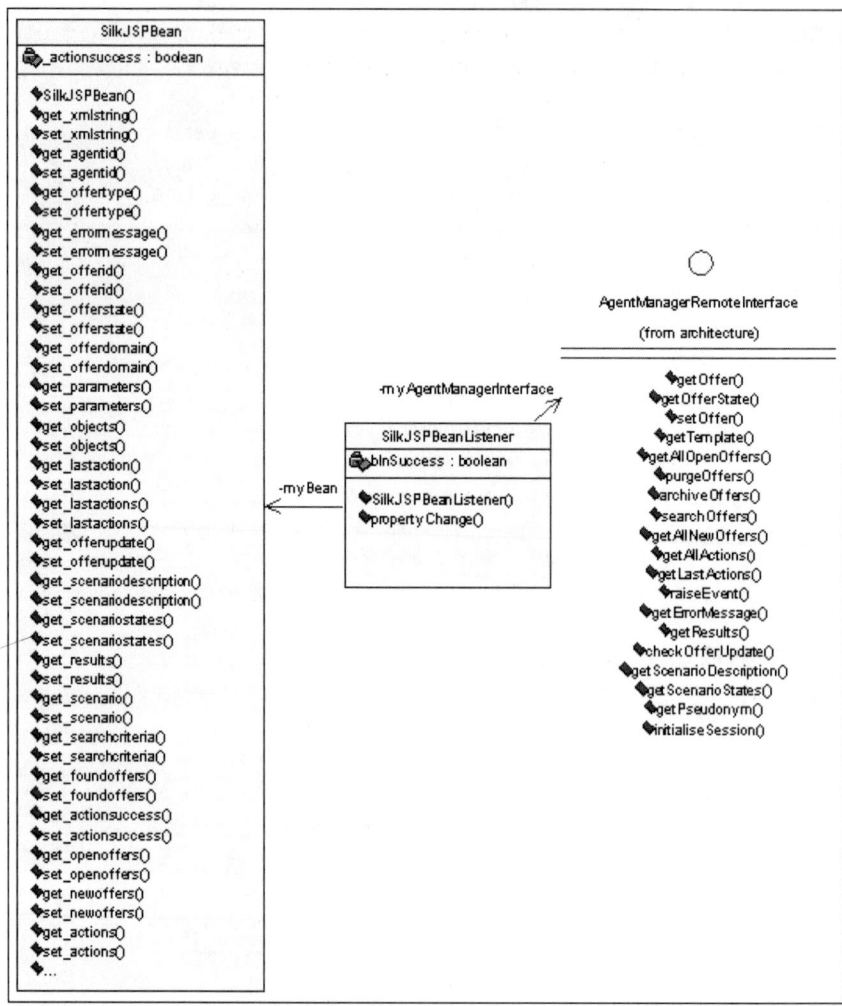

Figure 93. JSP agent adapter class diagram

5. XML SCHEMATA EXAMPLES

The following offer base schema in Code sample 1 is used as the foundation for the generation of state- and ontology-dependent offer schemata (see Section 5.4.1).

Code sample 1.
```xml
<?xml version="1.0" encoding="UTF-8"?>
<schema
   targetNamespace="http://www.silkroads.ch"
   xmlns:xsr="http://www.silkroads.ch"
   xmlns="http://www.w3.org/2001/XMLSchema"
   elementFormDefault="qualified">
   <element name="CONTAINER" type="xsr:CONTAINER">
      <unique name="AGENT_ID">
         <selector xpath="xsr:AGENT"/> <field xpath="@ID"/>
      </unique>
      <unique name="AGENT_TYPE">
         <selector xpath="xsr:AGENT"/> <field xpath="@TYPE"/>
      </unique>
   </element>
   <element name="OBJECT_CONTEXT" type="xsr:CONTEXT"/>
   <element name="TRANSACTION_CONTEXT" type="xsr:CONTEXT"/>
   <element name="AGENT_CONTEXT" type="xsr:CONTEXT"/>
   <element name="CRITERION" type="xsr:CRITERION"/>
   <complexType name="CONTAINER" abstract="true" mixed="false">
      <sequence>
         <element name="AGENT" type="xsr:AGENT"
            maxOccurs="unbounded"/>
         <element name="OFFER" type="xsr:OFFER"
            maxOccurs="unbounded"/>
         <element ref="xsr:AGENT_CONTEXT" maxOccurs="unbounded"/>
         <element ref="xsr:TRANSACTION_CONTEXT"
            maxOccurs="unbounded"/>
         <element ref="xsr:OBJECT_CONTEXT" maxOccurs="unbounded"/>
         <element ref="xsr:CRITERION" minOccurs="0"/>
      </sequence>
   </complexType>
   <complexType name="AGENT">
      <attribute name="ID" type="string" use="required"/>
      <attribute name="TYPE" type="xsr:AGENT_TYPE" use="required"/>
      <attribute name="SIGNATURE" type="string" use="optional"/>
      <attribute name="NAME" type="string" use="optional"/>
```

```xml
      <attribute name="URL" type="string" use="optional"/>
   </complexType>
   <complexType name="OFFER" mixed="false">
      <attribute name="ID" type="string" use="required"/>
      <attribute name="TYPE" type="xsr:OFFER_TYPE" use="required"/>
      <attribute name="SCENARIO_ID" type="string" use="required"/>
      <attribute name="STATE" type="string" use="required"/>
      <attribute name="CLASS" type="string" use="required"/>
      <attribute name="START" type="string" use="optional"/>
      <attribute name="END" type="string" use="optional"/>
   </complexType>
   <complexType name="CONTEXT" abstract="true" mixed="false">
      <sequence>
         <element name="NAME" type="string"/>
         <element ref="xsr:OFFER_CONSTRAINT" maxOccurs="unbounded"/>
         <element ref="xsr:COUNTER_CONSTRAINT"
            maxOccurs="unbounded"/>
      </sequence>
      <attribute name="NUMBER" type="integer" use="optional"/>
   </complexType>
   <element name="OFFER_CONSTRAINT" type="xsr:CONSTRAINT"/>
   <element name="COUNTER_CONSTRAINT" type="xsr:CONSTRAINT"/>
   <complexType name="CONSTRAINT" abstract="true" mixed="false">
      <sequence>
         <element ref="xsr:ATTRIBUTE_DOMAIN" maxOccurs="2"/>
         <element name="CONSTRAINT_OPERATOR" type="xsr:OPERATOR"
            minOccurs="0"/>
      </sequence>
      <attribute name="NEGOTIABLE" type="boolean" use="optional"/>
      <attribute name="MATCHED" type="xsr:MATCH_CODE"
         use="optional"/>
      <attribute name="IMPORTANCE" type="xsr:WEIGHT" use="optional"/>
      <attribute name="MEDIATED" type="xsr:MEDIAT_CODE"
         use="optional"/>
   </complexType>
   <element name="ATTRIBUTE_DOMAIN" type="xsr:ATTRIBUTE_DOMAIN"/>
   <complexType name="ATTRIBUTE_DOMAIN" abstract="true"
      mixed="false">
      <sequence>
         <element name="NAME" type="string"/>
         <element ref="xsr:OPERATOR" minOccurs="0"/>
         <element name="VALUE" minOccurs="0" fixed="*"/>
```

Appendix

```xml
    </sequence>
</complexType>
<element name="OPERATOR" type="xsr:OPERATOR"/>
<simpleType name="OPERATOR">
   <restriction base="string">
      <enumeration value="EQUAL"/>
      <enumeration value="UNEQUAL"/>
      <enumeration value="GREATER_THAN"/>
      <enumeration value="LESS_THAN"/>
   </restriction>
</simpleType>
<simpleType name="OFFER_TYPE">
   <restriction base="string">
      <enumeration value="O2B"/>
      <enumeration value="O2S"/>
   </restriction>
</simpleType>
<simpleType name="AGENT_TYPE">
   <restriction base="string">
      <enumeration value="BUYER"/>
      <enumeration value="SELLER"/>
      <enumeration value="INTERMEDIARY"/>
   </restriction>
</simpleType>
<simpleType name="MATCH_CODE">
   <restriction base="string">
      <enumeration value="MATCHED"/>
      <enumeration value="RANGE"/>
      <enumeration value="SINGLE_SIDED_NEGOTIABLE"/>
      <enumeration value="DOUBLE_SIDED_NEGOTIABLE"/>
   </restriction>
</simpleType>
<simpleType name="MEDIAT_CODE">
   <restriction base="string">
      <enumeration value="ORIGINATOR"/>
      <enumeration value="COUNTERPART"/>
      <enumeration value="ADJUSTED"/>
   </restriction>
</simpleType>
<!-- scoring section -->
<complexType name="CRITERION">
   <choice>
```

```xml
            <sequence>
               <element ref="xsr:CRITERION"/>
               <element ref="xsr:CRITERION_WEIGHT"/>
            </sequence>
            <sequence>
               <element ref="xsr:ATTRIBUTE_DOMAIN"/>
               <element ref="xsr:UTILITY" minOccurs="0"/>
            </sequence>
            <element name="UTILITY_FUNCTION"
                type="xsr:UTILITY_FUNCTION"/>
         </choice>
         <attribute name="SCORED" type="integer" use="optional"/>
      </complexType>
      <element name="CRITERION_WEIGHT" type="xsr:WEIGHT"/>
      <simpleType name="WEIGHT">
         <restriction base="integer">
            <minInclusive value="0"/>
            <maxInclusive value="100"/>
         </restriction>
      </simpleType>
      <element name="UTILITY" type="xsr:UTILITY"/>
      <simpleType name="UTILITY">
         <restriction base="float">
            <minInclusive value="0.0"/>
            <maxInclusive value="1.0"/>
         </restriction>
      </simpleType>
      <complexType name="UTILITY_FUNCTION">
         <sequence>
            <element ref="xsr:ATTRIBUTE_DOMAIN"/>
            <element ref="xsr:UTILITY"/>
            <element name="FUNCTION" type="xsr:FUNCTION"/>
         </sequence>
      </complexType>
      <simpleType name="FUNCTION">
         <restriction base="string">
            <enumeration value="LINEAR"/>
            <enumeration value="EXPONENTIAL"/>
         </restriction>
      </simpleType>
   </schema>
```

Appendix

An example for a complete state-dependent customisation is shown in Code example 2 (sample file *O2X_ADVERTISED_EXAMPLE.xsd*). The corresponding offer state design specifies, for instance, that no evaluation criteria or counters can be defined in this state and that a start date is required (see the comments in Code example 2).

Code example 2.

```xml
<?xml version="1.0" encoding="UTF-8"?>
<!-- example for an O2X.ADVERTISED schema with context typing -->
<schema
   targetNamespace="http://www.silkroads.ch/example"
   xmlns:example="http://www.silkroads.ch/example"
   xmlns:xsr="http://www.silkroads.ch"
   xmlns="http://www.w3.org/2001/XMLSchema"
    elementFormDefault="qualified">
   <import namespace="http://www.silkroads.ch"/>
   <complexType name="CONTAINER" mixed="false" abstract="true">
      <complexContent>
         <restriction base="xsr:CONTAINER">
            <sequence>
               <!-- Restriction applied - Only one AGENT -->
               <element name="AGENT" type="xsr:AGENT" maxOccurs="1"/>
               <element name="OFFER" type="xsr:OFFER"
                  maxOccurs="unbounded"/>
               <element ref="xsr:AGENT_CONTEXT"
                  maxOccurs="unbounded"/>
               <element ref="xsr:OBJECT_CONTEXT"
                  maxOccurs="unbounded"/>
               <element ref="xsr:TRANSACTION_CONTEXT"
                  maxOccurs="unbounded"/>
               <!-- Restriction applied - CRITERION omitted -->
            </sequence>
         </restriction>
      </complexContent>
   </complexType>
   <complexType name="OFFER" mixed="false">
      <complexContent>
         <restriction base="xsr:OFFER">
            <!-- Restriction applied - START required -->
            <attribute name="START" type="string" use="required"/>
         </restriction>
      </complexContent>
   </complexType>
```

```xml
<complexType name="CONTEXT" mixed="false">
  <complexContent>
    <restriction base="xsr:CONTEXT">
      <!-- Restriction applied: NAME omitted -->
      <sequence>
        <element ref="xsr:OFFER_CONSTRAINT"
          maxOccurs="unbounded"/>
        <!-- Restriction applied - COUNTERS omitted -->
      </sequence>
      <attribute name="NUMBER" type="integer" use="required"/>
    </restriction>
  </complexContent>
</complexType>
<complexType name="CONSTRAINT" abstract="true" mixed="false">
  <complexContent>
    <restriction base="xsr:CONSTRAINT">
      <!-- Restriction applied: minOccurs="0": context typing-->
      <sequence>
        <element ref="xsr:ATTRIBUTE_DOMAIN"
          minOccurs="1" maxOccurs="2"/>
        <element name="CONSTRAINT_OPERATOR" type="xsr:OPERATOR"
          minOccurs="0"/>
      </sequence>
      <attribute name="NEGOTIABLE" type="boolean"
        use="optional""/>
      <!-- Restriction applied - CODES omitted -->
    </restriction>
  </complexContent>
</complexType>
<complexType name="ATTRIBUTE_DOMAIN" abstract="true"
  mixed="false">
  <complexContent>
    <restriction base="xsr:ATTRIBUTE_DOMAIN">
      <sequence>
        <!-- Restriction applied: NAME omitted -->
        <element ref="xsr:OPERATOR" minOccurs="0"/>
      </sequence>
    </restriction>
  </complexContent>
</complexType>
</schema>
```

Appendix

The schema generation example is completed with the simplified state- and ontology-dependent schema in Code sample 3. In this example, ontology concepts such as a *WORKSTATION* with the attributes *CPU* and *HD* are encoded.

Code sample 3.

```xml
<?xml version="1.0" encoding="UTF-8"?>
<!-- example for an O2X.ADVERTISED ontology-dependent schema -->
<schema targetNamespace="http://www.silkroads.ch/example"
  xmlns="http://www.w3.org/2001/XMLSchema"
  xmlns:example="http://www.silkroads.ch/example"
  xmlns:xsr="http://www.silkroads.ch"
    elementFormDefault="unqualified">
  <include schemaLocation="O2X_ADVERTISED_EXAMPLE.xsd"/>
  <import namespace="http://www.silkroads.ch""/>
  <complexType name="WORKSTATION" final="restriction"
    mixed="false">
    <complexContent mixed="false">
      <extension base="example:CONTEXT">
        <sequence>
          <element ref="example:CPU_CONSTRAINT"/>
          <element ref="example:HD_CONSTRAINT"/>
        </sequence>
      </extension>
    </complexContent>
  </complexType>
  <element name="CPU_CONSTRAINT" type="example:CPU_CONSTRAINT"
    substitutionGroup="xsr:OFFER_CONSTRAINT"/>
  <complexType name="CPU_CONSTRAINT" mixed="false">
    <complexContent mixed="false">
      <restriction base="xsr:CONSTRAINT">
        <sequence>
          <element ref="example:WORKSTATION.CPU"/>
        </sequence>
        <attribute name="NEGOTIABLE" type="boolean"
          use="optional"/>
      </restriction>
    </complexContent>
  </complexType>
  <element name="WORKSTATION.CPU" type="example:WORKSTATION.CPU"
    substitutionGroup="xsr:ATTRIBUTE_DOMAIN"/>
  <complexType name="WORKSTATION.CPU" final="restriction">
    <complexContent mixed="false">
```

```xml
        <extension base="xsr:ATTRIBUTE_DOMAIN">
          <sequence>
            <element name="VALUE">
              <simpleType>
                <restriction base="float">
                  <minInclusive value="1.00"/>
                  <maxInclusive value="999.00"/>
                </restriction>
              </simpleType>
            </element>
            <element name="UNIT">
              <simpleType>
                <restriction base="string">
                  <enumeration value="MHZ"/>
                  <enumeration value="GHZ"/>
                </restriction>
              </simpleType>
            </element>
          </sequence>
        </extension>
      </complexContent>
    </complexType>
    <element name="HD_CONSTRAINT" type="example:HD_CONSTRAINT"
       substitutionGroup="xsr:OFFER_CONSTRAINT"/>
    <complexType name="HD_CONSTRAINT" mixed="false">
      <complexContent mixed="false">
        <restriction base="xsr:CONSTRAINT">
          <sequence>
            <element ref="example:WORKSTATION.HD"/>
          </sequence>
          <attribute name="NEGOTIABLE" type="boolean"
             use="optional"/>
        </restriction>
      </complexContent>
    </complexType>
    <element name="WORKSTATION.HD" type="example:WORKSTATION.HD"
       substitutionGroup="xsr:ATTRIBUTE_DOMAIN"/>
    <complexType name="WORKSTATION.HD" final="restriction">
      <complexContent mixed="false">
        <extension base="xsr:ATTRIBUTE_DOMAIN">
          <sequence>
            <element name="VALUE" type="float"/>
```

Appendix

```xml
                    <element name="UNIT" fixed="GB"/>
                </sequence>
            </extension>
        </complexContent>
    </complexType>
</schema>
```

6. ACRONYMS

Table 24. Acronyms

ACID	Atomicity, Consistency, Isolation, Durability
AHP	Analytic Hierarchy Process
AI	Artificial Intelligence
ASP	Application Service Provisioning
ATM	Automated Teller Machine
AW	Adjusted Winner
BATNA	Best Alternative To a Negotiated Agreement
CSP	Constraint Satisfaction Problem
DODE	Domain-Oriented Design Environment
DSS	Decision Support Systems
DTD	Document Type Definition
EJB	Enterprise Java Bean
EBNF	Extended Backus-Naur Form
FSM	Finite State Machine
FTP	File Transfer Protocol
GSS	Group Support Systems
HTTP	HyperText Transfer Protocol
JAR	Java ARchive
J2EE	Java 2 Enterprise Edition
JDBC	Java DataBase Connectivity
JNDI	Java Naming and Directory Interface
JSP	Java Server Page
JVM	Java Virtual Machine
MAUT	Multi-Attribute Utility Theory
MRM	Media Reference Model
NSS	Negotiation Support System
RFQ	Request For Quote
RMI	Remote Method Invocation
SOAP	Simple Object Access Protocol
TCP/IP	Transmission Control Protocol / Internet Protocol
UDDI	Universal Description, Discovery, and Integration
UML	Unified Modeling Language
URL	Uniform Resource Locator
WAR	Web Application aRchive
WSDL	Web Service Description Language
W3C	World Wide Web Consortium
XML	eXtensible Markup Language

Bibliography

[AlZi01] Alt Rainer, Zimmermann Hans-Dieter: Guest Editors Note. In: EM - Electronic Markets, Vol.11 No.1, 2001.

[Andr01] Andren Emily: Negotiation Software Helps Work Out E-Commerce Details. Gartner Group Research Note COM-12-7082, January 9 2001.

[AnGr01] Angelov Samuil, Grefen Paul: B2B eContract Handling - A Survey of Projects, Papers and Standards. University of Twente CTIT Technical Report 01-21, 2001.

[Arpi+00] Arpinar Sena, Dogac Asuman, Tatbul Nesime: An Open Electronic Marketplace Through Agent-Based Workflows: MOPPET. In: International Journal of Digital Libraries, Vol.3 No.1 2000, pp.36-59.

[Bako91] Bakos Yannis: A Strategic Analysis of Electronic Marketplaces. In: MIS Quarterly, Vol.15 No.3 1991, pp.295-310.

[BaLo00] Barbuceanu Mihai, Lo Wai-Kau: A Multi-Attribute Utility Theoretic Negotiation Architecture for Electronic Commerce. In: Proceedings International Conference on Autonomous Agents, New York, 2000, pp.239-246.

[BaPe76] Barclay Scott, Peterson Cam: Multiattribute Utility Models for Negotiations. Technical Report 76-1, Decision and Designs Inc., McLean VA, 1976.

[Beam+99] Beam Carry, Segev Arie, Bichler Martin, Krishnan Ramayya: On Negotiations and Deal Making in Electronic Markets. In: Information Systems Frontier, Vol.1 No.3 1999, pp.241-258.

[BeKe00] Benyoucef Morad, Keller Rudolf: An Evaluation of Formalisms for Negotiations in E-Commerce. In: Proceedings of the Workshop on Distributed Computing on the Web, LNCS Vol.1830, Springer Berlin, 2000, pp.45-54.

[Benj+99] Benjamins Richard, Fensel Dieter, Decker Stefan, Perez Asuncion: Building Ontologies for the Internet: A Mid Term Report. In: International Journal of Human Computer Studies, Vol. 51 1999, pp.687-712.

[Benn+99] Benn Wolfgang, Görlitz Otmar, Neubert Ralf: Enabling Integrative Negotiations by Adaptive Software Agents. In: Proceedings of CIA 99 - Third International Workshop on Cooperative Information Agents, Uppsala Sweden, 1999.

[Beny+00] Benyoucef Morad, Keller Rudolf, Lamouroux Sophie, Robert Jacques, Trussar Vincent: Towards a Generic E-Negotiation Platform. In: Proceedings of the 6th International Conference on Re-Technologies for Information Systems, Zurich Switzerland, 2000, pp.95-109.

[BeSe97] Beam Carry, Segev Arie: Automated Negotiations: A Survey of the State of the Art. CMIT Working Paper 97-WP-1022, 1997.

[Bich00] Bichler Martin: A Roadmap to Auction-based Negotiation Protocols for Electronic Commerce. In: Proceedings of the 33rd Hawaii International Conference on Systems Sciences (HICSS), 2000.

[Bich01] Bichler Martin: The Future of e-Markets: Multi-Dimensional Market Mechanisms. Cambridge University Press, Cambridge UK, 2001.

[Bich99a] Bichler Martin: Decision Analysis - A Critical Enabler for Multi-attribute Auctions. In: Proceedings 12th International Bled Electronic Commerce Conference, Bled Slovenia, 1999.

[Bich99b] Bichler Martin: An Experimental Analysis of Multi-Attribute Auctions. In: Decision Support Systems, Vol.29 No.3 1999, pp.249-261.

[BiSe01] Bichler Martin, Segev Arie: Methodologies for the Design of Negotiation Protocols on E-Markets. In: Computer Networks, Vol.37 2001, pp.137-152.

[Bish67] Bishop Robert: Game-theoretic Analyses of Bargaining. In: Quarterly Journal of Economics, Vol.77 1967, pp.559-602.

[BrDu00] Brown John, Duguid Paul: The Social Life of Information, Harvard Business School Press, Boston MA, 2000.

Bibliography

[BrTa99] Brams Steven, Taylor Alan. The Win-Win Solution. W.W. Norton & Company, New York, 1999.

[BrTa96] Brams Steven, Taylor Alan: Fair Division: From Cake-cutting to Dispute Resolution. Cambridge University Press, Cambridge UK, 1996.

[BuGo99] Budimir Miroslaw, Gomber Peter: Dynamische Marktmodelle im elektronischen Handel. In: Wirtschaftsinformatik, Vol.41 No.3 1999, pp.218-225.

[BuSh96] Bui Tung, Shakun Melvin: Negotiation Processes, Evolutionary Systems Design, and NEGOTIATOR. In: Group Decision and Negotiation, Vol. 5 1996, pp.339-353.

[Butt+00] Butt Joseph, Rutstein Charles, Kafka Steven, Kim Steve: Big Science Takes on Multiattribute eCommerce. In: The Forrester Brief, August 15 2000.

[CaMa96] Chavez Anthony, Maes Pattie: Kasbah: An Agent Marketplace for Buying and Selling Goods. In: Proceedings of the First International Conference on the Practical Application of Intelligent Agents and Multi-Agent Technology (PAAM'96), London UK, 1996.

[Card+99] Cardoso Henrique, Schäfer Max, Oliveira Eugenio: A Multi-Agent System for Electronic Commerce including Adaptive Strategic Behaviours. In: Proceedings of the 9th Portuguese Conference on Artificial Intelligence EPIA'99, Portugal, 1999.

[ClLe99] Clark Theodore, Lee Ho Guen: Electronic Intermediaries: Trust Building and Market Differentiation. In: Proceedings of the 32nd Hawaii International Conference on System Sciences (HICSS), 1999.

[CoSt98] Cortese Amy, Stepanek Marcia: Good Bye to Fixed Pricing. In: Business Week, May 4 1998.

[CrMa01] Crowston Kevin, MacInnes Ian: The Effects of Market-Enabling Agents on Competition and Prices. In: International Journal of Electronic Commerce, Vol.2 No.1 2001.

[Crot92] Crott Helmut: Verhandlungstheorie. In: E. Frese (ed.): Handwörterbuch der Organisation, Poeschel, Stuttgart Germany, 1992.

[CrPu99] Cranefield Steven, Purvis Martin: UML as an Ontology Modelling Language. In: Proceedings of the IJCAI-99 Workshop on Intelligent Information Integration, 1999.

[CrSc00] Crampton Peter, Schwartz Jesse: Collusive Bidding: Lessons from the FCC Spectrum Auctions. In: Journal of Regulatory Economics, Vol. 17 2000, pp.229-252.

[Davi97] Davis Morton: Game Theory - A Nontechnical Introduction. Dover Publication Inc., Mineola NY, 1997.
[DeGa87] DeSanctis Geradine., Gallupe Brent: A Foundation for the Study of Group Decision Support Systems. In: Management Science, Vol.33 No.5 1987, pp.589-609.
[DeMi+00] DeMichiel Linda, Yalcinal Uemit ,Krishnan Sanjeev: Enterprise JavaBeans Specification, Version 2.0. Sun Microsystems, Palo Alto CA 2000.
[ErSt99] Erdmann Michael, Studer Rudi: Ontologies as Conceptual Models for XML Documents. In: Proceedings of the 12th Workshop for Knowledge Acquisition, Modeling and Management (KAW'99), Banff Canada, 1999.
[Faya+99] Fayad Mohamed, Schmidt Douglas, Johnson Ralph: Building Application Frameworks - Object Oriented Foundations of Framework Design. Wiley, New York, 1999.
[Fens+00] Fensel Dieter, Horocks Ian, VanHarmelen Frank, Decker Stefan, Erdmann, Michael, Klein Michel: OIL in a Nutshell. In: Knowledge Acquisition, Modeling, and Management, Proceedings of the European Knowledge Acquisition Conference (EKAW), R. Dieng et al. (eds.), Lecture Notes in Artificial Intelligence, Springer Berlin, 2000.
[FeSi93] Ferstl Otto, Sinz Elmar: Grundlagen der Wirtschaftsinformatik. Oldenbourg, München Germany, 1993.
[FiHo98] Field Simon, Hoffner Yigal: ViMP – a Virtual Marketplace for Insurance Products. In: EM - Electronic Markets, Vol. 8 No. 4 1998.
[Fisc98] Fischer Gerhard: Seeding, Evolutionary Growth and Reseeding: Constructing, Capturing and Evolving Knowledge in Domain-Oriented Design Environments. In: International Journal of Automated Software Engineering, Vol.5 No.4 1998, pp.447-464.
[FoBa01] Fögen Malte, Battenfeld Jörg: Die Rolle der Architektur in der Anwendungsentwicklung. In: Informatik Spektrum, Vol.24 No.5 2001, pp.290-301.
[Fran96] Frank Robert: Microeconomics and Behavior. McGraw Hill, Boston MA, 1996.
[Gamm+95] Gamma Erich, Helm Richard, Johnson Ralph, Vlissides John: Design Patterns – Elements of Reusable Object Oriented Software. Addison Wesley, Reading MA, 1995.

Bibliography

[Gisl+99] Gisler Michael, Haeuschen Harald, Joehri Yvonne, Meier Arion, Mueller Otto, Schopp Bernd, Stanoevska Katarina: Requirements on Secure Electronic Contracts. University of St.Gallen, mcm Institute Working Report 99/01, 1999.

[Gomb+00] Gomber Peter, Schmidt Claudia, Weinhardt Christof: Pricing in Multiagent Systems for Transportation Planning. In: Journal of Organizational Computing and Electronic Commerce, Vol.10 No.4 2000, pp.271-280.

[Greu+00] Greunz Markus, Schopp Bernd, Stanoevska-Slabeva Katarina: Supporting Market Transactions through XML Contracting Container. In: Proceedings of the 6th Americas Conference on Information Systems (AMCIS 2000), Long Beach CA, 2000.

[GrWi73] Green Paul, Wind Yoram.: Multiattribute Decisions in Marketing: A Measurement Approach. The Dryden Press, Hinsdale IL, 1973.

[GuMa98a] Guttman Robert, Maes Pattie: Agent-mediated Integrative Negotiation for Retail Electronic Commerce. In: Proceedings of the Workshop on Agent Mediated Electronic Trading (AMET'98), Minneapolis MN, 1998.

[GuMa98b] Guttman Robert, Maes Pattie: Cooperative vs. Competitive Multi-Agent Negotiations in Retail Electronic Commerce. In: Proceedings of the 2nd International Workshop on Cooperative Information Agents (CIA'98), Paris France, 1998.

[Gull79] Gulliver, Peter: Disputes and Negotiations: A Cross-Cultural Perspective. Academic Press, New York, 1979.

[HaHo99] Handl Daniela, Hoffmann Hans-Jürgen: MALL2000 - A Document-Based Platform for Negotiations in Electronic Commerce. In: Proceedings of HCI International '99, Vol.2, Lawrence Erlbaum Associates, Mahwah NJ, 1999, pp.1142-1146.

[HaRe83] Haerder Theo, Reuter Andreas: Principles of Transaction-oriented Database Recovery. In: ACM Computing Surveys, Vol.15 No.4 1983, pp.287-317.

[HaSe87] Harsanyi John, Selten Reinhard: A General Theory of Equilibrium Selection in Games. MIT Press, Cambridge MA, 1987

[Hoff+01] Hoffner Yigal, Field Simon, Grefen Paul, Ludwig Heiko: Contract-Driven Creation and Operation of Virtual Enterprises. IBM Research Report 3328, Yorktown Heights NY, 2001.

[Hoff99]   Hoffner Yigal: Supporting Contract Match-Making. In: Proceedings of RIDE-VE'99, Sydney Australia, 1999.

[HoLo98]   Holland Christopher, Lockett Geoff: Business Trust and the Formation of Virtual Organizations. In: Proceedings of the 31st Annual Hawaii International Conference on System Sciences (HICSS), 1998.

[Hols+95]   Holsapple Clyde, Lai Hsiangchu, Whinston Andrew: Analysis of Negotiation Support System Research. In: Journal of Computer Information Systems, Vol.1 1995, pp.233-247.

[Hols+91]   Holsapple Clyde, Lai Hsiangchu, Whinston Andrew: Negotiation Support Systems: Roots, Progress and Needs. In: Journal of Information Systems Vol.1 1991, pp. 233-247.

[Hurw73]   Hurwicz Leonid: The Design of Mechanisms for Resource Allocation. In: American Economic Review, Vol.63, 1973, pp.1-30.

[Hust94]   Hustadt Ullrich: Do We Need the Closed World Assumption in Knowledge Representation? In J. Kunze (ed.) and H. Stoyan (ed.) KI-94 Workshops: Extended Abstracts, 1994.

[ISO96]   ISO/IEC 14977: Extended BNF. International Standard, 1996.

[Iwai00]   Iwaihara Mizuho: Supporting Dynamic Constraints for Commerce Negotiations. In: Proceedings of the 2nd International Workshop on Advanced Issues of E-Commerce and Web Based Information Systems WECWIS, 2000, pp.12-20.

[JeFo89]   Jelassi Tawfik, Foroughi Abbas: Negotiation Support Systems: An Overview of Design Issues and Existing Software. In: Decision Support Systems Vol.5 1989, pp.167-181.

[Kafk+00]   Kafka Steven, Temkin Bruce, Wegner Lisa: B2B Auctions Go Beyond Price. In: The Forrester Report, May 2000.

[KaKo01]   Kannan P.K., Kopalle Praveen: Dynamic Pricing on the Internet: Importance and Implications for Consumer Behavior. In: International Journal of Electronic Commerce, Vol.5 No.3 2001, pp.63-83.

[Kan95]   Kan Stephen: Metrics and Models in Software Quality Engineering. Addison Wesley, Reading MA, 1995.

[Kass00]   Kassem Nicholas: Designing Enterprise Applications with the Java 2 Platform, Enterprise Edition. Sun Microsystems, Palo Alto CA, 2000.

Bibliography

[Keen+83] Keeney Robert, Renn Ortwin, Winterfeldt Detlef: Structuring Germany's Energy Objectives. Social Science Research Institute Report, University of Southern California, 1983.

[KeMa98] Kersten Gregory, Mallory Geoff: Rational Inefficient Compromises in Negotiation. Interim Report IR98-024, International Institute for Applied Systems Analysis, Laxenburg Austria, 1998.

[KeNo99] Kersten Gregory, Noronha Sunil: Negotiations in Electronic Commerce: Methodological Misconceptions and a Resolution. Interneg Research Report INR02/99, 1999, http://interneg.org/interneg/research/papers/1999/02.pdf, visited 03/30/01.

[KeNo97] Kersten Gregory, Noronha Sunil: Supporting International Negotiation with a WWW-based System. Internet Research Report INR05/97, http://interneg.org/interneg/research/papers/1997/05.pdf, 1997, visited 03/30/01.

[Keph+98] Kephart Jeffrey, Hanson James, Sairamesh Jakka: Price-War Dynamics in a Free-Market Economy of Software Agents. In: Proceedings of ALIFE VI UCLA, MIT Press, Cambridge MA, 1998.

[Keph+00] Kephart Jeffrey, Hanson James, Greenwald Amy: Dynamic Pricing by Software Agents. In: Computer Networks, Vol. 32 No. 6 2000, pp. 731-752.

[KeRa76] Keeney Robert, Raiffa Howard: Decisions with Multiple Objectives. Wiley, New York, 1976.

[Kers+00] Kersten Gregory, Noronha Sunil, Teich Jeffrey: Are All E-Commerce Negotiations Auctions? Proceedings of 5th International Conference on the Design of Cooperative Systems (COOP '2000), Sophia Antipolis France, 2000

[Kers+91] Kersten Gregory, Michalowski Wojtek, Szpakowicz Stan, Koperczak Zbig: Restructurable Representations of Negotiations. In: Management Science, Vol.37 No.10 1991, pp.1269-1290.

[Kers00] Kersten Gregory: Modeling Distributive and Integrative Negotiations. Review and Revised Characterisation. Interneg Research Report INR02/00, http://interneg.org/interneg/research/papers/2000/02.pdf, 2000, visited 10/10/01.

[Kers98] Kersten Gregory: Negotiation Support Systems and Negotiating Agents. In: Proceedings Colloque SMAGET, Cemagref ENGREF, Clermont-Ferrand France, 1998.

[KeSz86] Kersten Gregory, Szapiro Tomasz: Generalized Approach to Modeling Negotiations. In: European Journal of Operational Research, Vol. 26 1986, pp.142-149.

[KeSz98] Kersten Gregory, Szpakowicz Stan: Modelling Business Negotiations for Electronic Commerce. Interim Report IR98-015/March, International Institute for Applied Systems Analysis, Laxenburg Austria, 1998.

[Kilg+99] Kilgour Mark, Rajabi Siamak, Hipel Keith: Water Supply Planning Under Interdependence of Actions: Theory and Application. In: Water Resources Research, Vol. 35 No. 7 1999, pp.2225-2235.

[Klei+00] Klein Michel, Fensel Dieter, van Harmelen Frank, Horrocks Ian: The Relation between Ontologies and Schema-Languages: Translating OIL-Specifications to XML-Schema. In: Proceedings of the Workshop on Applications of Ontologies and Problem-solving Methods, 14th European Conference on Artificial Intelligence, Berlin Germany, 2000.

[Klei95] Kleijnen Jack: Sensitivity Analysis and Optimization of System Dynamics Models: Regression Analysis and Statistical Design of Experiments. In: System Dynamics Review, Vol.11 No.4 1995, pp.1-14.

[KoBu00] Kowalczyk Ryszard, Bui Van Anh: FeNAs: A Fuzzy e-Negotiation Agents System. In: Proceedings IEEE/IAFE Conference on Computational Intelligence for Financial Engineering, IEEE, Piscataway NJ, 2000, pp. 26-29.

[KoBu01] Kowalczyk Ryszard, Bui Van Anh: On Constraint-Based Reasoning in e-Negotiation Agents. In: F.Dignum (ed.) and U.Cortes (ed.): Agent Mediated Commerce III, LNAI Vol.2003, Springer Berlin, 2001, pp.31-46.

[Koni01] Koning Jean-Luc: Designing and Testing Negotiation Protocols for Electronic Commerce. In: F.Dignum (ed.) and C.Sierra (ed.): Agent Mediated Electronic Commerce, LNAI Vol.1991, Springer Berlin, 2001, pp.34-60.

[KrDu80] Krzysztofowicz Roman, Duckstein Lucien: Assessment Errors in Multiattribute Utility Functions. In: Organizational Behavior and Human Performance, Vol.26 1980, pp.326-348.

[KuFe98] Kumar Manoj, Feldman Stuart: Business Negotiations on the Internet. In: Proceedings inet'98, Geneva Switzerland, 1998.

Bibliography

[KuLa00] Kunze Christian, Lamersdorf Winfried: A Rule Management Framework for Negotiating Mobile Agents. In: Proceedings 4th International Enterprise Distributed Object Computing Conference, IEEE Computer Society, 2000, pp.135-143.

[Lame+98] Lamersdorf Wolfgang, Merz Michael, Tu Tuan: Distributed Systems Technology for Electronic Commerce Applications. In: Lecture Notes in Computer Science, Vol.1521 1998, pp.135-148.

[LaSe86] Lax David, Sebenius James: The Manager as Negotiator: Bargaining for Cooperation and Competitive Gain. The Free Press, New York, 1986.

[Leak96] Leake David: Case-Based Reasoning: Experiences, Lessons, and Future Directions. MIT Press, Menlo Park CA, 1996.

[Lee+00] Lee Kyoung, Chang Yong, Lee Jae: Time-Bound Negotiation Framework For Electronic Commerce Agents. In: Decision Support Systems, Vol.28 No.4 2000, pp.319-331.

[Lee98] Lee Ho Guen: Do Electronic Marketplaces Lower the Price of Goods? In: Communications of the ACM, Vol.41 1998, pp.73-80.

[Lewi+97] Lewicki Roy, Saunders David, Minton John: Essentials of Negotiation. Irwin McGraw-Hill, Boston MA, 1997.

[LiDo00] Liang Ting-Peng, Dong Her-Sen: Effect of Bargaining in Electronic Commerce. In: International Journal of Electronic Commerce, Vol.4 No.3 2000, pp.23-43.

[LoMo97] Loui Ronald, Moore Diana: Dialogue and Deliberation. Draft intended for Negotiation Journal, 1997, www.cs.wustl.edu/cs/techreports/1997/wucs-97-11.ps.z, visited 03/30/01.

[Lomu+01] Lomuscio Alessio, Wooldridge Michael, Jennings Nick: A Classification Scheme for Negotiation in Electronic Commerce. In: F.Dignum (ed.) and C.Sierra (ed.): Agent Mediated Electronic Commerce, LNAI Vol.1991, Springer Berlin, 2001, pp.19-33.

[MaSm95] March Salvator, Smith Gerald: Design and Natural Science Research on Information Technology. In: Decision Support Systems, Vol.15 1995, pp.251-266.

[McMc96] McAfee Preston, McMillan John: Game Theory and Competition. In: Journal of Marketing Research Vol.33, 1996, pp.263-267.

[Milg89] Milgrom Paul: Auctions and Bidding: A Primer. In: Journal of Economic Perspectives, Vol.3 No.3 1989, pp.3-22.

[MoMa00] Morris Jane, Maes Patty: Negotiating Beyond the Bid Price. In: Workshop Proceedings of the Conference on Human Factors in Computing Systems CHI, The Hague Netherlands, 2000.

[Mouk+00] Moukas Alexandros, Zacharia Giorgios, Guttman Robert, Maes Pattie: Agent-Mediated Electronic Commerce: An MIT Media Lab Perspective. In: International Journal of Electronic Commerce Vol.4 No.3 2000, pp.5-21.

[MuVa00] Mudgal Chhaya, Vassileva Julita: Bilateral Negotiation with Incomplete and Uncertain Information: A Decision-Theoretic Approach Using a Model of the Opponent. In: Cooperative Information Agents IV, LNAI Vol.1860, Springer Berlin, 2000, pp.107-118.

[Nash51] Nash, John: Non-Cooperative Games. In: Annals of Mathematics, Vol. 54 1951, pp. 286-295.

[NeMo44] von Neumann John, Morgenstern Oskar: Theory of Games and Economic Behavior. Princeton University Press, Princeton NJ, 1944.

[Nuna+87] Nunamaker Jay, Applegate Lynda, Konsynski Benn: Facilitating Group Creativity, Experience with a Group Decision Support System. In: Journal of Management Information Systems, Vol.3 1987, pp.5-19.

[Oliv97] Oliver James: Artificial Agents Learn Policies for Multi-Issue Negotiation. In: International Journal of Electronic Commerce, Vol.4 No.1 1997, pp.49-88.

[PaCu01] Paurobally Shamimabi, Cunningham Jim: Specifying the Processes and States of a Negotiation. In: F. Dignum (ed.) and C. Sierra (ed.): Agent Mediated Electronic Commerce, LNAI Vol.1991, Springer Berlin, 2001, pp.61-77.

[Pars+98] Parsons Simon, Sierra Charles, Jennings Nick: Agents that Reason and Negotiate by Arguing. In: Journal of Logic Computation, Vol.8 No.3 1998, pp.261-292.

[PaUn00] Parkes David, Ungar Lyle: Iterative Combinatorial Auctions: Theory and Practice. In: Proceedings of the 17th National Conference on Artificial Intelligence (AAAI), Austin TX, 2000, pp.74-81.

[Phli83] Phlips Louis: The Economics of Price Discrimination. Cambridge University Press, Cambridge UK, 1983.

[Pico+97] Picot Arnold, Bortenlänger Christine, Röhrl Heinrich: Organization of Electronic Markets: Contributions From the New Institutional Economics. In: The Information Society, Vol.13 1997, pp.107-123.

[PrLe75] Pruitt Dean, Lewis Steven: Development of Integrative Solutions in Bilateral Negotiations. In: Journal of Personality and Social Psychology, Vol.31 No.4 1975, pp.621-633.

[Raif82] Raiffa Howard: The Art and Science of Negotiation. Harvard University Press, Cambridge MA, 1982.

[Rama+99] Raman Rajesh, Livny Miron, Solomon Marvin: Generic Matchmaking with Classified Advertisements. In: Proceedings of the 1st IAC Workshop on Internet-Based Negotiation Technologies, Yorktown Heights NY, 1999.

[RaSh97] Rangaswamy Arvind, Shell Robert: Using Computers to Realize Joint Goals in Negotiations: Toward an Electronic Bargaining Table. In: Management Science, Vol. 43 1997, pp.1147-1163.

[Rebs99] Rebstock Michael: Adding Complexity to the Electronic Market Model: Lessons Learned From an Oil Industry Case Study. In: Proceedings HCI International '99, Vol.2, Lawrence Erlbaum Associates, Mahwah NJ, 1999.

[Reev+00] Reeves Daniel, Grosof Benjamin, Wellman Michael, Chan Hoi: Automated Negotiations from Declarative Contract Descriptions. In: Proceedings AAAI-2000 Workshop on Knowledge-Based Electronic Markets, Austin TX, 2000.

[Roth+98] Rothkopf Michael, Pekec Aleksandar, Harstadt Ronald: Computationally Manageable Combinatorial Auctions. In: Management Science, Vol.44 No.8 1998, pp.1131-1147.

[RoZl96] Rosenschein Jeffrey, Zlotkin Gilad: Mechanisms for Automated Negotiation in State Oriented Domains. In: Journal of Artificial Intelligence Research, Vol.5 1996, pp.163-238.

[Rumb+99] Rumbaugh James, Jacobson Ingvar, Booch Grady: The UML Reference Manual. Addison-Wesley, Reading UK, 1999.

[Rung00] Runge Alexander: Die Rolle des Electronic Contracting im elektronischen Handel. Dissertation Nr. 2366, Universität St.Gallen, Difo-Druck, Bamberg Germany, 2000.

[Rung98] Runge Alexander: The Need for Supporting Electronic Commerce Transactions with Electronic Contracting Systems. In: EM – Electronic Markets, Vol.8 No.1 1998, pp.16-22.

[Saat96] Saaty Thomas: The Analytic Hierarchy Process. McGraw Hill New York, 1980, reprinted by RWS Publications, Pittsburgh PA, 1996.

[Sand00a] Sandholm Tuomas: Issues in Computational Vickrey Auctions. In: International Journal of Electronic Commerce, Vol.4 No.3 2000, pp.107-129.

[Sand00b] Sandholm Tuomas: Agents in Electronic Commerce: Component Technologies for Automated Negotiation and Coalition Formation. In: Autonomous Agents and Multi-Agent Systems, Vol.3 2000, pp.73-96.

[Sand99] Sandholm Tuomas: eMediator: A Next Generation Electronic Commerce Server. AAAI Workshop Technical Report WS-99-01, 1999, pp.46-55.

[Sark+96] Sarkar Mitra, Butler Brian, Steinfeld Charles: Intermediaries and Cybermediaries: A Continuing Role for Mediators in the Electronic Marketplace. In: Journal of Computer-Mediated Communication, Vol.1 No.3 1996.

[Schm00] Schmid Beat: Was ist neu an der digitalen Ökonomie? In: Belz (ed.), Bieger (ed.): Dienstleistungskompetenz und innovative Geschäftsmodelle. Thexis, St. Gallen Switzerland, 2000, pp.178-196.

[Schm98] Schmid Beat: Elektronische Märkte - Merkmale, Organisation und Potentiale. In: Sauter (ed.), Hermanns (ed.): Handbuch Electronic Commerce, Universität der Bundeswehr München Germany, 1998.

[ScQu01] Schoop Mareike, Quix Christoph: DOC.COM: A Framework for Effective Negotiation Support in Electronic Markets. In: Computer Networks, Vol.37 2001, pp.153-170.

[Sebe92] Sebenius James: Negotiation Analysis: A Characterization and Review. In: Management Science, Vol.38 No.1 1992, pp.18-38.

[Shef92] Sheffield James: The Effect of Bargaining Orientation and Communication Medium on Negotiation. In: Proceedings of the 25th Hawaii International Conference on Systems Sciences (HICSS), 1992, pp.174-184.

[Stol00] Stolze Markus: Soft Navigation in Electronic Product Catalogs. In: Journal on Digital Libraries, Vol.3 No.1 2000, pp.60-66.

Bibliography

[Stol99] Stolze Markus: Comparative Study of Analytical Product Selection Support Mechanisms. In: Proceedings INTERACT, Edinborough UK, IFIP/IOS Press, 1999, pp 45-53.

[Strö01a] Ströbel Michael: Design of Roles and Protocols for Electronic Negotiations. In: Electronic Commerce Research, Vol.1 2001, pp.335-353.

[Strö01b] Ströbel Michael: Communication Design for Electronic Negotiations on the Basis of XML Schema. In: Proceedings of the 10th International World Wide Web Conference, Hong Kong, 2001, pp.9-20.

[Strö00a] Ströbel Michael: On Auctions as the Negotiation Paradigm of Electronic Markets. In: EM – Electronic Markets, Vol. 10 No. 1 2000, pp.39-44.

[Strö00b] Ströbel Michael: The Effects of Electronic Markets on Negotiation Processes. In: Proceedings of the 8th European Conference on Information Systems, Vienna Austria, Vol. 1 2000, pp.445-452.

[Strö00c] Ströbel Michael: A Framework for Electronic Negotiations Based on Adjusted-Winner Mediation. In: Proceedings of the 11th International Workshop on Database and Expert Systems Applications (DEXA), IEEE Computer Society, Los Alamitos CA, 2000, pp.1020-1028.

[Strö00d] Ströbel Michael: Dynamic Outsourcing of Services. IBM Research Report 3236, Yorktown Heights NY, 2000.

[StSt01a] Stolze Markus, Ströbel Michael: Utility-based Decision Tree Optimization: A Framework for Adaptive Interviewing. In: Proceedings of the 8th International Conference on User Modeling, LNAI Vol.2109, Springer Berlin, 2001, pp.105-116.

[StSt01b] Ströbel Michael, Stolze Markus: A Matchmaking Component for the Discovery of Agreement and Negotiation Spaces in Electronic Markets. In: Proceedings of Group Decision & Negotiation, La Rochelle France, 2001, pp.61-75.

[StWe02] Ströbel Michael, Weinhardt Christof: The Montreal Taxonomy for Electronic Negotiations. To appear: Group Decision & Negotiation Journal, Special Issue 2002.

[Syca90] Sycara Katia: Negotiation Planning: an AI Approach. In: European Journal of Operational Research, North Holland, Vol.46 1990, pp.216-234.

[TaTh00] Tan Yao-Hua, Thoen Walter: INCAS: A Legal Expert System for Contract Terms in Electronic Commerce. In: Decision Support Systems, Vol.29 2000, pp.389-411.

[Teic+98] Teich Jeffrey, Wallenius Hanelle, Wallenius Jyriki: Multiple Issue Auction and Market Algorithms for the World Wide Web. Interim Report IR-98-109/December, International Institute for Applied Systems Analysis, Laxenburg Austria, 1998.

[TeMa00] Tewari Gaurav, Maes Pattie: Beyond Passive Bids and Asks: Mutual Buyer and Seller Discrimination Through Integrative Negotiation in Agent Based Electronic Markets. In: Proceedings of Knowledge Based Electronic Markets, Papers from the AAAI Workshop (Technical Report WS 00-04), Austin TX, 2000.

[Thom89] Thomson Leigh: Information Exchange in Negotiation. In: Journal of Experimental Psychology, Vol. 27 1989, pp.161-179.

[TsSy00] Tsvetovat Maksim, Sycara Katia: Customer Coalitions in the Electronic Marketplace. In: Proceedings of the International Conference on Autonomous Agents, New York, 2000.

[Tsve+01] Tsvetovat Maksim, Sycara Katia, Chen Yian, Ying James: Customer Coalitions in Electronic Markets. In: F.Dignum (ed.) and U.Cortes (ed.): Agent Mediated Electronic Commerce III, LNAI Vol.2003, Springer Berlin, 2001, pp.121-138.

[Tu+01] Tu Tuan, Seebode Christian, Griffel Frank, Lamersdorf Winfried: DynamiCS: An Actor-Based Framework for Negotiating Mobile Agents. In: Electronic Commerce Research, Vol.1 2001, pp.101-107.

[Tu+98] Tu Tuan, Griffel Frank, Merz Michael, Lamersdorf Winfried: A Plug-in Architecture Providing Dynamic Negotiation Capabilities for Mobile Agents. In: Proceedings 2nd International Workshop on Mobile Agents, Springer Berlin, 1998, pp.222-236.

[Tu00] Tu Tuan, Wolff E., Lamersdorf Winfried: Genetic Algorithms for Automated Negotiations: A FSM-based Application Approach. In: Proceedings of the 11th International Workshop on Database and Expert Systems Applications (DEXA), IEEE Computer Society, Los Alamitos CA, 2000, pp.1028-1033.

Bibliography

[Ulji+01] Uljin Jan, Lincke Andreas, Karakaya Yunus: Non Face-To-Face International Business Negotiation: How is National Culture Reflected in this Medium? In: IEEE Transactions on Professional Communication, Vol.44 No.2 2001, pp.126-137.

[VaMa94] Varian Hal, MacKie-Mason Jeffrey: Generalized Vickrey Auctions. Technical Report, University of Michigan, July 1994.

[Varian92] Varian Hal: Microeconomic Analysis. Norton, New York, 1992.

[VaSe00] Vakrat Yaniv, Seidmann Abraham: Implications of the Bidders' Arrival Process on the Design of Online Auctions. In: Proceedings of the 33rd Hawaii International Conference on System Sciences HICCS, 2000.

[Vick61] Vickrey William: Counterspeculation, Auctions and Competitive Sealed Tenders. In: Journal of Finance, Vol. 16 1961, pp.8-37.

[Whin+97] Whinston Andrew, Choi Soon, Stahl Dale: The Economics of Electronic Commerce, Macmillian Technical Publishing, New York, 1997.

[WiBe95] Benjamin Robert, Wigand Rolf: Electronic Commerce: Effects on Electronic Markets. In: Journal of Computer-Mediated Communication, Vol. 1-3, Special Issue on Electronic Commerce, 1995.

[Will+00] Willmott Steven, Calisti Monique, Faltings Boi, Santiago Macho-Gonzalez, Belakhdar Omar, Torrens Marc: CCL: Expressions of Choice in Agent Communication. In: Proceedings of the 4th International Conference on Multi-Agent Systems (ICMAS), 2000.

[Wong+00] Wong Wai Yat, Zhang Mei Dong, Kara-Ali Mustapha: Negotiating with Experience. In: Knowledge-Based Electronic Markets, Papers from the AAAI Workshop, AAAI Press, Technical Report WS-00-04, 2000.

[Wurm+01] Wurman Peter, Wellman Michael, Walsh William: A Parameterization of the Auction Design Space. In: Games and Economic Behavior, Vol.35. 2001, pp.304-338.

[Wurm+98] Wurman Peter, Wellman Michael, Walsh William: The Michigan Internet AuctionBot: A Configurable Auction Server for Human and Software Agents. In: Proceedings of the 2nd International Conference on Autonomous Agents, Minneapolis MN, 1998, pp.301-308.

[Wurm01]	Wurman Peter: Dynamic Pricing in Virtual Marketplaces. In: IEEE Internet Computing, Vol.5 No.2 2001, pp.36-42.
[Yoon+99]	Yoon Shim, Yun JuYoung, Kim SooWoong, Kim Juneha: Jangter: A Novel Agent-Based Electronic Marketplace. In: Proceedings AMEC'99, Springer Berlin, 1999, pp.102-112.
[Yuan+98]	Yuan Yufei, Rose Joseph, Archer Norm, Suarga: A Web-based Negotiation Support System. In: EM - Electronic Markets, Vol.8 No.3 1998, pp.13-17.
[ZaBr99]	Zarnekow Rüdiger, Brenner Walter: Diensteebenen und Kommunikationsstrukturen agentenbasierter elektronischer Märkte. In: Informatik Spektrum, Band 22 Heft 5 1999, pp.344-350.
[ZeSy98]	Zeng Dajun, Sycara Katia: Bayesian Learning in Negotiation. In: International Journal of Human-Computer Studies, Vol.48 1998, pp.125-141.

Bibliography

URLs

[Arib01]	http://www.ariba.com – visited 10/10/01.
[Band01]	http://www.band-x.com – visited 10/10/01.
[Barg01]	http://www.bargainandhaggle.com – visited 10/10/01.
[Dove01]	http://www.dovebid.com – visited 10/10/01.
[eBay01]	http://www.ebay.com – visited 10/10/01.
[Empt01]	http://www.emptoris.com – visited 10/10/01.
[Info01]	http://virtualairport.lufthansa.com – visited 10/10/01.
[Inte02]	http://www.interneg.org – visited 20/04/02
[Lets01]	http://letsbuyit.com – visited 10/10/01.
[Mene01]	http://www.menerva.com – visited 10/10/01.
[Kasb02]	http://lcs.www.media.mit.edu/groups/agents/projects/ – visited 20/04/02
[Moai01]	http://www.moai.com – visited 10/10/01.
[MobS01]	http://www.mobshop.com – visited 10/10/01.
[Perf01]	http://www.perfect.com – visited 10/10/01.
[Pric01]	http://www.priceline.com – visited 10/10/01.
[SOAP01]	http://www.w3.org/tr/soap – visited 10/10/01.
[WebS01]	http://www.w3.org/tr/wsdl – visited 10/10/01.
[Xerc01]	http://xml.apache.org – visited 10/10/01.

[DEXA01] Field Simon, Stolze Markus, Ströbel Michael: DEXA 2000 e-Negotiations Workshop, http://www.zurich.ibm.com/~mrs/dexa2000/, visited 10/10/01.

[Mont01] Kersten Gregory, Weinhardt Christof: eNegotiations and eMarkets Seminar, http://commerce.concordia.ca/gkersten/en_montreal.htm, visited 10/10/01.

[Scor01] Markus Stolze: Adaptive Commerce Components, http://www.zurich.ibm.com/csc/ebizz/acommerce.html, visited 10/10/01.

Index

agreement
    candidate **85**, 92
    process **42**, 225
    scenario 43
    space **53**, 86, 105, 223
application framework 155
auction 3, 12, 20, 23, 25, 69, **100**
automation 7, 74
    efficiency 78
    level 76

business model 68, 114

closed world assumption 221
constraint
    negotiable **49**, 83, 86, 122
    satisfaction **48**, 81, 223
    specification 47

decision-making 14, 76, 108, 224
    bundling **97**, 211
    criterion **88**, 224
    matchmaking **81**, 163, 196, 223, 236
    mediation 93, 105, 225
    model 74
    preference 90
    scoring **88**, 196, 223, 238

design meta-model **116**, 127
    protocol 124
    role 124
development action-model **112**, 134, 228
domain-oriented design environment 250

eCommerce 1, 23, 26, 109, 253
electronic contract 16, 42, **102**, 202
electronic market 1, 3, 6, 30, 33, **41**
electronic negotiation **43**, 253
    architecture 35
    architecture model 154, **157**, 183, 233
    directory service 251
    engineering 248
    hybrid **31**, 34, 76
    instance **43**, 70, 156
    intermediation 186
    medium 8, **43**, 56, 156
    ontology problem 118
    pattern 243
    process **43**, 74
    research 14
    scenario **43**, 56, 131, 171
    symmetry 27, **32**
    tasks 58
    use cases 161
enMedia framework 10, 111, 151, 164,
    184, 185, **220**, 243, 252

Index

finite state machine 116, **131**, 139, 149, 171, 232

game theory 12, 20, 92
    adjusted winner **92**, 105, 225, 240
    coalition formation 97

information system 74
    architecture 153
    component **73**, 157
    pattern 158
    quality 234

Java
    Enterprise Beans 165, 168
    Server Pages 165, 179

mechanism design 12, 20, 66, **78**, 243
medium **41**, 111
    communication design **118**, 172, 230
    integration design **134**, 174
    organisation design **124**, 172, 232
multi-attribute
    auction 204
    negotiation **26**, 31, 36, 108
    utility theory 12, 22, **88**, 89, 224, 238

negotiation 2, 11, **40**, 251
    analysis **13**, 21
    commercial 3
    distributive 21, **55**
    integrative **55**, 227
    intermediation **31**, 108
    model **35**, 116, 229
    opposition 54
    power 6, **99**
    process 5, **42**, 54, 85
    research 12
    service provider 188
    support component **73**, 122, 222, 240
    support systems **44**, 185

offer 41, **51**, 75, 118, 177
    exchange 58
    session 195
    space 50
    state 121, 127
    template 123

ontology **118**, 134, 144, 174, 190, 230
outsourcing 187

pricing
    dynamic 23, 26
    fixed 1

SilkRoad **164**, 170, 234, 247
    application architecture 168
    components 157
    deployment 167, 175
    technical architecture 165
software agent **17**, 22, 75

taxonomy **59**, 100
    endogenous criteria **60**, 243
    exogenous criteria **67**, 114
transaction **40**, 104, 119
    cost 6, 30, 101

UML 116, 132, 232

XML 139
    document 147
    generation 140, 175
    persistence 165
    Schema **139**, 142, 176, 231
Web Services 247